UNCOMMON
VALOR

UNCOMMON
VALOR

The Recon Company That Earned Five Medals of Honor and Included America's Most Decorated Green Beret

STEPHEN L. MOORE

Naval Institute Press

Annapolis, Maryland

Naval Institute Press
291 Wood Road
Annapolis, MD 21402

Library of Congress Cataloging-in-Publication Data.

Names: Moore, Stephen L., author.

    Title: Uncommon valor : the recon company that earned five Medals of Honor and included America's most decorated Green Beret / Stephen L. Moore.

    Description: Annapolis, Maryland : Naval Institute Press, [2018] | Includes bibliographical references and index.

    Identifiers: LCCN 2018019058 (print) | LCCN 2018042541 (ebook) | ISBN 9781682473122 (mobi) | ISBN 9781682473122 (epub) | ISBN 9781682473122 (ePDF) | ISBN 9781591145745 | ISBN 9781591145745?(alk. paper)

    Subjects: LCSH: United States. Military Assistance Command, Vietnam. Studies and Observations Group. | Vietnam War, 1961-1975—Commando operations—United States. | Vietnam War, 1961-1975—Reconnaissance operations, American. | United States. Army. Special Forces. | Medal of Honor. | Vietnam War, 1961-1975—Regimental histories—United States.

    Classification: LCC DS558.92 (ebook) | LCC DS558.92 .M67 2018 (print) | DDC 959.704/342—dc23

    LC record available at https://lccn.loc.gov/2018019058

♾ Print editions meet the requirements of ANSI/NISO z39.48-1992 (Permanence of Paper).

Printed in the United States of America.

26 25 24 23 22 21 20   9 8 7 6 5

CONTENTS

AREA OF KEY SOG OPERATIONS

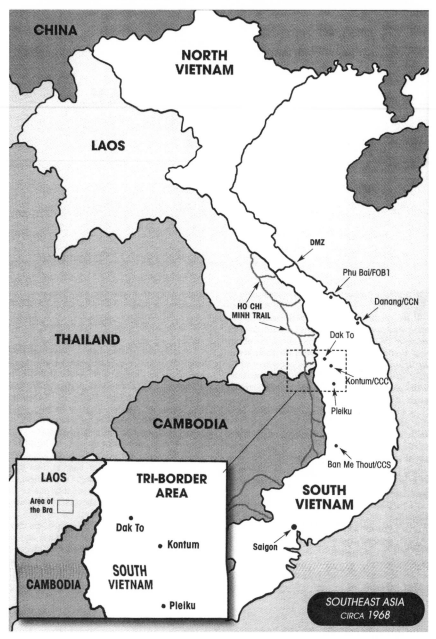

Map artwork courtesy of Joe Parnar

PROLOGUE

Sergeant First Class Bob Howard lay unconscious as hellacious volumes of semi- and full-automatic weapons fire made confetti of the dense green jungle foliage all around his crumpled body.

It was December 30, 1968, and Howard's thirty-three-man recon platoon was being shredded by two companies of North Vietnamese infantrymen. Near him lay his platoon commander, a young first lieutenant whose body had been ripped by bullets and grenade fragments. Four South Vietnamese members of Howard's platoon had also been cut down—one was already dead and the other three were writhing in agony.

Howard was raised in near-poverty by his grandmother in Opelika, Alabama; he was now a specimen of physical fitness—a powerfully built six-footer with a square jaw and a fierce sense of patriotism. A quiet, unassuming character, he was considered the epitome of bravery in combat. He had already been written up for the Medal of Honor twice, only to have the citations downgraded to a Distinguished Service Cross and a Silver Star.

But now the fierce warrior was in agony, with shrapnel wounds to his hands, groin, and lower legs. Blown backward by the force of a grenade, Howard fought to regain consciousness and struggled to see through the blood gushing from an ugly head wound. As his senses slowly returned, he detected the most vile stench—the scent of burning human flesh. He pulled himself upright and spotted a North Vietnamese soldier brandishing a flamethrower. The enemy infantryman was moving about the kill zone, roasting the bodies of Howard's wounded platoonmates with liquid fire.

The grisly massacre was playing out in Cambodia, far from any friendly troops in an area where the American government denied having any military presence. Bob Howard knew there would be no cavalry racing to his rescue. Most of the Green Beret's web gear had been ripped away and his automatic weapon was useless, blown all to hell by the enemy grenade. To the left of the soldier with the flamethrower, Howard spied his gravely wounded lieutenant screaming in agony. He fumbled to retrieve an M33 hand grenade strapped to his left side and struggled to remove the pin with fingers that had been slashed by red-hot shrapnel.

As he did so, the North Vietnamese Army (NVA) soldier spotted him and turned his flamethrower in Howard's direction. In the midst of rising smoke, rattling gunfire, and the screams of dying men, Howard and his opponent made direct eye contact. The American felt his enemy was experiencing a smug sense of satisfaction knowing he was about to burn a Green Beret to death.

Howard gripped his hand grenade as final thoughts rushed through his head: *I'm about to be burnt up or blown up, but I'm at least going to take this guy out with me.*[1]

◆◇◆

Sergeant Howard was stationed at Special Forces Forward Operating Base No. 2 (FOB-2), which was established in May 1966 near Kontum in the Central Highlands region of South Vietnam. This advanced base served as the operations center for a recon company of an elite U.S. military unit that fell under the auspices of the Military Assistance Command, Vietnam (MACV). The unit, code-named the Studies and Observations Group (SOG), was composed strictly of volunteers—Army Green Berets, a handful of Navy SEALs (Sea, Air, and Land), Central Intelligence Agency (CIA) field agents, and indigenous personnel.

SOG reported directly to the Joint Chiefs of Staff (JCS) and the White House, running "black ops" (top secret operations)—so classified that the very existence of the covert unit was denied by the U.S. government. SOG men took on the most dangerous assignments, working behind enemy lines to penetrate NVA facilities in Cambodia, Laos, and South Vietnam along the heavily defended Ho Chi Minh Trail. MACV organized SOG in 1964 to conduct strategic reconnaissance missions, capture enemy soldiers for intelligence, identify targets for bombing missions, conduct psychological missions (such as sabotaging enemy ammunition), and even to attempt the rescue of American prisoners of war (POW). SOG's recon men were also responsible for saving the lives of downed pilots during so-called Bright Light missions conducted deep behind enemy lines.

SOG's Green Berets operated in small recon teams of generally two or three Americans with three or more indigenous soldiers. The SOG teams were often inserted behind enemy lines by helicopter, with the American soldiers decked out in "sterile" uniforms (stripped of insignia) and carrying foreign weapons. If killed or captured, their existence in their area of operations (AO) would be denied by the U.S. government. In 1969, MACV-SOG documented its ratio of NVA soldiers killed to each lost Green Beret at 150 to 1—the highest documented kill ratio of any American unit in the war.

In many cases, the SOG teams went in under enemy fire and were pursued by NVA trackers from the moment they inserted into the jungle. They remained on the ground for days or even more than a week at a time with meager rations and only the ammunition each man could carry, often engaging platoon- to division-sized enemy forces until the surviving members could be extracted by helicopter. Sometimes entire teams were wiped out.

According to Major John Plaster, author of the first detailed history of SOG, the recon company at FOB-2 Kontum was the Vietnam War's most highly decorated unit, with five Medal of Honor (MOH) recipients. These five sky blue ribbons were awarded between February 1967 and January 1970. Within that same stretch, FOB-2 recon men also received eight Distinguished Service Crosses (DSC)—the nation's second-highest award for valor—and innumerable other awards. Purple Hearts were awarded by the unit at a pace unparalleled in American wars of the twentieth century, with team casualties sometimes reaching 100 percent. Oftentimes, Special Forces (SF) troopers declined the submission of paperwork for a Purple Heart or simply did not report minor shrapnel wounds—as far as they were concerned, it was all in a day's work.

It would be impossible to relate all of the covert missions run by the Kontum recon company in a book of this length. Many of the reports and documents pertaining to these missions were destroyed to maintain the secrecy of SOG. Reconstructing the story of how FOB-2 Kontum took shape was made possible largely through the knowledge of the original thirty-three Green Berets who began running operations from the base. These same men added improvements to the compound. The FOB slowly increased in size, incorporating more recon teams (RTs) and a reaction battalion until the number of American servicemen stationed there had doubled.

This small base would slowly grow in strength during its first two years of operation, and the records it would amass for the numbers of troops involved are inspiring. In the official language of the Medal of Honor citation, each of the five SOG recipients received the nation's highest award for "conspicuous gallantry and intrepidity at the risk of his life above and beyond the call of duty" while tending to the welfare of wounded comrades.[2] Some of these five perished in the course of the mission for which they were later honored. Bob Howard was wounded on fourteen occasions, received eight Purple Hearts, and emerged from Vietnam as the most highly decorated soldier since World War II's Audie Murphy.

However, this is not only the story of five MOH men, but also one about the eight Kontum-based DSC recipients and of dozens of other warriors who were acknowledged with other awards. In some cases, the most valiant received no formal recognition at all, either due to the eccentricities of the awards board process or the fact that there were often no surviving witnesses to the heroic actions of the man in question. The SOG warriors were supported by a wide variety of aviators flying prop-driven assault planes, single-engine Cessnas, fast-moving jets, and highly vulnerable choppers—all manned by personnel tasked with providing aerial cover, radio relay support, and life-saving extractions that often took heavy tolls.

Relating the true tale of Kontum's FOB-2 recon company is possible thanks to the participation of many. Because of the highly classified nature of SOG's existence, many of the missions remained unknown to the American public for decades after the close of hostilities in Vietnam. The author reviewed surviving military documents that have since been declassified but his primary sources were the veterans themselves—dozens of former Green Berets, airmen, and even a retired general who served two years as chief of SOG during Vietnam. They are the men who made the covert actions of SOG so highly successful. Their sacrifices were only sometimes later acknowledged with a military award, but their conduct under fire speaks volumes.

They were an uncommon bunch who displayed uncommon valor.

Chapter One

THE KONTUM THIRTY-THREE

Steve Goth suppressed an excited smile as he glanced over at Al Keller. He thought to himself: *This is it!* [1]

The two had known each other long enough that even such quick eye contact said it all. After long months of training and preparation, the close friends had finally reached the pinnacle of their short military careers—the chance to join a top secret Special Forces team so covert even its name was unknown to most.

It was the first of May 1966, and the room in which they were sitting was far removed from any bustling military compound where one might expect a clandestine force to be recruiting new members. Instead, they were on the second floor of a meager civilian villa in Da Nang that the U.S. government procured to serve as a safe house. The city was also the home of a major air base used by both the South Vietnamese and American militaries. The air inside the wood-floored structure was thick and muggy, same as it was outside.

Goth and Keller sat in silence, wearing the same standard-issue green fatigues that adorned the dozens of other Green Berets packed into rows alongside them. Most of the soldiers had arrived in Saigon just days before, where they had gone through in-country processing with the 5th Special Forces Group (SFG). There, Goth had learned about the potential new top secret assignment from Jim Hetrick, another buddy he and Keller had known since their training days.

The tension was broken only by the sharp delivery of a powerfully built Special Forces officer as he briefed his audience on their current options.

1

He was a blooded lieutenant colonel—commonly referred to as a "light colonel" or a "light bird" in military slang. But there was no disrespect shown to Lieutenant Colonel Raymond L. "Cherokee" Call as he outlined the daunting proposition facing his potential recruits.[2] A Hoosier with a serious demeanor, Call was selected to serve as a senior commander within the Army's most elite SF organization and oversee all operations at the Da Nang SF command and control headquarters, known as the C&C. The clandestine force he was to command was unknown to the men assembled before him. Some had heard rumors of its existence. Others had even heard its abbreviated name whispered: SOG.

Call did not utter the acronym but instead explained he was recruiting volunteers needed to staff two forward operating bases for the purpose of running recon missions into enemy territory. Special Forces personnel to be considered for the assignments were required to possess at least two years of service, multiple levels of specialized training, and a rank of at least specialist fourth class or corporal (E-4 pay grade).

Steve Goth and Al Keller, both of whom ranked as specialist fourth class, were the youngest Green Berets present. Goth, twenty-one, had enlisted in the Army in August 1964 after leaving college. The majority of his time had since been spent in one form of training or another. Goth and Keller met in jump school and then went through Special Forces Training Group (SFTG) together. After graduation, Steve went to the 3rd Group and Al went to the 7th Group, but both remained stationed at Fort Bragg.

The two had gotten to know each other well during that time. Keller learned that Goth was an Army brat born in New Jersey who had spent many years being raised in Europe during his father's tours of duty. At twenty, Keller was the youngest man in the room. He had grown up around Washington, DC, the son of parents who worked for the telephone company. Keller attended Hardin-Simmons College in Abilene, Texas. When his first true love didn't pan out, he joined the Army.

Some of the Green Berets seated near Keller and Goth learned of the unique assignment while still Stateside. Sergeant First Class Jim Stewart first heard of a list being quietly compiled by senior noncommissioned officers (NCOs) in the 3rd, 6th, and 7th Groups. Those who volunteered for the top secret assignment in Vietnam received no further information until they arrived in-country. Stewart penned his name to the list without hesitation. "Access to the list was closed before some of the guys even knew it was being circulated," he recalled.[3] Stewart and others were quickly gathered in San Francisco, placed on a Boeing 707 airliner bound for Saigon via Hawaii, and in-processed by the 5th Group headquarters in Nha Trang before being flown to Da Nang for their secret assignment briefing.

Among the Green Berets whisked from Fort Bragg, North Carolina, to Nha Trang in the previous week were a few with more experience. Twenty-eight-year-old Sergeant First Class Morris "Mo" Worley found the whole Vietnam "special project" to be intriguing. "We asked a lot of questions and got no answers," said Worley, who jumped at the chance nonetheless. He and his father did not see eye to eye, so Worley finished his senior year of high school living at the local Louisville, Kentucky, YMCA while working at a duplicating company in the afternoons to make ends meet. Upon joining the Army in 1956, he was open to new adventure.

Worley's initial service was with the 11th Armored Cavalry Regiment, which found him stationed in Germany off and on for the better part of five years. During the early 1960s, Worley also saw service in Korea's demilitarized zone and later back at Fort Knox as a drill instructor. He attended Airborne School in October 1964, and completed his Special Forces training in June 1965. Worley had more military experience than many of his fellow soldiers assembled at the Da Nang briefing, but he was equally green when it came to combat.

"Most of your operations will be conducted across the fence," Lieutenant Colonel Call explained. "This means you will be operating behind enemy lines."[4]

He further detailed that each man would go in sterile, meaning that they would wear no uniform and carry no weapon or accoutrements that could in any way identify them as being part of the U.S. military. Recon patrols would include a combination of Green Berets and indigenous troops called "Nungs," ethnic Chinese who had immigrated to Vietnam from China's Kwangsi Province. The Nungs had proven their fighting skills during the French Indochina War more than a decade prior. In some cases, the team might also include an officer of the Army of the Republic of Vietnam (ARVN) to assist with their mission.

Recon patrols could expect clashes in enemy-held territory with NVA soldiers or their allies, fighters of the People's Liberation Armed Forces of South Vietnam (PLF), who were referred to by American soldiers as Vietcong or VC. In the event that anyone was killed or captured while conducting covert missions "across the fence," the U.S. government would deny any knowledge of their activity. Their families would simply be notified that they were missing in action (MIA).

Such work was exactly why Steve Goth had gotten into Special Forces in the first place. His mind flashed back to the action-packed James Bond film *Goldfinger*, which he had seen at the base theater the previous year. Ian Fleming's fictional British secret agent thriller had first hit American theaters in 1962, with Sean Connery starring as agent 007. By early 1966,

American audiences had already been captivated by four James Bond films. *Goldfinger*, the third Bond film, had quickly become the highest-grossing movie of its time, surpassing $124 million worldwide.

Goth was still reliving James Bond action scenes as he considered the potential dangers he might face behind enemy lines. But the romance came to an end as he noted the briefing officer turn the meeting over to poker-faced men dressed in black suits with thin black ties. *Obviously CIA guys,* thought Goth.

One of the black suits reminded the volunteer group that everyone present had special clearance to even hear the secret details they had heard so far and before proceeding, each man had to make the choice whether this special assignment was something he was fully prepared to accept.

"Those who wish to move forward at this point will be committed for one full year," he said. "Anyone who wants to decline the opportunity can now simply raise your hand. You will be taken to another room for debriefing, and then will simply be sent back to 5th Group for a new duty assignment. No questions asked."

Jim Stewart glanced nervously around the room. No hands went up, but he felt if anyone had raised their arm to opt out, others would have followed suit. After a quiet moment, the briefing officers continued their presentation.

"I wanna tell you one other thing," Lieutenant Colonel Call added. "Take a look to your left and then take a look to your right. One of those two men beside you will be dead at this time next year." The officer let that fact soak in for a moment before continuing. "All right, let's take a break. Go downstairs, grab a Coke or a cigarette. Then, if you're still willing to stay with the unit, come on back up after the break."

Goth and Keller shuffled downstairs to talk during the short recess. *Well, if Steve will do it, I'll do it,* Keller thought. Goth was playing out the same scenario in his mind. He was prepared to move forward with the new Special Forces assignment since his former jump school buddy also seemed willing. Remembering the colonel's warning, a dark thought—unspoken to his pal—reverberated in Goth's head: *Poor ol' Al is going to be dead next year.*

The smoke break was short. Goth noted only one man, a Green Beret who had two young children, who declined to return to the briefing. Once everyone was reassembled back upstairs, the colonel resumed his briefing. His new volunteers were to be assigned to one of two forward operating bases: either the one at Kham Duc, located just ten miles from the Laotian border and sixty miles southwest of Da Nang, or a new FOB to be located in the Central Highlands near the town of Kontum.

At the conclusion of the meeting, a list was posted. Roughly half of the group were slated for service at the Kham Duc FOB. The remainder had their names written in for duty at the Kontum forward operating base designated as FOB-2. Jim Stewart scanned down the two lists and saw that two of his closest buddies, Harry Whalen and John "Ranger" Roy, were on the Kham Duc list.

He then ran his finger down the alphabetized names on the Kontum list: Billy Joe Anthony, Louis Austria, Jan Borek, Ronald Bowling, John Couch, Alex Fontes, Robert Franke, Stephen Goth, Jim Hetrick, Richard Jenkins, Alan Keller, Charles Kerns, Jerry Lee, James Lively, and Louis Smith. He hurriedly skimmed toward the bottom of the list: Charles Vessels, Morris Worley. Running his finger back up the sheet, he finally spotted his own name: Jimmie Lee Stewart.

Many of these men were complete strangers to each other, but the Green Berets would soon become very well acquainted. The two groups of new recon recruits were ordered to gather their gear and report to the airstrip, where a C-130 Hercules transport was waiting. Located on the eastern coast of the Republic of Vietnam, Da Nang had become the world's busiest airport by 1966. The C-130 was scarcely airborne before the pilot was landing at the FOB at Kham Duc. "When we landed at Kham Duc and I saw that camp, I was certainly happy that I had been assigned to Kontum—even though I hadn't seen it yet," said Stewart. "Whoever located the camp at Kham Duc certainly didn't consider defending it."[5]

From Kham Duc, the next flight was only seventy-five miles south to Kontum, where the C-130 landed on the concrete strip of the bustling civilian airport. The Green Berets grabbed their gear and clambered onto a pair of three-quarter-ton trucks for the short ride to their new base south of town. Steve Goth glanced about at Kontum, a small French colonial rubber plantation town nestled in the Annamite Mountains of the Central Highlands region. Its simple streets were sprinkled with white stucco, red tile-roofed buildings.

As their trucks approached the fence of a modest, gated compound, Goth was enjoying the moment. *The sun is shining and this looks like the start of a great adventure,* he mused. The truck jerked to a halt within the old base and the Da Nang transferees grabbed their personal effects and disembarked. They found that they were the first large contingent of permanently assigned men to arrive at FOB-2. They had been preceded by only a handful of other SF guys who had been similarly assigned from other bases. All told, the new Special Forces base would initially comprise fewer than three dozen men, who were soon calling themselves the original "Kontum thirty-three."

Leonard Tilley, a staff sergeant with nearly a dozen years in the Army to his credit, was one of the thirty-three who arrived separately from the big Da Nang bunch. A country boy from Arizona raised on hunting and fishing, Tilley had been with the 3rd Group in HALO (high altitude, low opening) training at Fort Bragg when he signed on for the special assignment. Despite his rank over some of the FOB-2 newbies, he was equally uncertain about the nature of his new assignment.

Tilley listened as a sergeant checked their names off a clipboard and reminded each man of the new radio code name he would use while on recon duty: "prince." Billy Anthony announced he was "swimmer," Jan Borek said he was "crossbow," and so on. Tilley knew that he was entering an entirely new level of security when he and the others were ordered to remove all the insignia from the uniforms they wore on base: Special Forces patches, name tapes, rank chevrons, and qualification badges—all had to come off.

All of their cross-border gear—from uniforms to rucksacks and web gear—was exchanged for items of Asian origin. The intel passed along in their Da Nang briefing was repeated. Should a team be captured, its members were to state that they had mistakenly crossed into Laos while searching for a downed aircraft near the border. In other words, they would be crossing into enemy territory on missions that were strictly denied by the United States. The prospect of now being a secret agent like James Bond was far removed from Tilley's mind at the moment.

All he could think was, *Oh shit!*[6]

Chapter Two

SPIKE TEAMS AND HATCHET FORCE

Although he tried to suppress his emotions, forty-four-year-old Colonel John Kirk "Jack" Singlaub was disappointed when he was handed command of a relatively new operation known as MACV-SOG. Having served in special ops in both World War II and Korea, he was hoping for a conventional command when his impending assignment to Vietnam was made known to him in the fall of 1965.[1]

His superiors considered Colonel Singlaub to be the perfect fit for the cloak-and-dagger job soon to be vacated by Colonel Donald Blackburn of MACV. Blackburn was the legendary commander of the World War II guerrilla network known as "Blackburn's Headhunters," which had been highly successful in disrupting the Japanese military in the Philippines. In May 1965, Blackburn assumed command of the joint unconventional warfare task force known as SOG. The Joint Chiefs created SOG in January 1964 to conduct operations in North Vietnam under direction of the unit's first leader, Colonel Clyde Russell, and his superiors in the Pentagon.

SOG was primarily composed of U.S. Army Special Forces personnel, but also included some Navy SEALs, Air Force personnel, CIA agents, and elements of the Marine Force Reconnaissance units. The United States had committed nearly two hundred thousand troops to South Vietnam by the end of 1965, but the war with North Vietnam was continuing to escalate. Defense Secretary Robert McNamara approved covert attacks on North Vietnam during 1963, and by early 1964 Lieutenant Colonel Raymond "Cherokee" Call had been assigned as one of the leaders of Operational

Plan (OP) 34A, the highly classified U.S. unconventional warfare program that developed into SOG.

Ray Call was commissioned in Germany during World War II and served in the infantry during the Korean conflict. In 1960, he took a military training team from the 77th Special Forces to Vietnam to set up one of three training teams of ARVN rangers. "The Vietnamese were not all that enthused about it so they sent me every misfit that they had in their roster," Call said. He immediately put the Vietnamese soldiers through a tough physical fitness regimen until he had only 19 worthwhile men remaining of the 110 he had been first assigned.[2]

President Lyndon Johnson used an attack on the destroyer USS *Maddox* (DD-731) in the Gulf of Tonkin in August 1964 to urge Congress to dramatically escalate the Vietnam War with more U.S. involvement. Lieutenant Colonel Call soon found more U.S. Special Forces collaboration in 1965 with the ARVN rangers he had trained, and he boldly issued plans for MACV-SOG OP-35. It called for direct action and long-range reconnaissance patrols into North Vietnamese territories by American-led recon elements to verify the existence of the Ho Chi Minh Trail and to disrupt the tremendous amount of supplies moving along "the Trail." The unpaved Laotian infiltration network had been created by the North Vietnamese Communist Party's Central Committee in April 1959, where the Truong Son Route (the name used by the NVA) wound covertly through mountains and jungles. During its height of use, the Trail would carry more than ten thousand camouflaged trucks along two thousand miles of hidden roads, protected by antiaircraft (AA) guns and tens of thousands of support troops.[3]

Call's OP-35 moved from his boss, Don Blackburn, on to General William Westmoreland, the MACV commander in charge of all U.S. forces deployed in South Vietnam. The chain of command for approvals continued all the way to Washington. SOG was given more flexibility to expand operations into Laos, an operation that was given the code name Shining Brass. These efforts were headed by Blackburn's chosen leader, Colonel Arthur David "Bull" Simons, a no-nonsense veteran of World War II's 6th Ranger battalion who had iron gray hair and a physique that fit his nickname. Simons began training volunteers from the 1st Special Forces Group on Okinawa in the summer of 1965 and then secretly moved the first sixteen of them into Vietnam for deployment.[4]

Don Blackburn's MACV-SOG operated out of Saigon, with its C&C headquarters at Da Nang Air Base on the eastern coast of Vietnam. In-country training was conducted near Saigon at the ARVN airborne training center (Camp Quyet Thang) located at Long Thanh, a well-guarded barbed wire compound with an asphalt strip big enough to accommodate C-130 transport planes. Training for U.S. personnel assigned to recon teams was conducted at Kham Duc, and SOG's Shining Brass operations into Laos commenced in late September 1965.

By that time, William Sullivan, the U.S. ambassador to Laos, had eased the restrictions slightly for recon teams inserting into Laotian territories. Instead of walking into just two small areas of the country, he authorized SOG teams to be inserted as deep as twelve miles across the entire two-hundred-mile border that separated Laos from South Vietnam. Don Blackburn's SOG teams were running regular Shining Brass missions to disrupt Communist efforts in Laos by the time he recommended Jack Singlaub to be his successor as chief SOG in April 1966.[5]

Colonel Singlaub's experience fit the job requirements to a tee. In October 1943, when the twenty-two-year-old UCLA graduate and lieutenant was serving as an airborne infantry patrol leader, he was recruited by the Office of Strategic Services (OSS) to become a member of Operation Jedburgh, a joint clandestine operation involving American, British, French, Dutch, and Belgian special operatives. In August 1944, Singlaub parachuted behind German lines to work with the Free French Resistance fighters after the D-Day invasion.[6]

Following World War II, he headed CIA operations in Manchuria during the Chinese Communist revolution, helped train Army Ranger companies for service in the Korean War, and commanded clandestine operations and an infantry battalion in Korea. Singlaub was a born fighter, ready to command a front-line brigade when he was assigned to Vietnam. His disappointment in being ordered to take over SOG was that it was an unconventional warfare, sabotage, and covert-action organization of considerably smaller size. But orders were orders, and Colonel Singlaub's orders had originated from General Westmoreland, who had specifically requested him as the new MACV-SOG commander.[7]

His duties thus cemented, Singlaub immediately decided what his command style must be. Hard-charging Green Berets,

Jack Singlaub, who had served in the OSS during World War II, was Chief SOG from April 1966 into early 1968. *U.S. Army*

Navy SEALs, and Air Commandos would respect a chief SOG who could lead by example versus pushing mimeographed orders from a distant headquarters. Jack Singlaub would do just that, making himself visibly available to his front-line SOG men.

He arrived in Saigon in April 1966, taking up residence with his deputy commander in a nearby villa in a quiet neighborhood. By all appearances, his duty was that of a staff colonel conducting routine studies on U.S. military operations. But his headquarters was in a guarded compound with air-conditioned operations and intelligence center vaults that closely guarded the identities of his agents. The locations of Singlaub's SOG teams were never marked on permanent maps, but instead on single-copy transparent overlays. As chief SOG, he reported directly to the Pentagon but kept General Westmoreland fully briefed on all of his operations.[8]

Singlaub's mission was to covertly take the war directly to the enemy's home and into his sanctuaries in Laos and Cambodia. His cross-border recon teams fell under the OP-35 group led by Colonel Bull Simons—a founding member of the Green Berets. During the Korean War, Simons had been the only man able to outshoot the new chief SOG on the pistol range. "He had a vocabulary that would make a drill sergeant blush," said Singlaub.[9]

MACV-SOG's new commander made trips around the country to meet his local commanders and inspect their units. During one of his observation flights in a command and control Bell UH-1 Iroquois (commonly known by the GIs as the "Huey"), Singlaub's pilot banked his chopper low enough over entrenched Vietcong positions that machine-gun fire clanged off the bottom of the helicopter. He was quick to expand the number of his cross-border teams, their staging areas, and forward operating bases, including the new facility coming together at Kontum. By mid-1966, Singlaub, Bull Simons, and Ray Call were authorized to increase their SOG recon teams to better explore their expanded operational area, with an authorization to up their five original teams to twenty teams.

Jack Singlaub soon became the biggest asset to the men running recon from the SOG bases, and the men of the new FOB-2 would grow to respect him immensely.

Mo Worley spent his first weeks at Kontum wondering when and if he would ever see action; his primary weapons were now a hammer, nails, and a saw. The site of his labor was just south of Kontum City, located only about forty miles southeast of the tri-border area where Cambodia, Laos,

An aerial view of Forward Operating Base 2 (FOB-2) at Kontum. The former ARVN (Army of the Republic of Vietnam) truck park was divided in half by Highway 14. *Joe Parnar*

and South Vietnam meet. He and the other new FOB-2 volunteers had been assigned to improve an older fortified camp first opened in early 1966 when the nearby Special Forces launch site at Dak To proved to be too small for expansion. The base at Kontum had been used by French forces as an ARVN truck compound during the French Indochina War. Split in two by Highway 14 south of Kontum City, the base had only a few sheds and some older, run-down buildings when SOG opted to convert it into FOB-2. There were no true barracks and no proper latrines. Rotting punji sticks—sharpened bamboo stakes protruding upward from the earth to deter enemy ambushes—were still scattered about the compound, hazardous remnants French troops had left in place in 1954 at the end of the First Indochina War.[10]

Many of the original thirty-three Kontum men were tasked with making quick improvements to the place. Sergeant First Class Fred "Huckleberry" Lewis was an engineer already at the base working on things when the newbies arrived. An easy-going country boy who often sported an old straw hat above his freckled face, Lewis could easily have played the part of the Mark Twain character for whom he was nicknamed.[11]

Huckleberry Lewis had been one of the first Special Forces men to be permanently assigned to man the new Kontum FOB. Prior to Lewis' arrival on the first of May 1966, Kontum had been staffed by temporary duty (TDY) soldiers on six-month assignment from the 1st Group on Okinawa. Many of these TDY troopers were still with Lewis, but their time was quickly drawing to a close. Lewis was a busy man. He found that Kontum's largest structure was a small building with two rooms about ten feet square each. He set to work walling in two large corrugated sheet-metal sheds that had originally been motor pools to create a mess hall for the Nungs. His next step was to hastily construct a number of barracks to be used by the American recon teams. Newbies like Mo Worley went a long way in assisting Lewis with the labor.[12]

FOB-2 was under the command of Major Charlie Norton, a well-seasoned Korean War veteran who had enlisted in the Army in 1944. As one of the first men to join Special Forces, Norton deployed to Vietnam in 1965, where he literally helped write the book on SOG's operational details. In addition to supervising the construction of improvements to the new Kontum compound, Norton was in charge of the equipping, training, briefing, deployment, and recovery of multiple recon teams—it was a tall order. He frequently flew with one or more forward air controller (FAC) reconnaissance flights, maintaining contact with deployed teams, often directing them to their exfiltration sites. During his early days of setting up FOB-2, he was assisted by Major Bobby Leites, another early SOG organizer.

Norton's value to SOG operations was obvious to his superiors, who would soon recall him to Da Nang to serve as the base executive officer (XO) under Ray Call and later Colonel Bill Rose. As commander of FOB-2, his shoes would be filled by Lieutenant Colonel Call's current XO, Major John Heuches Crerar. Being of Scottish ancestry, Crerar had picked up the nickname "Scotty" by age fourteen—a nickname that was even employed by his mother. Crerar went through SF training in the spring of 1965 and completed a six-month tour in Laos as an attaché working psyops (psychological operations) with other parties in-country. After a three-month rotation back in the States, he returned to Vietnam in 1966 and was processed through the 5th Group to SOG.[13]

Scotty Crerar's first visit to Kontum came in early May, when he flew down to meet Charlie Norton at Dak To, the launch site Norton was running to deploy FOB-2 recon teams. The officers traveled down to Kontum, where Crerar spent the next two weeks shadowing the man he was to replace before Norton left to assume his new billet at SOG's C&C headquarters and Major Leites was similarly reassigned.

Left to right: Major John "Scotty" Crerar, the base commander of FOB-2; Sergeant First Class Burrell "Rat" Wilson of Spike Team Texas; and Captain Frank Jaks, who arrived at Kontum in June 1966. *Jason Hardy*

Major Crerar found his first organizational duty at Kontum was to replace the TDY men with those assigned for full-year tours. He considered the initial logistics to be a "disaster" until he filtered out the remaining TDY soldiers for permanent subordinates. His only saving grace was an abundance of Vietnamese money, which he allowed his officers to use to buy and trade for the things they needed—mainly carbines and ammunition for the teams going into the field. Crerar's outfit started out with poor logistics, expanding in personnel much faster than in anything else. Nine-millimeter ammunition—among the most common ammo in the world—was so scarce at FOB-2 that it had to be scraped together for teams going into the field with Swedish K submachine guns and semiautomatic pistols by taking it from the teams coming out of the field.

Major Crerar used Vietnamese money to acquire most of what he needed from the locals. He resorted to whatever measures were necessary to get things done. "I even traded two pairs of jungle fatigues I had for a guy to build a defensive berm around the camp," he recalled. Crerar found his officer pool doubled with the arrival of Captain Fred Trzos, who became the base XO. "Fred worked on building the camp at Kontum while I was trying to run the launch site at Dak To," said Crerar. "We'd talk at night about what each of us had accomplished."

Several of the early noncommissioned officers would prove to be worth their weight in gold for Crerar and Trzos during the early days at Kontum. Among them were two master sergeants, Cole Eagle and Paul Darcy, who helped disseminate intelligence received from Saigon and prepare the teams as best they could for their missions. Crerar had no true intelligence officer for his base during its early months of operation. He similarly had no true medical division to care for anyone wounded in the field. The first two qualified medics to reach Kontum were a brace of staff sergeants, John

McGirt and Don Fawcett. "McGirt scrounged together what he could," Crerar said. The wily Green Beret horse-traded with other units, giving up yellow and black paint, cavalry insignia, and other desirables in exchange for basic medical equipment and supplies to stock Kontum.

The size of the small staff was of interest to Jack Singlaub when he made his first visit to the new FOB that summer. Chief SOG made a point of traveling to his forward operating bases with Bull Simons to meet his recon teams, debrief them after extractions, and absorb firsthand what weapons his Green Berets needed to better carry out their clandestine operations. At Kontum, Major Crerar walked along with SOG's commander-in-chief pointing out the various structures his men had completed. Leading NCOs like Darcy and Eagle briefed Singlaub on other aspects of their daily operations. At one point, Singlaub nudged Crerar to the side.

"Why are all these sergeants briefing me?" he asked.

"Because there are only two of us birds here, and the other one, Captain Trzos, is up running the operations at Dak To right now."[14]

Singlaub seemed genuinely shocked and also impressed that FOB-2 was being run by only two officers. The original thirty-three were literally moving mountains to ensure their base would soon be one that chief SOG would remember.

◆◇◆

Scotty Crerar's fledgling FOB-2 was one of three new SOG bases established during the summer of 1966. The original FOB-1 at Kham Duc was abandoned in favor of a new location in the northern region of South Vietnam at Phu Bai, originally commanded by Major James Vansickle. Major Fred Patton was dispatched to the Khe Sanh launch site with instructions to develop a new forward operating base at Khe Sanh that would become FOB-3. Base commanders Crerar, Vansickle, and Patton reported to C&C Da Nang chief Ray Call, who in turn reported to the Operation Shining Brass commander, Bull Simons, in Saigon and Chief SOG Jack Singlaub. Each of the three forward operating bases housed the Special Forces personnel separate from their nearby helicopter launch sites—from which the recon teams would be flown into their assigned target areas. Crerar's Vietnamese adviser at Kontum was a Captain Tan, an old veteran of the Vietnamese airborne and the French war. "We knew who they worked for and we assumed that everything they heard they were reporting," Crerar said of his local advisers. "We were a little bit careful of what they did know."[15]

By early June, Major Crerar's FOB-2 sported eight teams either in active operation in the field or in varying stages of training and preparation for active combat service. Each recon unit, or "spike team" (ST) consisted of two to three Americans—Special Forces Green Berets—with a small number of local tribesmen to fill out their ranks.

The initial SOG recon indigenous troops were all Nungs. During Vietnam's French Indochina War, these Nungs had proven to be exceptional fighters who were very familiar with the local terrain. The South Vietnamese government, however, saw the Nungs as inferior and did not force them into the required draft for this war. SOG's brass soon found plentiful recruits among the indigenous Nungs—who were only too happy to begin accepting U.S. recon work jobs with significantly higher pay than what was normally available to them. The lowest-ranking Nungs on a SOG team in 1966 were paid about sixty U.S. dollars, comparable to the monthly pay of a South Vietnamese captain.[16]

The early SOG teams thus operated with a mix of U.S. Special Forces troopers and Chinese Nungs. The new FOB-2 at Kontum was allotted 7 American officers and 70 enlisted men, plus 135 indigenous troops for its recon teams, although Crerar had nothing close to his 70 U.S. soldiers at the onset. Each of the eight Kontum spike teams was named after an American state: Colorado, Dakota (for both North Dakota and South Dakota), Hawaii, Iowa, Maine, Nevada, Ohio, and Texas.

The leader of each spike team was assigned the code number "one-zero." The title of one-zero was prestigious within SOG, indicating a man who was respected by his leaders for possessing the fighting skills and sound judgment needed to keep his team alive when faced with numerically superior opponents in enemy territory. The Green Beret serving as the assistant team leader was given the code designation of "one-one." Teams with a junior third American member (who often carried the team's radio) labeled that Green Beret as their "one-two."

Staff Sergeant Tom Livingston was one of the first of the new Kontum thirty-three to be pulled into a recon team. Fresh from his SOG orientation meeting, he reported in at the orderly room, an older building that had been standing since the French once occupied the compound. Livingston was told he would be the new radio-telephone operator (RTO), or "commo man," for one-zero Jerry Howland's ST Hawaii.

Master Sergeant Howland, thirty-four, and his one-one, Staff Sergeant Dave Fernea, were both veterans of the Korean War with extensive experience. Livingston found them both to be easy to get along with as he adapted to his new environment at FOB-2. The living quarters were cramped; the Green Berets all slept in one old barracks building partitioned off for the teams, with their Nung counterparts sleeping in separate areas of the same rickety French structures. Construction work was already under way to build proper barracks buildings with individual team "hooches," but for the moment recon life was rather crude.

"The American shitter got built rather quickly because the Nungs had a habit of squatting over the toilet," said Livingston. The foul remnants left by their Asian counterparts motivated the Green Berets to quickly build their own latrine for the sake of hygiene. Howland's ST Hawaii had less construction detail, spending most of May training on mission and weapons procedures. Scarcity of ammunition forced Howland to train his Nungs on the Carl Gustav m/45 (better known as the "Swedish K") submachine gun with very little live firing. Tom Livingston was eager for action. Two days into his training, he watched Master Sergeant Paul "Snuffy" Conroy's ST Maine exiting one of the returning choppers and listened to details of the action they had seen across the fence.

Just weeks into team training, Livingston would get his own chance to encounter the enemy in Laos. Howland briefed the team to prepare their field gear for insertion from another forward operating base, and ST Hawaii was flown by military transport to the new base at Phu Bai. There, Livingston found choppers waiting to whisk them away yet again to FOB-3 at Khe Sanh, from which they would stage their insertion.

Major Scotty Crerar normally had his spike teams flown by chopper up to Dak To, about thirty miles away, each morning to be ready to launch from the airfield. From Dak To, the spike teams could be inserted into the tri-border region of Cambodia, Laos, and North Vietnam. Most nights, the teams not inserted would be flown back to the Kontum base, leaving only Nung company guards and radio operators to run the Dak To launch site station through the nights. During the early days of FOB-2, many of the teams were inserted by twin-rotor U.S. Marine CH-46 Sea Knight helicopters, which were particularly noisy. Not only did this tip off the enemy of their approach, it also left the Green Berets and their indigenous cohorts virtually deaf during their first crucial moments on what might well be a "hot LZ" (landing zone).[17]

Major Crerar also enlisted the services of Vietnamese Air Force (VNAF) pilots of the Da Nang–based 219th Helicopter Squadron. This unit was sent to operate from Kontum and flew old Sikorsky CH-34 Choctaw helicopters, nicknamed "Kingbees." The Kingbees had old radial, nine-cylinder Wright Aeronautical Corporation "Cyclone" R-1820 engines used in the legendary World War II B-17 aircraft—that often leaked hydraulic fluid. They were larger choppers than the U.S. Army's UH-1 Hueys, allowing them to carry more men and absorb more ground fire hits than the Hueys. Personnel exited and entered a CH-34 through one side door and the chopper was equipped with only one door gunner who was often armed with an older .30-caliber machine gun for defense. The pilots of the 219th were particularly gutsy. "On occasion, they flew when an American pilot would not," Crerar said. "If a team was in trouble, they would go."

Many of the 219th's fearless pilots were college-educated men who were paid five hundred Vietnam piasters for every twelve hours or more away from their home station and an additional three thousand Vietnam piasters every time they crossed the border into North Vietnam—roughly twenty-five dollars U.S. for each insertion and extraction. These South Vietnamese pilots were highly respected for their can-do attitude when it came to extracting U.S. Special Forces personnel from the jungle under heavy fire. Two of the plucky 219th chopper pilots flying from FOB-2 were simply known to most by their nicknames, "Mustachio" and "Cowboy." Nguyen Van Hoang—Mustachio—was known for his finely trimmed mustache, grown to hide a bullet wound he had taken in the face during a 1965 extraction. Dai Uy ("captain" in Vietnamese) Loc, known to all simply as Cowboy, had earned his nickname from his preference for well-tailored flight suits, usually in some odd camouflage pattern.[18]

Jerry Howland's ST Hawaii would be inserted into a particularly hot area of Laos from FOB-3 instead of going in from the normal Dak To launch site. One-Two Tom Livingston was heavily loaded with gear as he scrambled into the lead CH-34 chopper with Howland and several of their Nung counterparts. He carried his Swedish K submachine gun, which was capable of firing thirty-six rounds from a double-stacked magazine. Recon men, however, soon learned not to load each magazine to capacity to prevent exerting excessive pressure on the spring that might result in a jam. Livingston packed six extra magazines for the K, a Browning Hi-Power 9-mm semiautomatic pistol (with a thirteen-round magazine capacity), and plenty of extra 9-mm rounds that could be used in either the Browning or the Swedish K.

Livingston also carried a hand-made Bowie knife, two fragmentation grenades, a smoke grenade, plastic water bottles that would not clink when brushing against metal, and all the supplies and rations he would need to survive for days in the jungle. He wore a boonie-style jungle cap and was dressed in green fatigues of Vietnamese manufacture that looked similar to the NVA's uniforms. Livingston carried less ammunition than other members of the team since he was the commo man and therefore had to carry the radio, a brick-like box called an AN/PRC-25 (or "Prick Twenty-Five" in Army jargon). Weighing more than twenty-three pounds, the radio gear was split into two metal boxes ("cans") that could be quickly buckled together to couple the radio with its battery pack. And since the battery was

Staff Sergeant Tom Livingston (*left*) with his new ST Hawaii one-zero, Master Sergeant Jerry Howland. *Tom Livingston*

only good for about a day's continuous use, Livingston also had to carry a spare—adding another five or six pounds to his ruck. Livingston would be responsible for communicating team info and positions to their air support team, a critical role. On the radio, he used the code name "Africa" for himself and "lion" for reference to Howland.

As the one-zero, team leader Howland was first to exit the Kingbee chopper as it nestled onto an open LZ in mountainous Laotian terrain near a small river. He was followed by Livingston and half of ST Hawaii's Nungs before a second CH-34 deposited One-One Dave Fernea and their remaining Nungs. Team Hawaii was going into an area that had already been occupied for days by another new Kontum team, Master Sergeant Gerry Wareing's ST Iowa. Before his team departed on the same Kingbees, Wareing was able to hurriedly pass along useful intel to Howland about the North Vietnamese troops in the area he had already stirred up.

It was already late afternoon, so ST Hawaii moved from the LZ through the dense jungle terrain toward the next large ridgeline in the Central Highlands chain. Tom Livingston noted that neither the humidity nor the heat were quite as oppressive as they felt in Saigon or lower-lying areas of South Vietnam. At ground level, there was quite a bit of waist-high elephant grass to move through as his team avoided obvious foot paths that might be booby-trapped or cause them to run directly into an enemy patrol. The lowest level of grass, vines, and brush was overshadowed by a blanket of smaller trees that formed a second level of canopy that stopped most sunlight from shining through. Towering above it all was a third layer of jungle trees reaching roughly a hundred feet that created yet another blanket from the sun. Collectively, the three levels of jungle forestation comprised what recon men referred to as "triple canopy."

Spike Team Hawaii moved forward, led by its indigenous point man, and a Nung grenadier toting a Springfield M79 grenade launcher. Team leader Jerry Howland followed, with another Nung between him and RTO Livingston. They were trailed by the indigenous team leader (their zero-one), who was in turn followed by One-One Fernea, his Nung assistant, another indigenous M79 man, and the Nung tail gunner. All movement was methodical and each step was carefully placed as each man scanned the jungle while holding his weapon ready to fire at any moment. Howland moved his team across a large creek and then advanced up the next hillside as darkness began to settle into the jungle.

He decided ST Hawaii should make its overnight camp near the crest of the hill, where they had the advantage of moving in either direction should they be surprised during the night. Such remain overnight (RON) sites were carefully chosen in areas of thick vegetation, with portions of both the American and Nung teammates splitting up the watch hours until dawn. The elevation of the Central Highlands made it cool enough during the night hours for Livingston to break out his locally procured sweater. Despite the apprehensions of sleeping in enemy-patrolled terrain, his exhaustion helped him drift off to sleep quickly.

Howland was on the move shortly after daybreak, taking one of his Nungs to recon the area below, back toward the creek. Upon his return, he dispatched assistant team leader Fernea with another indigenous trooper to sweep back down to the creek. Howland then ordered his men to pack their gear quickly and get ready to move out. Livingston, green to the situation, would only realize later that his one-zero was having a little fun with their one-one. Howland had detected a company of North Vietnamese Army (NVA) soldiers sweeping up the hill toward their position—and they were already across the creek.

When Fernea and his Nung raced back to the RON site moments later, Howland was fully prepared for his announcement.

"NVA!" Fernea whispered. "They're moving towards us. Lots of 'em!"[19]

Spike Team Hawaii moved swiftly through the triple-canopy jungle, over the crest of the hill and then up the side of the next hill. Chattering fire from North Vietnamese automatic weapons and the sound of little metal clickers (hand-held signaling devices) gave Livingston indications of the directions from which his opponents were advancing. Howland's men remained on the run as his one-two called in air strikes against the pursuing NVA soldiers. Air Force A-1 Skyraider "Spad" attack aircraft soon arrived to drop 500-pound bombs in the wake of the fleeing Green Berets. Livingston felt the ordnance make hellacious booms, and he prayed that their explosive force was not only ripping the jungle foliage but also killing the men who were chasing him.

Kingbee choppers swooped low over another open mountain ridge to extract Jerry Howland's ST Hawaii a short time later. His men had thoroughly stirred up their enemy, had called in air strikes on an NVA company, and had been extracted without loss. For rookie Tom Livingston, his first action across the fence was one he would not forget. Two of his closest buddies, Al Keller and Steve Goth, listened to his fresh adventure tales with the wish they could soon make their way out of commo duty and onto one of Kontum's recon teams.

✦◇✦

FOB-2 was initially home to three spike teams, all of which had seen prior service. Teams Dakota, Iowa, and Ohio had been in operation at FOB-1 in early 1966 before they were shifted from Kham Duc in early May down to Major Crerar's new Kontum FOB. Each of these units was headed by an experienced master sergeant: ST Dakota under Don Fowler, ST Iowa led by Gerry Wareing, and ST Ohio under Dick Meadows. These three went right to work at Kontum and continued running missions across the fence during May while five other FOB-2 spike teams completed their training.

Spike Team Ohio was already considered something of a hotshot team. Its one-zero, Master Sergeant Meadows, was considered the foremost prisoner snatcher operating with SOG at the time. The son of a coal miner, he was born in Johnson's Creek, Virginia, on June 16, 1931, as Bernard J. Meadows Jr. He was not fond of the name Bernard and was called "Junior" by his family. In time, he would change his name to "Richard J. Meadows," and he became known to most simply as Dick. He enlisted in the U.S. Army at age fifteen with the aid of his uncle, Oscar Meadows, who signed as a witness for him to enter the service.[20]

Dick Meadows originally failed to qualify for airborne training by being five pounds shy of the 125-pound minimum requirement. He worked to put on the necessary weight, completed Airborne School at Fort Benning, and joined the 187th Regimental Combat Team in 1951. By age twenty he was wearing the stripes of a master sergeant, an impressive achievement. He joined Special Forces during the 1950s and completed overseas tours of duty that included Bavaria and England.[21]

In addition to representing the Army on a British rugby team, he became one of the first two officially trained HALO jumpmaster-instructors. He and his wife Pamela celebrated the birth of their first son in 1964 and a year later, Dick volunteered for service in Vietnam. Meadows was clearly a man with a mission: behind his bright blue eyes burned an intense desire to be the consummate professional warrior. Assigned as an operations sergeant at Long Thanh, Dick soon caught wind of the top secret SOG project. He approached Colonel Bull Simons and expressed his desire to be a reconnaissance team leader, a one-zero, one who would build the best possible team through detailed training, planning, and physical fitness, augmented by boldly thinking and constant rehearsal of critical techniques and immediate action drills. Meadows swore he would do his best to make sure he never lost a man.[22]

Boldness was exactly the asset that Master Sergeant Meadows and his ST Ohio became known for. They quickly gained a strong reputation running targets from FOB-1. In January 1966, his team had engaged in a firefight with five NVA soldiers and managed to bring back two of them alive. On another mission, Ohio had a firefight with a party of NVA on the bank of a river. Meadows dropped his weapon and dove in after a wounded enemy soldier who was trying to flee, and thereby added to his growing tally of prisoners successfully snatched.[23]

During a target run from April 25 to 28, 1966, Meadows and his ST Ohio found what they deemed to be an enemy way station in the jungle. The route of infiltration into American areas of operation was manned by two Montagnard (literally "mountain dweller" in French) tribesmen who were apparently sympathetic to the North Vietnamese. The Montagnard are a diverse group of indigenous tribes inhabiting the Central Highlands region; they were recruited to fight by both sides of the conflict. Meadows had his team capture the men and destroy their banana tree crop and their water buffalo to foil the way station's operation.

On May 24, Ohio was inserted into another enemy-controlled area where Montagnard agents operated way stations to help the enemy troops. Team Ohio was credited with the destruction of three thousand bushels of rice and three villages of six houses each which were used as way stations.[24] Spike Team Ohio also captured a local Montagnard supply agent on this mission and located an NVA battalion. Meadows called in air strikes on the battalion and his men directed these strikes for eight hours. The enemy soldiers would at times move closer into the area of ST Ohio for their own protection. They came close enough that a member of Meadows' team killed one of the NVA. The incident compromised Ohio's position, so Meadows had his team fall back to a new location from which to direct the strikes. En route, they captured two NVA soldiers and after five days in the field Ohio was extracted with its three prisoners. Intelligence gathered from the POWs led to additional heavy bomber strikes in that area.

Dick Meadows and ST Ohio's success centered around their boldness, their training, and the proficiency of each man on the team. Meadows' team was exceptional, both when operating from Kham Duc and after its transfer to FOB-2. By early June, ST Ohio had taken on new team members from the original Kontum thirty-three. Meadows' one-one was thirty-one-year-old Sergeant First Class Charles Nathan "Chuck" Kerns, who helped fill the void soon created by the transfer of Raul Torres, a Hawaiian native who had been with ST Ohio for a while. During this time, ST Ohio added another new team member—thirty-three-year-old Sergeant First Class Jan (pronounced "yahn") Borek, a blooded veteran with thirteen years of Army service. His early years had been lived amid the turmoil of World War II, growing up in war-ravaged Poland under Nazi occupation. Borek's family moved to France seeking political asylum and it was here that he spent his teen years. In 1952, he was listening to a Polish radio broadcast coming out of England stating that people from behind the Iron Curtain with a good, clean record had been authorized by the U.S. Senate to join the American army. With that, Borek submitted his paperwork, hopped a train to Germany, and joined the U.S. Army.

Borek served in a variety of assignments with the Army during the next decade, including tours of duty in Panama with the 8th Special Forces Group. During his years in Panama, he had come to know two SF soldiers who were now part of his recon company at Kontum—Dick Meadows and Billy Joe Anthony. Borek joined ST Ohio as its RTO.

Meadows, Kerns, Borek, Torres, and their team of Nungs were inserted on the morning of June 18 to determine the location and activities of VC forces. They carried 9-mm Swedish K submachine guns, wore sterile uniforms (no rank or insignia), and humped gear that was largely Asian-made and untraceable. As soon as the sounds of their insertion choppers had faded away, Meadows had his team fan out on the move through the balmy jungle terrain.

The mission of ST Ohio was to direct air strikes against native way stations that were being used to support NVA troops. Meadows called in B-52 bombers to pound each reported enemy location, his team taking cover as the concussive shock waves of 500-pound bombs leveled trees, flattened structures, and left towering clouds of dust and dirty smoke drifting skyward. Once the strike craft had cleared the area, the recon men of ST Ohio swept in to perform bomb damage assessments (BDAs). These were Montagnard villages, but in one BDA area, Meadows' team found the bodies of three Vietcong killed by the strikes.

In one of the Montagnard shacks, they discovered a stashed 75-mm howitzer. Borek read the French language on the howitzer's ID plate and found that it had been made in Toulouse, France, during World War II. In another village, Borek was surprised when his team's interpreter suddenly opened fire with his Swedish K. Nguyen Canh Thach, known to ST Ohio as "Ted," skillfully dropped two VC opponents before running out to retrieve their two weapons.[25] Dick Meadows would receive the Silver Star for this patrol, during which his men had called in disabling air strikes and lay in hiding close enough to an enemy trail to photograph passing VC and their equipment. When his team was ordered to evacuate the area on June 23, Meadows was flown to Saigon to brief General Westmoreland on the types of weapons his team had discovered.

Meadows returned to Kontum with orders to lead ST Ohio back into the area to continue destroying the Montagnard way stations that were providing supplies and comfort to the enemy. They found one village with many bamboo hooches and a heavy concentration of animals that were undoubtedly supplying the North Vietnamese.

Meadows relayed the intelligence to Kontum, where Major Crerar ordered up a Hatchet Force platoon to complete the destruction of the way station. Air strikes leveled the vicinity before the choppers landed the next morning to finish off the livestock and search for potential prisoners. Jan Borek was shocked to see another of his old buddies from Panama days, Billy Joe Anthony, coming off one of the choppers.

"What the hell are you doing out here?" he asked.

"Well, I'm just here," Anthony replied. "I'm on the Hornet Force."[26]

Anthony had spent his early weeks on the Hatchet Force but he was eager to join a recon team, and he would soon get his chance, joining his buddies Borek and Meadows on ST Ohio. As the newest member of the team, Anthony was no raw recruit. A rugged North Carolinian, he was an Army brat whose father and brother were also servicemen. His dad reluctantly signed the papers allowing him to join the Army in 1958 right out of high school. He joined Special Forces and had already done tours in Germany and Central America before being assigned to the new FOB-2 at Kontum in May 1966. Like Meadows and Borek, Billy Joe had once served in the 8th Special Force Group in Panama before cycling back to the States. He soon became bored with the "ash and trash" of Stateside life and enlisted the aid of Billye Alexander in the Pentagon to land an assignment to SOG in Vietnam. Mrs. Alexander, the civilian administrator who oversaw Special Forces overseas assignments, quietly ran the SOG replacement pipeline from Washington for years, seeing to it that the most qualified Green Berets were hand-selected for rotation into the hot zones of Vietnam.

Spike Team Ohio already had the reputation for being the hottest team in terms of pulling prisoners during early 1966. With the new team of Meadows, Borek, and Anthony in place, it would not be long before Meadows was ready to try another prisoner grab.

✦◇✦

Captain Frank Jaks was a welcomed arrival at FOB-2. Base commander Scotty Crerar and his XO, Captain Fred Trzos, had been snowed under with work. Their spike teams ran targets while the base officers continued organizing new teams, running the nearby Dak To launch site, and continuing to improve upon the existing structures. Captain Jaks' arrival during June 1966 as a third infantry officer at Kontum would certainly help lighten the load for Crerar's staff.

As a teenager, Jaks had been an anti-Nazi resistance fighter in his native Czechoslovakia. He fled to America after the Communists seized power in 1948. Under the 1952 Lodge Act, he was able to secure American citizenship as a European refugee by enlisting in the U.S. Army—where he went into Special Forces. Jaks had received a Purple Heart during his first tour of combat in Vietnam during 1963.[27]

At FOB-2, Frank Jaks became the base operations officer (S3), in charge of the deployment of all men—American and indigenous—for recon missions. As such, he received a target list from SOG headquarters in Saigon, with approximately twenty-five to forty approved targets per month. From this list, Jaks and his staff selected teams to engage the targets by their priority order.[28]

The appropriate team leader for each mission was then given an initial briefing by one of Jaks' cohorts in S3. The team leader was then able to study maps, aerial photos, and other intelligence known of his target area. "After he has studied his target folder, he will then be programmed for a visual reconnaissance (VR)," Jaks said. "This is done with a U-17 type aircraft or an O-1, whichever is available." After visually surveying his target area, the one-zero then prepared his team for the specific mission. A final briefing was then given by one of Captain Jaks' S2 (intelligence) officers, this meeting dealing with the target area and flight route.[29]

Standard equipment during the early months of operation from FOB-2 included the Swedish K submachine gun, with approximately 350 to 450 rounds of ammunition per person. Each spike team carried a minimum of two M79 grenade launchers and forty to fifty rounds, with high explosive (HE) comprising at least two-thirds of the rounds. "Each team member carries two to three fragmentation hand grenades, one CS [teargas] grenade, and a minimum of two smoke grenades per man," said Jaks. "The U.S. members carry URC-10 survival radios and one PRC-25. Each remaining member of the team carries the following survival equipment: [fluorescent red and orange reversible signal] panel, signaling mirror and strobe light, and a pin flare."[30]

For team leaders, Jaks preferred Green Berets with ten years of service and a rank of staff sergeant or sergeant first class. He believed that one-zeros must serve on a truly voluntary basis, should be less than thirty years of age, and in top physical condition. He soon found that he had less than a five percent drop-out rate of SF men on his teams after the individual was fully briefed on the realities of the unit's mission.

By the time Frank Jaks joined FOB-2, Major Crerar had started forming a Reaction Force to help the spike teams break enemy contact so they could be extracted. As the number of Kontum-based recon teams increased, their rate of contact with NVA forces also increased. The use of such exploitation forces—to be deployed both for cases of necessity and opportunity—had been authorized during 1965. Each exploitation battalion or "Haymaker Force" could consist of as many as four companies. Each 138-man Hatchet Force company was to be formed of three platoons—better known as "Hornet Forces." Each Hornet Force platoon consisted of forty-two indigenous troops and four Green Berets, under the command of an American lieutenant. Each FOB was also to be assigned a separate rifle company as a security force.

It would take some time to bring Major Crerar's Hatchet Force companies up to strength. During late May 1966, he did not have enough Green Berets to fill out Kontum, much less any lieutenants to run Hornet Force platoons. Chinese Nungs made up the lion's share of the Hatchet Force. The old 1st Group TDY men from Okinawa were still in the process of being rotated out in favor of permanent team replacements, so Crerar and Trzos found willing recruits among some of the thirty-three permanent newbies still without a team. Jim Stewart jumped at the chance. Kontum's initial Hatchet Force was designated the First Raider Company. Its members were issued a patch featuring a white skull with glaring red eyes resting on green crossed arrows on a black background. "First Raider Company" was printed in red letters on a black tab across the top of the patch—which, of course, Stewart knew was forbidden to be worn on uniform in the field.[31]

Kontum's new Hatchet Force saw action right away in May. Jim Stewart had only been a part of the unit for about two weeks when Colonel Bull Simons put out a call for the Hatchet Force to be deployed in the Ashau Valley. Simons wanted four Americans and a Hatchet Force platoon to meet him immediately at the air strip in Da Nang.

Stewart, Sergeant First Class Alex Fontes, Staff Sergeant Don Fawcett, and Sergeant First Class Jerry Lee were told to grab their gear and their Nung platoon and head for the choppers. Simons was waiting for them on the ground when they reached Da Nang. He unfurled an area map and proceeded to brief Fontes' team and their Huey pilots on the mission. Colonel Simons wanted to make an onsite inspection of Camp Ashau, a former A-team camp that had been overrun by the NVA two months earlier.

"I noticed that the Huey pilots' eyes got a little bigger and there was a look of disbelief on their faces," said Stewart. "I'm sure they saw the same reaction from me."[32]

There were plenty of raw nerves as the four Americans and their Nung team members were flown across the fence into enemy territory. As the Hueys reached the former A-team camp, Fontes deployed his Nungs in a loose perimeter around the area. The Green Berets moved swiftly about the camp, on high alert for possible enemy contact. Stewart was much relieved to find no action this day. Instead, his team discovered many weapons, ammunition, and the skeletal remains of those who had been killed in action. Bull Simons' command slick (a helicopter with only defensive armament) dropped him on the ground once the perimeter was clear and his inspection time was no more than a half hour.

The four Huey slicks soon thereafter collected the Hatchet Force platoon and the colonel and were on their way back to Da Nang. Jim Stewart believed the North Vietnamese in the area had been caught off guard by "the audacity of four slicks coming in to Ashau without a gunship" to support them.

It was the second week of June before Scotty Crerar and Frank Jaks received the officers needed for Kontum's fledgling Hatchet Force company. Captain Arlen Cavin, a veteran of both World War II and Korea, would serve as the first company commander over the three platoons. Cavin, though respected for his years of army service, was not immune to jesting from his subordinates. He would soon earn the nickname "Quickdraw" after accidentally shooting himself in the foot with his service .45 en route back to camp one night from a Kontum bar.

The first Hatchet Force company of FOB-2 was composed of three platoons (each referred to as "companies" by HF personnel): Captain Dick Legate's 1st Company, First Lieutenant George Dias' 3rd Company, and First Lieutenant Hartmut "Mecky" Schuler's 5th Company. Two Green Beret noncommissioned officers were assigned to each of the companies. Schuler found that recruiters had gathered Nungs of all ages, "really young guys from sixteen all the way up to seventy." Schuler promoted the men on the spot that he felt had the most potential. They were all paid in Vietnamese money by Kontum's S1 (personnel officer), Captain Merritt "Willie" Wilson.

The American recon company at Kontum and its Hatchet Force company each relied heavily on locals to keep all phases of their operations going. The Vietnamese pilots of the 219th Helicopter Squadron and the ARVN soldiers operating with SOG played important roles, but the local indigenous people were another issue altogether. In some cases, the

First Lieutenant "Mecky" Schuler commanded one of Kontum's Hatchet Force companies. He is pictured here with his platoon at an NVA way station they have overrun whose defiant sign reads "Defeat the American aggressors and the Vietnamese traitors." *Hartmut Schuler*

Nungs worked out while other teams turned them over constantly, creating a training nightmare. The Nungs used by Kontum's teams were recruited in Saigon and delivered by the planeload. "Some of them would arrive with everything including small arms and others would arrive with nothing but a smile on their face," Crerar said. He allowed his team leaders to handle much of the training needed for the new recruits. "Dick Meadows ran training every moment he had control of them," he added. Other one-zeros ran so aggressively in the field that they struggled to retain their indigenous counterparts. "Gerry Wareing never had the same people more than one mission so he was always starting off cold," Crerar recalled. "They would quit after one mission with Gerry."[33]

Master Sergeant Gerry Wareing was highly respected as a recon man. He had served two previous TDY tours in 1959 and 1960 with the 7th SFG in Laos and a third with the 1st SFG assigned to the B team in Da Nang. In December 1965, Wareing became the one-zero of ST Iowa—one of SOG's five original teams created at Kham Duc. Team Iowa had been the first to cross into Laos under Operation Shining Brass but its original members had been reassigned to other duties by November.[34]

Once Wareing moved ST Iowa to FOB-2, he had two new Americans on his team: Sergeant First Class Alex Fontes, a three-tour and Korean War veteran, as his one-one, and Sergeant First Class Charlie Vessels as his one-two. The rest of their team was composed of Nungs, but Wareing had a way of going through them. Even Fontes and Vessels would soon shift to Hatchet Force duty. "Gerry would get into firefights and call in ordnance strikes dangerously close to his own team," recalled recon man J. D. Bath. "His own men would be hit by the blasted dirt. A lot of guys didn't want to go out with Gerry again after stuff like that." In time, Wareing settled in with two of the original Kontum thirty-three—Leonard Tilley and Dick Jenkins—as his permanent American team members.

The third Kham Duc team shifted to help open Kontum was ST Dakota, another of the five original SOG teams created in the fall of 1965. Dakota was an "old" team that had been running for three-quarters of a year. The Vietnamese men from the team were shifted intact from Kham Duc to Kontum in May. Their new one-zero, Master Sergeant Don Fowler, was also left to replace the former TDY Americans with some of the new thirty-three recon men at FOB-2. Fowler added Jim Stewart as his one-one, Lou Smith as his one-two, and Ronald "Bo" Bowling as his one-three.

Spike Team Iowa, ST Dakota, and ST Ohio hit the ground running and proved their worth in quick order. Operations officer Frank Jaks kept them plenty busy with recon missions and began deploying his other five teams as they came into their elements.

✦◇✦

Not all enemies encountered in the jungle were NVA. Lou Smith, the radio operator on Don Fowler's ST Dakota, found that his team was being stalked by an Asian tiger on one cross-border mission. Spike Team Dakota had just reached an extraction LZ when their Nung tail gunner went to investigate a loud noise from the bush on their back trail. Smith then heard loud thrashing and slapping sounds as the tiger batted at the horrified Nung—who stood frozen with the safety still on his Swedish K. Fortunately, the tiger did not pounce on the man and ST Dakota escaped intact.[35]

Jim Stewart only remained with the Hatchet Force for about a month before he was asked in late June to join Fowler's ST Dakota as the team's one-one. About a week later, ST Dakota was alerted that they would be making a trip across the fence. Master Sergeant Fowler flew a visual reconnaissance of the Laos target area to select an appropriate LZ for insertion. "The next day, we were flown to Dak To for our final operational briefing at the TOC [tactical operations center] located on the airstrip, and boarded the chopper for the flight and insertion into the target area," said Stewart.[36]

During the inbound flight, Stewart noticed his one-zero talking over the intercom with the pilot just minutes before they reached the LZ. Moments later, he saw the crew chief handing an M16 and a bandolier of ammunition to Fowler. Stewart then realized that his team leader had done the unthinkable: he had scrambled aboard the chopper and accidentally left his Swedish K at the TOC. Fowler had no choice but to go into enemy territory brandishing a regular U.S.-issue weapon—something completely against protocol.

Fowler's team inserted on June 30, a two days' walk from their target area so as not to alert their enemy that they were coming in. Spike Team

Dakota moved into their target area by late the second afternoon and prepared to make their RON spot. One-Two Lou Smith made radio contact with their FAC to give their final evening coordinates before settling in. At that moment, "all hell broke loose," said Stewart.

The outer perimeter Nungs on security detail returned fire well enough that Fowler was able to get his team on the move out of the kill zone. A company-sized NVA unit remained on their tail as the spike team men scurried back down a mountain they had just spent two days ascending. Smith was able to raise an airborne controller, who sent two propeller-driven A-1E Skyraider fighters into the area to help the team break contact.

The next morning, Smith made the usual morning contact with the early FAC on duty. Fowler hoped to have his team extracted but the jungle weather turned foul and they could not see the aircraft. Jim Stewart knew there was no way a helicopter could get low enough in the downpour to pull them out. The team thus remained on the run all day and through the following evening. The clouds fortunately broke enough on the fourth morning, July 3, that the FAC agreed to send in a chopper to extract them.

Stewart, Fowler, Smith, and their Nungs broke out survival saws and began clearing enough undergrowth to allow room for a smaller Vietnamese Kingbee chopper to lift them straight up. They were in for a rude awakening to find instead that the arriving chopper was instead a much larger HU-1E, a Marine Corps variant of the redoubtable Huey. (Stewart later learned that another Kingbee had crashed while carrying ST Nevada, killing all on board.) The brave Huey pilot maneuvered his big bird low into the canopy to extract ST Dakota. In the process, his blades chopped into some of the bamboo and broke off a piece of the rotor, but he skillfully managed to keep the chopper airborne.

Spike Team Dakota survived the mission and was soon safely back at Kontum. Stewart found their comrades ready and waiting at the base bar, eager to give Don Fowler hell about forgetting his Swedish K. Resident artist Bob Brown had already drawn a picture which was displayed behind the bar, unmistakably depicting one-zero Fowler straddling a barbed wire fence with his pants down around his ankles. Fowler and his ST Dakota would run more missions into Laos, but their FOB-2 recon buddies would never let the team commander forget the mission where he left his weapon in the TOC at Dak To.

The boozed-up vocalists at the Kontum base bar even greeted Team Dakota with a rousing chorus:[37]

Fowler went across today.
He forgot his Swedish K.

Chapter Three

THE MONTAGNARD CAMP
AND "OLD BLUE"

Scotty Crerar decided his new spike teams needed options. Aside from the Green Berets, the teams were all originally filled out with at least two-thirds of their members being Nungs. By mid-1966, SOG had been authorized to increase its original five SOG recon teams to twenty.

Colonel Blackburn instituted a recruiting program—and passed it along to his spring '66 successor Jack Singlaub—designed to include more of South Vietnam's largest ethnic minority, the Montagnard. The Montagnard people were organized in tribes, similar to the American Indians. Their skin color was darker than that of ethnic Vietnamese and the men were generally stockier in build. They embraced a modest lifestyle, living in simple villages in the hill country, where they sustained themselves by hunting, fishing, and foraging.[1]

Early SOG recruiters found that many Montagnard tribesmen wore handwoven loincloths and favored brass-ring bracelets crafted from scavenged shell casings. The numerous tribes—for example, the Rhade, Sedang, Koho, Bahnar, Jarai, and Bru—employed a variety of languages and their social structure was somewhat primitive; some had been converted to Christianity by missionaries. Their notable capability as trackers in the local jungles made them a valuable asset to the American servicemen. As the new FOB at Kontum was being developed, Major Crerar and Captain Jaks saw the need to recruit Montagnard men to help run their base and fill out their recon teams.

Captain Edward Rutledge Lesesne, who soon shifted over to Kontum, was detailed to develop a large pool of these indigenous fighters. Lesesne was a seasoned officer. The son of an airline pilot for Panagra (forerunner of Pan American Airways), Lesesne was born in Lima, Peru. He joined the Marine Corps in 1957 after completing high school but transferred to the Army two years later and received his commission from Officer's Candidate School in 1962. His middle name honored his mother's ancestor Edward Rutledge, the one-time governor of South Carolina and a signer of the Declaration of Independence.

Ed came from a fiercely patriotic family. His father flew bombers during World War II. The main gate of the Citadel—the Military College of South Carolina at Charleston—was named after his great-grandfather Charles Lesesne, who commanded one of the batteries that fired on Fort Sumter at the opening of the American Civil War. Captain Lesesne had already seen action with SOG at FOB-1, where he took over the Nung company after its commanding officer (CO) had been killed.

After running a few successful missions from Kham Duc, Ed "Insane" Lesesne was tapped to join the new group at Kontum to form a Montagnard company and build a proper camp for them. He was assigned Sergeant Morris Worley and a Montagnard interpreter, issued a pair of two-and-a-half-ton trucks (known in the Army as the "deuce-and-a-half"), along with sufficient weapons to arm a company and ample recruitment money. They loaded up and headed for the Montagnard's homeland in the highlands beyond Pleiku.

Worley was only too happy to lay down his hammer and saw to assist Captain Lesesne. In the mountains near Kontum, they met with the Montagnard district chief and were pointed toward the villages where they could recruit. "The people were more than willing to come work with us," Worley recalled.[2] He found the tribesmen eager to be paid to kill Vietnamese, who had abused this ethnic minority for centuries. Lesesne and Worley completed their recruiting in a matter of days and spent the next few weeks training their sixty new Montagnards in recon skills.

They built a proper camp for their Montagnards about two miles from Kontum, just off Highway 14, which ran right through FOB-2. "We moved all the Yards we recruited to our new compound, along with their wives, their chickens, their water buffalo, and everything else they owned," said Worley.[3] As he and Lesesne developed their Montagnard company, Kontum's spike teams were in various stages of organization.

The first three transferred over from FOB-1 to Kontum—spike teams Ohio, Iowa, and Dakota—were all running with Nungs. During early June, five other teams—ST Colorado, ST Hawaii, ST Maine, ST Nevada, and ST Texas—were either being organized or were in varying stages of training. Most of the newer teams were under the command of veteran master sergeants: ST Nevada was taking shape under the watchful eye of thirty-six-year-old Ralph Reno, ST Hawaii was under Jerry Howland, ST Texas was led by Foyle "Pete" Golden, and ST Maine was under Paul Conroy. Each of these units originally operated with Nungs as well.

Spike Team Colorado was the first of the newer five teams to begin running with some of Ed Lesesne's Montagnards. It was also the first Kontum team to be commanded by a sergeant first class, Ted Braden, in early June. Braden began his military career during World War II serving with the 101st Airborne Division. As the Vietnam conflict escalated, he entered the country in 1965 with Special Forces Project Delta, and by the spring of 1966, he had been assigned as one-zero of ST Idaho working out of Kham Duc.

Jim Hetrick was assigned as Ted Braden's assistant team leader. Hetrick also came into Kontum via Kham Duc. Born in Southern California and raised by foster parents, he was a family man with six years' experience in the Army. He was one of the few married men on recon assignment at the time, with three kids and a wife pregnant with their fourth child back at Fort Bragg. Braden and Hetrick's ST Idaho was short-lived at FOB-1, however. Braden had issues with his newly assigned Vietnamese team leaders regarding who was truly in charge of the team's actions. "I had run one operation with Idaho, when they changed our Vietnamese team leader," said Hetrick. "This kid looked like he was fourteen years old and he was all

Sergeant First Class Ted Braden, one-zero of ST Colorado, seen with his Swedish K submachine gun on patrol in the DMZ in 1966. *Alan Keller*

Sergeant First Class Jim Hetrick, one-one of ST Colorado in 1966. *Jim Hetrick via Jason Hardy*

hung up on who was in charge. When I would try to take the team to draw rations and ammunition from the S-4 to test fire our weapons, he wouldn't show up."[4]

Hetrick went in search of his indigenous team leader and found him stretched out on his bunk. The young Vietnamese lieutenant looked up casually and announced, "Mister Hetrick, if you want the team today, you must ask my permission."

Similar assertions of authority continued until Hetrick and Braden were reaching their breaking point. It climaxed one morning as Team Idaho was preparing their gear at the Kham Duc airstrip for an insertion. Braden's interpreter came up to him and said, "Mister Braden, the lieutenant says you must report to him."

"I'll report to that son of a bitch!" Braden snapped.

Hetrick watched in shock as Braden strode over and punched out his Vietnamese counterpart. The Kham Duc base commander had Braden and Hetrick relieved of duty at his base and they were shipped to Kontum, where Major Crerar assigned the duo to reorganize Spike Team Colorado. The previous one-zero of ST Colorado, Jerry Howland, had just taken over ST Hawaii following the transfer of one of its senior TDY men.

Braden and Hetrick soon added a third American to their new team as RTO, Sergeant First Class James David "J. D." Bath. The new commo man came from a large family, the oldest of seven brothers who had entered military service. Bath was already on his way to having a big family of his own: he had five kids back home when he headed to Vietnam. Although the junior team member on ST Colorado, Bath was several years older than Hetrick. Bath had served in the Army Reserves, gone into active service in 1956, and then returned to strip mining until the phosphate mine shut down, compelling him to rejoin the Army. Bath, assigned to the Kham Duc base for a matter of days in May 1966, had been among the original thirty-three to help fill out the new Kontum FOB-2.

J. D. Bath had initially been assigned to Ralph Reno's ST Nevada before tragedy struck that team. One of Reno's older men, Charlie Humble, was completing his tour of duty, so Bath had jumped at the chance to run recon as the unit's fourth American, or one-three. He began training with ST Nevada, learning the various hand signals and immediate action drills that could mean the difference between life or death in the field. Reno's team was tapped to run a target in late June but Bath was left behind. Inserted into Laos, Master Sergeant Reno's ST Nevada was composed of Nungs and two other Americans: one-one Don Fawcett, a twenty-five-year-old SF medic who hailed from Washington County, Pennsylvania, and the team's radio operator, Sergeant First Class Glen "Swede" Jensen, a ten-year Army veteran from northern Wisconsin who came into Kontum at the same time as Bath.

Spike Team Nevada completed a successful mission in Laos and was extracted to FOB-1 at Kham Duc near the border of South Vietnam. Kham Duc was already in the process of being closed out by SOG command due to constant NVA harassment and the fact that weather conditions at the site were not conducive to constant operations. Kham Duc would remain in operation as a reconnaissance training center for SOG and as an alternate launch site until 1968. During July a new FOB-1 was hastily opened at Phu Bai, near an ARVN training camp and airstrip.[5]

From Kham Duc, ST Nevada was to be transported to Kontum via the older Kingbee helicopters flown by South Vietnamese aircrews. The pilot assigned to fly Reno, Fawcett, Jensen, and their Nungs was Nguyen Van Hoang, better known as Mustachio.

As ST Nevada boarded Mustachio's Kingbee, the South Vietnamese pilots were urged to take on extra passengers. Among them was a staff officer, Major Edwin Joseph McNamara. The chopper Jensen was on was so heavily loaded with passengers and team members that it could not get off the ground. It taxied back, where Reno told Jensen to get on the other chopper with his gear. Mustachio lifted off with his overloaded Kingbee, carrying himself and fourteen other passengers, but his bird hit severe air turbulence over extremely rugged jungle-covered mountains approximately sixteen miles southeast of Kham Duc and fifty-seven miles north-northwest of Kontum. The chopper's tail boom—designed to fold for storage on aircraft carriers—came loose, swung around, and began ripping the helicopter apart in midair. It fell over fifteen hundred feet in a tight spiral, ejecting its passengers, crew, and debris over a large area.[6]

Everyone on board was killed in the crash. An extensive ground and aerial search over the next five days managed to recover the bodies of five Asians, as well as Fawcett and McNamara. The Americans' remains were positively identified and returned Stateside for proper burial. Search personnel were unable to find the remains of Master Sergeant Reno or the seven remaining Asians. Ralph Reno's status remains as Killed in Action/Body Not Recovered.

Glen Jensen was shaken by the loss of his entire team. For Major Scotty Crerar, the crash created the first personnel losses for his FOB-2. He had been planning a big Fourth of July party for his men to celebrate their weeks of hard work in shaping Kontum, but now he was having second thoughts. It was only through the urging of his senior sergeant, Paul Darcy, that Crerar agreed to go ahead with the base party to help his men push past the tragedy.

Nguyen Van Hoang (*left*), better known to SOG teams as "Mustachio," was a South Vietnamese pilot of the Da Nang–based 219th Helicopter Squadron. Mustachio and other Kingbee pilots are seated in the Kontum FOB-2 club with First Lieutenant Mecky Schuler. Mustachio and Spike Team Nevada were lost in a crash on July 3, 1966. *Hartmut Schuler*

Sergeant Jensen remained with ST Nevada as the team was rebuilt. Other recon men volunteered as "straphangers," fill-in team members who helped cover various slots for single missions. The one-zero position on Nevada was soon filled by Master Sergeant Charlie Hurley, a veteran recon man pulled from the new FOB-1 at Phu Bai to take over. Hurley kept Swede Jensen and soon added a third American, Jim Lively, to keep the legacy of ST Nevada alive.

Kontum was still only operating eight recon teams by early July, although ST Colorado was still in the training and organizational phase and now the wiped-out ST Nevada had to be regrouped. A ninth team, a "snake bite" team—composed of men on temporary duty from the 1st SF Group in Okinawa—was christened ST New York; it had a full complement of indigenous team members, but the TDY Green Berets had been sent back to Okinawa. Spike Team New York would remain inoperative for the next few months. The extreme dangers of running recon meant that one or more teams would often be in a state of rebuilding or even temporary nonexistence. Due to the incessant pace of SOG operations, the Green Berets could do little more than toast their fallen comrades, pick up the pieces, and carry on with the mission at hand.

◆◇◆

J. D. Bath had little time to mourn his fallen comrades. He was tapped by Ted Braden to join ST Colorado, where he was quickly immersed in intensive training and in the recruitment of new indigenous team members. Braden, Jim Hetrick, and Bath would be the first Kontum team to begin using Montagnard team members. Captain Ed Lesesne was actively recruiting and training Montagnard recruits in a new camp a couple of miles from the main base, so Braden sent his two junior Americans to the local villages to recruit their own Montagnard team.

In one village, Hetrick and Bath found the local chief unreceptive as they entered his hut. Local custom forbade them from entering with a weapon, so they met in the middle by simply removing their magazines. Bath soon realized the cause of the chief's poor disposition with the Special Forces men. An Army reaction team had come through the village some time before to dig a well. The major in charge smoked a pipe and he promised to get one for the chief. "Undoubtedly, the major forgot all about that pipe but the chief did not," Bath said. "He was thoroughly upset."

Quick on their feet by nature, Hetrick and Bath assured him: "You know, we've been looking for you! We've got your pipe."[7]

The Green Berets raced back to the base PX in their truck to buy a pipe and smoking tobacco to carry back to the chief. From that point on, Hetrick and Bath could do no wrong. Bath even wrote to his wife and had her mail over a corncob pipe from the States for the Montagnard chief. He was so pleased that he invited the two SOG sergeants to a special celebration.

The Montagnards introduced Bath and Hetrick to their fermented rice wine, which was sipped in large quantities through a notched banana stalk straw. "The Yards were sucking it down like ice water," Bath recalled. "After two times on that straw, Jim and I were throwing it up. They were rolling around like kids on the floor, laughing and pointing at us." Not to be shown up, Bath and Hetrick bought a large bottle of Jim Beam bourbon from the base and returned with it to teach the Montagnards how Americans could chug from a whiskey bottle. In short order, their new friends were the ones struggling to keep a foreign liquor down.

Spike Team Colorado was successful in recruiting Montagnards from several different tribes, which Bath found to be similar to different tribes of Native Americans back in the States. "We tried to pick one or two men from different tribes to keep them competitive," he said. "A Jarai is not going to run if a Bahnar is still shooting things. In the field, we learned to run with even numbers of them—never odd—because of their superstitions."

The presence of more Montagnards within the Kontum compound became commonplace as training proceeded. Sergeant First Class Lou Austria was of Hawaiian descent; he took advantage of the indigenous personnel's presence on occasion to wander about camp wearing Vietnamese-style black clothing, slippers, and a rice hat on his head. With his darker complexion and attire, Austria passed for a Vietnamese man, creating confusion among visiting VIPs until he finally elected to startle them by breaking into perfect English.

After assisting with recruiting Montagnards for his team, Bath settled into carrying the radio for Braden's team on recon patrols. Across the fence, his code name was "tub," Braden was "touchdown," and Hetrick was "raven." Bath adapted to Braden's team style, which included wearing sterile black uniforms on patrol and carrying untraceable Swedish K 9-mm submachine guns. "The SK was good but some of the ammunition we had was from 1943," said Bath. "The brass had that greenish mold on it. We tried carrying carbines and that was a mistake. When a carbine gets dirty, you're down to single shot bolt action. Then we got the M-16s and we used them until we starting getting in the Colt CAR-15 [the Colt Commando or XM177E2, a shortened variant of the M16]."

Braden's team proved to be as efficient in the field as they had been in recruiting the Montagnards. One of their first missions was run in-country to support the local Marines. Prior to their insertion, a Marine general inspected ST Colorado and advised them of the hot area they were to patrol. "He told Braden his teams couldn't stay in there forty-five minutes," said Hetrick. "We stayed in there four days and killed a couple of people."

◆◇◆

Kontum's eight core recon teams rotated into the field during July as missions were assigned from Saigon. Scotty Crerar, Fred Trzos, Frank Jaks, Paul Darcy, or Cole Eagle gave initial target briefings to the team leaders before each one-zero was left to prepare his team for the mission at hand. Only one team, ST Texas, managed to bring back enemy prisoners in early August. It was led by Pete Golden, with Green Berets Burrell "Rat" Wilson and Lloyd "Snake" Adams. They were ordered into the edge of North Vietnam, inserted from Khe Sanh to snatch any enemy soldier they could find. "After about five minutes on the ground, we fleeced up two Montagnards," said Adams. "The same choppers that put us in came right back, grabbed those Montagnards, and then extracted us." Spike Team Texas had encountered four Montagnards in the snatch attempt, but Adams was forced to gun down two who took off running.[8]

The recon teams of FOB-2 saw heavy action running targets, but in each case the men all returned without loss. The only casualties during the first two months of the base's operation had been the loss of Ralph Reno's ST Nevada. Kontum's sister base, FOB-1 at Phu Bai, was less fortunate.

Spike Team Montana, led by Sergeant Major Harry David Whalen with two other Americans and seven indigenous warriors, was conducting a recon in Laos southwest of Khe Sanh. The team was overrun by a company-size NVA unit on July 29 that ambushed the team with automatic weapons fire from its rear and flank positions. Whalen and his men had stopped at a small stream as they were climbing down the back slope of Co Roc Mountain. The last thing Whalen saw before the jungle erupted was his assistant team leader, Sergeant First Class Delmar Lee Laws, signaling that he had heard something to their rear.

Specialist Fourth Class Don Rue Sain and two Vietnamese team members were killed outright. The remaining men rallied to escape and evade, but Laws was not seen again. The only American to survive was Sergeant Major Whalen, who managed to evade the enemy by diving into a nearby river. He sloshed upstream under heavy fire as his teammates were pursued and cut down. Whalen hid himself in a grassy overhang of the riverbank as NVA soldiers searched in vain for him. The NVA apparently captured some of his team alive and tried to use them to compel him to come out from his hiding place. Whalen could only listen in horror to agonizing screams and gun shots as his comrades were tortured to death nearby.[9]

Whalen waited until after dark before he waded upriver and hiked to the Laos border. He finally opened up on his radio and was extracted by chopper the next day. A recovery team under Sergeant Major Billy Waugh, Major James Vansickle (commander of FOB-1), and several others was inserted to search for his other team members. They found only the bodies of two of their indigenous troopers and that of Don Sain—whose staked-down corpse had been crudely booby-trapped with a hand grenade. Waugh's team found a severed leg which was determined to be that of that of Delmar Laws when the rest of Laws' body was located in the jungle nearby. The team had not gone down without a fight: four dead NVA, stripped of weapons and clothing, were also found stacked at the base of an anthill.

The tragic mission marked the first casualties for the new Phu Bai FOB-1. The North Vietnamese had stripped Sain and Law's bodies of weapons, radios, maps, codes, and other SOG property that were likely the first such evidence they had obtained regarding the complex American recon force they were facing.

Harry Whalen, assigned as Kontum's sergeant major, suffered mentally from the loss of his teammates and spent his nights drowning his miseries at the newly constructed base bar. The loss of SOG men on operation compelled plenty of other recon men to gather in the NCO club to toast their fallen comrades. After many rounds of toasts, accompanied by stories in tribute to their brothers-in-arms, J. D. Bath listened as ST Colorado's Jerry Lee broke into a song of closure. The tune was "Old Blue," an American folk song about a possum-chasing dog that died and went to heaven.[10]

I had a dog and his name was Blue.
Bet you five dollars
He's a good dog, too.

The simple rhyme was slowly becoming something of a ritual for SOG men, who joined the singing as the tune related the death of Old Blue. "When I get to heaven, first thing I'll do, I'll blow my horn and call for Blue," they sang. "Dug his grave with a silver spade, lowered him down with a golden chain." At the end of the song, instead of calling Old Blue's name over his grave, the Green Berets substituted the names of their lost comrades. "Hey friends, you were good guys, you."

"Jerry had a good singing voice," Bath recalled, "so we started adding names to that song as we joined him in singing it." Among them were Reno and Fawcett, the first casualties for FOB-2, plus the fresh losses of Laws and Sain from FOB-1. Over time, verses would be added for new recon men, and the signing of "Old Blue" at the base compound would become one of SOG's most solemn traditions.

Chapter Four

PRISONER SNATCHING
AND WIRETAPS

"Good morning"—that was the signal that Sergeant First Class Jan Borek knew would start the action. His life and the lives of many others would depend upon how well he reacted to his enemy's first movements upon hearing those words.

Borek and the rest of ST Ohio had a plan. They were on their feet and ready long before daybreak on August 8. Spike Team Ohio crawled out of their tight RON position and checked their weapons and ammunition. Borek's one-zero, Dick Meadows, intended to bring back living NVA soldiers to prove once and for all that regular military personnel were heavily involved in operations in South Vietnam, Laos, and Cambodia.

Meadows had succeeded in previous missions in bringing in more than a half-dozen indigenous prisoners. During early August, Pete Golden's ST Texas had snatched two Montagnard enemy combatants and extracted them after only five minutes on the ground just inside the border of North Vietnam. This time, Meadows hoped to please his SOG bosses by rounding up NVA prisoners to discredit the North Vietnamese prime minister, Pham Van Dong, who had proclaimed to the world for months that no North Vietnamese regular soldiers were in South Vietnam. Orders were issued from the Pentagon directly to Colonel Jack Singlaub, chief SOG, to prove Van Dong was a liar.[1]

Spike Team Ohio was tasked with infiltrating an area containing numerous trails to seek out enemy installations worthy of heavy bomb strikes. In addition, Meadows was advised to bring back an enemy prisoner, something he felt confidence in doing based on his team's past successes. His ST

Ohio included One-One Chuck Kerns, One-Two Billy Joe Anthony (just two weeks shy of his twenty-sixth birthday), and One-Three Jan Borek. The other members of his spike team were Nungs, including interpreter Nguyen Kim Thach—Ted—and Lieutenant Le Minh, Ohio's zero-one, or indigenous team leader.

Inserted by Kingbee helicopters deep into Laos on August 6, Meadows and his team moved through the high mountains during the first day, traversing sharp rocks and continuing to climb until settling into their first RON site. The team was on the move again the following day, moving stealthily through the thickets toward higher ground. They finally came upon a heavily used trail and decided that it offered their best chance of surprising some NVA troops. During the evening, they observed small groups of soldiers moving at random.

"We crawled into a thick area and spent the night there within forty yards of the trail, ready to set the prisoner ambush after daybreak," Borek said.[2] Upon waking up the next morning, Billy Anthony realized the date was August 8, his brother's birthday. He would soon have another reason to remember the date.

Spike Team Ohio consumed a quick meal of canned fruit, rice, and ready-to-eat meat before burying their trash and moving away from their RON site near the trail. Borek made a quick inventory of his gear. He had one magazine in his weapon, eight more ready magazines with thirty-four rounds in each, plus extra boxes of ammunition in his rucksack. He had eight hand grenades, including one smoke grenade and one "willy peter" (a white phosphorous round). Each man wore olive-green color indigenous jackets and solid-color fatigue pants with no camouflage striping. Borek preferred the indigenous jackets because, unlike the American versions, they had no pockets to get hung up on the jungle foliage.

The team then moved to set their prisoner snatch trap. Anthony and two of his Nung teammates, Nueck and Duong, moved to one side of the

Members of One-Zero Dick Meadows' premiere POW-snatching Spike Team Ohio, seen in late 1966 in the FOB-2 club. Seated (*left to right*) are Green Berets Jan Borek, Billy Joe Anthony, and Navy SEAL Richard Ray. *Billy Joe Anthony via Jason Hardy*

trail on higher ground while Borek and two others prepared to be the "kill team" that would lay down the fire. Meadows and the remaining Nungs hid near a large tree and waited. Near Meadows was his assistant team leader, Kerns, and his trusted interpreter Ted.

Borek had his PRC-25 radio ready to call for extraction, hopefully with enemy prisoners in tow. Spike Team Ohio did not have long to wait. Just ten minutes after Meadows' team had taken up their positions, they heard the sound of approaching soldiers. Anthony considered it the perfect ambush site, as a high embankment rose above the well-worn trail. He was more than a little stunned at their luck when the approaching half-dozen uniformed North Vietnamese soldiers stopped right alongside the trail near the concealed Americans to take a break.

Glancing quickly to make sure everyone was ready, Meadows initiated contact. He stepped out from behind his tree and announced the phrase that both stunned his enemy and set his team in motion: "Good morning!"

Several of the relaxed NVA grabbed for their weapons, as Meadows and ST Ohio commenced firing. Anthony dropped one of the soldiers with his first burst while one of the other Vietnamese darted through the forest. Borek set out in pursuit, hoping to run down the soldier and take him alive but was forced to gun him down with his AK47. Interpreter Ted shot one of the other three before he could bring his rifle to bear as another one of the group crumpled alongside the trail. The fourth NVA crashed through the undergrowth in the direction of Anthony's trio. "One of them entered from my end of the trail," said Anthony. "He scared me when he stood up. He was pretty tall, a big, well-equipped son of a bitch."[3] Billy and his Nungs managed to knock down the NVA and overpower him without serious injury to either side.

The other members of ST Ohio pounced on and secured the fifth member of the enemy team who had survived the initial trailside firefight. It was over in less than a minute. Meadows, Kerns, Borek, and their Nungs stripped their prisoner of all weapons as Anthony emerged from the bamboo with the second prisoner. Ted began a hasty interrogation of the two prisoners while Borek opened up on the radio to call for an emergency extraction.

Spike Team Ohio moved toward a mountaintop area with their two restrained NVA prisoners. Extraction choppers moved in close enough to touch their wheels on the edge of the mountain as Meadows and his men leaped in for the flight back to their Khe Sanh staging area. Their pair of NVA would provide Chief SOG Jack Singlaub the smoking gun that Hanoi was lying about its involvement in the tri-border area. Meadows was a consummate master at snatching prisoners; when he finally finished his service in Vietnam years later, he and his teams had pulled thirteen POWs from behind enemy lines. During 1966, his closest competition was ST Iowa under One-Zero Gerry Wareing, who brought back more than a half-dozen prisoners from within Laos.[4]

By the close of 1966, elements of Operation Shining Brass had managed to capture a total of fifteen prisoners—most hauled in from Laos by Kontum recon men—and had killed seventy-two enemy soldiers, a number that was verified by body counts. Friendly losses had been three U.S. servicemen killed in action, along with sixteen of their Vietnamese counterparts. Five additional Americans and twenty-five Vietnamese were listed as "missing in action" (MIA), including some of the casualties of ST Nevada's July chopper crash.

◆◇◆

By August, Kontum's original thirty-three men had been serving at the base for nearly four months. Several of them, like Tom Livingston, had been pulled into recon teams quickly. Others had spent those months assisting Hatchet Force missions or carrying out other base and launch-site duties. Major Crerar originally had senior NCOs running the teams when some of the original Kontum thirty-three came in as lowly specialists, like Keller and Goth. "It was difficult to get guys to take them on teams," said Crerar. As older recon men completed their enlistments, were injured, or fell ill, the younger Green Berets were afforded the opportunity to rotate into action with a team.

Each one-zero had his own method for preparing new team members for missions across the fence. Dick Meadows schooled his team around a sand table mock-up of their area. Each member, American and indigenous, had to be able to point out LZ sites and alternates where they would meet if the team had to split in the field. They also had to memorize all kinds of details. "Dick prepared his team to the Nth degree," said Crerar. "The opposite was Gerry Wareing. He would just grab his team, tell them they were going to go out, and that was it. When they came back, they threw down their weapons and quit. They wouldn't go with Wareing again. He got a new team every time he went out."[5]

Al Keller was involved with radio duty and supervising various construction projects during his early weeks at Kontum. At age twenty-one, he was the youngest recon man on base, followed by his two closest buddies, Livingston and Goth. "I badgered Major Crerar every day of his life about getting me on a team," Keller said. "Finally, J. D. Bath went home on leave, and I was given my chance."[6]

Bath left Kontum in mid-September on emergency medical leave. His younger brother Tommy, a twenty-six-year-old Air Force veteran, was born with only one kidney and now his other was failing. "I was only home a couple of weeks," Bath said, "but I got to spend a couple hours with him before he went into a coma the next day."[7] During Bath's leave, his young replacement would be well broken-in.

Specialist Keller seized the chance to serve as the one-two for Ted Braden's ST Colorado. For his first mission, Keller found that his able leader had orders to stage their team out of Phu Bai for a recon into the demilitarized zone (DMZ), where several teams had been forced to abort their landings due to stiff enemy resistance. The prospect of going in under heavy fire made Keller a bundle of nerves as they jumped from the chopper onto the LZ. His mouth was so dry he could not form words to speak into the radio. But he shook off his nerves and made it through. Spike Team Colorado remained in the area for three days. They encountered several indigenous types and recovered a pay book from a female. "It turned out this female was a prostitute, and the book we lifted from her was a record book of the North Vietnamese she had been servicing," said Keller.[8]

Keller's second mission with Braden in early October would be even more memorable. On September 28, one of the FOB-3 Khe Sanh teams was nearly overrun by an aggressive NVA force. The team was split, leaving Staff Sergeant Danny Taylor and two Nungs unaccounted for. Five days later, on October 3, two spike teams were inserted into the same area (Target MA-10) near Khe Sanh. The first team in was ST Colorado, led by One-Zero Ted Braden, One-One Jim Hetrick, and One-Two Keller. They were going in to do a wiretap, inserting an alligator clip onto a NVA communications cable to tape-record enemy transmissions. "We went in just two hours ahead of darkness because another team was coming in after us, one hour later," Keller said. Braden led his men from the choppers into heavy elephant grass to take cover.

The same choppers returned to the staging area at Phu Bai and picked up the second team of seven men, ST Arizona. It was led by Master Sergeant Raymond Louis Echevarria, with Master Sergeant James Emory Jones as his one-one, and Staff Sergeant Eddie Lee Williams as his one-two. The CH-46 Sea Knight carrying ST Arizona and its four Nungs settled into an LZ to deposit the team just a few miles from the position of Braden's ST Colorado. Arizona was inserted three miles west of the Laos/South Vietnam border and twenty-four miles northwest of Khe Sanh.[9]

Spike Team Arizona was inserted amid an entrenched NVA unit. Just as the CH-46 lifted away, the team encountered an enemy soldier and opened fire. The team was soon taken under fire and surrounded by an estimated one hundred NVA troops. The team was pinned down from all directions and one of the Marine choppers suffered fifteen hits. Air strikes called in on the NVA failed to suppress their hellacious firing.

Miles away, Al Keller and Jim Hetrick heard Echevarria shouting on the radio for the helicopters to pull them out, but heavy enemy fire drove off each attempt. Keller desperately wanted to help in some way, but Braden informed him the distance was too far and that the other team would have to rely on their air assets.

Covey Rider Paul Darcy listened in despair as ST Arizona's one-zero soon grasped his fate. "It's all over," Echevarria radioed. "Don't come in. You haven't got a chance." The enemy force was too powerful and the brave team leader knew that many would die if a chopper tried to extract them. Echevarria then called back to Darcy with a final plea to "put the shit right on us."[10]

Fighter bombers screamed in to deliver loads of ordnance right on ST Arizona's position. Seven choppers that had tried to retrieve the team were hit, along with an A-1 Skyraider. Darcy heard no further transmissions from Arizona—the first entire SOG team to be wiped out. Details of the fate of ST Arizona were learned three days later when a recovery team found the team's interpreter, Bui Kim Tien, still alive. He said that he and One-Two Eddie Williams had evaded capture after Ray Echeverria and Jim Jones were mortally wounded.[11]

Williams, hit in the thigh with an AK47 bullet, moved through the jungle with Tien through the night. They spotted some caves and Williams sent his interpreter to investigate them as a possible hiding spot. As he

moved forward, Tien was spotted by enemy troops and was forced to flee under fire. He raced through the jungle and heard heavy gunfire emanating from the direction of Sergeant Williams, an African American, had last been seen. A search and rescue (SAR) operation spent thirty-six hours searching for the downed team but only recovered Tien.

SOG interrogators heard from an enemy POW a month later that he had seen a black recon man with a wounded thigh. He was led

Specialist Fourth Class Alan Keller worked in the commo bunker for months before he was able to land a position as the one-two on ST Colorado at age twenty. *Alan Keller* through villages for public mockery with a noose around his neck and his hands tied behind his back until he could no longer walk. According to the POW, the American was then executed.[12]

✦◇✦

Miles away, Al Keller suffered through the night, wishing there had been some way his team could have aided ST Arizona.

Ted Braden had his ST Colorado make their RON site in the slit trench of an enemy antiaircraft defensive position to wait for dawn. "During the night, we heard a shot at the bottom of the hill and another shot at the top of the hill above us," said Keller. "They were out looking for us."[13] The following morning, October 4, Braden's men continued with their wiretap mission.

Jim Hetrick and one of his indigenous teammates moved to the base of a nearby telephone pole while the remainder of their team provided cover support from a nearby trench. Hetrick and his teammate climbed up the pole and strapped on the wiretap receptacle. Keller informed his team that the wire they had tapped was actually a telegraph line. Hetrick removed the wiretap device and Braden then led his team along a trail in search of fresh water and a telephone wire.

En route they encountered four Vietcong clad in the simple black attire of the Vietnamese peasant. Braden's team evaded contact and regrouped that evening to RON in the same antiaircraft position. The following day, ST Colorado was successful in locating a phone line running along the ground. After installing their device in the afternoon, the team took cover for the night to listen and to record. Lieutenant Vic, the team's Vietnamese translator, monitored the transmissions through the night during a heavy rain as the team collected seven cassettes of North Vietnamese conversations.[14]

The intelligence gathered from their successful wiretap indicated that an important NVA leader, General Kiop, was in the area. On the morning of October 7, Ted Braden received word that it was time to pull out. And just in time: the team had observed an increased number of enemy soldiers in their vicinity. "We went light, dumping all our food, and moved swiftly to the nearest LZ to be extracted," Keller said.[15] Braden moved his men swiftly through tall elephant grass past the enemy patrols to reach the top of a ridge where their choppers would extract them. ST Colorado's four nights in the jungle and the swarming mosquitoes they endured had taken a toll. Keller and Hetrick were diagnosed with malaria and moved out to the hospital at Da Nang to recover.

Team Colorado's Green Berets suffered from the conditions experienced across the fence, but they held the honor of completing the first successful wiretap for SOG during Shining Brass.

✦◇✦

Keller's best friend, Steve Goth, made it onto a team soon after him. Goth had remained on radio duty, running both the Kontum base and Dak To launch site stations, until his break finally came during an important rescue operation. Throughout the day, he coolly manned the commo bunker radio and kept intelligence flowing between the FAC and the teams in trouble on the ground. For the better part of the day, Major Charlie Norton, the FOB-1 commander, and Colonel Bull Simons from SOG headquarters were draped over his shoulders, listening to the drama.

By day's end, the teams were successfully extracted. On his way out of the bunker, Simons acknowledged the young radio operator. "Kid, you did a good job today. How you doing?"

Without hesitating, Goth leapt on the opportunity. "Sir," he blurted. "I'm trying to get on a recon team."

Simons looked at Norton and simply said, "Do it."[16]

One week later, Specialist Steve Goth had been assigned to Kontum's ST Maine. His one-zero, Snuffy Conroy, did not seem overly pleased to be handed one of the two youngest men in camp as his new radio operator. Goth realized his team leader was likely given little choice in the matter, so he was wise enough to not make any waves with his new team.

By early October 1966, command of FOB-2 changed hands when Major Scotty Crerar received new orders to a position at command headquarters. His replacement, Major Francis Joseph Sova, enjoyed roughly a week overlap getting accustomed to the base and its launch site at Dak To. Crerar found Frank Sova, a soldier who had enlisted during World War II, to be very competent and he felt sure he was leaving Kontum in good hands.

One of the first mission priorities handed to Major Sova for his recon teams was to work over a military road designated as Route 110. This east-west infiltration road ran through the tri-border region where Cambodia, Laos, and South Vietnam meet. SOG teams had been sent in to evaluate and mine Route 110 during May and Kontum men had continued to monitor the newly discovered route during the summer of 1966. Ted Braden's ST Colorado—having completed its successful wiretap along Route 110 in early October—paved the way for a larger operation.[17]

Braden's intelligence pointed toward a large concentration of NVA troops in that area. Major Sova's men were thus tasked with conducting

SOG's first so-called SLAM (Search, Locate, Annihilate, Monitor) mission during the second week of October 1966. The specific target area chosen was a sector of Route 110 about two miles in diameter that was immediately struck by B-52s and followed by 7th Air Force tactical strikes and propaganda leaflet drops. This first coordinated assault came to be called SLAM I by the SOG leadership.

The results were convincing enough that SLAM II was initiated on October 13. It was conducted close to Route 110 where other teams had discovered the bivouac areas of two NVA battalions. After the strikes, SOG had its first opportunity to launch a platoon-sized bomb damage assessment of a B-52 strike area in Laos. Hornet Force platoons carried out several BDAs in the SLAM II area, but the results were far from encouraging. The men found little evidence that the raids had killed either humans or animals. Most of the explosive force of the ordnance had been spent in the overhead canopy and the teams found that BLU-3 cluster bomb units (CBU) had left craters less than a foot in diameter on the ground.[18]

More than three months would pass before SLAM III would be authorized by SOG to hit a major target complex along Route 110.

◆◇◆

By October 13, FOB-2 Kontum had sixty-one Americans assigned to the base, including command staff.

Major Sova and his XO, Captain Frank Jaks, had four staff captains under their direction: Arlen Cavin, Dick Legate, Ed Lesesne, and an adjutant, Merritt Wilson. First Lieutenants George Dias and Mecky Schuler each headed up one of the Hatchet Force companies. Sova's base had eight spike teams remaining in operation as of this date. A ninth, ST Dakota, had been reassigned to FOB-1 by the end of July. Green Beret Lou Smith remained behind but the other three Americans of ST Dakota (Don Fowler, Jim Stewart, and Bo Bowling) had moved with their team.[19]

The eight remaining spike teams were: ST Colorado under Ted Braden; ST Hawaii under Jerry Howland; ST Iowa under Leonard Tilley; ST Maine under Snuffy Conroy; ST Nevada under James Lively; ST New York under Burrell Wilson; ST Ohio under Dick Meadows; and ST Texas under Pete Golden. The newest team, New York, had been formed when thirty-three-year-old Sergeant First Class Rat Wilson was shifted from ST Texas in the fall of 1966. He assumed command of indigenous team members who had previously served under a Snake Bite team but had remained intact for several months. Wilson took on Bob Franke as his one-one and Clarence McCormick as his one-two.

The recon base was still far below its approved operating level in terms of active teams. Sova and Jaks were continually tasked with finding team replacements or straphangers who could assist a short-handed team suffering from men who had been wounded, had fallen ill, or were on temporary leave. Al Keller and Jim Hetrick had both contracted malaria while out in the field and were recovering in the Pleiku hospital. Another spike team member, J. D. Bath, returned to Kontum in early October after attending the funeral of his younger brother.

Bath found that some of the spike teams had brought on Navy SEALs as temporary team members to help fill the void. Ted Braden used SEAL Gary Shadduck to serve as his interim assistant team leader. Braden and Shadduck went out with ST Colorado to attempt a wiretap mission but were compromised by the enemy before it could be completed. Only a handful of SEALs would run as SOG team members from FOB-2 in the fall of 1966.

Noncommissioned officers Shadduck, Richard Ray, and Dever Cunningham had been assigned to MACV-SOG from SEAL Team One for cross-training exercises with the Green Berets. Their small unit of Navy frogmen had been sent to Vietnam in February 1966 to conduct direct-action missions. Ray was assigned to ST Ohio as its one-four under Dick Meadows, where he joined fellow Americans Chuck Kerns, Billy Anthony, and Jan Borek. Ray ran with ST Ohio into early October before being returned to his base at Da Nang.[20]

The third SEAL, Dever Cunningham, was assigned to Leonard Tilley's ST Iowa as the one-two alongside One-One Dick Jenkins. Cunningham was put to the test on his first mission when Iowa's ten men became engaged in a bloody firefight with a platoon of NVA on September 22. One of the Vietnamese members of ST Ohio was badly wounded in the exchange. Tilley ran to treat the wounded man while under fire. He and Cunningham then moved toward the heat of the action to suppress the enemy's fire while other ARVN teammates carried the injured man to safety. Tilley and Cunningham killed at least two of their opponents and continued to hold off their enemy while the rest of ST Ohio retreated roughly 325 yards to an extraction LZ.

Tilley was written up for the Silver Star for this mission and he in turn cited Cunningham for the SEAL's heroism. The tenure of the Navy SEALs at Kontum was short-lived, but their willingness to jump right into action was appreciated.

Chapter Five

CODE NAME BRIGHT LIGHT

Billy Joe Anthony spotted the flattop as the big Sea Stallion chopper he was riding aboard settled in for a landing. He realized this mission—inserting a SOG recon team from a U.S. Navy aircraft carrier—was going to be anything but ordinary.

Spike Team Ohio was landed on board the USS *Intrepid* (CV-11) around midnight on October 14, 1966. Deck hands assisted Anthony, One-Zero Dick Meadows, One-One Chuck Kerns, and eight of their Nungs below decks for another briefing. The Green Berets from FOB-2 had been called upon to insert from the *Intrepid* into a very dangerous area of North Vietnam to search for and attempt recovery of a downed American pilot.

Meadows was without the help of one of his reliable teammates, Jan Borek—who had contracted falciparum malaria, the deadliest strain of the mosquito-borne disease, in early October. Borek was medevaced to a hospital in Cam Ranh Bay, where he would spend months recovering, along with Snake Adams from ST Texas, who had also contracted the nasty bug.

Meadows and his team absorbed the latest mission intelligence from the specialists onboard the *Intrepid*. Their downed pilot was hiding near a ridgeline but foul weather and dense jungle had foiled previous attempts to extract him. After studying aerial photographs of the area, Meadows spotted a point about 875 yards from the pilot's location where he believed that choppers could insert his men. This rescue attempt would be the most ambitious yet to be attempted; it was an interservice effort involving the Army, Navy, and Air Force. It was also the first effort to be undertaken by a new top-secret recovery program that became known as Bright Light.

◆◇◆

Lieutenant Robert Deane Woods was piloting an A-1 Skyraider of his squadron, VA-25—based on the carrier USS *Coral Sea* (CVA-43)—when his plane was hit by ground fire south of Than Hoa. Woods was forced to eject near the South China Sea on October 12. He landed in a heavily jungled ridgeline about halfway between the cities Vinh and Hanoi, roughly nine miles from the coast. Not seriously injured, Woods released himself from his parachute harness and shimmied down the tree he landed in. He ditched his helmet and gear and tried to put some distance between himself and his telltale parachute billowing from the treetops.

"I kept going for about fifteen minutes and then I just collapsed from the shock and fatigue," said Woods. By late afternoon, he had managed to make radio contact with another Navy A-1. An SAR helo was vectored in close to nightfall, but the rescue attempt was unsuccessful. The chopper came under fire from NVA troops that had moved into the area and Woods was forced to flee.[1]

Major Les Hansen in Saigon was closely monitoring the downed pilot's situation and the first failed rescue attempt. He went to work on employing a SOG team to join in the recovery mission. The code name Bright Light was assigned to such rescue attempts—the recovery of downed airmen, remains of those who had fallen in combat, or potentially even prisoners of war. Bright Light mission duty, soon to become a mainstay of Kontum's recon men, was the brainchild of Hansen's boss, Colonel Harry "Heine" Aderholt, a special operations officer challenged by the Air Force to come up with a new rescue operation. Search and recovery efforts often failed because of slow reaction times by helicopters. Intelligence had shown that downed Americans usually only had high extraction rates if a SAR team could get to their position within the first fifteen minutes. After a half hour, the odds plummeted. Colonel Aderholt determined that SOG was the perfect vehicle for pursuing post-SAR actions to attempt rescues of downed aviators or even POWs. He had been assigned the command SOG's OPS-80 section on September 16 to coordinate with many non-SOG entities. One month later, the attempt to recover Lieutenant Woods became Aderholt's first Bright Light mission.[2]

With Colonel Aderholt out of town, Major Hansen sought and received the approval of Chief SOG Jack Singlaub to deploy one of their teams. Hansen then met with the local Navy commander at Tan Son Nhut to explain the rescue concept. The carrier task force commander on Yankee Station, Admiral Roy L. Johnson, approved of the Bright Light mission. Foul weather had moved in over the North Vietnam coast, preventing further rescue attempts of Lieutenant Woods. Political approval was reportedly sought all the way to the White House as Singlaub called on Major Frank Sova to prepare a Kontum team for the mission.

It was little surprise that approval was given on October 14 to one of FOB-2's most experienced recon men, Master Sergeant Dick Meadows. Dick told his ST Ohio to prepare to move out pronto on a classified recovery mission. They were first flown to Da Nang for a briefing on the new Bright Light operation before being ferried out to the carrier *Intrepid* shortly before midnight. Meadows was told to be prepared to deploy the next morning. He was not prepared for the next order, however. Major Hansen reported that Admiral Johnson was unwilling to put Americans on the ground into North Vietnam to recover Lieutenant Woods. The situation was delicate and Dick was to instead insert only his indigenous team members.

"Dick protested strongly," said Billy Anthony. "He questioned the idea of putting our Nungs on the ground with no Americans. They had been trained to run missions with us, not on their own."[3]

Meadows was surprised to find that his Nungs were willing to go on their own, but he had no such intentions. He pleaded his case with the admiral. Johnson ultimately came back with a thumb's up from General Westmoreland. Spike Team Ohio would go in as one, Americans and all.[4]

In the meantime, Deane Woods had suffered through his third full day without food on October 15. He had narrowly dodged NVA patrols searching for him thus far, but his luck ran out that day when three North Vietnamese soldiers found and captured him. "As soon as I saw them, I broke the antenna off my survival radio," he said. He knew that even without its antenna, his radio would continue to emit a weak signal.[5]

Foul weather prevented the Bright Light operation from proceeding on October 15. Billy Anthony was seriously questioning how the U.S. pilot could still be free in North Vietnam. "I just had a gut feeling that he had been taken by the enemy by this point," he said. "He had been on the ground for too long, and too many attempts had been made to go get him. His area had certainly been pretty well pinpointed by the people trying to get him."

The weather cleared early on October 16, and all elements involved in the Bright Light were given the nod to proceed. Unknown to them, the NVA now holding Lieutenant Woods prisoner had the upper hand; the pilot believed his captors were using his damaged beeper to lure other Americans into a trap.

Two Navy Sea King helicopters—code-named Indian Gal 66 and Indian Gal 69—lifted off from the *Intrepid* with the eleven men of ST Ohio and headed inland over North Vietnam. The Navy crewmen had already flown missions into the area of Lieutenant Woods' loss for four consecutive days. Indian Gal 66 (IG 66) was piloted by Lieutenant Robert Burnand Jr. with Lieutenant (junior grade) Ross Mordhorst as his co-pilot. On their Sea King were Meadows, Anthony, and half of their Nungs. The assistant team leader, Chuck Kerns, climbed aboard Indian Gal 69 (IG 69) with the remainder of ST Ohio's Nungs. His chopper was crewed by Lieutenant Commander David Rodney Murphy, Ensign Edward G. Marsyla, Petty Officer First Class Vincent F. Vicari, and Aviation Antisubmarine Warfare Technician Petty Officer Second Class William Stephen Caple. Gunner Caple felt the Nung mercenaries and their three Special Forces Americans looked like "little guys with big rucksacks and Swedish ... machine guns."[6]

Anthony wondered what kind of reception his team would face as they crossed the coastline and moved more than two dozen miles inland. The Navy pilots made several false insertions to throw off any nearby NVA ground troops before IG 66 and IG 69 dropped into hovers and began depositing the team. "We went in on jungle penetrators, got on the ground, and began moving," Anthony said.[7]

Meadows' team moved near a well-worn trail en route to the ridgeline where they expected to find the pilot. Their air support was still receiving signals from Woods' transponder, though Billy Anthony had doubts. *The Vietnamese have probably taken him by this point*, he thought. *They may be hoping to take us prisoner, knowing we'll come to get him out.*

Spike Team Ohio had moved only about eight hundred yards from their insertion point when their air support indicated the pilot's transponder was perhaps two hundred yards away. Before they could reach the area where Woods was believed to be, Meadows and his men encountered an NVA officer and three enlisted men. As he took position, hoping not to be spotted, Meadows noted that the enlisted men were chattering away without a care in the world. But the NVA point man spotted him and began to raise his weapon.

"Good morning." Meadows utilized the action call now familiar to his teammates as he opened up with his AK47 from the edge of the dense foliage. Before the NVA soldiers could return fire, Meadows and two of his Nungs, Song and Kon, had mowed down all four with their automatic fire. His team quickly searched the bodies and Meadows pocketed a pistol recovered from the NVA officer. His hopes of silently searching for Lieutenant Woods were dashed. Spike Team Ohio started to pull back. They began to hear voices all around them and the blare of signaling bugles. "They were looking for us," said Anthony. "They were expecting us. The shit was on."[8]

The game was up. Meadows initiated contact with the air support as his team hustled through the jungle. The enemy had clearly gotten to the pilot first. There was little hope of surprising the NVA and liberating Woods at this point. Everyone in the vicinity knew that Americans were on the ground and they undoubtedly hoped to add more American prisoners—or bodies—to their tally.

Meadows used the call sign "sugarfoot" to alert the Navy Sea Kings to move in. Pilots Dave Murphy and Bob Burnand had been running racetracks nearby while the recon team was on the ground. Team Ohio reached an area with low scrub brush and only a few taller trees, and Meadows vectored in the first chopper with his marker panel. Lieutenant Commander Murphy moved in with his Indian Gal 69 to begin pulling the team. "They were in a grove of banana trees, cutting an opening with a little chainsaw," said crewman Steve Caple. "I lowered the jungle penetrator, they folded out the seats and got on two at once."[9]

Murphy's chopper pulled up Kerns and three others of ST Ohio, two at a time on the hook-like penetrator. From the ground, Meadows felt that the effort seemed to take an eternity. Two more Nungs jumped into the seats as they were lowered a third time. At that moment, the jungle suddenly erupted with small-arms fire. Bullets slammed into the chopper as Murphy quickly lifted away. "Abort! Abort!" shouted Meadows. Bullets hit one of Indian Gal 69's engines, causing fuel to stream out. Navy gunners Caple and Vicari returned fire on the NVA until they were clear.[10]

Meadows, Anthony, interpreter Ted, and Nungs Song and Nueck were still on the ground, and they were in peril. They took cover in dense bamboo while Meadows directed in support aircraft to create noise by swooping in on their position. Anthony lost his Remington chainsaw and his favorite boonie cap in the process of thrashing through the thick bamboo in such haste. "When I finally crawled down to the bottom of the thicket, Dick thought I had been hit," he said. "Turns out the little bottle of soy sauce I had in my pocket had been crushed in the bamboo."

Meadows used the air support and gunfire as the necessary distraction for his team to flee as the NVA took cover. They reached their original insertion point and called in the other Sea King, Indian Gal 66. Bob Burnand held his SH-3A in a steady hover as his crew worked the penetrator hoist with a fury. His gunners, Powell and Roberts, provided covering fire while Dick Meadows and the remainder of the men were hoisted up. Then Burnand took off for the coast.

About fifteen minutes later, Indian Gal 69 neared the heavily fortified coastline and came under heavy AA fire. Murphy jinked his bird about as best he could with only one operational engine. Door gunner Steve Caple was battling a jammed ammunition belt when an antiaircraft round struck the leading edge of the chopper's horizontal stabilizer with a resounding bang. Then another hit the tail cone and cut the tail rotor cables. A third shell struck aft of the Sea King's cargo door and blew up just inside the skin with a big orange ball of fire. Shrapnel from the exploding rounds injured every man on board the helicopter to varying degrees and knocked gunner Caple unconscious. Chuck Kerns had wisely donned a life preserver as they neared the coast and he had ordered his Nungs to do the same. The extra padding undoubtedly shielded them from more severe wounds but Kerns still suffered injuries and realized he might quickly be swimming in a life vest that was badly pierced with metal shavings. Crewman Vicari later snapped photos with his Polaroid revealing that at least 252 shards of shrapnel or bullets had perforated their bird.[11]

The fuel tanks began dropping toward zero and pilot Murphy and co-pilot Marsylva wrestled with the controls of their wounded bird in a valiant effort to keep their stricken Sea King in the air. They made it about fifteen miles out to sea toward the Navy destroyer *Collett* (DD-730) before their tail rotor cable finally parted. It took all they had to control the chopper enough to make an emergency forced ditching as they plunged toward the waves. The heavy bird hit on its belly and skidded into the ocean with a big splash, somehow managing to stay upright. The nearby *Collett* quickly lowered a motor whaleboat to rush to the aid of the downed aviators and SF recon men.

The Navy crew hurried to get the recon men out of the sinking chopper as Tonkin Gulf water rushed in. Everyone on board had shrapnel wounds from the AA shell explosion, including one of the team Nungs who had suffered a nasty thigh wound. The crew deployed a shrapnel-punctured six-man life raft that co-pilot Marsyla—suffering from a wounded right arm—used to move some of the Nungs aft of the chopper, drifting toward the approaching whaleboat.

Pilot Dave Murphy remained at the controls, working them to make sure the blades did not hit the water and potentially kill any of the men. Once everyone was clear—either in the raft or with life jackets—Murphy bailed out his window and swam clear. A UH-2 from another Navy frigate dropped in to help pull Caple and Marsyla from the water with a cable line. The two Navy airmen were treated for shrapnel injuries on the frigate and were later flown back to the *Intrepid*.

The operation had failed to recover the downed pilot but the valor displayed by all involved did not go unnoticed. Murphy later received a Navy Cross and his three crewmen all received a Silver Star. General Westmoreland sent a letter to Chief SOG Singlaub on October 19 in which he praised

Dick Meadows and ST Ohio. "The entire team demonstrated a complete professional competence and the utmost in personal courage." Westmoreland further praised Meadows for "his superb performance under fire deep in enemy territory" as being "the highest order of courage and devotion to duty. His superb professional conduct should be an inspiration to all of us serving in Vietnam."[12]

Singlaub decided to reward Meadows with a battlefield commission, but the Army informed him that the twenty-eight-year-old Green Beret was too old to become a second lieutenant. Chief SOG appealed directly to Westmoreland, using the general's prestige to overwhelm objections from Washington bureaucrats. Meadows accepted the commission and would step down as one-zero of ST Ohio in November 1966. His actual promotion would take several months to be realized, and by that time he was back Stateside serving with the 6th Special Forces Group at Fort Bragg. On April 14, 1967, Meadows was awarded his captain's bars and a third Army Commendation medal by Bull Simons.[13]

Lieutenant Deane Woods spent six long years in captivity but survived the war. He later had the chance to meet with Meadows, who presented him with the Tokarev pistol he removed from the body of the NVA officer he had killed on October 16.[14]

✦◇✦

Two days after attempting to rescue Deane Woods, Kontum recon men would undertake their next Bright Light mission.

Its planning had been in the works for weeks. Colonel Heinie Aderholt's Joint Personnel Recovery Center (JPRC) had been tipped off to the possible location of an enemy POW camp in the Mekong Delta of South Vietnam, about 18 miles west of Soc Trang. Aderholt personally overflew the location on October 8, while a sergeant snapped intelligence photos. Aderholt believed a recon company could assault the camp and potentially rescue an American POW. In honor of his beloved University of Alabama, he code-named the mission Crimson Tide.[15]

Planning had commenced on Crimson Tide shortly after August 30, 1966, when a seventeen-year-old Vietcong guerrilla named Pham Teo had defected to the South Vietnamese government. Teo claimed to have seen a black American prisoner just five days before. The first intelligence photos taken of the camp area described by the defector proved to be of the wrong area. Colonel Aderholt then overflew the correct area on October 8, after many weeks of wrestling with Army bureaucracy over the mission. SOG intelligence pointed toward the black POW being James E. Jackson, a medic captured on July 5, 1966, but Sergeant Alden Egg, JPRC's intelligence analyst, believed the prisoner to be Edward R. Johnson, a black sergeant captured in South Vietnam in July 1964.[16]

The defector, Teo, was given a lie detector test by SOG and passed. He pointed out the POW camp from low-level photos during early October, so plans were put in motion to land a Bright Light raiding party. Major Frank Sova, base commander of FOB-2, was tasked with organizing the force; he selected his operations officer, Captain Frank Jaks, to lead the mission. The men had reason to be suspicious of a trap, knowing that SOG's intelligence had come from a deserter. Sova and Jaks made final coordination of Operation Crimson Tide with the American senior adviser of IV Corps (the military region covering the Mekong Delta). The colonel told Sova his men could expect little resistance and should be able to pull off their rescue mission in half an hour.

Jaks assembled three platoons from his Hatchet Force Raider Company but opted to leave many of the senior officers behind. Each of the Hornet Force platoons was normally composed of forty Nung mercenaries and several American Green Berets. Only Lieutenant Mecky Schuler, who commanded the 5th Raider Company, would take his entire platoon and serve as second in command of the mission. Captain Dick Legate, commander the 1st Raider Company and Lieutenant George Dias, CO of the 3rd Raider Company, remained behind.

Mecky Schuler was a five-foot-six man of Germany ancestry who came of age during World War II. He came from a big family of six boys in Ludwigsburg, Germany, that immigrated to Reading, Pennsylvania; Schuler was drafted only six months after his family's arrival in the States in 1957. Unlike many Germans his age, Schuler sported a short haircut that his girlfriend and future wife thought made him look like a popular cartoon character of the day, a porcupine named Mecky. His platoon included two other Americans staff sergeants: Donald "Curly" Brown and Ralph Phillippi.

Captain Jaks was approached by Kontum's camp engineer, easy-going country boy Fred "Huckleberry" Lewis. Eager to see to see his first "real combat," Lewis begged to be allowed to tag along. Jaks allowed it, since little opposition was predicted. Lewis would accompany the 1st Raider Company, led by an experienced NCO, Sergeant First Class Charlie Vessels.[17]

The raiding party of more than a hundred men assembled at Kontum on the morning of October 18, just three days after first learning of Crimson Tide. After a two-hour delay as their Air Force transport plane off-loaded cargo, the force was moved to the city of Can To, where Frank Jaks received a final intelligence briefing. His raiding party then moved via C-130 Hercules to Soc Trang, the staging base in the Mekong Delta, to prepare for insertion. The only American well-briefed on the mission, Jaks was led to believe that his men would be in and out in short order. He therefore ordered them to go light on food rations and to double up on ammunition.

Around 1330 on October 18, the Bright Light party began boarding a dozen Huey helicopters. More than a hundred Nungs and nine Americans packed into the choppers. Captain Jaks was surprised to see the VC defector, Teo, climb aboard one of the nearby Hueys to accompany the men on the raid. Another surprise came in the fact that the Seventh Air Force opted to send along F-100 jets to accompany the mission. Recon men normally preferred the slower, more maneuverable, prop-driven A-1 Skyraiders when monsoon rains yielded a low cloud ceiling—like it was that day.[18]

Three lines of four Hueys each headed south from Soc Trang. They approached the LZ near the Vietcong prison camp around 1425. Frank Jaks was in the lead UH-1 as it came in to land on the flat, grassy field of the Delta terrain. The rice paddies were intersected by water-filled canals and the VC camp was only about five hundred yards away. Jaks quickly found that the enemy had been expecting his men's arrival. Machine-gun fire from the nearby tree line commenced, joined by small-arms fire. The helicopters began maneuvering to avoid the gunfire while quickly depositing the platoons. Jaks and the 3rd Raider Company—which included Green Berets Lou Smith, Francis Fitzgerald, and Lou Austria—jumped down onto the rain-soaked field to take cover.

Mecky Schuler and his 5th Raider Company also made it onto the ground without casualties. He, Phillippi, Curly Brown, and their Nungs did not receive any fire, but Schuler could hear the firing several hundred yards away.

Good fortune, however, did not shine on the 1st Raider Company under Charlie Vessels. His chopper commander found the LZ too small to land all twelve Hueys at once, so he shifted and set down Vessels' platoons across one of the canals in another LZ, located at the edge of the enemy camp. They were immediately caught in a mass of .50-caliber machine-gun fire. The pilots had unwittingly deposited the two Americans and their Nungs between two hidden VC units. Even worse, the 1st Raider Company was separated from the other two platoons by a small canal. Huckleberry Lewis, the camp engineer who had begged Captain Jaks to be allowed to join the mission, was cut down by machine-gun fire across his chest as he exited his chopper.[19]

Vessels and his remaining Nungs tried to set up a defensive position, but the men were steadily mowed down by the fierce enemy attack. Vessels was soon hit and his Nungs began falling as machine-gun fire, small-arms rounds, and mortars pounded their open position. Some five hundred yards away across the canal, Jaks and Schuler heard Nung voices from the 1st Platoon screaming for help over the radio.

Jaks and his men took cover in small thickets of bamboo and in thin scrub bushes as the 3rd Platoon was also taken under fire. Jaks gathered his platoon and assaulted the VC position in the nearby tree line. His men swept through the area of the suspected POW camp but were disappointed. Defector Teo pointed out an underground hospital complex, but there was no camp to be found and no American prisoners.

The 1st Raider Company did manage to take two prisoners. Mecky Schuler's men encountered one enemy soldier who tried to hide in a large clay pot sunk into the earth to collect rain water. Schuler had his Vietnamese interpreter issue the warning: "If you don't come out now, a grenade will come in there."

Failing to find any American prisoners of war, Captain Jaks got on the radio to direct air support in to help his pinned-down 1st Raider Company. He was frustrated to have been denied slow-flying Skyraiders. The overhead FAC, circling in a slow-moving Cessna O-1 Bird Dog two-seater prop plane, could only direct in the Air Force F-100 Super Sabre jets to drop bombs on the heavily entrenched enemy. Loud explosions rocked the area as a pair of F-100s raced in low and fast. The pilots missed their mark, causing casualties among the Nung platoon, as the FAC furiously called off the jets from dropping any more bombs.

Darkness was settling in. The Crimson Tide raiders realized they would have to fight off enemy attacks through the night to have any chance to make it out the next morning. The first POW recovery mission launched under the auspices of the JPRC was turning out to be a disaster. Jaks and his interpreters learned from their two VC prisoners that his men had landed in the middle of a rest area for two battalions, including the elite U-Minh 10 Battalion—one of the most feared units in the Mekong Delta.[20]

Jaks was unable to raise anyone on radio from the doomed 1st Platoon. He led his own 3rd Platoon through a swampy area and rendezvoused with Mecky Schuler's 5th Platoon before darkness had settled. Together, the seventy men formed a defensive perimeter and prepared for an enemy assault. It was a long night without food or mosquito repellent in leech-filled marshes. Air Force flare ships kept the area illuminated through the night by dropping continual streams of parachute flares. It was enough to keep the Vietnamese soldiers from mounting a full assault.[21]

After daybreak on October 19, Jaks led his platoons across the canal. Only six Nungs out of the thirty-six-man 1st Platoon were found alive.

Body bags of the fallen are collected during the extraction of the Crimson Tide mission platoons on October 19, 1966. Two Kontum Green Berets and eleven Nungs were killed and another seventeen Nungs were listed as MIA. *Hartmut Schuler*

They found Huckleberry Lewis and many Nungs dead where their 1st Platoon had been overrun. Charlie Vessels and the bodies of other Nungs were found clustered in a little cemetery where they had made their last stand. The final tally stood at two POWs taken at the cost of two dead Green Berets, eleven Nungs killed, and another seventeen Nungs listed as MIA.[22]

Choppers moved in during the morning to extract the survivors and their two VC prisoners. They were flown to Vi Thanh, the capital city of Chuong Thien Province, and there loaded on a C-130 for the flight back to Kontum. It was a somber return trip as Nungs and Americans rode in company with the body bags shrouding their dead comrades. Frank Sova welcomed his returning men. "We were absolute wrecks," said Captain Jaks. "I was devastated by the losses, especially Lewis, who just wanted to come along to see a little action."[23]

The superstitious Nungs refused to step foot in the 1st Raider Company indigenous barracks at Kontum, as they believed it to be inhabited by the spirits of their deceased comrades. Some Green Berets finally soaked the wooden structure in kerosene, torched it, and watched one of the barracks assembled by Lewis reduce to cinders. In his honor, the Kontum club was christened that evening as the Huckleberry Inn. The now-familiar "Old Blue" SOG memorial drinking song stretched a bit longer as new verses for Lewis and Vessels were tagged on.[24]

✦✧✦

The failure of Crimson Tide rippled through Saigon. General Westmoreland and Jack Singlaub were bitter over the personnel and helicopters lost on October 18. Colonel Heinie Aderholt of the JPRC felt the Air Force had botched the job with improper air support planes and at least one bomb load that been dropped on the 1st Platoon by an F-100. The Joint Personnel Recovery Center was left smarting over Crimson Tide. But Aderholt found a way to turn things around a week later.[25] Once again, FOB-2 personnel were involved in the next Bright Light mission on October 27, 1966.

Major Sova was flying rear seat in a SOG-assigned Cessna O-1 late that afternoon near the town of Attapeu in Laos. He happened to witness the destruction of an F-105 Thunderchief that was hit by ground fire near his Bird Dog. The pilot bailed out and drifted down in his chute. Sova radioed back to the Dak To launch site: "I can see the parachute and I'm closing in."[26]

The pilot, using the call sign Kingfish 2, was Major Robert Earl Kline, part of a flight of four F-105Ds that launched from the new Korat Royal Thai Air Force Base in northeast Thailand at 1520. He was forced to eject when the AA fire caused all his controls to freeze up. Kline drifted down and became entangled in a tree. He decided to shimmy down the tree but was unable to hold on when he pulled the quick releases on his harness that detached him from his canopy. He ditched his helmet upon hitting the ground and attempted to raise his squadronmates via radio.[27]

Kline then headed for a clearing he had seen on his way down but left his survival kit behind in his haste. He was finally able to make contact with the aircraft overhead and advise them he was unhurt. Sova replied back that he had Kline in sight and would have a chopper on the scene within fifteen minutes. It was approximately 1720, two hours after his Thunderchief had been downed.

Captain Frank Jaks was on duty at Dak To when his CO's radio call came in. He learned that the downed pilot was about six miles from Attapeu, far beyond the operating range of an extraction chopper. Jaks explained the situation and Sova radioed back: "Figure something out." Jaks improvised: he sent out two choppers from the VNAF 219th Squadron to land fifty-five-gallon fuel drums and hand pumps on an LZ in Laos nine miles from the pilot. He positioned gunships and A-1 Skyraiders to protect the fuel cache and then Jaks boarded one of the two Hueys that departed to recover the pilot.[28]

Major Kline had hidden himself between two felled trees to wait for his rescuers. He turned on his radio about 1735 and was advised that the chopper would be longer than expected in arriving. Around 1755, he finally heard the welcome sound of chopper blades but was unable to make radio contact with either the FAC or the chopper. It was nearly dark, so he began signaling with his pen light and finally lit a night flare as the chopper buzzed his position at two hundred feet. "The chopper then came

Captain Frank Jaks, operations officer for FOB-2, led both the ill-fated Crimson Tide mission and the first successful Bright Light pilot recovery in October 1966. *Jason Hardy*

in and hovered near the ground about a hundred yards from my position," said Kline.[29]

Hundreds of NVA were closing in on the location but the Bright Light team was able to land their HU-1B and pull Kline aboard. Sergeant First Class Luke Nance, an SF medic flying on the chase medic chopper, saw NVA only a hundred yards away as the pilot was spirited away. During the return trip, the Hueys settled down in the grassy field in Laos to hand-pump more fuel back in their aircraft. They departed with the pumps but left the empty fuel drums booby-trapped for whoever discovered them.[30]

Pilot Kline was amazed to be recovered so quickly. "I didn't realize American choppers were in this area," he said.

"We aren't," replied Captain Jaks. "Just be happy we're here and forget the whole thing."[31]

Jaks put the rescued pilot on an O-1 and had him flown to Pleiku for examination by the flight surgeon and an intelligence briefing. Fast thinking had saved the pilot's life, and Jaks would spend considerable time explaining to Saigon exactly what his men had managed to pull off. Colonel Aderholt considered the Kontum Bright Light mission to be the first-ever night recovery of a downed pilot—even if the 7th Air Force gave him hell for using Army choppers to pull it off. After a series of mishaps and failures for Bright Light, it was a relief to finally celebrate a success.[32]

By the end of 1966, only four Bright Light missions had been conducted by SOG: one in-country, two in North Vietnam, and one in Laos. Based on the successful pilot recovery during late October, Bright Light duty would become a mainstay for the Kontum recon company.

Chapter Six

HEAVY DROP

One-Zero Ted Braden simply disappeared from Vietnam in December 1966. His Spike Team Colorado had been revamped when he led his last mission that month. Two of his men, Jim Hetrick and Al Keller, had been laid up with malaria in the late fall. After Keller returned to Kontum, he fell in with Jerry Howland's ST Hawaii as the acting one-one, where he was pleased to be paired with his buddy Tom Livingston. J. D. Bath, who returned to Kontum after his emergency leave in October, was back on Braden's team as the radio operator with Navy SEAL Gary Shadduck serving as ST Colorado's one-one.

Braden, Shadduck, Bath, and their Montagnard team were inserted in mid-December for a wiretap mission. When their mission was complete, they were sent to Saigon for a debriefing. After their separate interviews and debriefing, they met at SOG's safe house in Saigon, House 10. There Braden announced to his team that he was under orders to take R&R. He departed, leaving Shadduck and Bath to return to Kontum alone.

Braden later explained that he was at the Caravelle Bar in Saigon when he first heard that white mercenaries were being hired to work in Africa. "Christmas 1966 was four days away," he said. "I'd been in Vietnam 23 months, had worked with some good men, enjoyed my share of women, probably drank more than my share of good liquor and had done interesting work. But I was fed up. It wasn't the work—leading a small group in the jungle on the prowl to find other men is what I enjoy and do best. In part it was hassling with chair-bound commandos in Saigon, empire builders, bureaucratic bunglers and incompetent Vietnamese officers and officials."[1]

Braden told his teammates that he was going on R&R, but that was a lie; he went AWOL—he simply disappeared. He already considered himself to be a poorly paid mercenary; now he jumped at the chance to be paid at least twice as much. Though his teammates didn't know it, he left Vietnam for the States, partied through Christmas and New Year's, and headed for London in January 1967 to begin his new life as a soldier of fortune.

Ted Braden assumed the identity of Joseph Edward Hornet, a SOG man killed at Camp Long Thanh in 1965, and made his way to Johannesburg, South Africa, to fight as a mercenary with the 5th Commando. Braden was later tracked down by U.S. federal agents, who extradited him to face desertion charges in a court martial. At the same time, congressional hearings were beginning regarding SOG activities. Seeing Braden as a potential embarrassment to the U.S. government, he was offered an honorable discharge in return for swearing not to disclose anything about SOG activities. It was a sweetheart deal, and Braden jumped on it. He disappeared again and this time he was never heard from again.

He became a kind of mythical character in Special Forces circles. Some of his comrades later heard—and believed—that he was the legendary D. B. Cooper, a hijacker who parachuted from a commercial airliner in November 1971 with $200,000 in cash and vanished in the heavily wooded terrain between Portland and Seattle. Many suspects were considered by the FBI in the wide-ranging investigation, but the definitive identity of D. B. Cooper remains a mystery to this day.

◆◇◆

Ken Sisler was eager for action and ST Colorado's one-zero had gone AWOL. He was only too happy to accept the position.

First Lieutenant George Kenton Sisler had served four years in Air Force intelligence during the late 1950s before entering college at Arkansas State University. Known to his friends as Ken, he was a former smoke-jumper and an avid skydiver who won the National Collegiate Skydiving Championship in 1963 with his leg in a cast. After graduation, he enlisted in the U.S. Army in August 1964, graduated from the Army's Intelligence School at Fort Holabird, Maryland, in November 1965, and was commissioned a second lieutenant. Sisler arrived in-country in Vietnam in June 1966, leaving his wife and two sons in his hometown of Dexter, Missouri.[2]

Sisler was assigned to intelligence duties at C&C as an S2 officer during his first months in Vietnam. Being an avid parachutist and Special Forces man, he could not help but have a desire to run recon. He got his chance to go on his first missions after being transferred to FOB-2 Kontum in late

1966. His hooch mate, Lieutenant Mecky Schuler, found Ken to be a good friend in short time. To him, Sisler had a certain eagerness for action. "He had it in his blood, I guess," said Schuler. "He told me he was related way back to one of the early American western heroes."[3]

Schuler related the ill-fated Crimson Tide mission and offered Ken the chance to run targets with him. They did just that during early December, when Schuler took Sisler out to serve as assistant team leader with his platoon. As commander of the Hornet Force, Mecky was landed first. "We were barely on the ground when they said they had new intelligence," he recalled. "The choppers came back in to get us but they picked up Ken Sisler first and moved his men a few miles away to where enemy action was." The platoon came under fire from a large caliber anti-aircraft piece almost immediately after landing. The 5th Raider Company was pulled out without casualties. "Sisler was down on a slope and these big guns couldn't depress down far enough to hit him," Schuler said. "I'll never forget how he ran with his head up when they finally pulled him out."[4]

As Christmas approached, new songs popped up in the base bar. J. D. Bath particularly enjoyed the SOG version of the Twelve Days of Christmas:[5]

On the twelfth day of Christmas,
The VC gave to me,
A sniper in a palm tree . . .

Some of the spike teams at Kontum were in transition as the new year of 1967 fast approached. After seven months in operation, FOB-2 had only two of its original one-zeros in place: ST Hawaii under Jerry Howland and ST Maine under Paul Conroy. Spike Team Dakota had long since been transferred and Larry Spitler was actively training a replacement team, ST Wyoming. Another new team, ST New York, was under One-Zero Burrell Wilson, while Dick Meadows had turned ST Ohio over to Chuck Kerns in November. Jim Lively had become ST Nevada's one-zero following the transfer of Charlie Humble and Glen Jensen, the latter having contracted a severe case of malaria that would result in his being medevaced out for a month-and-a-half stay in the hospital. The senior Americans running ST Texas were Bruce North and John Taylor, while Leonard Tilley, one of the old Kontum thirty-three, was one-zero of Gerry Wareing's original ST Iowa.

FOB-2, with nine recon teams in operation, was still running below its allocated numbers. Ted Braden's disappearance in late December was the open door of opportunity for Lieutenant Ken Sisler, who became team leader of ST Colorado. His intelligence background would prove vital for SOG: just days into his new assignment, he was working on a plan to establish a new communications relay site to aid the recon teams in the field.

Sisler spotted the perfect ridgeline in late December as he was flying visual reconnaissance (VR) over his team's next target area in southern Laos, in the Golf-5 region. He believed the rugged mountaintop would be an ideal location to set up a radio relay site to communicate between the teams, the Dak To launch site, and Kontum. Returning from his VR, Sisler pulled his one-one, J. D. Bath, off to the side and explained his excitement over the spot.

"Get a bird and go check it out," Sisler said.

Bath arranged for his own visual recon of the Laos peak and returned equally optimistic. "Yeah, I can put a wire up there and make a commo site out of it," he informed Sisler.

Spike Team Colorado then geared up for their mission that was scheduled into that area. Sisler, Bath, Jerry Lee, and their Montagnards were tasked with observing a certain village near the ridge. "It seemed like it had a lot of people in it but not a lot of crops to support such a village," Bath said. "So, they suspected it might be an R&R center or some kind of headquarters."[6]

The NVA were aware that an American team had inserted the previous evening because of all the commotion caused by the choppers feinting landing runs and then finally inserting ST Colorado. Once the team was inserted, the men took up station near the village to observe. Sisler took Lee and a point man in closer to set up a key recon position, while Bath stayed back with the Montagnards to maintain a defensive perimeter.

An NVA patrol sent out to search for the Americans succeeded in stirring up a fight the morning after ST Colorado moved in toward the suspicious village. Bath's first indication of trouble came when he spotted one of his Montagnards, a man named Joey, running back from his post position. Bath had just changed the batteries on his radio and was adjusting the frequency.

"What are you doing, Joey?" he called as the indigenous trooper ran past.

"Bu-ku, VC! Bu-ku VC!" Joey cried back.

All hell suddenly broke loose. The jungle erupted into gunfire as the NVA took the fleeing Montagnards under fire. Bath shouted "Kill! Kill!" in Vietnamese as he admonished his men to return fire. Bath and his indigenous cohort took cover and laid down accurate return fire until they were able to break contact without taking any casualties. In the process, Bath could not help but find humor in the stress of war. "Our Yards were duck-walking from one tree to another," he said. "They didn't jump or roll. They just duck-walked from one tree to another. You could get killed doing that. But they just hollered back and forth at each other and duck-walked forward."

Once the smoke from the firefight had cleared, Bath asked one of the Montagnards what all the yelling was about. A Bahnar tribesmen replied nonchalantly, tongue in cheek: "Oh, I tell the Jarai, he can go home now. I take care of everything."

Bath enjoyed a laugh as he realized that all the shouting had come from rival Montagnard tribesmen talking trash to each other under fire, trying to show up one of their own teammates in terms of who was the bravest. Lieutenant Sisler, Jerry Lee, and their point man soon rejoined the team to find out what the ruckus had been about. "Ken was thoroughly ticked off that he missed out on that firefight," Bath said.

"Let's go get 'em!" Sisler insisted. "Let's go!"

Bath knew that his men had not wiped out their resistance. In fact, he felt the enemy would quickly be reinforced. "Let's get the hell out of here," he implored. Spike Team Colorado soon heard signal shots coming from a Vietnamese trail watcher.

"Any time we moved in a direction other than straight ahead, we would come under fire," Bath said. "They wanted to work us into an old slash and burn area where they could annihilate us. They were bringing in more people as they attempted to direct us."

Bath opened up on his radio and called for an extraction and fire support. He was very impressed with the gunships that came in firing newer Gatling guns, a sound he had never experienced. A deafening roar of guns filled the air as the gunships zoomed past to pound NVA spotted to the left of ST Colorado. Spent brass cartridges rained down on the Americans, causing Bath to dive so hard for cover that he buried the barrel of his M16—approved for recon use as of 1967—deep into the soil.

A Marine helicopter settled in the nearby slash and burn area. Sisler, Bath, and Lee provided cover fire while they sent their Montagnard teammates racing for the chopper. "The door gunner told me later that he nearly crapped himself," said Bath. "All he could see were all these little people running toward him, a couple of them with AK47s. He told me it was lucky he couldn't get his gun around fast enough or he would have killed our Yards before he realized they were with us Americans."

✦◇✦

Sisler's team made it out without loss but he was eager to pursue the commo site on the Laos mountaintop in Golf-5 he and Bath had surveyed
before their trip across the fence. J. D. Bath realized the importance of the
site. He believed the NVA had become wise to the ways of the SOG recon
teams. "We would go in just before dark, get off the chopper, move rapidly
out about a hundred yards, and then button-hook around to see if we had
anyone on our tail," he said. "If we didn't, we'd tell the birds we were okay,
and then they would go home." The battle-wise North Vietnamese platoon
leaders often learned it was best to lay low and wait for the American air
cover to retire for the evening. Then they would follow the spike team and
hit it sometime during the night or during the next morning. Tucked down
into canyons or along steep mountainsides, the recon teams more often
than not had no chance of calling in air support or extraction choppers
unless they could survive until the next morning.

Sisler and Bath thus realized the golden opportunity of being able to
establish a radio relay site in the Laos mountains. "Ken decided if we could
set up a PRC-25 radio to communicate with Dak To, then teams could in
turn communicate with Kontum in case they needed emergency support,"
said Bath.

In early January 1967, Sisler traveled to Saigon to personally visit with
Colonel Singlaub, taking photos of the nearly vertical peak in southern
Laos with him. He proposed that SOG occupy it and he told the Chief SOG
that he could stay on top of that rock indefinitely. Singlaub had met Sisler
years before in a skydiving school and he appreciated the young lieutenant's innovation and initiative. Sisler explained how the radio relay point

Sergeant First Class Jerry
Lee of ST Colorado watches
for enemy movement atop
Leghorn—a Laos mountain-
top on which a radio relay
site was established with
the code name Heavy Drop.
Alan Keller

An H-34 of the South Vietnamese 219th Helicopter Squadron seen landing atop the steep pinnacle of the Leghorn radio relay site. *Alan Keller*

would be crucial for teams in trouble to communicate to the launch site and to their FOB.

Singlaub was in support of the plan, but William Sullivan, the U.S. ambassador to Laos in Vientiane, was not convinced. He and Singlaub exchanged cablegrams before a compromise was reached. Sullivan would allow one small SOG team to use the pinnacle, provided they were armed with obsolete World War II–era weapons that could be denied to be American, such as the M1 carbine and .30-caliber machine guns.[7]

Armed with the support of Colonel Singlaub and the new Kontum base commander, Major Frank Sova, Lieutenant Sisler led a team out from Dak To on the morning of January 15. J. D. Bath went to work as soon as the choppers had cleared. He set up his PRC-25 radio with a double antenna and then worked with Jerry Lee and other recon specialists to erect four other antennas around the key peaks of the mountaintop. Initially, the relay site was called the "Eagle's Nest" and was given the radio call sign of "Heavy Drop."

Once Bath had his radio gear up and running, it was clear that Operation Heavy Drop was an instant success. He put in a call to the Dak To launch site and was stunned by the return call he heard.

"Heavy Drop, this is White Horse. We read you."

"White horse" was the code name for FOB-2, Kontum!

"My, my," Bath replied, smiling. "We don't have to do a relay after all."[8]

His radio signals were not only picked up by the nearby Dak To site but were being received all the way back at Kontum. Sisler's Eagle's Nest radio relay site was a thing of beauty. His team was scheduled to build out the site and spend ten days on the mountaintop to establish a working system. They ended up spending more than two weeks on the lonely mountain, where choppers occasionally dropped fresh supplies to the Heavy Drop relay team.

North Vietnamese troops tried probing toward the Americans atop the mountain but had no success. The terrain was far too steep and rugged for any team to assault from below. Sniper scopes could be used to easily pick out enemy movements below Heavy Drop, and such intrusions were quickly beaten back with air strikes called in from the PRC-25.

Passing Air Force fighter pilots could not resist dropping in low to get a peek at the new top secret relay site. "They would mess with us," said Bath. "The Air Force guys would fly maneuvers just above the trees and then they would kick in their afterburners and corkscrew while they climbed it on up." The fighter pilots got a kick out of the low-level flash passes. At times, the unexpected zooms left Bath and his comrades "almost having to scrape out our underwear."

Sisler's SOG relay site paid almost instant dividends. Just days into its existence, a recon team had just inserted when they were hit hard by the NVA. The team was in an area where radio contact would not normally have been possible. The Heavy Drop commo team, however, was able to communicate with the beleaguered team and Sisler recalled the choppers to come in and whisk his fellow Americans to safety.[9]

Bath was sitting out sunbathing one afternoon on the mountaintop when he heard someone call, "Hey, we've got a VIP coming in."[10]

Ken Sisler was pleasantly surprised to find that his overall commander, Jack Singlaub himself, decided to pay a visit to the isolated Heavy Drop relay site. Singlaub had donned a sterile uniform that gave no indication of his importance. Accompanied only by a handful of Montagnard body-guards, Singlaub recalled that he "felt obligated to do a personal recon before committing more men and equipment" to the limestone peak. As his Vietnamese-piloted chopper touched down, several NVA antiaircraft tracers rose up from the surrounding valley. "Heavy machine-gun rounds thudded into the limestone cliff face," Singlaub said. "We were protected by the steep angle of the pinnacle. I saw how easy it was to defend this site."[11]

The chief SOG had confidence in Eagle's Nest. One of the recon men passed him a sniper's scope to take in the green jungle terrain visible from the mountaintop. "He peeked through it, down on the trail where we could see movement sometimes or vehicles going by," said Bath. "He was thoroughly impressed with what we had."[12]

Singlaub was gone hours later, leaving a small group of SOG men more than a little impressed that their commander would put his own life at stake to see their new forward mountaintop base. General Westmoreland, who had forbidden his chief SOG from accompanying any team into Laos, later learned of the little escapade when Singlaub explained how he knew that Eagle's Nest was so thoroughly defensible.[13]

Forgetting momentarily his pledge to never expose himself to enemy capture, Singlaub admitted, "I did a recon myself, sir."

Westmoreland was shocked momentarily, but then broke into a grin. "I should have guessed as much, Jack," he said.

The radio relay site would be continually manned by a commo recon team for five years.

Though it would officially come to be known by the code name "Leghorn," the site was always recalled as Heavy Drop by those intrepid Special Forces troopers who first manned it.

Spike Team Colorado sat on Heavy Drop from January 15 through the end of the month; ST New York then took over and guarded the commo post until February 14 and was replaced in turn for the balance of the month by Larry Spitler's ST Wyoming. The men were charged with maintaining static surveillance and providing radio relay for the operational teams, and they assisted the 7th Air Force through UHF communications in their night work.

Steve Goth, who spent two weeks on Heavy Drop in early 1967 running the radio for ST Maine, immediately understood why the site had been chosen. "There wasn't even a proper LZ," Goth said. "With the CH-34s, there was one spot where they could get the front tires of the landing gear down on the ground. We came off the chopper onto a small, relatively flat area and scooted away."[14]

✦◇✦

Sergeant First Class Mo Worley proved that he was as capable with his machine gun and Bowie knife as he was with a hammer and a saw. As one of the original Kontum thirty-three, he had been instrumental in applying his labor to improving his base's facilities in the early weeks. He had since joined Captain Ed Lesesne in recruiting and training Montagnards at their nearby camp, and that's where he was working in January when Jim Lively, the one-zero of ST Nevada, came calling. Lively needed a good recon man to fill in as his one-two. The man who usually filled that role, Clarence McCormick, was sidelined with a nasty case of malaria. Lively found Worley to be more than willing. Spike Team Nevada—Lively, Worley, one-one Bob Marple, and their Nungs—was inserted deep into Laos near Highway 110 in mid-January. They scouted the road and dodged trackers for days while watching cargo bicycles ride past their position. By January 19, Lively opted to have his worn-down Nungs extracted by chopper. A Kontum-based Hatchet Force—a thirty-three-man platoon of Nungs led by First Lieutenant George Dias and Sergeant First Class Bob Franke—was brought in to help continue the mission.[15]

Assisted by Lively, Marple, and Worley, the Hatchet platoon under Dias had come in with the goal of snatching an NVA prisoner. Kontum's recon men had not brought in a POW since the ill-fated Crimson Tide mission in October. Their chance came the next day, January 20. Worley was leading the platoon's lead squad when he suddenly sensed an odd calm in the jungle. There were no chattering monkeys. Something was wrong. Worley instinctively deployed his Nungs and then laid down a base fire.

He charged forward firing his Swedish K as he ran. Worley's action inspired his cohorts, who assaulted the unmasked enemy positions and captured a North Vietnamese soldier. There was a little hiatus in the action. Dias and Lively moved their platoon down the trail. Just eighty yards farther, they were attacked again. Worley again charged through a hail of bullets, laying down a punishing base of fire as his squad scrambled for cover. Mo exhausted his ammunition more than once. Each time, he tossed his Swedish K back to Bob Franke, who was loading for him. He was out of bullets when the enemy suddenly sprang from their cover and began to flee. "I had just broken the assault line of an ambush and I could see that a person was lying behind a log," he said. Before Franke could pass him an M16, Worley instead drew his Bowie knife, scrambled toward the log, leaped over it, and seized the North Vietnamese soldier by his hair. He pressed his blade to the man's throat and growled, "Come on boy! I've got someone who wants to talk to you!"[16]

Lively immediately called for a helicopter exfiltration, and choppers already standing by were able to quickly settle in to haul the two prisoners away. Spike Team Nevada and Dias' Nung platoon remained on the ground through the night in hopes of creating more chaos. They found action again the next day, January 21, when Mo Worley again volunteered to take the point squad. For the third time in two days, he broke an enemy ambush he alertly detected before their assault was launched. Worley killed two enemy soldiers in the firefight he initiated, then dauntlessly remained on the trail to engage the NVA positions. Three of the platoon's Nungs perished in the fight, some while trying to protect Worley.

This band of NVA was not giving up as easily. They launched their own counter-assault. Worley's good luck soon ran out. He continued to fight until his weapon was shot away and he was riddled with a burst of AK47 fire. One of the bullets passed through his right arm, traveling up the bone before coming out the other side. Another bullet grazed his face, while a third hit a branch or some other obstruction. The bullet broke up and ripped into his chest in several places, one fragment lodging just outside of his pericardium. Grenade fragments sliced through Worley's legs as well.

Worley struggled to compose himself enough to continue fighting. "I tucked my arm inside my stabo gear [an extraction harness], cinched it down real good and tight," he said. Bob Franke, lying just yards away, found that the enemy fire was too intense for him to even dare lift his head. He just kept Worley supplied with ammunition and grenades by tossing them to his severely wounded comrade. Using his good left arm, Worley drew his Browning pistol and emptied the magazine. He killed the soldier who had shot him, fired into other NVA, and then lobbed a grenade that silenced the hostile position.[17]

The NVA resistance was shattered. No other Americans had been hit. Extraction choppers were immediately called in to remove the dead and wounded SOG men. In spite of his life-threatening wounds, Worley refused to be carried. He walked the three hundred yards to the LZ with his shredded left arm tucked tightly into his STABO (STAbilized BOdy) gear. The medical chopper was already hovering when he arrived. A husky black medic, Sergeant First Class Charlie White, lifted Worley over his head into the Kingbee chopper, where Special Forces medic John McGirt began working to save his life.

The Kingbees soon landed at Dak To, where Captain Ed Lesesne was waiting, while other choppers extracted the remainder of Lieutenant Dias' Nung platoon. Lesesne was concerned that Sergeant Worley might expire if much more time was wasted on bringing in another H-34 to move him to the Pleiku hospital. He pulled his .45 automatic and ordered another Kingbee pilot—scheduled to deliver supplies to another team—to forget about his intended mission. He had his fellow Green Beret loaded on board and ordered the pilot to fly straight to Pleiku, where doctors fought to save Worley's life. "Waiting on another chopper probably would have killed him," said One-Zero Leonard Tilley. Fortunately for Ed Lesesne, the sympathetic pilot opted not to file a complaint against him.[18]

✦◇✦

Mo Worley would spend many months in recovery. He was moved from Pleiku to the Philippines and then spent more months in rehab in a Japanese hospital. When he was finally shipped back to the States, he spent a year in recovery in Ireland Army Hospital at Fort Knox, Kentucky. During that time, the military processed paperwork to have Sergeant First Class Worley awarded the Distinguished Service Cross for breaking three enemy assaults, capturing a prisoner single-handedly, and saving many lives at great personal cost. He was Kontum's first SOG man to be awarded the nation's second highest military honor.

Worley was still undergoing treatment at Fort Knox when he was presented with his DSC. He proudly put on his uniform and went to the parade field for the ceremony, still wearing various bandages and a long cast on his right arm. He stood at attention as Brigadier General Alvin F. Nrzyk read his citation for "extraordinary heroism and devotion to duty."[19]

Worley spent considerable effort fighting for things important to him. He even employed a lawyer to help him pass a physical review board at Walter Reed Hospital. He fought to keep his shattered right arm when doctors recommended that it be removed and he be medically discharged. The chairman of the review board finally leaned forward over his table and asked bluntly, "Son, why do you want to keep that arm so bad?"

Without skipping a beat, Worley replied, "Well, sir, it fills out my sleeve so well."[20]

The recalcitrant sergeant won the battle to keep his arm. Surgeons removed a section of bone from his right leg and some vascular material to help repair his shattered arm with a steel rod. He slowly regained some use of his right arm although median nerve palsy left him with no sense of touch in parts of his right hand. He fought to remain in Special Forces, completing periodic jumps to maintain his airborne status. One of his close friends, Special Forces Sergeant Major Robert K. Miller, appealed to Billye Alexander at the Pentagon to have Worley assigned as a Special Forces instructor at Fort Bragg. Miller rolled Mo's wheelchair out of Ireland Army Hospital and used his own vehicle to drive his determined friend back to Fort Bragg in December 1967.[21]

Once on base, Worley insisted on going to work each day. It took special effort just for him to don his uniform. His former recon teammate Bob Franke, also assigned to Fort Bragg, picked Worley up each morning and squired him to the base. "One of the overly large guys would pick up a chair with me in it and sit me up on a platform, where I would teach for hours," said Worley.[22]

Such dedication to his calling did not go unnoticed by the young men he was training. One of them, John Plaster, watched Worley fearlessly struggle to write on the blackboard with his casts and bandages. During a break, he heard that his instructor had earned the Distinguished Service Cross while serving in some top secret Special Forces group called SOG. Plaster could hardly imagine that in a matter of months he would be in the same group, running targets from the same forward operating base. He was left with a strong impression of those men and their courage. "Worley was a man of humility and indomitable spirit," he wrote. "He was a hell of a soldier."[23]

It was little surprise that Worley later returned to MACV-SOG to participate in Operation Heavy Hook, a downed pilot recovery program, with Ed Lesesne. Even as Worley suffered through his painful recovery, other Kontum recon heroes were in the making.

◆◇◆

Ken Sisler was still itching for a good fight in late January 1967. Major Frank Sova's FOB-2 remained heavily engaged in Shining Brass, recon operations across the border into southern Laos. That year would see 187 recon missions into Laos and 71 platoon-sized operations, from which the Shining Brass program would generate 774 intelligence reports. Ten communist prisoners were taken, including the two snatched by ST Nevada and Mo Worley.

The U.S. embassy in Saigon informed Ambassador William Sullivan on January 21 that an estimated seven thousand People's Army of Vietnam (PAVN) troops had entered South Vietnam during the month, most through Laos. This intelligence helped lead Jack Singlaub to initiate SOG's third SLAM operation against troops moving on the main east–west supply artery, Route 110. On January 30—more than three months after SLAM II's conclusion—SLAM III was launched against a target complex near Route 110, about five miles west of South Vietnam's Kontum Province.[24]

Ground teams provided photo reconnaissance, which was followed by two large B-52 bombing missions and massive tactical aircraft strikes. Three separate Hornet platoons were inserted into the target area, and they reported ample targets for more air strikes. Kontum's ST Maine (One-Zero Paul Conroy with One-One John Couch and One-Two Steve Goth) was inserted on February 2, and they reported more NVA activity. While performing a BDA in the Highway 110 area between February 3 and 5, Hornet platoons Delta and Echo from Kontum found an ammo cache and called in air support, resulting in thirty-five secondary explosions.[25]

Sisler had scarcely returned to Kontum from Leghorn before he seized the chance to take part in another mission tied to SLAM III. On the morning of February 5, a recon team was needed to conduct a BDA in the wake of a B-52 bombing raid. Sergeant First Class Leonard Tilley, the one-zero of ST Iowa, was tasked with the mission. Being a thorough leader, Tilley had always flown a VR of his target areas prior to leading in a team. This time, he was assured, it was merely a recon and the intel was needed right away.

Tilley had been assisting Ed Lesesne in training their Montagnard charges, so they were able to organize the force expeditiously. Tilley was asked to take a company in with him, but he opted to move in with a lighter force. He would use only a platoon of Montagnards, plus a few Green Berets, leaving the balance of his company at the Dak To launch site. If trouble was found, Tilley could quickly call in his cavalry to come to the rescue.

He handpicked his platoon of thirty-three skilled Montagnard soldiers, as well as two experienced Green Berets: Specialist Fifth Class James M. Wood and Sergeant William J. Ernst Jr. As Tilley was hurriedly assembling his team, Lieutenant Sisler offered to go along as a volunteer.

Sisler wanted to try out a rocket pistol, a new special ops toy called a Gyrojet. The stamped steel and plastic weapon weighed mere ounces but was capable of firing a thumb-sized 13mm mini-rocket propelled by solid fuel in its base. It fired with a noisy *whoosh!* like a Roman candle, clearing the barrel at 1,300 feet per second. In the SOG compound, such Gyrojet rocket rounds had been test-fired through sandbag walls, tree trunks, and an old truck door with impressive effect.[26]

J. D. Bath, Sisler's teammate on ST Colorado, felt that the first lieutenant was eager to prove himself in combat. Sisler had been irked at having missed the team's NVA scrape in the jungle in December. "Ken wanted to get into a firefight," said Bath. "A friend of his in Airborne had sacrificed himself on a grenade in 1966 and got the Medal of Honor. Ken was always talking about him. He wanted to mix it up with the enemy."[27]

Tilley's team was going into a known hot area. First Lieutenant Mecky Schuler's 5th Raider Company had just been extracted from the area, where they had been run off by NVA. "We found 61mm mortar shells stacked in wooden boxes," Schuler said. "We blew that stuff up with our [M18A1] Claymore mines and then got into a firefight with some of the enemy guards who had taken off when they heard us coming."[28] He found his hoochmate Sisler standing by an H-34, preparing to insert into the same area with a portion of Schuler's own platoon of indigenous warriors.

Sisler asked his buddy to point out on a map exactly where they had come out from. "I'm going right back in there where you came out of," Sisler insisted.

"No, don't do that, Ken," Schuler warned. "It's overrun by NVA. Just let the Air Force bomb the shit out of them."

Vietnamese Kingbee choppers flew the team twenty miles north to Dak To on the morning of February 5. After refueling, they carried the team to its insertion point at the bomb site, near Laotian Highway 96, located only about a ten minutes' flight from Dak To. Tilley and Sisler's men moved forward to perform their BDA and spent two nights in the area. On the afternoon of February 7, an aerial resupply was sent in for them. Captain Frank Jaks was flying as covey in an O1E Air Force aircraft that had launched from Dak To at 1005. He saw Sisler's unit place their identification panels, and Jaks then directed in the resupply chopper. It landed at 1230 to deliver more water and other supplies to Sisler and Tilley's recon team.

A half-hour later, Tilley's team was hit by an NVA platoon. The enemy attacked from three sides simultaneously. Specialist Wood estimated the enemy to be a company-sized unit. Sisler, as senior recon man present, shouted orders to the American and Montagnard fighters to pull back up the hillside and form a tight perimeter. "When we reached the top, he moved around the perimeter continuously exposing himself to heavy enemy fire, to encourage his men to return the fire and stay in place," said Wood.[29]

Frank Jaks was still overhead in his covey bird as the ambush ensued. "Sisler came up on the air and calmly reported that his unit had been hit from three sides," Jaks said.[30] Jaks called for immediate air support from available support aircraft. Having been in the air for three hours, his O1E then headed back to Dak To for fuel as another O1E piloted by Major Jim Leatherbee arrived on station. Master Sergeant Paul Darcy occupied its rear seat as covey rider.

Leonard Tilley assessed their situation. He, Sisler, and their men were near a hilltop that rose near the B-52 strike area they had been sent in to assess. The area around them was heavily covered with woods to the north and east. The LZ where the resupply choppers had landed was over a big hill to their east. Tilley could tell they were facing a numerically superior opponent that was perhaps company sized. Two Montagnards were seriously wounded in the initial burst of fire.

Lieutenant Sisler opened up on the radio and transmitted the code words "prairie fire" to Darcy. Such a call meant that a team was in imminent danger of annihilation. Thanks to the legwork of Chief SOG Singlaub in early 1967, fighter-bombers deployed over Laos and North Vietnam would immediately respond to the prairie fire call and be diverted to support any SOG recon men who were either running for their lives or on the brink of being overrun.

Sisler sent out the call and informed Darcy that he had casualties. Major Leatherbee called for TAC air while Darcy asked that the remaining aircraft at Dak To be launched. While waiting for their arrival, Sisler marked the enemy's location with a white phosphorous grenade. Leatherbee rolled his O1E in and fired two smoke rockets in the general area of the enemy force. Lieutenant Sisler called in correcting coordinates from the rocket strikes and the first flight of fighters put five-hundred-pound bombs on the enemy. Sisler then requested that his casualties be evacuated.

The two seriously wounded Montagnard were unable to move. Both had been left exposed when the balance of the men formed their perimeter. Sergeant Tilley asked Sisler to cover him so he could go out and check on the downed men. Before he could move, Tilley saw Sisler leap up and charge down the hill under heavy fire as his team covered his advance. The lieutenant found that one of the Montagnards was already dead. Wood watched as Sisler returned with the other wounded Montagnard, only to come under heavy fire from two sides as he approached the team's perimeter. Sisler dropped the wounded man, began firing his M16, and cut down three NVA that were advancing on him. From his left flank, a machine gun also opened up, but Sisler lobbed a grenade in that direction and effectively silenced the enemy crew. Tilley later felt that his own life may have been spared by the lieutenant's instant actions.

Darcy kept up with the situation on the radio with Tilley while Sisler was away. Sisler returned to the radio and informed Darcy that he could not pull back without his downed teammates. "More air support was on the way and again he asked for [the ordnance to be dropped] as close as possible," Darcy said. Sisler then advanced under fire to pull the wounded Montagnard back into their perimeter. His next thoughts were to retrieve the slain Montagnard.[31]

"Cover me," said Sisler. "I'm going back for the other guy." Before he could move out to retrieve the body, a canister of napalm exploded to the front of the platoon, preventing him from going. "The enemy's fire picked up tremendously now and our left flank was taking the worst beating," said Wood. Sergeant William Ernst, already wounded, was in charge of the left flank, five men whose position was in danger of being overrun.

Sisler fought back during the opening minutes of this latest assault, lobbing grenades with his left hand and firing his M16 with his right. The enemy onslaught was temporarily broken up, allowing Sisler to move back to his radio to talk to Darcy. Sisler was standing exposed, coaching in the air support to bring in close bombing runs; he was talking to his teammates when he was hit. The bullet struck him in the head just above his left eye and passed out just above his ear. Sisler crumbled to the ground; the round killed him instantly.

Sergeant Tilley, the veteran one-zero of ST Iowa, shouted to his men to tighten their perimeter as a merciless hail of automatic fire chewed through their ranks. Tilley took over the radio again and barked at Darcy to have his air support land their ordnance within twenty meters of his team's position. Time and again, he exposed himself to devastating enemy fire while encouraging his defenders and treating the wounded. Minutes turned into hours as the recon men tried to conserve their ammunition while beating back fierce enemy assaults.

Only three men out of the entire platoon were not wounded. "All of my Yards were wounded, some with serious head wounds," said Tilley. "I was covered in blood, but it was the blood of my Montagnard first sergeant. He was hit by a bullet that cut a groove right across his forehead." As Tilley lay beside his seriously wounded indigenous leader, he realized that his companion was still alive. *We've got to get out of here now or we're all going to die*, he thought. *There's more of them than I've got bullets!*

The only chance for the survivors, most of them badly wounded, was to break through the enemy forces and reach the pick-up zone. He called for close air strikes again while preparing his men to move. Tilley found that he and Sergeant Wood were running desperately low on ammunition. The NVA suddenly began charging their position in force. It was now or never.

"When they get close enough to battle, I'm going to jump up and scream," he announced. "When I do, everybody jump up, shoot one. Cover me and run north. Everybody is to take one of these little bastards out!"

Ignoring the danger, Tilley leaped to his feet screaming and charged headlong toward the onrushing NVA. He fired as he ran and lobbed grenades into groups of opponents. His aggressive, single-handed assault so astonished the enemy that they broke off their attack. Tilley ordered his men to follow him past the hill to the landing zone as choppers were brought in. After leading his platoon to the LZ, he made two return trips to make sure that the most severely wounded had been pulled to safety. Others helped drag the bodies of Lieutenant Sisler and two Montagnards to the extraction point. Tilley remained on the ground until every man of his platoon had been extracted, except for the bodies of two dead Montagnards.[32]

Once the platoon was clear, Paul Darcy called in relentless air strikes to continue pounding the enemy troops. Further exploitation of the area Sisler had probed resulted in the location and destruction of a large NVA weapons and ammo cache. "The team that went in the next day said they found a lot of blood trails," said Tilley. "The enemy took their bodies with them, but there were blood trails everywhere. We hurt them bad."[33]

Kontum recon captain Ed Lesesne considered the work of all involved in this Hatchet Force operation to have been far beyond the call of duty. He wrote up both Ken Sisler and Leonard Tilley for the nation's highest award, the Medal of Honor. He additionally recommended James Wood for the Silver Star and William Ernst for the Bronze Star with "V" device (for valor). Tilley had little desire for such commendations and helped heap praise on the valiant fighting spirit of Lieutenant Sisler during the opening actions of their fight. The paperwork was pushed through the Army's numerous layers of protocol during the ensuing weeks and by April 11, 1967, Sisler's award was approved.

Sergeant First Class Tilley's Medal of Honor recommendation was downgraded to the nation's second highest honor, the Distinguished Service Cross. The only thing he requested after the February 7 mission was a case of Crown Royal whisky—"and I got it."[34] Tilley had helped save many lives and badly whip his opponents in the process. His DSC was approved and awarded to him by late March. The second Kontum man to receive the Distinguished Service Cross, Tilley was still serving FOB-2 by helping to run the Dak To launch site.

After giving a mission debriefing in Da Nang, Tilley escorted Ken Sisler's remains back to his hometown in Missouri for proper military burial with honors. Following his thirty-day leave, Tilley returned to Kontum but was restricted from running missions across the fence. Weeks later he was surprised to receive orders to report to the base parade grounds in dress uniform, where he was honored with both a Silver Star and his Distinguished Service Cross.

Jane B. Sisler was an honored guest at the Pentagon on June 27, 1968, to finally receive the Medal of Honor on behalf of her late husband. Secretary of the Army Stanley Resor presented the nation's highest honor to the widow and her two young boys, ten-year-old David and two-year-old James during the ceremony.

SLAM III, the coordinated operation in which Lieutenant Sisler had been killed, ended on February 13. Its success ensured a follow-up with the overlapping SLAM IV operation, which spanned the period of February

10–27, 1967. Eight more platoons entered the area along Route 110 and the 7th/13th Air Force responded with 1,526 tactical sorties and 256 B-52 strikes.

By February 22, two of the Shining Brass operational areas in Laos were approved for extensions to twelve miles in depth. Even the reluctant Ambassador Sullivan could not deny the success of SOG's efforts during these two latest SLAM operations. MACV-SOG's size and responsibilities would be increased based on these results. More helicopter assets were made available, the number of recon teams were increased, and the number of missions rose proportionately.[35]

February 1967 proved to be a bloody month for the recon men of Kontum as the consecutive SLAM operations were carried out. Just one week after Ken Sisler was killed, a Hatchet Force team suffered a casualty on Valentine's Day. Staff Sergeant Andre Joseph St. Laurent was making one of his first missions across the fence near the Ho Chi Minh Trail in Laos. St. Laurent, a French Canadian who was born in Quebec, had immigrated to the United States at age five. He entered the Army at age twenty-six, with five years of prior service with the U.S. Marines. He arrived at Kontum in January after transferring to SOG from Delta Project in Nha Trang.

St. Laurent's platoon had just crested a hill in the jungle when they were attacked by NVA snipers. He was hit in the upper leg by a bullet and a grenade exploded nearby. St. Laurent lobbed back his own grenade and saw its explosive force blow off a North Vietnamese soldier's hat. His platoon managed to break contact and spent the next day on the run as he struggled with a tourniquet on his leg. St. Laurent and his teammates were successfully extracted but his wounds required hospital time that put him out of commission after only a month serving with Kontum's Hatchet Force.

Captain Ed Lesesne was also badly wounded during the SLAM IV operations. He didn't remain around Kontum long enough to see how the awards he had written up for Sisler, Tilley, Wood, and Ernst fared with the Army's recommendations board. Just ten days after the mission involving Sisler, Lesesne took part in another bloody Hatchet operation on February 17. His team came under fire before they could be extracted and he was badly wounded when an RPG (rifle-propelled grenade) exploded behind him. "Shrapnel went into my back, groin, and legs," he recalled. He was bleeding profusely but was able to apply a tourniquet around the more delicate region of his body that had been shredded. "I had to administer morphine to myself as the pain was excruciating."[36]

Captain Lesesne slipped into shock and had to be extracted by his teammates on the first chopper they could safely coach into the LZ.

When Lesesne came to, he was on the operating table at the Pleiku Field Hospital.

"Do you have any kids?" the surgeon asked.

"Three," mumbled Lesesne.

"Do you want any more?"

"No, why?" he asked.

"Well," said the doctor, "You've already got half a vasectomy from that RPG. Would you like me to properly finish the job?"

"Go for it," said Lesesne.

The Pleiku doctors tended to Lesesne's wounds as best they could and then evacuated him to Japan for further treatment. Once he was sufficiently stable, he was flown back to the States to recover near Fort Jackson. He was awarded his third Purple Heart for the February 17 fire-fight, and Ed Lesesne would be back in action at Kontum by mid-1968.

Chapter Seven

DANIEL BOONE AND BOB HOWARD

Operation Shining Brass took on a new identity in March 1967. The long-standing code name for covert operations across the Laotian border was changed in March from Shining Brass to Prairie Fire. The choice of the new name was intended to confuse outsiders who had learned the meaning of Shining Brass. The operational designation Prairie Fire bore no connection to the radio call used to request emergency air support and swift recon team extraction.[1]

Recon teams could be extracted in a variety of ways and innovative new options were periodically created. Chief SOG Jack Singlaub opted to be the first to test a new ground snatch invention called the Fulton Surface-to-Air Recovery System, or "Skyhook." It involved an agent or downed pilot wearing a harness that was attached to a helium balloon by a thick nylon rope lanyard. The balloon apparatus was snagged by a low-flying transport plane using a V-shaped yoke. Wild though this may sound, the Skyhook operation only suffered one fatal accident in decades of employment. On February 28, Colonel Singlaub took a seat alongside a runway at Long Thanh; he was trussed up in a Skyhook harness and was successfully snatched from the ground by a passing MC-130 Blackbird. Singlaub was winched on board without incident.[2]

Most SOG teams were extracted from hostile territory by hovering helicopters. In cases where the jungle canopy was too thick for a Huey to descend to the ground or deploy its two thirty-five-foot ladders, the air crews dropped extraction lines through the trees to the recon men. The teams running in early 1967 generally used an emergency extraction device called the "McGuire rig," a contraption invented by Special Forces Sergeant Major Charles T. McGuire (who was assigned to Project Delta). It was little more than a hundred-foot rope with a six-foot loop at the end fitted with a padded canvas seat. Each Huey carried four rigs ("strings"), two on each side, to pull four men from a hot LZ simultaneously. Over time, injuries and deaths suffered using the McGuire rig would compel other Green Berets to don Swiss seats (an improvised arrangement of knotted rope used for rappelling) instead of sitting in the string. A more sophisticated STABO rig was later developed that utilized a special webbing harness to allow the riders' hands to be free to wield weapons.[3]

Many missions became "hot" from the initial insertion and required tricky, immediate extractions. Sergeant First Class Billy D. Evans and some of his Vietnamese teammates were jumping from a chopper onto an LZ on March 29 when their team was hit by a hail of machine-gun fire. The remainder of the team was unable to land, leaving Evans and his men to defend themselves through the night. A mass enemy assault the next morning disabled all of the men in his sector and severely wounded Evans. Nonetheless, he repelled the enemy assault single-handedly until reinforcements could be shifted to his position. Another determined NVA assault broke through the perimeter, but Evans fiercely charged the onrushing soldiers, killing several and destroying a machine-gun position. "His actions inspired his men to greater heights to defeat the enemy and allow exfiltration of the unit," reads the citation for Billy Evans' Distinguished Service Cross.[4]

Prairie Fire operations continued to be launched into Laos from all three FOBs at an accelerated pace during the spring of 1967. Kontum base commander Frank Sova and his staff were taxed with keeping their spike teams operational as men were wounded, fell ill, or reached the end of their service periods. The old-timers at FOB-2 were largely filtered out during the ensuing months.

Al Keller, now a blooded veteran, was running as the one-two on ST Hawaii under Staff Sergeant Dave Doughty—who had assumed command of the company after Jerry Howland's tour ended. Keller survived a number of harrowing brushes with the NVA, including one attempted prisoner snatch that turned into a fierce firefight. Although a junior team member, Keller ably took control of the situation, calling in close air support and rallying his indigenous teammates to form a solid perimeter. He finally supervised the team's extraction from a nearby riverbed. The covey rider flying air support for the mission, Paul Darcy, sought out Keller and said, "Junior, you did all right out there."[5] Keller considered that to be high praise.

Keller was soon transferred to Da Nang, where he would complete the remainder of his one-year service period as a radio operator. Other Kontum old-schoolers were moved out of running recon for other reasons during March 1967. Jan Borek, a veteran of Dick Meadows' successful ST Ohio, spent the balance of his tour working at the Dak To launch site after recovering from a nasty bout of malaria. One of his ST Ohio teammates, Billy Joe Anthony, was commissioned from sergeant first class to second lieutenant and was stood down from running missions in March due to his pending commission. "I felt like I had been busted, instead of getting a battlefield commission," Anthony said.[6]

Major Sova began utilizing new Green Berets who had recently arrived at Kontum to keep his spike teams operational. Spike Team Wyoming was handed over to a pair of sergeants first class, Tom Corbett and Joe Messer, its new one-zero and one-one. Both men arrived at Kontum in February, after processing through Nha Trang with other recon men like Fred Zabitosky and Robert "Squirrel" Sprouse. Zabitosky was originally sent out with a group to FOB-1, while Messer, Corbett, Sprouse, and a handful of others were transferred to Kontum to help fill voids on the FOB-2 teams. While his buddies Corbett and Messer revamped ST Wyoming, Sprouse began straphanging with other shorthanded teams.

Messer hailed from the coal mining country of Kentucky. He came from a strong military family, including two uncles who fought in World War II. Messer joined the Army Reserve at age seventeen, completed jump school and Special Forces training, and had completed his first tour in Vietnam in 1963. At age twenty-five, he was already an old man by service standards, with seven years in the Army. His buddies tagged him with the nickname "Dirty Joe," because he blended right in with some of his team's Montagnard complement. "I was Yard size, and had a tan as dark as a Yard," he said. "I wore my hair longer and had a Fu Manchu mustache that dripped down on the sides all the way to my chin."[7]

During one of his first recon missions on April 22, Messer was wounded as his H-34 approached the LZ. Bullets suddenly ripped through the chopper's floor and one passed through his leg. The wound did little to slow Messer, who took over ST Wyoming in May when One-Zero Corbett left the team to oversee the construction of a new mess hall for the indigenous personnel at Kontum. Mounting casualty rates would push other Green Berets into team leadership positions at an accelerating pace. Among them was J. D. Bath, who was advanced to one-zero status shortly after two veteran Kontum team leaders were lost during one week in March.

The first casualty was Master Sergeant Paul Conroy, who had served as the one-zero on ST Maine from its earliest operations at FOB-2. He was temporarily away from the base on March 18, teaching a training class at the C&C detachment at Kham Duc. Conroy had an old willy peter grenade he was using to teach his class how to booby-trap a grenade. During his demonstration, the grenade exploded in his hand and severely wounded the veteran of two wars. Conroy was medevaced to a hospital in Japan, but died of his injuries five days later.

Tragedy next struck Bath's ST Colorado on March 25. Command of the team had passed to Captain Dick Legate, a former Hatchet Force platoon leader, following the death of Ken Sisler. One-One Bath found that Legate had developed his own style of working with his Montagnards based on his reaction battalion experience. The captain drilled his team on rapid disassembly and reassembly of weapons, compass drills, and other standard military procedures expected of recon men. Bath tried to intervene, explaining that the team's Montagnards were natives of the jungle who simply did not possess any formal training. "They all wear wristwatches, but if you look at them, every one is set to a different time," Bath explained to his one-zero. "They only bought the watches because they're pretty."[8] Bath was less concerned with their ability to absorb formal U.S. military field tactics; what impressed him was the their prowess at spotting enemy soldiers in the jungle long before he could even sense the danger.

Bath was still training with his team when Captain Legate volunteered to go out with a Hornet Force group to assault an NVA battalion base camp deep in enemy territory. Other Americans hastily assembled to run the target included Kontum veteran Snake Adams and straphanger Squirrel Sprouse, a relative newcomer to the base. Adams had just returned to Kontum the previous day after emergency family leave back in the States. The next morning, after being asked to tag along with the battalion assault, he made a quick stop at the supply room to grab a rucksack and a Swedish K machine gun before heading for the launch pad.

Choppers inserted Legate, Sprouse, Adams, and their indigenous force on March 25 near the suspected area of the NVA base camp. The team was engaged by NVA en route, but they appeared to withdraw after only a brief firefight. Captain Legate led his patrol over a ridge line and entered the enemy's seemingly abandoned camp. It appeared to be a well-maintained bivouac site capable of accommodating a hundred troops. The sharp eyes of the recon men, however, spotted discarded clothing and a bowl of rice that was still steaming. Legate was preparing to document the camp with photographs when the silence was shattered by automatic weapons fire erupting from well-concealed bunkers.[9]

Several bullets ripped through Legate's leg, severing his femoral artery. Squirrel Sprouse sprang into action, rushing forward to organize his troops' defenses and direct fire on enemy emplacements. His team leader was bleeding out—Legate's wounds were mortal. Sprouse then exposed himself to enemy fire, crawling twenty-one feet down a steep incline to recover Legate. He found that his captain was already dead but refused to abandon him. Assisted by Snake Adams, he dragged Legate's body back into the team's perimeter.

Just as they returned with the body, the NVA unleashed a furious assault. Sprouse gunned down several soldiers who charged within mere feet of his position. He realized the enemy was being reinforced. He opened up on the radio, directing air strikes on the advancing forces while directing his own troops toward an LZ for immediate extraction. His men encountered another NVA bunker complex during this maneuver. Sprouse directed Adams to continue moving the team toward the LZ, while he held off the enemy by charging several bunkers and killing more NVA in a heated battle. Even the extraction was contested by harassing fire from a lone enemy sniper.

Sprouse again saved lives by exposing himself to draw the sniper's fire. He spotted the firing point of the NVA and then disposed of the enemy sniper with a burst from his weapon. Once the choppers had extracted the team, along with Dick Legate's remains, air support moved in to pound the enemy position with nine bombing sorties. Sergeant First Class Sprouse was awarded the Silver Star for his valor on March 25, and he would soon prove to be an able recon team leader of his own.

✦◇✦

J. D. Bath was back at base when word came that Captain Legate had been killed. When it came to his luck with team leaders, Bath was feeling snake-bit. His first, Ralph Reno, had been killed in a July 1966 chopper crash. Later that year, Ted Braden had gone AWOL. In February, his One-Zero Ken Sisler had been killed. Now—a mere month later—his new one-zero, Legate, was dead.

Sergeant First Class Bath reluctantly took command of Spike Team Colorado. He had lost so many men on his teams that he began to become a little more rigid with his relationships. "After you'd lost a few teammates, you just quit asking about their families and personal stuff," he said. "You didn't want to know anything about them."[10]

Soon after taking over as one-zero, Bath and his team were inserted into a hot area another team had just been pushed out of. Accompanying him for this target were Jerry Lee and their Montagnard contingent, along with Bob "K9" Brown, a skilled artist and the dog handler for the base's German

Kontum's recon dog Buddha seen with his able handler, Bob "K9" Brown. *Larry Spitler*

shepherd, Buddha. Bath was initially unhappy about having a canine assigned to go out with his team. He had never seen a dog trained to work with troops and could only imagine the shepherd racing about trying to flush birds. Buddha, however, would soon convince him of the merits of such a recon companion.

Team Colorado came upon a massive rice cache used to sustain the NVA. "We cut rice bags all day until we were standing knee-deep in it," said Bath. By morning, they were exhausted from having slashed bags through-out the night. Air strikes proceeded to napalm the cache as Bath took his team down a trail to further reconnoiter the area and to escape the counterattack that he fully expected. Everyone was exhausted and their fatigue was nearly fatal. Canine-handler Brown missed a key signal when Buddha went ahead and lay down, a signal that he had spotted something in the direction his body was pointing.

Brown tried calling Buddha back, but the dog refused to move. An irritated Brown finally moved forward and bent down to grab Buddha by the collar. As he did so, enemy bullets suddenly ripped through his ruck-sack and knocked him over backwards. Brown scrambled back toward his team, as Bath and his companions laid down covering fire. Colorado had been compromised, but they were very fortunate. Had Buddha not dropped down to point out the nearby enemy, his human companions would have walked right into an ambush.

Jet fighters moved in to blast the NVA position while Bath pulled his men away from the area. Covey Rider Paul Darcy struggled to find a hole in the canopy large enough to pull Bath's team through. He finally resorted to using a jet to blast an opening with a five-hundred-pound bomb. Spike Team Colorado was extracted and Bath was left with a whole new appreciation of Buddha.

By April, J. D. Bath was physically and mentally spent from running targets. He had been at Kontum for nearly a year and his time in country was coming to an end. His decision to hand over ST Colorado to Jerry Lee was approved when more devastating news arrived from home. Another of his younger brothers, Marine veteran Gerald Bath, was killed by a drowsy truck driver while Gerald was riding his motorcycle. Bath flew home for his second emergency leave in mere months and was greeted by his wife and kids as he stepped off the plane in Tampa. "I stood five-foot-nine," he said, "but I was so skinny by this point that my kids hardly recognized me."

Bath helped his family move past the anguish of having lost a second family member in less than six months. He would spend several years of service stateside before returning to Vietnam in 1971 for another tour of duty. Bath was typical of the brave men who had sweated out the first year at the Kontum forward operating base. The resolve possessed by such Green Berets was contagious to the newer recon men now charged with carrying FOB-2 into its second year of operation.

+◇+

The base commander position at Kontum was also a revolving door during the late spring and early summer months of 1967. When Major Sova was transferred in May, his place was filled briefly by one of his veteran officers, Major Jerry Kilburn, who had spent nearly three years as a POW during the Korean War. One of the more amusing anecdotes of Kilburn's command tenure at FOB-2 was his requisition of a draft animal for use by the base—Kilburn had discovered a note in the fine print of Table of Organization and Equipment that authorized the use of a draft animal for a field company, so he took advantage of it.

Base XO Frank Jaks, charged with procuring such an animal, had Bob Leites in Da Nang write the distribution approval document, which granted Kontum the use of three horses per company. "Horses were hard to come by in Vietnam," said Jaks, who finally turned to Green Beret Rat Wilson to help him buy a horse from some of the locals.[11] Although the mount was intended to be used for carrying equipment, it was an instant source of amusement for the recon company. Wilson even rode it into the base club, where he demanded drinks for both himself and his mount.

The Green Berets found the whole episode even more outrageous when one of their own rode the horse into Kontum City two days later seeking the services of a local prostitute and left the equine hitched to a post outside while he conducted his business. He returned to find his ride home had been liberated by thieves. Just days after entering a company pack horse into his usual reports, an irritated Captain Jaks found himself filing documents to account for Major Kilburn's stolen property. Queries from Saigon forced him to declare, "We've been rustled."

Kilburn soon received orders to serve as the executive officer of Company C of the 7th SFG at Fort Bragg, and he turned temporary command of FOB-2 over to Major Frank Leach. That officer in turn was replaced on July 21, 1967, by thirty-six-year-old Georgia native Major Roxie Ray Hart, who would command the Kontum recon base for the next nine months. As Hart's tenure commenced, SOG was actively engaged in SLAM V, a concentrated assault against targets in the tri-border region that ran through August 16. A sixth SLAM operation commenced later that month with seven B-52 strikes carried out by the Air Force in conjunction with spike team troops and Hornet Force elements to conduct the usual BDAs to assess the damage.[12]

Chief SOG Jack Singlaub was intent on disrupting his enemy's operations with any means at his disposal, including unconventional tactics. One of his new programs, code-named Project Eldest Son, involved the placement of booby-trapped cartridges into NVA ammunition caches that his recon teams discovered. Singlaub knew that air strikes would only scatter small-arms ammunition and booby-trapping the cases would be difficult for his men to accomplish without leaving a trace. He instead turned to his CIA deputy for assistance. Technicians in the U.S. assembled approximately 14,000 rounds of AK47 rifle cartridges, 12.7-mm machine-gun cartridges, and 82-mm Type 67 mortar shells that would detonate in the weapon when firing was attempted.[13]

Mortar ammunition was supplied in four-round cases while tainted AK47 rounds were distributed as singles to spike teams. SOG teams soon found the least detectable method of planting Eldest Son rounds was to plant them on the bodies of ambushed enemy soldiers. This psychological warfare "salting" tactic implemented by Singlaub helped create distrust among North Vietnamese soldiers, who thought that some of their exploding rounds resulted from quality control problems within the factories of their ammunition-supplying ally, the People's Republic of China.[14]

Operation Prairie Fire, the new code name for Shining Brass, continued to expand in scope. The recon teams of FOB-2 were well versed in running missions into Laos and even occasional Nickel Steel targets (missions run into North Vietnam with the teams staging temporarily from FOB-1). SOG's operations continued to expand, with cross-border missions into Cambodia becoming a priority by mid-year. The North Vietnamese Army had long been acquiring thousands of truckloads of rice from Cambodian farmers without being subjected to air assaults or SOG team raids. MACV's intelligence officers also estimated that a thousand metric tons of Chinese military hardware had been moved quietly through Cambodia by 1966 to reach enemy forces on Vietnam's frontier. It was not until May 1967, however, that General Westmoreland and his associates convinced Washington that SOG should be allowed to penetrate the Cambodian border to disrupt the Ho Chi Minh Trail supply line there.[15]

In June 1967, a new strategic program code-named Daniel Boone commenced with SOG teams now being permitted to conduct cross-border operations into Cambodia. Colonel Singlaub was pleased, as the nearly half-million American troops on the ground in South Vietnam had been plagued by attacks from the NVA, an enemy who could push steady streams of replacements and matériel down the Ho Chi Minh Trail. During the second half of 1967 (beginning July 1), spike teams conducted ninety-nine Daniel Boone missions. Cambodian missions were previously assigned to Project Omega, a 5th SFG outfit officially known as Detachment B-50. The Joint Chiefs transferred Project Omega to SOG in 1967 and it was this detachment that began running the first operations into Cambodia to help disrupt things.[16]

The rules of engagement in Cambodia were initially quite strict. Recon teams could not exceed a dozen men, no more than three of whom could be Americans, and no more than three teams could be across the fence at any given time. They were sent in to merely gather intelligence; combat should be resorted to "only as a last resort to avoid capture." The Daniel Boone operatives were divided into two separate forces operating out of base camps at Nha Trang and Ho Ngoc Tau. While a proper command and control center was being established for these groups at Ban Me Thuot, their operations were temporarily controlled by FOB-2 at Kontum for a five-month period in late 1967.[17]

Spike teams running from FOB-2 were always named after states, whereas the B-50 teams of Project Omega were named for hand tools and inanimate objects, both during their operation at Kontum and after their eventual transfer to a new FOB. Project Omega teams that ran in late 1967 bearing tool names were: Auger, Awl, Ax, Bench, Brace, Bucket, Chisel, Drill, File, Fork, Hammer, Hatchet, Level, Mallet, Mattock, Miter, Nail, Pail, Pick, Plane, Rasp, Saw, Screwdriver, Shovel, Square, Trowel, and Wedge.

The first Project Omega spike team to enter Cambodia returned without serious incident in early June 1967. The second Daniel Boone operation, carried out by one of the eight B-50 spike teams operating from Kontum, was conducted on June 15. The six-man team, led by Sergeant First Class Lowell Wesley Stevens as the one-zero, was picked up by trackers on its first day and soon found itself surrounded. Stevens called for an extraction but his inexperienced FAC was reluctant to pull them out. When Vietnamese Kingbee crews did finally arrive to extract the team, the choppers were greeted by an NVA assault.[18]

Stevens had just begun to lift his Nung point man into the waiting arms of Sergeant First Class Ben Snowden—a twenty-nine-year-old

Kontum recon man assigned to Project Omega—when an NVA machine gun opened fire. The Kingbee staggered away toward Dak To with sixty-eight bullet holes and Snowden's lifeless body torn by nine bullets. The second chopper to land scooped up the remainder of Stevens' team but had its tail rotor shot off as it lifted thirty feet into the air. The Kingbee slammed into the ground. Stevens and his one-one, Staff Sergeant Roland Nuqui, pulled the Vietnamese crew and Nung recon men to safety and formed a defensive perimeter while the enemy machine gun kept them pinned down.

Stevens was soon able to direct a Pleiku-based 6th SOS (Special Operation Squadron) A-1 Skyraider pilot in to silence the gun with a napalm canister, but the aircraft and its pilot were lost to fire from another enemy gun crew. More gunships arrived overhead to keep the enemy suppressed until the bullet-riddled first Kingbee returned from Dak To after delivering Snowden's body and the first Nung extracted earlier. Stevens, Nuqui, and their remaining Nungs were extracted without further loss.

Green Berets toasted the fallen Ben Snowden in the Kontum bar that night, including a new verse to the now-familiar "Old Blue" tribute song. In his honor the men also renamed the new FOB-2 recon company office "Snowden Hall." Forty-five years later, the brave Texan was finally awarded a posthumous Silver Star for his actions.[19]

◆◇◆

Project Daniel Boone continued in earnest through the second half of 1967. The SOG teams penetrating Cambodia turned up valuable intelligence: roads, communications lines, caches, base camps, and dozens of enemy trails. The eight B-50 teams continued their operations from Kontum until November 1967, when the detachment was transferred to the newly completed Ban Me Thuot base. Originally known as FOB-5, the name was changed during 1968 to Command and Control South (CCS).

The most famous of the Project Omega team leaders to operate from Kontum in the fall of 1967 was Sergeant First Class Jerry Shriver, one-zero of RT Brace. His courage under fire was unquestionable, and he soon became known among the SOG community as "Mad Dog" Shriver. During his time running targets from Kontum with his Detachment B-50 team, Shriver was awarded a Silver Star, three Bronze Stars, and an Army Commendation Medal with "V" device. Shriver's awards continued to pile up long after he left Kontum in November for FOB-5.

Shriver and other Project Omega teams saw plenty of action running from FOB-2 in June and July. Kontum's permanent spike teams and

Hatchet Force platoon were equally busy with Prairie Fire missions during this time, and July would prove to be a record month for Green Beret casualties. The first loss came on July 3, when Spike Team Texas was inserted into Laos. The team included three Green Berets, a complement of Nungs, and a South Vietnamese sergeant, all led by One-Zero Staff Sergeant Leo Earl Seymour from Towanda, Pennsylvania.[20]

Seymour had been moving his team in an easterly direction when he stopped during the late morning on July 3 for a break to eat. "During this halt, we heard voices and saw approximately seventeen enemy forces moving down a trail, approximately twenty-seven yards from our position," recalled One-One Charles Henderson.[21] Seymour contacted the FAC for an air strike against the enemy troops, which was carried out during the next half hour. The area was located eleven miles inside Laos, northwest of Ben Het in the Dak Xou river valley.

When Seymour led ST Texas in to do a bomb damage assessment ten minutes after the air strike had cleared, his men became engaged in a hot firefight that split the team. Henderson emerged from a thicket an hour later with only his point man, Duong Van Bac, still with him. His one-zero had not been seen since the start of the fight. Henderson called in air support and extraction choppers, which managed to retrieve him, Sergeant First Class Joe Phillips, and two of their Nungs. The team's zero-one, Sergeant Nguyen Cong-Cu, was rescued by chopper around 1800, while two other indigenous members of ST Texas were extracted three days later on July 6 in the vicinity of Heavy Drop. One-Zero Leo Seymour was officially listed as missing in action. Subsequent efforts made to search the area of action turned up no traces of him, and his remains have never been recovered.

Just one day after Seymour's loss, Major Hart's Kontum recon base suffered further tragedy in the form of a deadly mid-air collision of Vietnamese CH-34 helicopters on the Fourth of July. Spike Team New York was returning from a cross-border operation toward Kontum when their two choppers collided. The team's one-zero, Sergeant First Class Marlin James Goodhue, and his one-one, Sergeant First Class Thomas L. Terry, were both killed, along with four of their indigenous team members and the Vietnamese chopper crewmen. The remainder of the men in the second chopper were seriously injured in the crash. The survivors and the bodies of the victims were recovered by UH-1 aircraft from the 170th Assault Helicopter Company.

The men of FOB-2 had less than two weeks of respite before they were mourning yet another recon team member loss on July 15. Spike Team Florida, originally created at Phu Bai in 1966, had only recently been shifted to Major Hart's forward operating base. By mid-July, Florida was led by a new one-zero, thirty-two-year-old Sergeant First Class James Junius Gray from North Carolina, along with One-One Willard Payne Jr. As Gray and Payne were newcomers to FOB-2, they were assigned a veteran SOG man, Sergeant Larry Spitler, to run radio on their first mission. Spitler, a two-year Special Forces veteran who had served in Panama with Paul Darcy and Dick Meadows in 1965, had run targets from Kontum with ST Wyoming and other teams in late 1966. Spitler had just returned to FOB-2 from an extended leave when he agreed to run a target with Gray as his assistant team leader while also carrying the radio.

Spike Team Florida inserted to perform a trail watch but walked right into an NVA ambush. In the midst of the firefight, Gray jumped up to lob a grenade but took a bullet in the chest as he did so. "He was almost dead before he hit the ground," said Spitler. He quickly pulled Payne and their Vietnamese team members into a defensive circle while calling over the radio to Covey Rider Paul Darcy for air support. "I talked him in with the air strikes and they bombed the shit out of them," he said.[22]

Napalm and CBU drops beat back the NVA enough for ST Florida to break contact. Spitler was able to get Sergeant Gray's body hoisted out via McGuire rig while his team continued to hold off the enemy. The balance of the recon team then fought their way to a more open area to be extracted by two Hueys.

July had been a tough month for Major Hart's FOB-2 with the string of losses of Seymour, Goodhue, Terry, and Gray. Aside from the temporary Project Omega teams, Major Hart had twelve permanently assigned spike teams: Arizona, Colorado, Florida, Hawaii, Illinois, Iowa, Maine, Nevada, New York, Ohio, Texas, and Wyoming. Some were transitioning under new one-zeros and others, like ST Arizona, were still forming up. Fortunately for Hart, his base was populated by well-qualified men, some of whom would become Kontum legends.

✦◇✦

Robert Lewis Howard was among those legendary men. Some who first encountered this stout Southerner could scarcely imagine the raw fearlessness that coursed through the veins of the soft-spoken Green Beret. Powerfully built, square-jawed Bob Howard had fierce courage hidden behind his quiet, unassuming character. Born July 11, 1939, in Opelika, Alabama, he came from a proud military family. His father and four uncles had given their lives while serving as paratroopers in World War II. His great grandfather had been killed in service during World War I.[23]

Following his father's death, Bob and his sisters picked cotton to help support their mother and maternal grandparents. He was primarily raised by his grandmother, whom he considered to be "a great influence in my life. She taught me in a simple old way to appreciate my country and the love of our country. She used to tell me, 'Every time you see the American flag, you see freedom, liberty, and Almighty God.'"[24]

At the time, Bob Howard did not realize he had been born into poverty. In spite of wartime rationing, his grandmother regularly filled syrup cans full of homemade cookies and had them shipped to the troops fighting overseas. She taught him to stand his ground when a gang of boys challenged him on the way home from school for his new pair of shoes. Due to his better shape, he outran the bullies by charging straight uphill to his home. Breathless, he explained to his tough grandmother why he had been running.[25]

"Boy, don't you ever run from anything again," she said as she looked him in the eyes. "Next time, you walk up that hill and look those boys straight in the eyes."

The next day, young Bob steeled his nerves and took her advice as he walked toward his home with his head held high. In later years, Howard never said much about that day's confrontation with the bullies other than he returned to his grandmother's home a bit beaten, with torn clothes, wearing a smile on his face and shoes on his feet.

It was little wonder that when Howard finished high school at age seventeen in June 1956, he followed in his father's footsteps by enlisting in the Army the next month in Montgomery, Alabama. A star football player at Opelika High School, Howard could have opted for a college scholarship but he chose the Army.

"I can remember being trained by rough old sergeants who loved their country but they didn't have the resources," he said. "When we trained we had to in basic training use training weapons, wooden weapons. And then when they finally issued us our M1 rifles, they only gave us three rounds of ammunition to zero our weapons." Howard moved through basic training and advanced infantry school before progressing into more specialized training. His resolve to wear paratrooper wings like his father and his uncles before him kept him motivated. "The first time I flew on an airplane, I jumped out of it," he said.

By 1965, Howard had been in the Army nine years when he was sent to Vietnam for his first tour of duty as a member of the 101st Airborne Division. In one of his first heavy actions, he was seriously injured by a rifle bullet that ricocheted off a tree and hit him in the face. During his time spent recovering in the hospital, he was particularly moved by the brotherhood he witnessed among Special Forces men. One of the men lying near him was an SF sergeant Howard had previously served with during airborne training. Howard was impressed that Colonel William A. McKean, commander of the 5th Special Forces Group, took the time to come visit Howard's wounded buddy. "I was shot up worse than he was, but nobody came to check up on me," Howard said.[26]

As McKean chatted with Howard's wounded buddy, the sergeant remarked to the colonel, "I have a good friend here I've known quite a while. He'd make a good Special Forces soldier."

"What unit are you in?" McKean asked Howard.

The colonel listened carefully as Howard answered. Days later, before he was even discharged from the hospital, Howard had orders transferring him into Special Forces. Once he was physically able to return to collect his gear from the 101st, he moved into SF training. Right away, Howard knew that this was his calling. The men were much better trained than the normal airborne or infantry soldiers he had previously trained with. "They taught me that you could take a small number of people and if you've got cohesion and good training, you can defeat a much larger foe," said Howard.

He was impressed that in SF, he was evaluated on how well he could train other people—even where language barriers could prove to be an issue. He was also instilled with a physical fitness belief that he would carry with him throughout his military career—often to the chagrin of the men who would serve under him. He learned that fitness could mean the difference between life and death. "When you're given an 80-pound pack, told

Sergeant First Class Bob Howard (*left*) is seen with Specialist Fourth Class George Bacon in the compound in late 1968. During his time at Kontum, Howard would be recommended three times for the Medal of Honor. *Dan Lindblom via Joe Parnar*

to move six miles and get there in two hours, then go into a fighting position and fight, you've got to be able to fight," he said. Howard learned that those who could not cut it would end up as casualties on the battlefield. He maintained his own stamina by making daily running an important part of his life.

Bob Howard was not loud or boastful. He was physically fit, morally strong, and more than willing to charge into any enemy encounter without a second thought. Ironically, when he arrived at Kontum in the late spring of 1967, he was initially assigned to the S4 section as the new supply sergeant. The FOB-2 command, in need of help in handling the supplies and paperwork, learned that Sergeant First Class Howard had once been a supply sergeant. Being relatively new to SOG, he did not complain and handled the duty with pride, but his eagerness to get back into combat did not go unnoticed.

Howard volunteered to go out as often as possible as a straphanger with other teams. Joe Messer, one-zero of ST Wyoming, was the first to take him out with his team during the summer of 1967. During a four-day recon, Wyoming discovered an area along a river with well-worn trails that indicated recent enemy use. The supply sergeant let Messer know that he wanted to pursue the trails up into the hills. The team leader knew that by doing so, his men would have to enter a triple-canopy area where the forest coverage would make extraction difficult in the event of a firefight. Messer had to insist to Howard that the team had recon duty to perform and was not looking to stir up an unnecessary fight. Bob Howard made no comment, but Messer could clearly see the disappointment in his face. Here was a man itching for a fight any day of the week.

By September 1967, Howard was joined in supply by Sergeant Gene McCarley, who also spent his first weeks at FOB-2 as part of the S4 section. A native of Wilmington, North Carolina, McCarley was an old-timer who had been in the Army since 1955. He took over ST Florida in the fall of 1967, and brought Howard along with him as a straphanger on one of Howard's first recon missions. "Howard just loved combat," McCarley said.

Action just seemed to follow Howard from his earliest months at Kontum. Even seemingly routine in-country operations had a way of turning into skirmishes for him. He accompanied McCarley in a deuce-and-a-half into Kontum one day. As they crossed a makeshift bridge over a little stream, their truck broke down and left them stranded. While the pair worked to sort out their dilemma, they became the targets of potshots from a pair of VC soldiers firing on them from the trees. "You couldn't call that a firefight," McCarley said. "But Bob and I took care of them pretty quick. The action didn't last thirty seconds."[27]

Many similar actions in which Sergeant Howard found himself engaged did not result in any awards for valor, but his heroics were noticed and appreciated by his brotherhood in the Kontum recon company. One Green Beret recalled the time when a VC terrorist riding on the back of a motorbike tossed a hand grenade at a GI chow line. Howard sprinted into action, grabbing an M16 away from a stunned camp guard. He then calmly dropped to one knee, took careful aim, and killed the motorbike's driver. Howard then pursued the terrorist passenger for a half-mile before he was able to shoot him down as well.[28]

Bob Howard continued straphanging on missions both with recon teams and Hornet Force platoons. On one occasion, he sprinted up alongside a moving NVA truck on Highway 110, tossed a mine in among the startled troops, and then detonated it as he raced away. Such an action seemed almost trivial to the man who believed he was simply doing his job. To others, he clearly went above and beyond the call of duty on every single mission. Those who knew him well found it to be no surprise that FOB-2 commanders wrote Howard up on three separate occasions for the nation's highest military award, the Medal of Honor. The third time was the charm.

Chapter Eight

INTO THE HORNET'S NEST

Fred William Zabitosky was another new arrival at Kontum whose coolness under fire became as well respected as that of Bob Howard. Zabitosky was not one to shy away from trouble. He had become familiar with it during his youth in a poor Polish community in Trenton, New Jersey. Zabitosky ran away from his tough home life more than once, and as a teen he spent time in a reformatory for vandalism and petty theft. His father left home when young Zabitosky was only fifteen, forcing him to help support his mother, younger brother, and two sisters. When he joined the U.S. Army in 1959 at age seventeen, Zabitosky found the home he had never had. He simply loved the discipline and the pride, since it was the first time he had experienced either.[1]

He had never even left his home state until he headed to Fort Benning, Georgia, for his first training—he traded reform school for "Benning's School for Boys." His early years in the Army were spent in infantry and artillery, with assignments taking him from Oklahoma to Germany. He continued supporting his family in New Jersey while he was in Europe by sending home forty dollars out of his sixty-eight-dollar monthly pay. During his two-and-a-half years overseas, Zabitosky completed high school, achieved status as the Outstanding Soldier of the Month for his company, and advanced in pay grade from E1 to E4.

Zabitosky— "Zab" to his buddies—found a certain allure in the growing reputation of Special Forces. He volunteered in 1963, completed Special Forces training at Fort Bragg, and spent four months in Alaska training on intelligence and infiltration methods. In September 1964, Zabitosky and his team were sent to Vietnam; his first tour of duty found him assigned to a Special Forces A camp in the Central Highlands. His first firefight came in February 1965 while on a security patrol with two Montagnard companies. His men walked into an ambush but Zabitosky survived the ordeal, recovering a Chinese weapon from a dead soldier in an NVA uniform in the process.[2]

Zabitosky completed his first tour in Vietnam in September 1965. He volunteered for a second tour in April 1966, was assigned to MACV-SOG; he spent the next year training South Vietnamese soldiers for infiltration and recon missions into North Vietnam, Laos, and Cambodia. When Staff Sergeant Zabitosky reached Kontum in September 1967, he was already into his third tour in Vietnam. From FOB-2, he would eventually complete fifteen cross-border operations either into Laos on Prairie Fire missions or into Cambodia on Daniel Boone missions.[3]

Zabitosky was soon assigned to take over ST Maine—commanded by One-Zero Johnny Arvai until he was rotated back to the States. Sergeant Zabitosky proved resilient under fire and well in command of his team. By late 1967, he had been joined by a new one-one, Staff Sergeant Doug Glover. Zabitosky's new assistant team leader turned out to be a hard-luck soldier. During his first cross-border operation with ST Maine, Glover was hit in the arm as their chopper was shot out of the LZ before being able to insert the team. On Glover's second mission, in November 1967, he was injured again; this time his team spooked an elephant in the jungle that had been following them for some time. The massive beast charged the men and stepped on Glover, breaking his foot. Aside from this unusual casualty, it was not uncommon for recon men to return from such insertions with a wide variety of enemy-inflicted wounds or other injuries—sometimes the team's extraction alone took a toll on a man's body.

Such was the case for Staff Sergeant Albert Erickson during the fall of 1967. He and his one-zero were nearly lost while on a Daniel Boone mission with ST Texas to attempt a wiretap near an NVA encampment. Erickson had joined ST Texas in September; the team was under command of Staff Sergeant Sherman Corren, an old-timer who began his Special Forces service in Germany in 1953. Corren first served on One-Zero Robert Marple's ST Arizona as its radio operator in 1967 before taking command of the team.

Corren and Erickson moved their team close to the NVA camp and Corren sent two men forward to perform the wiretap. They were spotted, however, by a North Vietnamese soldier before they could complete the work. Erickson opened fire but suffered a jammed gun. Fortunately, his teammates managed to kill five soldiers as they pulled back. His wiretap efforts compromised, Corren moved his team swiftly downhill toward their planned extraction point while Erickson called for a fast extraction.

Spike Team Texas came under fire again near the LZ and was forced to call in air support. The gunships began blasting the area with bombs and rockets, some placed so close that Erickson was knocked senseless by one blast; shrapnel sliced through his legs and back. Corren called in the first chopper to pull out their indigenous troops. Because of a heavy canopy, the Hueys were forced to drop McGuire rigs in order to pull team Texas out of the Cambodian jungle.

Corren and Erickson snapped into the McGuire rigs on the second chopper. Corren helped to secure his injured radioman, then snapped himself in and signaled "go!" as bullets flew around the area. The men were battered as they were ripped through the trees; Erickson's radio pack absorbed an enemy round in the process. He was left only partially secured in his McGuire rig and spinning out of control below the chopper.

He and Corren swung past each other twice, yelling to each other to grab the other for support. "The third time, we slammed together," said Erickson. "He grabbed me and I grabbed his leg with my two feet. Then we were slammed up against a tree and I nearly passed out from the pain."[4]

Corren wrapped himself around Erickson and the pair clung to each other for a half-hour before they could be set down. Erickson had suffered shrapnel lacerations in his back and rope burns on his neck from the McGuire rig. His arms had been jerked out of socket and he had suffered dislocated shoulders. Corren pulled ligaments in his own legs while trying to keep Erickson wrapped up.

In the wake of this mission, Sherman Corren was transferred to FOB-3 to take over another team and Erickson was sent for medical attention. Command of ST Texas passed to Sergeant First Class Clarence Harold Webb from Rochester, New York, in late October 1967. At age forty and with more than a dozen years in the Army, Webb was commonly known to his younger comrades as "Pappy." Like Zabitosky and Howard, Webb would soon gain a reputation at Kontum for his fearlessness.

Webb retained Erickson as his one-one but added Staff Sergeant Bob Van Hall as his one-two and Staff Sergeant Richard Adams as his one-three. On October 29, 1967, Webb's ST Texas came under enemy assault while on a mission in Laos. The spike team was moving up a ridgeline when an estimated platoon of NVA opened fire on them with heavy automatic weapons and grenades. Webb rallied his troops, moved them up the hill, and formed a defensive perimeter to repel the pursuing enemy. The NVA assaulted through bamboo thickets while Webb hurled grenades and sprayed them with fire from his weapon. Spike Team Texas managed to force the enemy to temporarily withdraw.

Van Hall had established communications with the FAC and called for air support for their perilous situation. The NVA soon discovered the location of the patrol's radio operator and unleashed a second, more furious assault, determined to overrun his position and silence his requests for air support. During their first attack, the NVA killed two of ST Texas' indigenous team members, leaving a dangerous gap in the line near Van Hall's radio. A withering hail of bullets chopped down bamboo all around him as Webb leaped to his feet and began killing NVA who were threatening his one-two. Van Hall rallied the team's other men for support as enemy soldiers were gunned down so close that Van Hall dropped one at a range of mere feet—point blank.

Ten NVA were believed to have been killed from Webb's fire. The remainder were forced to flee down the hillside, leaving weapons and equipment behind. Spike Team Texas was extracted without further loss. Webb, on his way to becoming one of the most respected one-zeros to run recon from FOB-2 during this time, was awarded a Silver Star for his valor on this mission.

◆◇◆

Kontum's Green Berets held their aviation comrades in high regard. Their lives literally hung in the balance of the skilled airmen who risked everything to extract them time after time from harrowing jungle firefights.

By late 1967, a new unit had arrived at Kontum to support the operations running from FOB-2. The 57th Assault Helicopter Company, organized early in the year at Fort Bragg, North Carolina, was deployed to Vietnam and began setting up camp at Kontum in October. Countless sand bags were filled and stacked to build bunkers around a revetment area to protect the unit's new UH-1H model Huey slicks and eight UH-1C Huey gunships. The first two months were relatively trouble-free but the NVA soon began firing mortars and rockets down on the new Kontum Army Air Field. By early 1968, it was frequent enough that the men of the 57th AHC ruefully dubbed it "Rocket City."[5]

The Huey slicks of the 57th that were used to insert SOG recon teams were nicknamed the "gladiators," while the gunship division under Major Curtis D. Green went by the call name "cougars." Each Huey was appropriately dubbed with a corresponding radio call sign (such as "Gladiator 167" or "Cougar 23"). The 57th had two platoons of slicks, maintaining eight Hueys per platoon with several spares available as needed to replace choppers that had been damaged or had maintenance issues. The first group of pilots and co-pilots—men like Rick Griffith, Joe Pagan, Jack Koshinsky, Kenneth Haan, Steve Sullivan, Dean Taylor, Darrell Anthony, Robert Tobey, and dozens of others—arrived in November. "When we got there, we began flying resupply missions to get familiar with the country before we started inserting SOG teams during December," said Griffith. "We slept in tents out there at the airfield during that first year at Kontum."[6]

The 57th AHC would quickly become a vital lifeline for the SOG recon team based at FOB-2. Many of the pilots and their crews were known only to the Green Berets by their radio call signs. Others became better acquainted in between missions at the base bar or because of shared ordeals in the field. But no one doubted the value or the determination of the young aviators who risked their lives time and again both during insertions and the often perilous extractions under fire.

Lives depended upon the teamwork shared by the ground and aviation units each day. Some would liken the cross-border operations to stirring up a hornet's nest. The fighters and B-52s were called in by recon teams to bomb the "hornet's nest" when a particular enemy area was discovered. Then, the spike teams were inserted for BDAs—which some likened to going onto the ground beneath the disturbed nest to count dead hornets. Inevitably, many of these teams ran afoul of greatly disturbed NVA or VC units. When they became too hotly engaged, they signaled a prairie fire emergency.

Their fate among the "hornets" was thus relegated to the U.S. or Vietnamese chopper crews who put their necks on the line to pull them out each time. Major Hart would find the further development of the Kontum airfield by the 57th AHC to be a godsend for his operations.

◆◇◆

With Zabitosky's one-one, Doug Glover, resigned to serving in supply thanks to his broken foot, Zab used straphangers as his assistant team leaders. In early November ST Maine was tapped for a Laotian mission into target area India-9, and Zabitosky found a willing volunteer in Captain Warren "Bud" Williams—recently assigned as the new Kontum Hatchet Force commander. At age thirty-two, Williams was a capable airborne officer, but he felt compelled to run a mission under fire to prove his mettle both to his new men and to Major Hart. *Good leaders never ask their men to do something they themselves are not prepared to do*, Williams reasoned. He felt little apprehension going in with Sergeant Zabitosky, whom Bud considered to be "one team leader who definitely had his shit together."[7]

Zabitosky and Williams went into India-9 heavy, taking a twelve-man team that included nine Montagnards and Sergeant First Class Bill Boyle as their one-two. Zabitosky and Boyle were already on the ground with half the team as Williams felt his Huey go into a hover above the designated LZ. Clutching his gear, he motioned for his Montagnards to follow and leaped off the skid into the dancing elephant grass. To his horror, the waving vegetation was six feet taller than he realized, and Williams slammed into solid ground so hard that he was initially afraid he had broken a leg.

Williams realized his rookie mistake, gathered his indigenous soldiers, and hustled away a few hundred yards from the LZ. He grouped quickly in thick brush with Zabitosky, Boyle, and the balance of ST Maine to confer. The news relayed from the FAC above was not good: one of the pilots had spotted an enemy tracker squatting near the edge of the grassy field. "It was a good bet that the enemy already had an accurate fix on our location," said Williams.[8]

Boyle argued that ST Maine should call for an emergency extraction before the NVA could hit them, but Zabitosky was not convinced. Captain Williams settled the discussion by making his first combat decision: the team would continue with their assigned mission but would use plenty of back tracking while remaining alert for ambushes. Spike Team Maine spent its next three days slipping through the mountains of India-9, a dozen men in olive green fatigues and floppy boonie hats, whose gear was secured with black electrical tape to conceal any noise or reflection. Zabitosky's men were being tracked the entire time, but his team managed to gather

One-Zero Fred Zabitosky's Spike Team Maine survived two treacherous Bright Light missions in late 1967 and early 1968. Zab (*left*) is seen here in November 1967 at the Dak To launch site with Captain Warren "Bud" Williams (*center*) and Sergeant First Class Bill Boyle. *Walter Williams*

intelligence on NVA troops and roadways for three days without blundering into a deadly firefight.

On the third day, Zabitosky arranged with his FAC to have the team extracted from a large bomb crater close to where ST Maine was already engaged in a sporadic firefight with their enemy. Some F-4 Phantoms and gunships did their best to suppress the NVA fire enough for slicks to pull the team out, but the first Huey pilot was forced to abort his attempted extraction after his chopper was riddled with small-arms fire. The second slick attempted to drop a rope ladder but a large tree prevented the pilot from descending low enough for the recon men to reach the ladder.

Zabitosky, Boyle, and Williams positioned their Montagnards to cover the perimeter of their LZ and set out Claymores to at least slow the advance of any charging enemy. Williams was the first to spot an NVA soldier forty yards away, emerging from the jungle into the bomb crater clearing. Two quick rounds from Williams' CAR-15 took care of him, but other soldiers soon crept close enough to the crater that they and ST Maine were soon exchanging grenades. In the midst of exploding grenades and small-arms fire, Williams soon began to question his fate. *I'm not sure that any of us are getting out of this hell hole.*[9]

He soon realized how well Zabitosky's Montagnards had been trained. Williams was taken aback when one of the team's point men calmly crawled over, asked for a light for his pipe, and then crawled back to his position to resume firing at the NVA with his pipe in his mouth. Spike Team Maine was finally pulled out by McGuire rigs, three men at a time until only Zabitosky, Williams, and Boyle remained for the final extract. "The enemy, by this point in the cross-border dueling, were pretty familiar with the SOG modus operandi," said Williams. "They knew that Americans would be the last ones to leave the battlefield."[10]

Three of ST Maine's Montagnards had been wounded during the firefight, but the brunt of the enemy's assault came as the three Green Berets were jerked skyward in their McGuire rigs. Williams waved to his opponents as he was pulled through the triple canopy and then spent the next forty-five minutes dangling below a helicopter, pondering his first Prairie Fire mission, until he was dumped at Dak To. Williams would run two more cross-border missions into Laos with ST Maine, one of which saw Zabitosky's team being driven out of the LZ before they could fully deploy.

✦✧✦

Supply sergeant Bob Howard continued to run missions whenever he got the chance. He carried the radio as a straphanger for Sergeant First Class

Johnnie Gilreath's ST Colorado on more than one mission. Gilreath, who was assigned to Kontum in April 1967 from the 10th SFG in Germany, had taken over ST Colorado by summer with Sergeant Larry Williams as his one-one.

The target Howard ran with Gilreath and Williams on November 21 was a hot one. They had already proven to be effective in the field during their early missions together. They had broken contact with an enemy unit in September after a firefight and had directed bomb strikes against an estimated two dozen NVA in October while attempting to run a wiretap. On November 19, ST Colorado was inserted into southeast Laos in target area Hotel-9. After two days across the fence, the team was running low on water. Gilreath and Williams consulted their maps, found a stream in the area, and moved toward it, taking position on a hillside. Williams took one of their Montagnards and eased down the hill to stock up on water. As they filled their canteens, Williams noticed a large cache of rice, stacked in massive bags, along with stockpiles of salt.

He hurried back to report to Gilreath. Spike Team Colorado reported their discovery back to base and requested a Hatchet Force platoon be sent in to help destroy the cache. Kontum scrambled to dispatch Hatchet Force Athens, led by volunteer Bob Howard. His men were to insert and rendez-vous with Gilreath's team, while Howard scouted for approaching NVA.[11]

Sergeant Williams used a Claymore to blow down a large tree to make room for the choppers. As Howard's Hatchet Force was landing, Williams took one of his indigenous troopers to recon the rice cache while the rest of his team remained on the hillside. As they approached the site, Williams motioned his Montagnards to sweep to the right. They encountered an NVA and exchanged fire with him. The seemingly peaceful jungle suddenly came to life.

"All hell broke loose," said Williams. "We had stirred up a hornet's nest."[12] Three of the choppers were badly damaged by ground fire as the Hatchet Force was inserted. Howard then avoided NVA ambushes while leading the recon platoon safely to Gilreath's position. The Hatchet Force team proceeded to destroy the cache, while Sergeant Howard took out a security patrol. They encountered four NVA, all of whom Howard took down with a single magazine, but his team then became pinned down by a camouflaged machine-gun bunker.

The Hatchet platoon worked feverishly to destroy the mounds of rice and salt, while Gilreath and Williams assaulted enemy pillboxes. Williams escaped uninjured, although his fatigue jacket was ripped in places by bullets. While the Hatchet Force men were destroying the food cache, they also discovered a thousand rounds of recoilless rifle ammunition and seven hundred rounds of AK47 ammunition. They used mortars to detonate the ammunition.

Recon men did not shy away from danger, but many avoided unnecessarily exposing themselves. Team leader Gilreath recalled of Howard: "He ran *toward* the enemy at all times."[13] After gunning down the four NVA, Bob Howard and his men were pinned down by a hail of gunfire erupting from a nearby machine-gun emplacement. Disregarding his safety, he crawled forward. En route, he killed a North Vietnamese sniper who was firing at him. Howard then charged forward with his M16 and gunned down the entire machine-gun crew at point-blank range.

A second machine-gun emplacement then unleashed a savage barrage. Sergeant Howard pulled his men back to a covered position and directed in an air strike against the fortified bunker. After the explosions, Howard crawled forward to assess the bomb damage. The machine gun began chattering away, as the angry occupants in the bunker sought to kill the advancing American. He was pinned to the ground with machine-gun bullets flying six inches above his head. Howard lobbed a hand grenade into the nest, killing the gunners and temporarily silencing the weapon.

Howard then raced back to his platoon as more NVA swept in to take over the machine-gun nest. He grabbed a light antitank rocket launcher as the bunker roared to life again. Amid a hail of bullets, he rose and fired the rocket into the nest, destroying the gun and its crew in a devastating blast. Howard's one-man assault had taken down two machine-gun nests and allowed the rest of his platoon to ease back out of harm's way.

The area was soon deemed too hot to handle. Gilreath and Howard found that it was a large logistical area surrounded by a battalion of enemy, who had the advantage of using a seemingly impenetrable bunker system. No casualties were suffered by the Americans, although Howard was wounded during his rampage. Gilreath finally had his team and the Hatchet Force fall back toward the LZ while calling in air strikes against the enemy forces and their cache.

After returning to Kontum, Howard and Gilreath were summoned by Chief SOG Jack Singlaub. They were ordered to fly to Saigon to brief General Westmoreland on their mission. The four-star was so impressed that he asked the two men if there was anything he could do for them. Gilreath replied that his ambition was to attend flight school and become an aviator. His wishes would be granted, but not before Gilreath completed another mission in December. Sergeant Howard only asked to be given the chance to see more action. He, too, would get his wish.

Larry Williams earned the Silver Star for his efforts on this mission, and Bob Howard collected another Purple Heart. His solo assault on the

NVA machine-gun nests so impressed Major Hart that he submitted his supply sergeant for the Medal of Honor. Howard simply shrugged off his actions, patched up his wounds, and continued in his role as base supply sergeant and recon straphanger without any boasting.

The Army's awards board in time would downgrade the Medal of Honor submission for Howard to the Distinguished Service Cross, the nation's second highest honor for valor. The humble warrior was presented with the medal in a Kontum awards ceremony months later, as his commanding officer read the citation proclaiming "his fearless and determined actions" of November 21, 1967.[14] The awards committee responsible for pushing through Medal of Honor recommendations, however, had not heard the last of Robert Howard.

◆◇◆

Fred Zabitosky was another who never flinched when he was called upon to risk his life to help save fellow soldiers. His name, in fact, would be called fairly often to take on perilous Bright Light missions.

His first such deployment came in late fall, when another recon team was overrun in the Kontum Province of South Vietnam. Master Sergeant Samuel Silver Theriault, a thirty-three-year-old from New Hampshire, had led a platoon of Nungs and Green Berets on a mission on November 26. The following day, his team was assaulted in dense jungle by a large VC force firing small arms and machine guns. Theriault was wounded but moved through heavy fire to deploy his men's defense and organize them for a counter-assault. He then led the charge through vicious fire and was mortally wounded in the process.

Five other men of the team were killed in the violent exchange, including Staff Sergeant Rudolfo Chavez and Sergeant William Wallace McGrew. The next day, Fred Zabitosky's ST Maine was inserted into the area of the firefight to conduct a Bright Light mission to look for survivors and recover bodies. As they approached the ambush area, Sergeant First Class Bill Boyle and his indigenous team members found three bodies that had been left for them as bait. Boyle sensed that the VC were lying in wait, ready to ambush. He alerted Zabitosky, recommending that they split the team, flank the ambush, and catch their enemy in a crossfire.

Boyle took half the men and maneuvered them to the flank of the VC before triggering the counter-ambush. For the next twenty minutes, he and his men were in heavy contact with the superior force. Boyle killed four enemy soldiers in the exchange and the resulting crossfire was hot enough to force the balance of the Communist force to retreat. Boyle continued to direct heavy fire while sending some of his indigenous troops forward to retrieve the bodies of four of the slain recon team men. Boyle hauled one of the bodies himself as the Bright Light team retreated 550 yards to a safe LZ for extraction. Once on the LZ, the team was hit again. Boyle helped direct the fight that carried on for another twenty minutes.

Tactical air support was successful in pounding back the VC forces long enough to get the Bright Light team extracted. Zabitosky, Boyle, and their Bright Light team escaped without injury, thanks only to the swift thinking they made in avoiding the baited kill zone. Master Sergeant Theriault was later awarded the Distinguished Service Cross post-humously for his heroism in directing his team even after being mortally wounded. Bill Boyle received the Bronze Star for heroism on the November 27 mission.

Boyle and Zabitosky were left with a new appreciation of how the North Vietnamese Army was prepared to lure SOG teams in for the kill by using their own fallen comrades as bait. Spike Team Maine would be called in to perform another Bright Light mission, again facing enemy booby traps, within weeks.

✦✧✦

Three weeks after meeting with General Westmoreland and being recommended for the Medal of Honor, Sergeant Bob Howard was out of the supply room and running recon once again.

He went out with Spike Team Colorado, but this time Johnnie Gilreath was no longer its one-zero—he had been summoned to Command and Control North (CCN) at Da Nang in December to handle a mission in the Ashau Valley in conjunction with the 1st Cavalry Division. Gilreath performed with such valor that he received a Bronze Star and a battlefield commission. On January 18, 1968, Gilreath was pinned with his second lieutenant bars and was soon on his way to the flight school training Westmoreland had promised.

Sergeant Larry Williams took over the one-zero position for ST Colorado and pulled in Sergeant Paul Poole as his new one-one. On December 7, Williams, Poole, and their team were flown once again into the hot area of Hotel-9, with Bob Howard straphanging as their third Green Beret. Their long-range patrol was assigned to recon the NVA battalion headquarters and supply area that they had so recently discovered. Williams kept his men moving stealthily over rugged mountainous terrain the next day, pausing long enough to call in air strikes against a dozen NVA troops they encountered, before ST Colorado continued moving.

On December 10, Williams' team made a significant discovery when they came upon a battalion-size enemy camp, complete with twenty-one bamboo structures and twenty tons of rice. Poole called for an air strike to wipe out the village, and once the destruction was complete, the team moved into the camp to perform a BDA. Bob Howard noticed several huts and cache points that had not been destroyed. He began pillaging and burning the remaining structures and supplies, destroying more than twenty tons of rice, a ton of medical supplies, and thousands of pounds of ammunition and weapons. The team then moved out of the area, only to be halted by an extremely steep ridge.

Pausing momentarily to select the best route to take in search of an extraction LZ, ST Colorado was hit by a wave of NVA. Larry Williams took over the radio to call in for aerial support and an extraction while Howard rallied his frightened indigenous teammates and led them in a successful stand. The North Vietnamese force was estimated to contain between thirty and fifty soldiers but the smart offensive work by the men of FOB-2 was estimated to have killed at least twenty of the enemy while repelling a heavy assault. Williams then moved the majority of his team toward their LZ area, leaving Bob Howard behind to hold their perimeter until the Hueys could begin the extraction process.

Howard would be awarded the Bronze Star with "V" device for leading the effort to destroy the enemy supplies and for continually exposing himself to hostile fire while his team was being extracted. Awards meant little to him, but it was the fearless resolve of men like Howard that helped SOG teams carry out ninety-seven missions into Cambodia by late 1967.

To continue supporting Operation Daniel Boone and other cross-border work, Colonel Singlaub had authorized the construction of two more forward operating bases: FOB-5 at Ban Me Thuot and FOB-6 at the Sigma base at Ho Ngoc Tau. SOG's fourth base, FOB-4, had opened for business in November on the beach at Da Nang, adjacent to Marble Mountain; its original recon teams were named after deadly snakes.

Radio relay sites continued to be manned at Eagle's Nest in Laos and at Sledgehammer, overlooking the Plei Trap Valley in the Pleiku Province. The Joint Personnel Recovery Center had launched sixteen prisoner recovery operations during the year but had enjoyed only one success— twenty ARVN POWs had been freed, but no Americans were recovered. The North Vietnamese by year's end were reducing the number of supply and maintenance personnel on the Ho Chi Minh Trail by increasing their use of mechanized equipment. MACV later estimated that from October 1967 through January 1968, some 44,000 NVA troops had been infiltrated south through the Trail system to take part in the early 1968 Tet Offensive.[15]

The recon teams operating across the border into Laos and Cambodia had primarily fought North Vietnamese regulars and VC guerrillas during the past year and a half. By the new year of 1968, however, there was evidence that the NVA had added more reliable counter-recon units to engage SOG's spike teams. Spike Team Python, based out of the new FOB-4, encountered one such enemy counter-recon unit on January 4, 1968, with horrific results.

The team was led by Sergeant First Class Paul Herman Villarosa, who was considered by one of his SF buddies to be "a brilliant commo man" who could decipher twenty words per minute in each ear. He sported spider web tattoos on his elbows and a dotted line tattooed completely around his neck with the gory admonition to "cut on dotted line." Paul Villarosa had served four years in the U.S. Navy during the Korean conflict, returned to civilian life, and then joined the Army in 1960. By late 1967, Villarosa was on his third tour in Vietnam and was leading a long-range reconnaissance patrol in Laos. Due to bad weather at the FOB-4 launch site, his team was inserted from FOB-2 in Kontum. As his men moved through the jungle on January 4, it became apparent to him that an enemy force was attempting to flank ST Python.[16]

Villarosa halted his team and was preparing to establish radio communications with base when an enemy force suddenly ordered his team to throw down their weapons and surrender. The Vietnamese counter-recon team quickly overpowered Spike Team Python and disarmed them. Only the one-one, Nathaniel Pipkins, managed to escape through the jungle and was later rescued. Villarosa, his young one-two, and the team's indigenous troops were lined up. An English-speaking NVA officer told the American radio operator to watch carefully as Villarosa's belly was slashed open. The officer then inserted a flamethrower and burned the Green Beret to death. The NVA then proceeded to incinerate ST Python's Montagnards while the one-two watched in horror.[17]

The surviving American was allowed to remain alive so that he could tell his fellow Green Berets what they might expect from their enemy. His radio calls for help were picked up by a covey FAC flying over Laos and an extraction team was sent in. The NVA allowed the young specialist to be extracted by McGuire rig through the jungle canopy so that he could relate the macabre experience.

Fred Zabitosky's ST Maine was on Bright Light duty at Dak To when the cries for help were heard coming from the frightened young American left alive. After the one-two was pulled out of the jungle, Zabitosky's team made several attempts to insert near the site of the overrun LZ on the afternoon of January 4. The NVA responded with heavy firepower that damaged Zabitosky's chopper and finally forced it to limp back to Dak To. Upon his return, Zabitosky was infuriated to learn that some of the men who were debriefing the lone survivor of the massacre had doubts about the accuracy of his story. Zabitosky challenged a visiting SOG lieutenant colonel to join his Bright Light team the next morning to go recon the site where Team Python had been executed.[18]

Spike Team Maine boarded choppers at Dak To on the morning of January 5 and returned to the scene of the war crime. Accompanying Zabitosky and his Montagnard teammates were Staff Sergeant Gene Bettis as his one-one (filling in for Doug Glover) and Sergeant Bill Boyle carrying the radio. The disbelieving SOG senior officer did ride out to the site with Zabitosky and his team, but refused to leave the chopper when the recon team landed. One of the circling Hueys spotted ST Python's one-one, Nathaniel Pipkins, in the meantime and pulled him out alive.

From the time ST Maine landed on the ground, Zabitosky was aware of enemy elements close behind his men. He led his team toward their objective in spite of occasional sniper fire. Zabitosky responded by setting a very fast pace to evade their attackers throughout the day. Upon reaching the ambush site, they found the casualties of the attack: the team leader and three burned Montagnards.[19]

Spike Team Maine made their RON about twenty-one feet from the site. Throughout the night, they listened to probing fire from the enemy trackers. Gene Bettis remained awake throughout the night to listen for close enemy movement while his comrades tried to rest. At first light on January 6, Zabitosky moved his team to the massacre site and had them search thoroughly to make sure the NVA had not set up an ambush. Once the bodies were determined to be clear, Fred had his men set to the gruesome task of hauling the remains to a safe LZ, some 650 yards through mountainous terrain. They had traveled only a short distance when enemy troops opened up on them with automatic weapons fire. Bettis and Boyle fell back to exchange fire with the NVA while Zabitosky and his Montagnards continued hauling their fallen comrades through the treacherous mountains.

Sporadic sniper fire and the burden of moving fast with their sacred burden made the journey excruciating. It took three hours to cover the football field–sized area but they finally reached the LZ. Zabitosky requested exfiltration and then set up his ST Maine in a defensive perimeter. He felt certain their movements had been observed by the enemy.

He was right. As their extraction choppers began circling the LZ, the NVA opened up from well-entrenched positions. Brave pilots brought their slicks in to begin pulling out the remains and the members of ST Maine.

Zabitosky and Boyle returned fire on the NVA throughout the loading process and managed to hold them off; Zabitosky was the last man to board the last slick out.

Zabitosky, Bettis, and Boyle would each receive the Bronze Star for their successful Bright Light. But awards did little to cure Zabitosky's seething anger over the officer who had refused to assist with the Bright Light mission. His only solace was that Paul Villarosa's family could now bury him with proper honors. Villarosa, who displayed great courage while his NVA captors burned him alive, posthumously received the Distinguished Service Cross.

Chapter Nine

"THEY WON'T TAKE US ALIVE"

Doug Glover was ready to take command. He had been serving as Fred Zabitosky's one-one for ST Maine, and by late January 1968 his foot (broken in the elephant incident) had sufficiently healed. Zabitosky, still troubled by the January 4 mission in which Villarosa's team was slaughtered, was nearing the conclusion of his latest six-month tour of duty extension. He began working with Glover to pass command of ST Maine to his able assistant team leader.

On January 21, another Kontum recon unit was very nearly overrun by the enemy. Master Sergeant Steven Ward Comerford, a thirty-three-year-old New Yorker, had been inserted with a Hatchet Force platoon to conduct a bomb damage assessment. In addition to his Montagnards, Comerford went in with three other Green Berets: Sergeant First Class Donald Kainu, Sergeant First Class Roland Marquis, and Sergeant Oran Bingham. In the midst of conducting their BDA, the platoon was ambushed by an NVA force of approximately two companies.

In the course of a lengthy battle, all three of the Green Berets were wounded, and more than half of their Montagnards were wounded, one fatally. Comerford, bleeding profusely from a head wound, called in tactical air support to drop their loads within ten yards of his position. The swarming NVA were so close to overrunning his team that Comerford finally ordered, "Drop your next load right on us!"

The resulting strikes inflicted more frag wounds to his team, but it succeeded in suppressing the enemy's advance enough for Comerford to lead his troops to an acceptable extraction LZ. Sergeant Marquis, wounded in the leg and back, covered his platoon's retreat, killing four more NVA in the process and calling in additional air strikes to pound their old position—thus effectively halting pursuit by the NVA.

Bingham, Kainu, and Marquis were each awarded the Silver Star for their actions on January 21, and Steve Comerford became Kontum's fifth man to receive the Distinguished Service Cross, the nation's second-highest honor. Bingham would later be killed in action in August 1971, a fight for which his team leader, First Lieutenant Loren Hagen, was posthumously awarded the last Medal of Honor for an action that occurred during the Vietnam War.

✦◇✦

Just a week after Comerford's escape, an equally outmatched recon team sent Fred Zabitosky's ST Maine into Bright Light action once again.

On January 29, a CCN recon team staging out of Kontum was inserted into the extreme northeastern corner of Cambodia. The Daniel Boone team included Sergeant First Class Charles Edward White, a recon patrol medic from Bessemer, Alabama, who was normally assigned to Company B from CCN. White's team was engaged by NVA but fought their way to a small clearing in the dense jungle to be extracted by McGuire rigs. He and his last two indigenous men, Nang and Khong, climbed into the rigs while the Huey above them hovered about a hundred feet over the canopy. The pilot began lifting off, pulling the men up through the trees. "I'm having a problem with the rig!" White suddenly radioed. He was a big man, standing six-foot-four and weighing 280 pounds. Those on the chopper watched in horror as White was flipped upside down in his McGuire rig. He fell free and crashed to the ground some twenty-five feet below.[1]

Because of the large number of NVA below, no immediate search and rescue (SAR) operation was possible. Charlie White had dropped into a densely forested mountain region in extreme northeastern Cambodia, approximately two miles south of the Cambodia-Laos border. Forty-nine miles southeast at Kontum, orders were received the next day to prepare a team to go in and search for White's body.

Early on January 31, a veteran Bright Light team was en route from Kontum. It was led by Fred Zabitosky and included Sergeant First Class Dallas Longstreath, a twenty-five-year-old Texan who had moved from ST Florida to become the one-zero of ST Illinois. Zabitosky, Longstreath, and their team rappelled into the same LZ where medic White had fallen the previous day. They scoured the area, finding enemy tracks where the NVA had apparently gotten in line and swept up the hillside. All of their boot prints came together at one spot.

Zabitosky and Longstreath found where the husky African American medic had fallen through the jungle canopy into a clump of thick bamboo that had been crushed by his fall. They determined that Sergeant White must have survived, as there was no blood on the ground or any of the bamboo. The team was extracted empty-handed and disappointed. Charlie White was officially listed as "missing in action," although the Defense Intelligence Agency added a note that he was possibly dead due to being "impaled." Zabitosky was left frustrated, convinced White had survived his fall. He had seen no blood trails to indicate the medic had been impaled (though he could have broken his neck or perished from internal damage). He was convinced that White had been seized by the NVA, although Hanoi would deny any knowledge of him. His remains were never recovered.

Charlie White had only three days remaining on his tour of duty when he became the first member of MACV-SOG to become MIA in Cambodia.

◆◇◆

The night Zabitosky and Longstreath returned to Kontum, the Tet Offensive was already in full swing. Tet, the Vietnamese New Year that was celebrated on January 31, had been selected as the date for one of the largest military campaigns the NVA would initiate during the Vietnam War. More than 80,000 Communist troops were scheduled to simultaneously make surprise attacks against military and civilian command and control centers throughout South Vietnam. Due to a calendar error, some of the attacks actually started during the late hours of January 30 in the I Corps and II Corps Tactical Zones of South Vietnam. Nha Trang was hit first, followed later that day by assaults against Pleiku, Kontum, and Da Nang.[2]

Captain Bud Williams and First Lieutenant Ken Etheredge were seated atop the sandbag perimeter wall, listening to radio chatter on Kontum's command radio network, when several Vietcong rockets sailed into the compound and exploded. Gunfire chattered throughout the night, but the enemy made no serious effort to breech FOB-2. "The enemy just wanted to keep our heads down while they moved past us in the direction of Kontum City," Williams said. After daylight, Williams led five other Green Berets and indigenous members of his Hatchet Force out toward Kontum to investigate South Vietnamese guard stations that failed to respond to radio communication. His unit was taken under fire by rebels clad in the common black garb of the Vietnamese peasant as they crossed a river bridge just outside FOB-2.[3]

Williams ordered a flat-out charge across the bridge. On the other side, he threw himself to the right to avoid the withering machine-gun fire. He rolled over and realized he had taken cover behind an Esso gas pump as an NVA rifleman continued shooting at him. "Fortunately, I got him first," said Williams. Three men from his Hatchet Force were wounded in the process of sweeping toward Kontum City through Vietcong-held bunkers and buildings, killing at least six VC in the process.

On the night of January 31, the North Vietnamese launched their attacks against more than 150 other cities as the Tet Offensive exploded. The shooting was close enough for General Westmoreland to hear it from his residence in Pleiku, the MACV headquarters dubbed "Pentagon East." Chief SOG Jack Singlaub was in Saigon, in the home he shared with MACV chief of staff, General Walter T. "Dutch" Kerwin. Both officers raced from their upstairs bedrooms in their underwear when a shell fragment came through Singlaub's window. Chief SOG quickly dressed, armed himself, and drove to MACV headquarters.[4]

The initial attacks of the Tet Offensive caught the allied forces off guard. The Communists managed to take control of several cities, although they were eventually beaten back after taking heavy casualties. The fighting around the U.S. military base at Khe Sanh would rage for two months. By that time, the Tet campaign had resulted in more than 9,000 U.S. and South Vietnamese soldiers killed, more than 1,500 missing, and more than 35,000 people wounded. In return, an estimated 17,000 North Vietnamese combatants were killed and another 20,000 were wounded in the initial months of the Tet Offensive. Civilians in the city of Hue suffered greatly, with thousands killed and 116,000 people rendered homeless.[5]

The Vietcong were being decimated in suicidal attacks on the cities of South Vietnam while the NVA were being pulled back to sanctuaries in Laos and Cambodia, except for the units committed to attacks on Hue and Khe Sanh. Amid these assaults, General Westmoreland asked Singlaub's SOG to determine whether the NVA was grouping for a massive thrust into the Central Highlands at Kontum or Dak To.

In late January ST Colorado was inserted for a long-range recon mission. Supply sergeant Bob Howard, ever eager to see his fair share of action, volunteered to straphang with One-Zero Larry Williams and One-Two Paul Poole. Williams, having drawn the hot-spot area of Hotel-9, was only too glad to have the familiar backing of big Bob Howard as part of his team. On the last day of the mission on February 1, the team was hit by a larger NVA force and pinned down by automatic weapons fire.

Howard immediately began moving the indigenous troops into effective firing positions and placed himself into exposed areas while doing so. He killed many enemy soldiers while Poole worked the radio to raise air support and request a prairie fire emergency extraction. The team used

Howard's covering fire to withdraw back to the protection of a bomb crater where they held off the enemy until air support arrived. Kontum's humble supply sergeant did not seek recognition for his efforts, yet the FOB-2 command continued to write him up for his valor under fire. For this mission, Howard and Poole would later be awarded the Army Commendation Medal for heroism.

✦◇✦

Two weeks into the Tet Offensive, the hottest area of operation for SOG teams was a region known as "the Bra." This well-known aerial reference point on the Dak Xou River was distinguishable as a set of double bends resembling a woman's brassiere.[6] Highway 110 ran along the river at this point as it snaked its way back into the Central Highlands of South Vietnam near Cambodia's northern half. At one of the bends of the Bra, Highway 110 split northeastward from the Ho Chi Minh Trail's major north-south route, Highway 96. This area was heavily defended by the NVA and contained some of the deadliest Kontum target locations—Hotel-9, India-9, Juliet-9, November-9, and Quebec-1. The NVA's Binh Tram 37, a major base of stockpiles defended by masses of antiaircraft guns and counter-recon units, was also hidden in the Bra.[7]

In mid-February, five spike teams were ordered in to check out various target areas in this region along the edge of Cambodia and Laos. The plan was for the teams to stay on the ground for five days to call in B-52s or tactical air units to destroy any NVA units located in the target areas. From Kontum, ST Florida, ST Wyoming, and ST Maine were ordered on February 18 to prepare to insert as three of these five teams the following morning.

Spike Team Maine was to insert into the Bra target area, about fifty-five miles west of Dak To. The Laotian region consisted of heavily wooded, mountainous terrain covered by very dense undergrowth, with head-high patches of elephant grass periodically breaking the various bamboo thickets and wooded expanses. Spike Team Maine's mission was to learn whether the NVA were pulling back, reinforcing, or resupplying their Tet Offensive activities in the Central Highlands.

On the evening of February 18, the new one-zero, Doug Glover, had apprehensions about the following day's mission. Normally, he was a fairly good-natured, easy-going guy. But he pulled Zabitosky aside and shared, "I had a dream that I'm going to get killed. I know I'm going to die tomorrow."

Zabitosky tried to reassure his friend, "Doug, I'll go in with you as your assistant team leader."[8]

On the morning of February 19, the 57th AHC choppers picked up ST Maine and ST Wyoming from Kontum. At Dak To, One-Zero Joe Messer, One-One David Hause, and the indigenous members of ST Wyoming boarded Hueys for their flight into Laos. They were inserted in the vicinity of Heavy Drop, the radio relay station, where they found the area to be overrun with NVA. The mission was a disaster from the start: ST Wyoming was on the run as they shot it out with pursuing enemy soldiers.

Hause opened up on the radio, calling for assistance as they evaded their pursuers. Messer led his men along a high ridgeline, hoping to find a suitable place for extraction. Messer decided if they could not be picked up along the ridge, his men would have to continue running all the way to Heavy Drop. A pair of H-34s soon appeared as their FAC directed them toward a suitable LZ. As the first chopper settled in, Hause and his indigenous troopers leaped aboard. Messer was the last man on the ground, but the crew chief delivered heart-sinking news.

"You can't get on! You'll have to wait for the next one!"

As one-zero, it was Messer's duty to be first off and last back on the choppers for each mission. Automatic fire zinged around him as he scrambled for cover. In the distance, he could see the chase ship banking around to come in for him. His only chance was to shoot it out until the pilot could drop in.

Messer realized that the NVA were fully expecting the teams this morning. He was in an unenviable position, with his team chased out of their recon area and leaving him as the lone man on the ground. Over his radio, he could now hear frantic shouts. His buddy Fred Zabitosky was also calling for help. Recon Team Maine was obviously experiencing its own prairie fire emergency. Messer hoped for the best for his comrades, but at the moment his own skin was in jeopardy.

◆◇◆

Spike Team Maine had boarded two unmarked Hueys minutes behind Wyoming for the short flight into The Bra. One-Zero Doug Glover had Zabitosky straphanging as his one-one, and a new one-two, Staff Sergeant Percell Bragg, who was making his first cross-border trip. Their six Nungs were solid fighters who had been operating from Kontum for twenty months. Their point man was a forty-seven-year-old, cross-eyed Nung who towered over his counterparts at six-foot-three inches. Glover's tail gunner, who stood only four-foot-nine inches, was even more experienced: the fifty-four-year-old had previously fought with a French parachute regiment in Vietnam and Algeria.[9]

As the slicks made their final run into the LZ, Zabitosky thumbed his throat mic to offer some advice to Glover. From the second chopper, Zabitosky relayed to the new one-zero that he had noticed a stream running north off the LZ that went right up into a box canyon. He advised Glover to stay away from the box canyon.

Glover's half of the team inserted first. By the time Zabitosky's Huey hovered over the LZ long enough for him and his three Nungs to leap to the ground, he could already see Glover's section disappearing up the stream. Zabitosky moved his section at fast pace to catch up to the leading group, hoping to stop them from entering the canyon. Before he could make it, his fears were realized, as automatic fire from NVA soldiers opened up on ST Maine's forward section.

By the time Zabitosky reached the contact point, he could see that the AK fire was coming from enemy bunkers and from soldiers moving through the bamboo. He directed Glover, Bragg, and the Nungs to return fire with their CAR-15s and to throw grenades to break the attack of the onrushing NVA. It was quickly apparent to Zabitosky that they were facing superior numbers. Their only hope would be to break contact, then evade and escape.

Zabitosky could tell right away that Glover was uncomfortable and asked him what he wanted the team to do.

"You take over the team," Glover said. He instinctively trusted Zab's ability to pull them through the perilous situation.[10]

"All right," he said. "Move the men back to the LZ and I'll stay here and cover."

In the brief lull after repelling the first rush, Zabitosky quickly set up Claymore mines with white phosphorous grenades and attached them along a line aimed toward the bunker complex. Zabitosky later learned from SOG intelligence that the box canyon he was trying to block contained a regimental command post—possibly the headquarters of Binh Tram 37 itself. He then grabbed the radio from Bragg, who had never called in air strikes under duress, and handed it to Glover.[11]

Zabitosky told Glover to call in the standby Skyraiders to bomb any white smoke that erupted from the Claymores. Glover, Bragg, and their Nungs raced back down the stream. As they did, Zabitosky could already hear the NVA crashing through the bamboo toward him. He triggered the first Claymore as the first green-and-khaki-fatigue clad NVA regular came into view.[12]

The first device erupted with a mighty roar, producing a cloud of willy peter smoke that rose above the canopy. During the next half hour, Zabitosky tossed grenades and burned through fifteen magazines to keep the NVA bottled up. He moved laterally to the advancing enemy, creating the illusion that a larger force of Americans was making the attack. Finally, he heard the welcome sound of more A-1E Skyraiders moving over. They dropped their first load of napalm over the drifting smoke. He then called for the A-1s to dump their ordnance. Zabitosky opened fire with his CAR-15 as more NVA appeared, and then he triggered the second Claymore. He turned to run as the second mine exploded but became entangled in the thick growth. Zabitosky could hear the next Skyraider screaming down. He lunged forward, pulling free from the bamboo, and took cover behind a rock as a 750-pound bomb detonated nearby.

The force of the blast knocked the wind out of him. Zabitosky scrambled to his feet and raced through the splintered bamboo before the wounded NVA could recover. At the LZ, he found that Glover had arranged his Nungs in a tight defensive perimeter and was calling in more Skyraiders. The news from the FAC overhead was not good. The other spike teams inserted that morning were already in contact and there were only so many slicks available to extract them all at once. The FAC told Glover that Hueys were going in to extract ST Florida under Captain Gene McCarley. Spike Team Maine was to hold on until more slicks could be freed up to come and get them.

✦◇✦

Joe Messer could hear over the radio that ST Maine was in dire straits, but he was in his own jam. His ST Wyoming had been extracted, leaving him the lone American on the ground on a high ridgeline in the vicinity of Heavy Drop. He could see and hear Vietnamese soldiers closing in on his position across a large clearing. The chase ship H-34 was coming in fast. *Charlie's all over me*, he thought. *I've only got one chance to make it on board.*

As the chopper settled into a hover, Messer could see friendly faces on board. Master Sergeant Roy Pace was blazing away with an M16 on a strap and One-Zero Robert Sprouse was pounding away with an M60 out the other window. Messer made a running leap as the chopper slid by close to the clearing. Pace and another recon man grabbed Joe by his web gear and pulled him in.

Messer was exhausted but uninjured. As he was flown back to Dak To to rejoin his team, he continued to hear the chatter over the radio as many others labored to save ST Florida and ST Maine.

✦◇✦

Zabitosky moved around the perimeter, checking on his team. There was little downtime before the thoroughly aroused NVA were moving down on them. The covey rider radioed down that he could see entire companies of soldiers forming up to assault the relatively open LZ. As the first NVA broke from the thickets, Zabitosky moved from team member to team member, encouraging them to use slow, deliberate fire to conserve ammunition.

Bodies began stacking up outside ST Maine's perimeter. Overhead, the two A-1Es made repeated passes on the onrushing NVA company. They dropped more 750-pounders around ST Maine's position. The first bomb triggered a long string of secondary explosions as it landed amid an NVA rocket supply cache near the enemy's division headquarters. The Skyraiders unleashed CBUs and napalm on their next run. The numerous bomblets, carried in dispensers that burst open at predetermined heights above the ground, mowed down more of the NVA company.

Glover, Bragg, Zabitosky, and their six Nungs fired in short bursts to thwart numerous frontal assaults during the ensuing ninety minutes. None of the Green Berets had been in such an intense, prolonged firefight. The FAC estimated that ST Maine held off twenty-two assaults and killed more than one hundred NVA from four companies on the LZ by the time he had word that two slicks were inbound with a medevac chase ship to rescue the team. Covey called down to Glover and directed him to move his team about fifty-five yards south of their location to a new extraction point.

The area was simply too hot for the slicks to come in. Zabitosky and Glover knew their only chance was to fight their way toward the new LZ and pray for some luck.

◆◇◆

Fortunately, the Gladiators were on their way. Spike Team Maine's extraction slicks were UH-1Hs assigned to the 57th Assault Aviation Company, 52nd Aviation Battalion, 17th Aviation Group, 1st Aviation Brigade. Their squadron nickname was the "Gladiators." Each slick was manned by four men: the pilot, co-pilot, crew chief, and door gunner.

The four Hueys were piloted by veteran Gladiator pilots this day: Captain John Foster "Jack" Koshinsky Jr., First Lieutenant Richard Joseph Griffith (known to his comrades as Rick or Griff), Warrant Officer 1 Robert S. Tobey, and Warrant Officer 1 John A. "Herbie" Herbold. Griffith and Herbold's slicks had initially inserted Glover and Zabitosky's ST Maine. They had barely reached Dak To after the insertion and refueled when word came in that Glover's team needed to be extracted. They took off again, with second Gladiator platoon commander Koshinsky leading slick pilots Griffith and Tobey, with Herbold flying the chase medic ship.

Lieutenant Griffith—an original member of the 57th AHC since it was formed in 1966 at Fort Bragg—was at the controls of the second chopper. The twenty-three-year-old pilot from Detroit had moved with the squadron to Vietnam in September 1967. He moved over to the 119th AHC briefly "to learn to fly the right way" for the hazardous duties he had inherited and then shifted back to the 57th at Kontum. Ferrying SOG teams to and from hot LZs was dangerous work but Griffith's job did have its lighter moments. At one point, he had the pleasure of being the personal pilot for Martha Ray—"Colonel Maggie," the darling of Special Forces—when the actress moved from one SF base to another. He flew her from Pleiku to Kontum and other camps before taking her back to Saigon. Griffith was impressed with how Maggie could play cards and drink with the best of the Green Berets.

It was serious business, however, on February 19 as he and two other Gladiator crews raced back to extract ST Maine from its peril. Griffith's routine, including regular crew and chopper, had been disrupted from the start this day. "I wasn't even supposed to fly this day," said Griffith. "They woke me up and told me I was going to have to take this mission."

Warrant Officer John W. Cook, a twenty-one-year-old from Long Beach, California, had been slated to fly routine missions this day. Cook had flown as Griffith's co-pilot for only a week. Because of the urgent scramble to insert several Kontum recon teams, Griffith was ordered to take the mission as pilot with Cook as his co-pilot again. To further frustrate matters, the pair reached the pad to find that Fred Herbold had already lifted off with their regularly assigned Huey—along with Griffith's regular crew chief, Specialist Fifth Class Henry Heberlein.

Heberlein had been forced to grab another man, John J. "Joe" Billings, in place of his regular gunner in the haste. He and Billings were joined by Special Forces medic Luke Nance for the flight on Herbold's borrowed slick. For Heberlein, already an old-timer at Kontum, it was his first flight to take part on a chase medic slick. Griffith and Cook grabbed another bird and were joined by their regular door gunner—Staff Sergeant Robert Smith "Bobby" Griffith (no relation to the pilot) from Hapeville, Georgia—who swapped with someone else in order to fly with pilots Griffith and Cook. Still short a crew chief, Lieutenant Griffith asked Staff Sergeant Melvin Carnills Dye of Carleton, Michigan, to join as their replacement.

"But, lieutenant," Dye pleaded. "I've only got 30 days left on my enlistment, and I'm not slated to fly. I shouldn't be on this."

"I know," said Griffith. "But we've got to go now."

Griffith and Cook brought their UH-1 in toward the landing zone for the second time this day, ready to help extract Glover's ST Maine. In the rear of their bird, reluctant fill-in crew chief Dye stood ready while Bobby Griffith was swinging his machine gun at the ready in the door. Behind them were slick pilot Bob Tobey and chase ship pilot Herbie Herbold.

Ahead of Griffith was Jack Koshinsky, who was already settling his Gladiator 3 down toward the hot LZ.

✦◇✦

Zabitosky and Doug Glover made a quick inventory of their situation as they moved toward the second LZ. Each member of ST Maine normally carried forty-five magazines with twenty rounds each, but there was little ammo remaining now. The eight-man team raced 150 yards southeast along a streambed and through a wood line to the safer new LZ. They made it without further contact but the covey rider's update to Glover was not encouraging: another company of NVA was closing in.

As the hum of the rescue slicks approached from the distance, Zabitosky had the team ring the perimeter of the new LZ with the last of their Claymores. The first slick, Captain Koshinsky's Gladiator 3, dropped in on the narrow opening, and Bragg scrambled on board with three of the Nungs. As one-one, Zabitosky normally would have boarded the first Huey, but roles had been reversed. Glover had asked him to manage the team until they were recovered.

No sooner had the first slick lifted away than the nearby NVA opened up with an assault on the five remaining members of ST Maine. Glover, Zabitosky, and their three teammates were faced with an estimated hundred NVA against them. Glover directed the gunships in while Zabitosky and his Nung teammates managed to shoot down the first assault wave that charged them. First Lieutenant Steve Sullivan, the platoon leader of the 57th AHC's Cougar gunships, led the assault in his Cougar 13 Huey. He and his wingman, Dean Smith, had been flying from Kontum since the squadron became based there in late 1967. Their mini-guns and rockets chewed up the converging enemy soldiers.

The North Vietnamese were determined, however, and two more charges quickly followed. Zabitosky and his indigenous troops held them off but his men were soon down to only two magazines each. Glover had to get off his radio to join in the shooting to knock back a fourth assault. Zabitosky dropped the last assailant only when he was within arm's reach. With ammunition nearly expended, Glover hollered desperately for the next chopper to land.[13]

Rick Griffith's extraction chopper, which had been keeping its distance during the heated firefight, raced in to save the team. Zabitosky knew this was his best hope—his only hope—for salvation. The NVA were still firing sporadically, but the team was nearly defenseless. They would be dead in minutes if this extraction attempt failed. A fifth NVA assault wave swept in on the LZ as Griffith settled his slick down into the short elephant grass near the center.

Glover and his three Nungs raced for the right side of the UH-1D. As they did, Zabitosky spotted an NVA break into the LZ and race for the left side of the slick. Zabitosky moved that way and caught the enemy soldier so close to the chopper that he appeared to be trying to board it. Zabitosky dropped him at point-blank range and leaped onto the Huey. Gladiator crewmen Melvin Dye and Bobby Griffith were mowing down advancing enemy soldiers all around the perimeter.

Griffith and Cook lifted their heavy bird out of the grass with Zabitosky still standing exposed on the left skid. The Huey made it only seventy-five feet into the air before an RPG slammed into Griffith's chopper with devastating effect. The force of the explosion turned the slick on its left side, swinging the tail boom around violently. It caught the main rotor, ripping through the chopper, and the Huey fell in two huge sections. Zabitosky, who was leaning over to yell to the two pilots, was blown clear of the chopper through the open door. As he plummeted toward the earth, he could hear screams coming from the plunging Huey. The bird slammed into the jungle a mere twenty feet from where Zabitosky hit the ground.

As he came to, Zabitosky wondered hazily. *I must be dreaming. I feel like I'm out in the sun somewhere.*

He quickly realized the "hot sun" was the wrecked chopper blazing nearby—and that his fatigues were also ablaze. His body had been ripped by shrapnel and the force of the impact had crushed vertebrae in his back and his ribs. His thoughts were immediately those of escape. *Hell, they're not going to take no damn prisoners. We just killed enough of those sons of bitches that they aren't going to take any prisoners.*[14]

Zabitosky started crawling toward the nearby bushes. He looked back to see the crumpled Huey turned over on its right side. The pilot, Rick Griffith, and his co-pilot, John Cook, were still in their normal sitting positions in the cockpit. The chopper was already in flames and Zabitosky could hear some of the ammunition on board exploding. The six men in the back—Doug Glover, crew chief Melvin Dye, door gunner Bobby Griffith, and Spike Team Maine's three Nungs—were still in the wreckage, apparently each badly injured. "They were already on fire and I could hear them screaming," Zabitosky recalled. Lying there immobile, writhing in pain from his burns and his broken back, he felt very helpless. "But the screams got to me," he said.[15]

Overhead, the covey could see that no one was moving on the LZ but the NVA. The FAC radioed orders to two waiting F-4 Phantoms. Luke Nance, the medic riding in Fred Herbold's chase ship, was stunned. He could see the blazing Huey on the ground below and felt great anguish that his friend Zabitosky had been killed. Gunner Joe Billings was busy blasting away from the left side of Herbold's slick and did not see the impact. On the right side, crew chief Henry Heberlein had seen the RPG slam into Griffith's Huey. "It just exploded and everything crashed down," said Heberlein. "I didn't think anybody could be left. There would only be pieces to find."[16]

Zabitosky was still very much alive, however. He smothered out his smoldering fatigues and mustered the necessary strength to run to the blazing Huey. He could barely breathe from the pain of broken ribs, crushed vertebrae, shrapnel wounds, and the burns he had suffered. The screams of severely injured men burning to death in the white-hot rear compartment pierced the air as he reached the twisted helicopter where it lay on its side. The flames had not yet reached the two injured pilots, so he staggered forward and struggled with the scorched door handle until it gave.

Lieutenant Griffith was dazed and burned but still alive. The Green Beret extracted the pilot from the fiery wreckage, stumbling as he moved him toward safety. In the process, he noticed that co-pilot Cook was still alive as well. Zabitosky asked Griffith to help him go back to the chopper. Live ammunition was exploding as the heat consumed the cartridges.

"You can't go back in there," Griffith warned. "The fuel cells are going off and there is still ordnance on it. Nobody is alive in there anyway."[17]

Undeterred, Zabitosky left his CAR-15—bent from his long fall—and ran back on his own. He crawled into the flaming Huey and wrestled to free Cook. He could feel his own flesh burning as he worked the co-pilot free from his harness. He was just pulling Cook free from the chopper when one of the fuel cells exploded with a tremendous blast. The force of the blast and a rush of fire propelled Zabitosky and the co-pilot clear of the wreckage. His body further burned, Zabitosky picked himself up and then dragged Cook away from his downed bird.

Then, he turned and raced back to the chopper for a third time. This time, there was nothing the Green Beret could do. "The ship was all melted and the guys were gone," he said. Glover, Dye, Bobby Griffith, and three Nungs of ST Maine were already dead, incinerated in the Huey. As Zabitosky stared in a daze at the roaring heap of twisted metal, his sense of self-preservation suddenly kicked in. The Cougar gunships piloted by

Steve Sullivan and Dean Smith were coming in low, strafing the LZ and firing their rockets near the recon team's perimeter. Zabitosky instantly realized that under the circumstances, the pilots above certainly believed that no Americans could have survived such an inferno. Their intent now was likely to bomb and strafe the hell out of the NVA clustered around the landing zone.

As Sullivan circled around, his Texan co-pilot, Warrant Officer Tony Yoakum, took the opportunity to snap several photos of Griffith's helicopter as its wreckage burned in the jungle below. Herbie Herbold's chase ship was orbiting high above the action playing out on the ground. Medic Luke Nance had seen a body fly free as Griffith's UH-1 went down. The FAC, buzzing the LZ in the O-1 spotter plane, had seen Zabitosky rush back to the chopper to pull one of the wounded pilots free. Captain Jack Koshinsky saw that Bob Tobey's slick had been forced out of position when he had to avoid Griffith's crash. He ordered chase-ship pilot Herbie Herbold to move in to attempt to rescue the survivors.

As Herbold's slick approached, Zabitosky seized his chance, even if the odds were against him. Numerous NVA soldiers were firing away between his position and that of the settling Huey. To further sour his odds, he saw other NVA start moving onto the LZ. He was down to a 9-mm pistol and a single hand grenade. The thought flashed through his mind momentarily: *They won't take us alive. I'll take us out with my last grenade rather than being taken prisoners.*[18]

Zabitosky pulled the pin on his grenade, hesitating for a split second. *What the hell?* he thought. A renewed will to live took hold, and he lobbed the grenade toward the approaching NVA. He emptied his pistol, then grabbed the wounded co-pilot. Weighing little more than 130 pounds, Zabitosky struggled to lift Cook onto his shoulder—crushed ribs, spine, burns, and all. Cook was a tall, hefty man nearly double the weight of the battered Green Beret. But Zabitosky was determined to get his man out, regardless of the cost.

He struggled toward the chopper, half-carrying, half-dragging the horribly wounded Gladiator pilot. "Cook was really burned bad," said pilot Griffith. "He had nothing left but his boots and his gun belt. All his clothes were gone and his skin was coming off." Zabitosky stumbled and they both went down in the mud, which suddenly felt soothing on his burned body. Most of his own clothing had been burned away except for a piece of his fatigue pants. The NVA had turned much of their attention toward firing at the freshly landed Huey as Zabitosky struggled forward again with the co-pilot. Continuing their agonizing movement, the pair staggered past Lieutenant Griffith—who appeared to be in shock, still clutching

Zabitosky's twisted CAR-15. "I grabbed hold of his vest and guided him toward the rescue ship," Zabitosky recalled. His strength finally gave out within ten feet of Herbold's bird. Crew chief Henry Heberlein announced to his pilot over the headset, "I'm going to help these guys."

"No!" snapped Herbold. "You guys stay in the helicopter!"

But Herbold and gunner Joe Billings were already out. Billings assisted Zabitosky, Griffith, and Cook on board while Heberlein offered cover fire. After helping the Green Berets on board, Billings ran back to assist co-pilot Cook. "All he had on was boots with no clothes," Billings recalled. "All his clothes were burned off and his boots were melted to his feet. As I was putting him on the chopper, the NVA were coming down the mountain." Heberlein then noticed more enemy soldiers rushing toward the chopper about sixty yards away. "Here comes three more!" he called.

Heberlein cut them down with his M16 and then noticed a swarm of men advancing from the jungle above his Huey. "I was afraid of shooting our own rotor blades, so I dropped to my knees and began shooting uphill," he said. "Once they got everybody on board, I jumped on and we got out of there."[19]

Medic Nance, who began offering first aid as Herbold pulled clear of the hot LZ, could hardly recognize his buddy due to Zabitosky's blackened and burned face. Small-arms fire pinged off the steel bird's sides as the pilot hauled them free. Staff Sergeant Zabitosky collapsed on the floor, burned, bleeding, and thoroughly spent.

◆◇◆

Captain Koshinsky's Huey landed at Dak To a short time later, with Percell Bragg and the first Nungs who had been extracted. Landing close behind him was Fred Herbold's chase ship, carrying the wounded Griffith, Cook, and Zabitosky.

Helping hands lifted the severely injured men out. They were immediately sent on to Pleiku because of the severity of their injuries. Lieutenant Griffith was in the best shape of the three. Zabitosky was terribly burned, punctured by shrapnel, breathing heavily from broken ribs, and suffering from his broken back. Co-pilot John Cook was in equally bad shape, severely burned from head to toe.

Once the rescue choppers had pulled the survivors free from the besieged LZ, the FAC called in B-52s to thoroughly pound the NVA division that had nearly annihilated ST Maine. Later that day, Sergeant First Class Pappy Webb led his ST Texas in to the crash zone to try and retrieve the remains of the Americans and Nungs who had perished in the chopper crash. Webb's team counted 109 NVA casualties around ST Maine's original LZ and another 56 enemy bodies around the two LZs where the extractions had taken place. Because of heavy enemy fire from the surviving NVA, Webb's team could not properly assess the number of casualties inflicted at the initial contact point up in the canyon, or in the thickets where the air strikes had pounded.[20]

Spike Team Texas photographed the bodies in the chopper for proof of death but were unable to extract them due to heavy enemy contact. The area proved to be so hot that it would be another month before a second team could be inserted into the area. They found no remains. It was not until 2007 that a joint U.S.-Lao People's Democratic Republic team successfully recovered human remains from the wreckage site. Forensic technicians were able to identify the remains of door gunner Bobby Griffith using dental x-rays; he was buried that fall in Fairburn, Georgia. The group remains of two other Americans—Doug Glover and crew chief Melvin Dye—could not be individually identified.

John Cook, the severely burned co-pilot, managed to find the strength at Dak To to offer his thanks to his Green Beret savior before he was medevaced to Pleiku. Fred Zabitosky would never see him again. He and Griffith remained in the Pleiku hospital together for a week before Zabitosky was moved on to Japan for further treatment of his burns and other injuries. Cook was medevaced to Japan for treatment soon after arrival at Pleiku but he died days later from his extensive burns. Herbold, who had successfully extracted the survivors, was later given a Bronze Star for this mission—as were crew chief Heberlein, gunner Billings, and medic Nance. Lieutenant Griffith, pilot of the downed Huey, received a Purple Heart and was back to flying in just over a week.

Zabitosky spent six weeks recovering in hospitals. He was written up for the Medal of Honor, a process that took another year to run the course of the military and political channels before his grateful nation's highest award would finally find the fearless warrior. During that time, the indomitable Fred Zabitosky recovered sufficiently from his wounds to return to duty at Kontum.

Chapter Ten

NEW FACES AT FOB-2

The Kontum base lost the services of two great warriors with the death of Doug Glover and the injuries suffered by Fred Zabitosky. Fortunately for the post commander, there was no shortage of fresh Green Berets arriving at FOB-2 during February and March of 1968, and the number of recon teams there literally doubled from the base's early days two years prior.

By March, Kontum had sixteen state-name spike teams in various stages of operation, training, or running missions across the fence: Arizona, Arkansas, California, Colorado, Delaware, Florida, Hawaii, Illinois, Iowa, Kentucky, Maine, Nevada, New York, Ohio, Texas, and Wyoming. Newcomers like Robert Kotin, Lou DeSeta, John Kedenburg, Tom Cunningham, Terry Dahling, and Wilson Hunt began making their mark at FOB-2, and the journeys of some of these men prior to Kontum are stories in themselves.

Louis Joseph DeSeta was looking for a way out of the jungle. Assigned to the 173rd Airborne Brigade Combat Team, DeSeta arrived in Vietnam in January 1967. After a brief rotation home following his first year in-country, he was not relishing another tour of duty when he returned to Vietnam. He told his company sergeant in March 1968 that he planned to "ten forty-nine"—submit transfer request form 1049—for the 5th Special Forces Group.

"That was like a slap in the face," Lou said of the old paratrooper sergeant's reaction to his desire to transfer out.[1] When he reached Nha Trang in early March 1968, Lou's orders had still not come through. The NCO in charge of replacements told him to go to the base club, have a burger and a beer, and return in the afternoon. DeSeta visited the Nha Trang base club and fell in love with it. "They had a soft serve ice cream machine," he said. "I thought that was the greatest thing in the world."

By the next day, the assignment sergeant handling DeSeta's pending transfer orders offered him the chance to work for him at Nha Trang, arranging transfers for men to and from the airstrip. In his mind, Lou figured he would be working right next to the base ice cream machine and would be in hog heaven. The young Delaware native, prior to joining the Army, had lived a pretty simple life. His father died when he was young, leaving his mom to raise four children. Lou had never traveled more than eighty miles from his New Castle home until he entered the service.

DeSeta's cushy life near the ice cream bar was short-lived, however. He reported in the next morning and was told, "Son, I've got some bad news for you."

"What's that?" DeSeta asked.

"You're going to C&C battalion."

"What's that?"

"You'll find out when you get to Da Nang," the sergeant replied.

DeSeta felt the whole SOG operation sounded crazy as he listened through his briefing in Da Nang, but he was not one to question orders. He selected the call name "jake three-zero," and was flown into Kontum in mid-February. The first person he met up with at FOB-2 was Specialist Howard Taylor, the one-one of ST Nevada. DeSeta was not an imposing giant at 120 pounds and standing only five-feet-four, but the 173rd patch on his right shoulder caught Taylor's eye.

"You wanna get on a recon team?" Taylor asked.

"Yeah," DeSeta replied, with no knowledge of what that might entail.

Lou followed Taylor to ST Nevada's hooch and dropped his bag on an open bunk. The previous team leader, Staff Sergeant Albert Bradford, was transferring out that day and Taylor would be taking over the team as one-zero. DeSeta gained experience running the radio and serving as assistant team leader in the ensuing weeks as he, Taylor, and their Nungs ran some in-country missions to help break him in. In preparation for his first trip across the fence, DeSeta was told to stop bathing two days in advance. "We stunk while we were out on a target," he said. "But it wasn't the stink of soap. The mosquito repellent had a smell to it, also, so we didn't wear it. I just put a rag around my mouth, tucked my pants into my boots, and buttoned down my sleeves at night."

DeSeta's first insertion into enemy territory with Taylor came on March 19. Their assignment was to insert into Cambodia on an Eldest Son

Lou DeSeta (*left*) of Spike Team Nevada, team interpreter Chang (*wearing hat*), another Nung team member, and John Kedenburg, seen in spring 1968 at Kontum. *Louis DeSeta photo, courtesy of Wilson Hunt*

mission to plant booby-trapped 7.62-mm rounds in AK47s that would be used by NVA. "We got trackers on us pretty quick," he said. "We weren't off the LZ an hour before they were on us." DeSeta was nervous as they prepared their RON the first night near the Ho Chi Minh Trail. "There was no light," he said. "But I could hear people talking in the distance and motors starting up." His already rattled nerves were shattered moments later when an elephant erupted into a trumpet blast in the dark. It took some time to shake off his trembles as DeSeta clutched his CAR-15, hoping nothing would trigger the Claymores rigged around their RON site during the night.

As his team moved out the next day, he found the NVA trackers were even closer. "Someone was on our back trail and it got to where they were firing shots every five minutes," DeSeta said. As the distance between the recon team and their trackers narrowed, Taylor prepared his men for action. During their first brush with the enemy, ST Nevada handed out a considerable score of casualties. Taylor was wounded in the firefight but his team broke contact and ran like hell. DeSeta was relieved to be extracted on March 21 without injury after three days in "Indian country." He found his one-zero to be a bit stiff and hard to get to know, but his next teammate proved to be more complementary to his own nature.

Specialist Fifth Class John James Kedenburg—an athletic twenty-three-year-old from Brooklyn who had lettered in football, soccer, and track in high school—joined Taylor and DeSeta on ST Nevada in late March as their new one-two. "I liked him right off," DeSeta said of Kedenburg. "John and I were both East Coast guys and had a similar sense of humor. I also came to know two of his buddies at the FOB—Tom Cunningham and Dennis Mack. They were known as 'The Three Musketeers.'" Cunningham had made it to Kontum thanks to his friend Kedenburg, from his home state of

New York. "John and I went through training together and were real good friends," Cunningham said. "He grew up in Long Island and I grew up in the Bronx. He got into Kontum several months before me because I was on an A Team down in the Delta. He and Dennis Mack kept busting my chops to get into SOG and join them at their FOB."[2]

Lou found that Kedenburg was a good talker and a slick horse trader. When U.S. convoys came down Highway 14, which ran right through FOB-2, Kedenburg would "liberate" M1 carbines from the base supply shack to use as trade goods if he learned a truck was carrying ice cream. "He never missed talking those drivers out of it, or any other thing we could use," said DeSeta.[3]

The first target run by the new team of Taylor, DeSeta, and Kedenburg was in-country. The team was trucked north out of the FOB and remained in a target area in the tri-border region where South Vietnam, Laos, and Cambodia met. On the second day in the field, one of ST Nevada's Nungs became ill. Taylor decided to call off the mission and had Kedenburg radio the FOB. Unable to secure an extraction, Taylor's team then attempted, without luck, to hitch a ride with a passing convoy.

Recon Team Nevada finally came upon a South Vietnamese encampment about five miles from their Kontum compound. Taylor found that the camp was deserted and his Nung was unable to receive medical attention. "We came across a jeep that still had the keys in it, so we loaded the team onto it and drove back to FOB-2," said DeSeta. "Afterwards, the jeep unofficially belonged to ST Nevada."

Shortly thereafter, One-Zero Taylor ran his second recon mission with his two new teammates in the tri-border region in one of the Echo target areas in Laos. Spike Team Nevada was scheduled for a five-day road-watch along the Ho Chi Minh Trail, but they were spotted by the NVA on the third day. DeSeta heard gunshot alerts from trackers on their trail and then Taylor put his team on the run. Kedenburg called for extraction and the team waited near the LZ. "While on the LZ and then as we were pulling out, we received a lot of small-arms fire, mostly from AK-47s," said DeSeta. No one was wounded and DeSeta came away impressed with the team's new one-two. He found that Kedenburg "remained totally calm the entire time, even when we were on the run and while we were under fire."

✦◇✦

The missions were nonstop in March 1968. Bob Howard—always looking for action—was not alone in joining teams who needed extra hands for a mission. Another answering the call was Lionel Francis Pinn, the husky first sergeant of recon company. A cigar-smoking, whiskey-drinking Massachusetts native, Pinn was the son of an American Indian who had fought in World War I. At age forty-five, and a veteran of World War II and Korea, Pinn was an old man among the Green Berets at Kontum, most of whom were half his age. Some of his fellow soldiers nicknamed him "Chief" because of his Indian heritage, but the sobriquet more commonly used for Pinn was "Choo-Choo" or "Chooch." One of his lieutenants in World War II commented that he looked like a train while running with his trademark cigar smoke trailing behind him.[4]

By October 1963, Chooch had earned his third award of the Combat Infantryman Badge for his service in Laos and was returned Stateside to Fort Bragg to train new men coming through Special Forces. Norm Doney, one of his recruits who would also serve at Kontum, recalled of Pinn's physical training regime: "He ran us all over the place. We would be running forward and Lionel would be alongside us, running backwards, smoking a cigar." Military life was hard on his personal life, as Pinn suffered several failed marriages. He retired from the Army in 1965 at the age of forty-two with more than two dozen years of military service under his belt.[5]

In early 1966, he was recalled to active duty after less than a year of civilian life. He spent much of his time filling out reports and keeping up with casualties, but the veteran sergeant enjoyed going out to the field so he could carry grenades and a Tommy gun. He narrowly escaped one mission in 1967 when his chopper was hit by a rocket and downed. Only Pinn and one other man survived the blazing crash, after which they were forced to shoot their way to the extraction LZ as NVA troops swarmed toward the crash site.[6]

Pinn wanted more than anything to be in Special Forces. His wish was finally granted in December 1967, when he was transferred to the Green Berets and flown from the 4th Division to Kontum. He volunteered for missions, and on March 4, Pinn accompanied Sergeant First Class Bill Boyle and Specialist Fourth Class Thomas O'Grady into Laos. Their team had scarcely been deposited onto a grassy knob when Pinn noticed that their "nine Vietnamese guys melted away." The three remaining Green Berets were instantly taken under fire by upwards of twenty NVA soldiers, who were obviously prepared to ambush the SOG team thanks to the turncoat South Vietnamese who had abandoned them.

Pinn, Boyle, and O'Grady began tossing grenades and running for heavier cover. They made it fifty yards to a large clump of trees, where they were pinned down by concentrated fire and grenades. Pinn transmitted the prairie fire code as his trio was hammered. "It was Custer's last stand all over," he recalled. Boyle and O'Grady were both wounded in the firefight and then Pinn was hit in his lower left back just above his buttocks. Pinn was knocked down and lay senseless as blood darkened his fatigues. His comrades laid down covering fire and administered morphine to the wounded man until the extraction choppers were able to pull the overrun recon team. The chase ship medic found that Sergeant Pinn had a live, unexploded rifle grenade lodged in his lower left side.

Upon arrival at the Pleiku field hospital, Pinn was put under anesthesia for the delicate operation. "The brave surgeons placed a heavy metal bracket around the thing and very gingerly removed it," Pinn said. He would spend several weeks in recovery at the hospital, where he received his seventh Purple Heart. Lionel Pinn—the indomitable "Chooch"—would make his way back to Kontum and resume his duties as recon first sergeant a month after the incident.[7]

◆◇◆

Bob Kotin arrived at FOB-2 in February, just days after Fred Zabitosky had been badly wounded. "He was the only guy I knew there and I come in to find he's been shot down," said Kotin, who had pulled guard duty with Zabitosky back at Fort Bragg. Kotin was promptly assigned as the second American on ST Ohio. He was a short man who sported a jaunty handlebar mustache. Despite this flashy touch, he was a reserved individual with a serious mien.

His one-zero was Gerry Denison, who had previously run three months of recon in late 1967 with ST Nevada. Known by his code name "grommet," Denison had been picked in January to reactivate Ohio, a long-standing Kontum-based team. "I hired the indig I wanted to work for me and I did something no one had ever done up to that point," Denison said. "I ran a mixed team of Vietnamese, Nungs, and Yards. My team sergeant was a Vietnamese who had been abandoned by his parents. He was then raised by Montagnards and he hated Vietnamese with a passion."[8]

Kotin took on the role of assistant team leader and radio operator as the team began running missions in late February. When ST Ohio was tasked with a special operation on March 15, Denison picked up a third American to help run radio—Specialist Fifth Class Frank Ruane, a straphanger. Denison's team was inserted that day into the Plei Trap valley close to the Cambodian border for a specific job. "We were there to ambush a truck convoy we had noted and observed on a previous mission into the area," said Denison.

Spike Team Ohio moved quietly over the rugged mountains to a position near the Ho Chi Minh Trail to observe enemy vehicle movement.

They gathered intelligence through the night before Denison contacted a FAC on March 16 to relay their finds. "When the plane got overhead he was opened up on by machine guns approximately two hundred meters from our position," Kotin said. Denison boldly advanced his team to within twenty yards of the concealed roadway. As expected, Vietnamese supply truck movements commenced after dark as Denison prepared his ambush.

Denison began calling in artillery strikes against that area of the road and on a truck stop his team had discovered. The pounding from the artillery halted all truck movement for the night and caused twice as many vehicles to be holed up the next day at the truck stop—the very area Denison had pre-planned to ambush the next night. Spike Team Ohio conducted detailed reconnaissance of the area throughout March 17. That evening, he put Kotin, Ruane, and his indigenous troops on point to watch for enemy troop movements.

Denison then eased down to the roadway to place land mines and white phosphorous booby traps along the road. He had only moved his team a short distance away when the first truck was heard rumbling toward their position. Just as planned, the first supply truck struck one of Denison's land mines and exploded with a mighty roar. The smoldering wreckage effectively blocked the roadway and trapped the vehicles that were following. Denison elected to remain in the area and began calling in heavy-caliber artillery strikes from the 4th Infantry Division to help finish off the other trucks.

Rounds from this thunderous barrage landed as close as fifty yards from the team, as Denison helped coach in the artillery. Bob Kotin was wounded by shrapnel in the process but the team stayed awake the entire night. After daylight on March 18, Denison moved in close for a post-strike assessment of their handiwork. Kotin reported that four NVA trucks had been demolished, ten enemy bodies were seen, and that numerous other enemy soldiers were believed to be killed and wounded. Spike Team Ohio then called in air strikes to finish pounding the truck stop and nearby troops, in spite of the certainty that enemy troops must be searching their vicinity to locate the American forward observers.

"Denison gave them coordinates, the artillery really gave it to the enemy, and then we got the hell out of there," said Kotin. The team was thoroughly exhausted by the time choppers extracted them that afternoon. Gerry Denison's valor had effectively shut down NVA traffic along the trail for at least a day and he had pulled off a feat that would only later become a more routine part of SOG history.

◆◇◆

Twenty-eight-year-old Staff Sergeant Terry Dahling, another of the new Kontum Green Berets, would never forget his first recon mission in March 1968. Raised in California, Terrell Alexander Dahling joined the Army in 1963 after finishing his finals at San Fernando Valley State College. He completed his Special Forces training and proudly donned his green beret—authorized by President John F. Kennedy the previous year as the official headgear of U.S. Army Special Forces. Stateside, Dahling found that most uninformed civilians who saw an SF man wearing his beret asked one of two questions: "Do you play in the band?" or "What country are you from?" To the latter, Dahling always replied, "I'm Canadian."[9]

Dahling served with the 10th SFG in Germany for three years before he was assigned to his first tour in Vietnam in 1967. By January of 1968, he was operating from Kontum where he spent a rotation as a commo duty man, relaying incoming radio traffic from Leghorn site atop a mountain in Laos. Dahling heard the exasperation of various teams in contact in the field as they attempted to communicate their situation to their command staff. He noted that the staff always wanted to know more about what kind of fire the team was taking and if they had exhausted all possible solutions before declaring an emergency.[10]

During January, Dahling heard an emergency request radioed in by Pappy Webb, the one-zero of Kontum-based ST Texas.

"I have a company of NVA surrounded from the inside," Webb called. "I gave them three minutes to surrender or we are going to attack."

Staff Sergeant Terry Dahling assumed command of RT Delaware when his one-zero was killed in action on March 22, 1968. *Jason Hardy*

The staff realized the situation behind Webb's tongue-in-cheek black humor. "Get your panels out," they replied. "We are on the way!"

Staff Sergeant Dahling learned a lot while monitoring and relaying these transmissions that would benefit him later. He became the one-one for Spike Team Delaware and his first call for action in-country came on March 20, 1968. He and his team leader, husky, thirty-year-old Sergeant First Class Linwood Dwight Martin from Virginia, had only that day to prepare their team on formations, movements, and other plans.

On the morning of March 21, Martin and Dahling attended the air briefing and were flown to Dak To with their nine Montagnards. Spike Team Delaware was inserted around 1400 and Martin released his air assets once the situation looked good. Three hours later, the team came across a classic high-speed trail, smooth, clean, and more than four feet wide. Martin's team began looking over the trail and the nearby river as darkness approached. As the Montagnards procured water for the team, Dahling noted fresh bunkers overlooking the trail as well as squared-off, man-made "rabbit holes" dug into the bank.[11]

Martin and Dahling decided it was best for their team to pull back and observe the trail overnight. One of their Montagnard troopers planted an M14 "toe popper" mine on the trail as ST Delaware heard the sounds of people joking and talking as they moved along the trail. The eleven-man recon team moved back into the woods and had only moments to wait. One of the unlucky NVA stepped on the mine and it detonated.

The team escaped after a brief firefight and spent the night hiding in deep jungle as NVA troops tried to flush them. With the arrival of dawn on March 22, Martin and Dahling heard their enemy blowing whistles, beating sticks, and creating enough noise to make it known they had the Americans surrounded on three sides. The fourth side of the box was formed by the nearby river. The Green Berets decided it was better to try easing through one of the enemy's flanks rather than moving in the direction the enemy was attempting to push them. After slipping through the NVA lines unmolested, Martin announced that he would fall back and photograph the trail for intelligence purposes. "I was dead set against it," Dahling said.

As team leader, Martin's wishes prevailed and the team eased back toward the high-speed trail. They found the shoe of an NVA—with a foot still in it—who had stepped on their toe popper. Martin motioned to his team to set up a perimeter. No sooner had ST Delaware gotten situated than the jungle erupted in a high volume of fire from the Vietnamese. "All hell broke loose," said Dahling.

He was face to face with his one-zero when a round from the first burst caught Martin over the left eye. His team leader appeared to be conscious, so Dahling took out his first aid compress to apply a dressing. When he lifted Martin's head, however, he could feel the fatal damage of the head wound. His one-zero was gone.

Dahling assembled his PRC-25 and called in a prairie fire emergency, before collecting his Montagnards and moving to the center of a clearing the size of two baseball fields. His FAC, First Lieutenant Jerald D. Henderson, kept up a steady stream of communication with Dahling as gunships and F-100s were called in. Henderson's pilot fired rockets and his automatic weapon to keep the NVA suppressed until his air support arrived. The gunships then took over, laying down gunfire and napalm so close and so hot that Dahling felt it sucked the air from his lungs. As things settled down for a moment, he made a desperate run back twenty meters to retrieve his downed one-zero, dragging the large man by his feet.[12]

Covey Rider Dallas Longstreath sent slicks in three different times to try and extract ST Delaware, but the Hueys were driven off each time. Finally, another slick made it through the ground fire and nestled in low. Dahling's adrenalin was pumping hard and he literally tossed Martin's hefty body into the chopper. "I then commenced to grab the Yards by the ass and collar and throw them into the chopper," he said. "I'm surprised I didn't throw a couple in one door and out the other."

Spike Team Delaware was flown back to Dak To, where Dahling found Major Roxie Hart, his FOB commander, waiting on the pad. Many willing hands were standing by to perform a Bright Light to retrieve the body of Linwood Martin—a hazardous duty not needed since Dahling had already recovered his own team leader. Terry would be awarded the Bronze Star for his actions and Linwood Martin would be posthumously awarded the nation's second highest honor, the Distinguished Service Cross. In less than two years of operations, FOB-2 recon men had been awarded six DSCs.

Dahling's first mission across the fence was tragic and full of life lessons. His frazzled nerves were not improved when his chopper out of Dak To lost hydraulics upon approach to Pleiku. Coming in hot at seventy knots upon landing, he found the chopper "must have made sparks a quarter mile long."[13]

✦◇✦

Wilson Hunt had already cheated death on several occasions before joining SOG. The first time was in 1960. Wilson was a reservist who had been making parachute jumps regularly with the 101st Airborne Division. Earlier that year, he had helped form the first skydiving team in Tulsa, Oklahoma, and made the first sixty-second delay jump in his state with two others on the Fourth of July. The farm boy who once had a profound fear of heights had long since gotten over that after surviving jump school at Fort Campbell, Kentucky, in 1958.

Wilson's reserve unit had been called to Fort Bragg in August 1960 for two weeks. On their final Saturday at the base, his unit was scheduled for a large demonstration jump in honor of a senior NATO official, Lieutenant General Hans Speidel—the first German NATO commander during the Cold War. The paratroopers were to make a mass jump over the fort from C-123 Providers. Hunt's plane carried forty-six paratroopers, split evenly into two "sticks" to exit from each side of the aircraft.

As the C-123 approached the drop zone, one of the opposing stick leaders put forth a friendly wager: "I'll bet a case of beer that our stick clears the plane first!"

"You're on!" came the reply.

At the signal, the twenty-three men of the left stick began leaping from the plane simultaneously with the men of the right stick. Hunt was the last man to leap from his side. He literally rode the backpack out of his buddy ahead of him in line, Dean "Grumpy" Glasgow. Shortly into his descent, Hunt knew he was in trouble when his main canopy failed to deploy—a high-speed malfunction. *I'm going to have to pull my reserve!*

Hunt's rate of fall was so fast that he caught up to Glasgow (who was now suspended beneath his open canopy). Hunt plunged through Glasgow's suspension lines, became tangled, and had his descent violently checked by a hard jerk that caused him to bounce several times like a marionette. Hunt's main canopy was too tangled for him to deploy his reserve, so Glasgow pulled his. As the reserve chute snapped open, Glasgow was yanked upward, but several of his lines snagged on Hunt's canteen.

"They caught on my web gear and pulled my canteen around behind my back," said Hunt. "I was left hanging, draped over my cartridge belt that my canteen was attached to." Hunt, hanging upside down, began twisting around as the tangled suspension lines slowly worked themselves free of his gear. With each twist, he slipped, and he feared what would happen when his last spin might finally free him from Glasgow's suspension lines.

"The last twist came out, I picked up speed, and away I went," he said. The ground was so close he knew his reserve chute would not deploy in time. With more than two hundred feet to the ground, Wilson Hunt plummeted down. He still had the presence of mind to run through split-second decisions in the same manner that a person races through them in the milliseconds before a violent car crash.

Some on the ground thought Hunt looked like a panicked cat, clawing at the air. He had decided that instead of breaking his legs, he needed to

Staff Sergeant Wilson Hunt, who narrowly survived a parachuting mishap years earlier, prepares for a practice jump from FOB-2 in 1968 with his RT Maine indigenous team leader Kiep. *Wilson Hunt*

turn onto his side to absorb the impact by making a "parachute landing fall"—the controlled roll he had learned in jump school—to spread the impact over a larger portion of his body. Officials, wives, and families watched in horror as the young parachutist slammed into the ground behind a sand dune beyond the grandstands. Those above him saw what looked like a splash of sand as his body hit the ground and bounced up again.

"The next thing I knew, I was laying on the ground and everything was kinda gray," Hunt said. His steel pot helmet with its plastic liner did little to prevent his head from violently impacting the earth. Likely suffering a concussion, he came to with adrenaline still rushing through his body. He glanced over at his buddy Dean Glasgow, who had landed nearby, and both men began giggling. They were so shocked to still be alive that their emotions poured out in laughter. The first man to reach them, a lieutenant with the parachute riggers, yelled at them. "What are you laughing at? You both ought to be dead!"

By some miracle, Hunt survived this accident with a concussion, torn muscles in a severely wrenched back, and a badly swollen knee and arm. He refused to be taken to the hospital because of his fear of missing the return flight to Tulsa the next morning with his reserve unit. His buddies treated him to a steak dinner in Fayetteville that night, where they sat around laughing at all the talk they overheard about the parachutist who had been killed at Fort Bragg that day.

The next morning, Wilson was unable to even move from his bed. His company mates literally carried him onto and off of the planes en route back home. He was driven that night to the base hospital at Fort Sill, Oklahoma, where he would spend a month in recovery.

✦◇✦

George Wilson Hunt's seemingly charmed life started in Shawnee, Oklahoma. He became known to his family and friends by his middle name since the first name George was so commonly used by the Hunt family in naming his cousins and other relatives—including his grandfather and great-grandfather.

Wilson's father, Lloyd Hunt, earned his keep as the manager of a laundromat until he joined the U.S. Navy Seabees during World War II. Wilson's family lived for a number of years in Rhode Island while his father was in the service. Shortly after the war, his father saved enough money to purchase a farm in Cobb, Oklahoma.

Farming life was tough in the early 1950s due to a severe drought in the area. The Hunt family lived in a modest, two-bedroom farm house without indoor plumbing or a telephone during Wilson's youth. Lloyd Hunt raised corn for cattle silage for two years before switching his crops to cotton and peanuts.

Wilson was the oldest of three brothers, followed by Roy, eighteen months his junior. The youngest sibling, David, recalled: "Wilson was a natural leader who always had lots of friends."[14] Wilson knew early on that the taxing life of farm work was not his calling, so he joined the Navy ROTC in high school and did well enough on a college scholarship exam to earn a full ride to the University of Oklahoma. In college, Wilson found that his meager education in the rural Cobb school had done little to prepare him for the rigors of advanced education with a heavy course load. He resigned his scholarship after one semester and reported to work in January 1957 in the Santa Fe Railroad Company's yards in Chicago. He worked in the switch yard throughout the year until he suffered a dislocated shoulder when he was thrown from the top of a rail car in a near collision in the yard.

Hunt returned to Tulsa on injury leave at age nineteen in late 1957. He and his buddy Travis Jones signed up for the Army draft just before Christmas and he was flown to Fort Carson, Colorado, to begin basic training. At five-foot-ten and 145 pounds, Hunt was large enough to qualify for infantry but his scrawny, lightweight buddy Travis was shipped off to the artillery. Learning that he could double his pay with an extra fifty-five dollars per month by going airborne, Hunt signed on with the 101st Airborne Division in 1958. He completed his Army service by late 1959, opting for an early out due to budget constraints. He saw no future in the military at the time. "I hated the Army," he said. "Coming out of the main gate at Fort Campbell, Kentucky, I gave the MPs the finger as I rode the bus out of there. I was never going back to another day in the Army."[15]

Hunt went to work in Tulsa selling insurance but spent little time as a civilian before the military caught his interest again. He survived the near-fatal jump in August 1960 and continued in the reserves, where he became qualified during the ensuing years as a light weapons sergeant with Special Forces.

By the spring of 1967, Wilson and his wife Sandra had three young sons, Randy, Paul, and Wilson Jr. Continuing in the Army Reserves, Hunt graduated top of the class from a Special Forces operations intelligence course at Fort Bragg and then completed the Army Intelligence School at Fort Holabird, Maryland. When he received a letter from the Department of Army asking him to consider a twelve-month tour in Vietnam on active duty, he felt torn between his family, his life insurance job, his reserve duty, and the opportunity to serve his country again. His younger brothers Roy and David had shipped off to Vietnam years before with the U.S. Navy. By the time Wilson decided he was primed and ready to go serve in the summer of 1967, he received a second letter from Fort Benjamin Harrison at Indiana. The personnel center's notice informed him that his specialty and grade was not needed.

Hunt was both dejected and angry by this rejection. He and a reserve buddy drove to Washington, DC, to straighten out the mess. Wilson asked to see Mrs. Billye Alexander, who was in charge of all Special Forces assignments at the Pentagon. She was impressed that he had traveled all the way to the Pentagon from Oklahoma to protest his rejection letter for Special Forces duty, and within hours Sergeant First Class Hunt had orders to report to Fort Sill in late October for active duty.

By early November, he was on a plane for Vietnam. Hunt was soon assigned as the operations sergeant at the B Detachment at headquarters level at Cai Cai, where he saw action during some of the fighting during January 1968. His buddy Stan Gann then told him about SOG, a top secret Special Forces outfit supported by the greatest assets in the world. Hunt was intrigued and put in a 1049 reassignment request, but his transfer was delayed by the start of the Tet Offensive. In the interim, his base came under mortar attack in February and he was wounded by shrapnel from an RPG explosion.

Hunt would later be awarded a Purple Heart and the Bronze Star for his actions during the siege. Before these could be presented, he had finally received his coveted SOG orders in late February. He was being transferred to FOB-2, the Central Highlands area SOG base at Kontum.

◆◇◆

Wilson Hunt and six other new recruits surveyed the green terrain below as their Air Force C-123 touched down on the Kontum airstrip.

He and his companions tossed their duffel bags onto a waiting flatbed truck, climbed up, and took a seat for the ride across the river into their new forward operating base. They were dropped at the base headquarters, eager for their next Army life experience. Hunt could tell immediately that standard protocol was all but forgotten in this strange new world. As he prepared to climb off the truck, he spotted two black NCOs in a heated argument. "They were out in the quadrangle, faced off like two guys in an old western movie," Hunt said. "They almost had a shoot out. I'd never seen anything like that in my life."

Several Green Berets broke up the argument, but Hunt was left wondering just what kind of assignment he had gotten himself into. As he gathered his bags to report in, he was relieved to see a friendly face in the form of Sergeant First Class Gene Bettis. The two had gone through an Office of Naval Intelligence course in the fall of 1966 and had been in the same Army intel school in 1967 at Fort Bragg. Bettis had earned a Bronze Star during the successful January Bright Light mission as Fred Zabitosky's one-one. Spotting Sergeant Hunt, Bettis made a beeline for him.

"Come on with me, Hunt," Bettis called.

"Well, I can't," Wilson offered. "I've gotta go inside and process in first."

"No, you don't," Bettis announced. "I've already talked to them. You're with me now. Just bring your bags."

Hunt grabbed his gear and followed Bettis into the little hooch for Spike Team California. He tossed his bags onto one of the three cots, took a seat, and was introduced to ST California's one-one, Jack Bagby. Bettis informed Hunt that he would be serving as the team's one-two, carrying the PRC-25 radio on their next mission using his assigned code name "sardine." He was quick to upgrade the old M2 carbine issued to him at Fifth Group for an M16 at Kontum, which he traded off for a CAR-15 as soon as he could.

During the first days of March, he was indoctrinated into the team's procedures. Bettis and Hunt spent hours discussing SOG operations in the Kontum base bar, talking over old times and getting acquainted with other key members of the recon base. Within days, ST California was given an assignment for what would prove to be Wilson's first target. Bettis returned from his briefing with maps of the target area and related the intelligence he had been given by the base S3 officer.

"We're heading out at first light tomorrow," he said. "Hunt, you and Bagby swing by the supply shack and draw the equipment we'll need."

Spike Team California boarded choppers the next morning and flew from Kontum into Dak To. The Hueys topped off with fuel and then the team was on its way into Cambodia, to the southwest of Ben Het. Their insertion into the target area was uneventful, but nerves played a part for Wilson Hunt as he peered down at the blur of the jungle canopy. Ahead, he could see a slash and burn in the rain forest where Montagnards had opened up a tiny clearing. The insert choppers went into a series of lazy circles, as if they were making laps on a race track. "I could feel that change in pitch as our chopper made its break for the LZ," Hunt said. "The butterflies were going around in my stomach."

Okay, here we go. We're headed in.

Wilson glanced down at the approaching slash and burn and then back at the Huey's door gunner. He marveled at how truly exposed the chopper crew was during such an insertion. They stood ready with rockets and machine guns but he realized that one accurate burst from a concealed NVA soldier could mean the end for some—or all—of the slick's occupants. As soon as the chopper broke for the LZ, Gene Bettis scooted into the open door with his legs hanging out. The pilot came in quick, hit his hover, and started to settle down near the ground. Bettis stepped out onto the skid with his CAR-15. Bagby held the one-zero's web gear for the moment, allowing his team leader to cover the area forward of the slick where the door gunner could not easily fire.

Bettis then grabbed his gear and leaped to the ground. Hunt was next. As his feet slammed into the jungle rubble below, he took off running across the opening toward the nearby undergrowth. Spike Team California's six Montagnards came out in the order Bettis had assigned to them. Last off the slick was Jack Bagby, bringing up the rear as each team member took cover at assigned points near each other close to the edge of the LZ.

As Hunt raced across the slash and burn, the area suddenly seemed much larger. Instinctively, his muscles tightened up as he imagined being shot in the back as he raced through the opening. He ran faster but it felt like an eternity before he finally reached the protective cover of the jungle. He was gasping for air and began hyperventilating as he reached Bagby and Bettis. His team leader instantly realized the stress his new one-two was suffering from and grabbed Hunt's hat off his head. "He crammed it over my [face] and gave me first aid for hyperventilation," said Hunt. "It really worked, just like breathing into a paper sack." Bettis could not suppress a chuckle as his green recon team member finally composed himself.

Bettis then moved his team away from the LZ, took cover, and had his new RTO contact covey. "It's a good day," Hunt said into his radio, indicating to the orbiting covey rider that the team had no trouble and planned to proceed with their area recon mission. The rest of the mission, in fact, went fairly smoothly. They heard signal shots at times but never encountered any NVA groups close enough to get into a firefight.

By the time ST California was safely extracted five days later, Wilson Hunt had gained valuable experience in the field. He would carry radio for ST California on two more missions, including one in which Bettis and his men were shot out of the landing zone, forced to hang back in their Hueys while air support worked over the area well enough to get them safely inserted. Sergeant Hunt proved his aptitude in the field so thoroughly after his first few missions that Colonel Smith soon decided he was seasoned enough to begin training his own team.

The need for veteran men to lead was great. Personnel losses piled up in the spring of 1968 as FOB-2's spike teams saw considerable action. On February 22, Sergeant Paul Poole was awarded the Bronze Star for valiantly guiding his ST Colorado through a fierce enemy assault. Five days later on February 27, another Kontum team was shot up as their chopper entered the LZ. Staff Sergeant Chester Domingue was forced into acting command when his one-zero leaped from their slick as it was riddled with fire and injured his back in the thirty-foot fall. Domingue spread out his team into two parties once on the ground, found their one-zero, and carried him some four hundred meters to an acceptable LZ. There, he directed the team in fighting off advancing NVA while calling in air strikes to within thirty meters of their perimeter. Domingue and his team were successfully extracted but another team was soon in peril.

The action had thoroughly stirred up the North Vietnamese. Staff Sergeant Bob Van Hall's ST Iowa ran into an enemy unit forced in his direction due to the action with Domingue's team. Van Hall placed his team in a bomb crater and set up a defensive perimeter. When the first enemy assault was broken, extraction choppers moved in and pulled out half of Iowa, but a renewed NVA charge drove the second Huey away. Van Hall again rallied the defensive fire efforts of his men while Specialist Fourth Class Albert C. Walker worked the radio during the next two hours. Air strikes helped Van Hall's men hold off the enemy assaults until a second chopper could be directed in. Finding only four hoisting rigs, Van Hall placed three of his indigenous troopers in the slings, secured himself to the fourth, and shouted for Walker to join him. Van Hall wrapped his arms around Walker and clutched him as they were dragged through jungle canopy so violently that the one-zero suffered severe bruises and a broken nose.

During recon missions in the first three weeks of March, nine more Kontum men were wounded to varying degrees. Gene Bettis, one-zero of ST California, was among them. He received a bullet in his leg as ground fire punctured the floor of his Huey during descent into an LZ. He called off the mission but Bettis and his team were placed on the inactive list at Kontum when he was transferred from FOB-2 for better medical care.

Such climbing casualty rates created new headaches for Colonel Smith and First Sergeant Pinn. New recon men continued to come in from Saigon, forcing them to shuffle the teams that had fresh voids, and use straphangers to keep other missions moving forward. The necessary shuffling offered an open door of opportunity for proven veterans like Wilson Hunt to take on team leadership roles.

Chapter Eleven

"THE BIG ONE"

SOG team nomenclature was revamped during the spring of 1968 and "spike teams" became known as "recon teams," though some operators continued to refer to larger-size insertions as spike team ops. Around this time, supply sergeant Bob Howard was continuing to straphang with FOB-2 recon teams as often as possible. In late March, he inserted as assistant team leader for his buddy Paul Poole's ST—now RT—Colorado, along with Specialist Fifth Class Charles Dunlap, who carried the radio as their one-two. When Poole's small team made contact on March 30 with a large NVA force sweeping down a hillside, he set his team in a covered position and then raced through a flurry of gunfire to plant a Claymore mine in the path of the aggressors. Poole was shot through the hand in the process but he managed to plant his mine, then waited until the advancing soldiers were almost on him before he detonated it, killing eight instantly and forcing the remainder to seek cover.

Poole then took the point position and led his men down a ravine toward an LZ. He was hit a second time as the NVA poured on automatic fire and fired rifle grenades at the team. Howard was also wounded en route, ensuring he would soon add another Purple Heart to his growing collection. When a rifle grenade landed between two team members, Poole pushed them away from it, only to find that the device failed to explode. Recon Team Colorado members continued running for their lives, with the enemy hot in pursuit.

Howard had learned a number of tricks to slow his opponents, however. He removed his bloody shirt as pursuers began gaining on him and

148

draped it over a bush—pausing long enough to plant a few toe poppers in front of it. He raced ahead and, as expected, the NVA approached his discarded shirt minutes later. The detonation of the toe poppers slowed their advance as the NVA took new casualties. At the LZ, Poole fell back to keep the enemy in check with his M79 grenade launcher as Dunlap radioed in the choppers. Only after his indigenous element and two Americans were safely rigged did Poole secure himself in the final harness for extraction (Poole later received a Silver Star for his actions).[1]

Sergeant Howard's wounds did not keep him grounded long. Two weeks later, he was back in action serving as a platoon adviser for a company of indigenous troops led by Captain Gene McCarley. The men of this Hatchet Force company were just finishing their noon meal on April 16 when they were ambushed from the rear by a superior-size enemy unit. During the opening minutes of the firefight, many of the young indigenous soldiers became frightened and fled to the top of the mountain. A disgusted McCarley suddenly found himself quite alone as his Montagnards scattered up the hill.

He charged up the hill, laying down covering fire as he attempted to collect his frightened sheep. In the meantime, Howard placed the remaining Montagnards in a defensive perimeter and exposed himself to enemy fire to help deflect the heat from McCarley. The captain made it only halfway up the mountainside before the Montagnard perimeter was assaulted by a barrage of mortar rounds.

Howard coolly advanced with his grenade launcher and laid waste to the NVA manning the mortars, exposing himself to automatic-weapons fire and flying shrapnel. McCarley, who did manage to regroup his spooked Montagnards, thought enough of the brave supply sergeant's actions to write him up for an Army Commendation Medal for heroism. The Hatchet Force team survived the affair, thanks also to precise direction of air strikes coordinated by another of their former recon men, First Lieutenant Ken Etheredge—who served three straight days flying FAC in the area.

✦◇✦

Prairie Fire operations into Laos were becoming increasingly bloody, and newer team members found themselves advancing into one-zero roles sooner than expected.

Such was the case for Specialist Fourth Class John Kedenburg, the one-two for RT Nevada. During late April, he ran his third mission in company with One-Zero Howard Taylor and One-One Lou DeSeta over the tri-border region into Laos. They were to observe traffic on the Ho Chi Minh Trail and plant a listening device. As with their previous mission, they were spotted by trackers on their third day in-country and had to run for it. This time, the area was too hot with small-arms fire for choppers to land to pick them up; the team was extracted on McGuire rigs without incident. Weeks later, in early May, DeSeta was transferred to FOB-3 and Taylor took temporary leave for R&R. Just like that, RT Nevada belonged to Kedenburg, who had arrived at Kontum less than two months prior.

Just days after RT Nevada's run through the jungle, RT Illinois was beaten up on another Prairie Fire mission. One-Zero Bill Watson's team was inserted sometime around April 20 for a long-range reconnaissance patrol. His one-one was Sergeant First Class Sherman Richard Batman, a thirty-seven-year old from West Virginia who completed his first tour in Vietnam in 1965 and had previously served in the Korean War. Batman—undertaking his third mission with Watson—felt a sharp sting as he exited the chopper. *Damnit, I've been shot!*

Fortunately, the burning sensation proved to be a yellow jacket sting and the team proceeded on its recon for the next two days. On April 22, RT Illinois was assaulted by a company of NVA. Watson's Montagnard point man was felled by grenade fragments that perforated his head with more than a dozen pieces of shrapnel. Another Montagnard was seriously wounded in the initial assault and One-One Batman's arm was ripped open by a grenade fragment. Watson charged through the hail of gunfire to help his three wounded men to a safer position. Batman helped move the point man with the multiple head wounds, hauling his own gear and weapons along with those of his teammate, and then performed first aid on both of his wounded teammates amid continuing heavy fire.

Watson rallied his team to lay down a hail of return fire that routed the NVA and broke their assault. Air support soon moved in, but the team's new one-two, Sergeant Duane Chilson, had also been hit by shrapnel. Batman took over his radio, calling in coordinates as the gunships napalmed the enemy's positions. Watson used the ensuing attacks as a chance to move his men through the enemy's ranks toward a landing zone for extraction. Upon arrival, he found that several of his men had become separated while moving through the heavy smoke of the napalm fires. Watson raced back alone into the enemy area, gathered his lost men, and directed them to the landing zone.

When the choppers arrived, Watson placed Batman and his wounded Montagnards on the first bird out. He continued firing back until a second chopper loaded the last of his men. When the Hueys reached Dak To, Batman was concerned for the proper treatment of his fatally wounded point man. He directed one of the new Green Berets working the launch site, twenty-year-old Specialist Fourth Class Mike Tramel, to accompany the man (so he would not be alone), and to return his remains to his family for proper burial. "That was Mike's first mission, flying a dead man back to his family," Batman said. "They paid the family a bonus of ten thousand piaster, which amounted to only about ten dollars in American money."[2]

Sergeant Batman, awarded the Silver Star for his actions with RT Illinois on April 22, inherited command of the team after this mission when Watson decided he had had enough. Batman opted to take on Tramel, freshly arrived at Kontum, as his new one-one. Together, they became a tight team that would run another half-dozen missions in the next two months without further injury.

✦◇✦

Other recon teams at Kontum were similarly forced to revamp themselves after personnel were lost to injuries or when senior men rotated home. Recon Team Florida, led in April by One-Zero Ron Fanning after Gene McCarley moved into Hatchet Force, received two new American Green Berets in April. Sergeant First Class Bill Hanson, on his third tour in Vietnam, joined as the new one-one along with a new one-two, Specialist Fourth Class Ralph Rodd—who arrived at the base on the same day as Hanson. The new team was only together for a matter of weeks before Hanson took command of RT Florida from the outgoing Fanning. Such experienced men often needed only brief overlaps in order to continue running an already successful team without a hitch.

Sergeant First Class Wilson Hunt had made only a few missions with RT California before he received the chance to take on his own team. He was approached by the recon company first sergeant, Lionel Pinn, recently returned from Pleiku after recovering from the injuries he sustained in March.

"Hunt, we're moving you from Team California," said Pinn. "We need someone to re-form Team Maine and get it operational again."[3]

Hunt found that his new team was filled with Vietnamese, and he had been assigned a Vietnamese interpreter named Tommy who appeared to be in his late twenties. To further assist him in training his new team, Wilson was given a special adviser—Fred Zabitosky, freshly returned to FOB-2 from his stay in the hospital. He had been nominated for the Medal of Honor for his February mission, but the approval process was grinding forward. In the interim, Colonel Smith forbade Zabitosky from making another recon mission. He was not about to have a potential Medal of

Honor winner get killed in action on his watch. Hunt could see that Zabitosky was still recovering from treatment—his burn scars obvious when his shirt sleeves were rolled up.

Hunt and Zabitosky spent only a short time with the Vietnamese assigned to Recon Team Maine before they decided that the whole lot was utterly worthless to them. Wilson had worked with Montagnards on RT California and he wanted the same for his new team. With the support of Zabitosky, he stripped the equipment from his Vietnamese soldiers, marched them to the main gate of Kontum, and fired them. He arranged with Gene Bettis to borrow RT California's interpreter to help him with interviewing recruits until he could select his own interpreter.

Hunt's move did not sit well with his newly arrived base commander. Major Hart, transferred to other duty, had been replaced at FOB-2 by Lieutenant Colonel Donald L. Smith, a veteran paratrooper who had served with the 82nd Airborne Division before being transferred to the 10th SFG in Germany in 1957. In 1960, Smith had attended the Infantry Officers Advance Course and gone on to graduate from Cornell University with a masters in international relations in 1963. After receiving his degree, Smith volunteered for a tour of duty in Vietnam (1963–64), then served at the Special Warfare School at Fort Bragg (1965–67). He returned to Vietnam in 1968 and joined SOG, where his peers saw Don Smith as a first-rate soldier, an intellectual with a love of history.

His new Green Berets nicknamed him "Whiskey" for his fondness of said libation, and more than a few would face his ire over various actions. When Smith learned that new One-Zero Hunt had dismissed his entire team, he was boiling mad. Hunt was summoned to the new base commander's office, where he received a severe dressing-down. "That was my team!" Smith screamed. "It was not your team to fire!"

Hunt remained silent while his CO ranted about how he had not received any permission from him before firing an entire team. "I assumed I was going to get pulled off the team," Hunt said. "He finally yelled that if I ever did anything like that again, he would have my ass." By the end of the ream session, the new one-zero agreed that he would never make another such move without obtaining Smith's permission first. Hunt was finally released to return to organizing his team. The fact that he remained one-zero made him think that Fred Zabitosky's approval of his mass firing must have carried at least some weight with Colonel Smith.

Using RT California's interpreter, Hunt returned to interviewing Montagnards, a smooth process that enabled him to assemble a solid team. He found able men in Zero-One Kiep, his indigenous team leader, and in Hinh, the indigenous assistant team leader or zero-two. Hunt then added two grenadiers, Munh and Wung, who would carry the team's M79 grenade launchers. Wung, in his mid-twenties, was one of the few Montagnards who could understand and speak some broken English. The oldest indigenous man he hired was thirty-four-year old Hep, a tall, skinny Montagnard rifleman who spoke fluent French and had fought with the French in Vietnam's previous civil war. The youngest rifleman of the new RT Maine was called Check. Childish and prone to be the team clown, Check loved to be around the team's hooch just to be close to the American Green Berets.

Hunt finally returned California's interpreter when he found the right man to handle that duty for his team. Some of the Montagnards he had run with on RT California brought in their own recommended friends, from which Hunt ultimately selected a seventeen-year-old named Andre, who had been raised in a French mission school. Andre was extremely valuable, thanks to his language skills: he spoke good English in addition to French, Vietnamese, and various Montagnard tongues.

Hunt took on Staff Sergeant David Warrum as his one-one and together they began training with their Montagnard team. In addition to work on weapons drills, RT Maine ran through countless immediate-action drills, using a different painted beer can to represent each team member. "We would sit on the covered porch of our barracks and go through different actions, moving our cans," said Hunt. "We covered each of the scenarios: if we were attacked from the left, or from the right front, or if we were trying to break contact, or if we were setting an ambush."

The team rehearsed, practiced, and rehearsed again. Zabitosky stayed involved as a mentor as the team progressed into live-fire drills with each scenario—including the roles of each team member for the actions that might be required in a prisoner snatch. After weeks of training, RT Maine finally went out on a recon training mission into an unsecured area of South Vietnam. Captain Amado Gayol, a short, muscular company commander from Kontum, accompanied Hunt's team on the choppers that took them in. Gayol, a Cuban who had joined the Marines before the 1961 Bay of Pigs invasion, had since been commissioned as an Army Special Forces officer. As the team's insertion choppers went into a hover and Hunt's men began rappelling down the ropes, they drew some enemy fire from the bamboo near a river bottom.

Sergeant Warrum froze up on the ropes as the gun shots erupted, causing Captain Gayol to begin barking at Hunt. He proceeded to instruct the new one-zero on how he should be running his operation, both during the insert and once on the ground. "He kept telling me how Rangers would do things," said Hunt. "I told him that's not how we'd been trained to do it with SOG. The Yards stayed out of it, but Gayol and I had a running disagreement the whole time we were out there about how we should conduct ourselves."

Warrum caused tense moments for both the team and the chopper crew as he whipped around on the ropes in the bamboo. Once the team returned to Kontum, Hunt kept Warrum only long enough to train a replacement one-one, Staff Sergeant Roger Loe. The team was forced to run back through their training scenarios again until their newest American Green Beret was up to par with all of their immediate-action drills.

Team Maine began running targets during May, called upon to observe enemy troop movements, either performing trail watches or truck convoy counts. Each time, Hunt's team managed to get their job done while avoiding serious NVA contact and without any injuries. He found Loe to be a proficient assistant team leader in the field but a whole new set of challenges arose during his down time. In between missions, Loe did little to stay in the good graces of Kontum's sergeant major, Rupert Stratton, thanks to his habit of creating small explosions and indiscriminately firing weapons just for fun.

One such event became a regular ritual that did not amuse Wilson Hunt. His new one-one had a habit of laying in his bunk drinking beer until midnight, at which time the Armed Forces Radio Vietnam would play the national anthem of South Vietnam, followed by the "Star Spangled Banner." "When they played the U.S. national anthem, Loe would jump off his bunk and stand at rigid attention," said Hunt. "As soon as the last note was played, he'd pull his .45 out of his holster and fire three rounds through our roof."

Hunt's remedy for his own nerves and anger was to order his badly hung-over assistant team leader on top of their hooch early the next morning to patch the fresh bullet holes in their roof.

◆◇◆

After months without a casualty, FOB-2's run of good luck played out on April 29. An indigenous Hatchet Force company led by First Lieutenant Terry Hamric was attacked as it moved down a mountain side toward an area of dense vegetation. Hamric's men were caught in an ambush just as they crossed a wide stream, and many of the indigenous troops fled once the firefight commenced. One was killed instantly, while another indigenous soldier fell wounded across Hamric's legs, pinning both in an open area until he could crawl free to administer first aid. Hamric coordinated effective fire down on the NVA ranks before dragging his wounded man to safety across the open field. Bob Van Hall, serving as an adviser for Hamric's team, bravely exposed himself to enemy fire while helping carry the wounded.

Extraction choppers soon hauled out the most seriously injured. Reinforcements were called in from Kontum, specifically the platoons under Captain Gene McCarley, First Lieutenant Joseph Linwood Shreve, and First Lieutenant Paul S. Spilberg. The area was stirred up from the recent fight and Shreve's Hatchet Force was ambushed by a large NVA unit on May 1 near a stream. Van Hall was in the process of placing demolition charges near a well-used enemy road when his men and their security element, under Lieutenant Shreve, were caught in a crossfire ambush as they forded the wide stream. There were many wounded in the battle, including Shreve, McCarley, Spilberg, and Master Sergeant Horace Ford.

Shreve, although seriously wounded in the initial grenade barrage, continued to place devastating fire on the NVA while medic John Probart and others moved the wounded. The Americans had successfully dragged most of the seriously wounded to relative safety, when the NVA suddenly began sweeping the area with automatic weapons fire. Those still crawling about in the open were pinned down. Shreve, ignoring his wounds, moved across the field and began directing fire on the enemy. In the process, he received additional—and mortal—wounds.

Van Hall was exceptional, carrying one of the most seriously wounded men out to the defensive perimeter before going back into the firefight to help recover Lieutenant Shreve. He placed the mortally wounded squad leader on his back and crawled back to the perimeter although Shreve, later awarded a Silver Star for valor, soon expired. The balance of the Hatchet Force men were extracted, but eight Americans were wounded in the process. It was a somber group that assembled in the Kontum bar to mourn the loss of Joe Shreve. Wilson Hunt and some of the other relative newcomers to Kontum would thus be exposed to the "Old Blue" traditional song that night for the first time. It would not be the last for most of them.

✦◇✦

Early May also proved costly to the airmen who daily risked their lives inserting and retrieving recon teams. The most profound loss occurred on May 4 when the Kingbee pilot "Cowboy" was lost. The smiling CH-34 pilot who preferred to dress in American Western garb and wear a trademark white World War I–style scarf when he flew was a member of Air Marshal Nguyen Cal Ky's 219th Vietnamese Air Force. Although most knew him simply as Cowboy, he was Captain (dai uy—pronounced "die we" in

Vietnamese) Loc. A stout muscular man, Cowboy had worked many SOG operations in his time—including the first SOG recon mission in 1965—and he went in with his Kingbee on May 4 after a SOG recon team that his American comrades had all but written off. He made the extraction, successfully delivered the team to FOB-2, and took off to fly back to his own base in a heavy overcast. Tragically, Cowboy became disoriented, crashed into a mountain, and was killed, leaving behind a young wife and son.

Pulling live prisoners out of Laos was proving to be exceptionally difficult for SOG's Kontum teams in 1968. Bob Kline's RT New York nearly accomplished a successful snatch on May 10 while scouting a well-worn trail leading to the crest of a hill. Kline sent One-One Dennis Mack ahead while the rest of the team moved to within twenty yards of the main trail. Kline spotted a second trail and then efficiently deployed his men as they heard an NVA patrol moving in their direction.

Mack managed to overpower a lone enemy soldier that was leading the patrol, but then a second appeared over the crest of the hill. Again, Mack took him down and subdued him without a shot being fired. Before he could move, the main body of the NVA patrol suddenly came into view. Remaining in an exposed position, he opened fire, dropping two of his opponents and sending the others fleeing for cover. Mack remained under hostile fire long enough to strip the bodies of all valuable intelligence information before he cleared the scene. Kline and his team finished breaking up the enemy platoon by directing a hail of grenades and small-arms fire into their ranks. Recon Team New York beat a hasty retreat while calling for an emergency extraction. Kline then directed a thunderous air strike in on the remaining NVA elements they had outrun but pulling their prisoners out alive proved to be too great a risk under the intense gunfire they faced.

Some of the more experienced men stepped into other roles during May, paving the way for newer recon men to advance. Green Berets like Dallas Longstreath moved into the role of covey rider, flying support in small prop-driven planes for recon teams on the ground. Longstreath was one of the few who chose not to use his given code name on the radio, going with "Dallas" instead. Gerry Denison, one-zero of RT Ohio, was also approached by Ken Etheredge to consider becoming a covey rider during May 1968.

Denison, who became familiarly known to teams on the ground by his code name of "grommet," was taken under Etheredge's wing. Within weeks, he was flying missions in Cessna O-2 Skymaster planes, twin-engine observation craft with much faster cruising speeds than the earlier O-1 Bird Dogs. After relinquishing RT Ohio to One-One Bob Kotin,

Denison moved out of his team hooch and was assigned a new hootch-mate, twenty-five-year-old Sergeant Joe Parnar, a Kontum newbie.

Parnar, who had dropped out of the University of Massachusetts during his junior year to become a Special Forces medic, was itching for combat with a recon team. But medical supervisor John Probart advised him that his services were more desperately needed in Kontum's dispensary as a medic. Probart did offer Parnar hope that he could see some action by flying duty as chase medic and by accompanying the Hatchet Force and SLAM operations when needed. When he was not in the dispensary, Joe often eavesdropped on conversations between Denison and Longstreath. "It was like hearing a nightly news commentary on the day's operations," he said.[4]

Disappointed to be relegated to a support role, Parnar found fellow newbie Bob Garcia and other FOB-2 fresh recruits to be similarly dejected to have been sent to work in the commo bunker. "Since we all had a common gripe, we formed what amounted to an unofficial support group and would sit together in the club many nights bitching about our plight," said Parnar. "Some of these included, in addition to Garcia, Larry Stephens, Billy Simmons, Ron Bozikis, William Copley, and Ken Worthley."[5] They would all get their shot at combat soon enough, though few of this group would survive their SOG tours.

✦✧✦

Specialist Fourth Class John Kedenburg had been assigned to FOB-2 less than two months when he ascended into the one-zero position for RT Nevada. After the May 1968 transfers of teammates Howard Taylor and Lou DeSeta, Colonel Smith assigned a Korean War veteran, Staff Sergeant James Richard McGlon, to take over the team. McGlon, however, soon departed for the States on a short leave when he agreed to extend his service period. During the interim, young Kedenburg was left as the acting one-zero of RT Nevada, tasked with reorganizing his indigenous team members. Without his veteran buddy DeSeta around to watch his back in the field, Kedenburg was wise enough to know he would benefit from the presence of another experienced recon man until McGlon returned. He thus sought out one of DeSeta's buddies, Sergeant Wilson Hunt, to strap-hang with RT Nevada on his first mission as acting commander.

Hunt readily agreed to assist Kedenburg, under one condition: he had no desire to carry radio for him. They were able to recruit one of the newer officers, First Lieutenant Tom Jaeger, who was recently transferred in. Recon Team Nevada was tasked with tracking an NVA unit that had ambushed a convoy on Highway 14 between Pleiku and Kontum. They inserted by helicopter and trailed the NVA unit for several days as it moved west through the jungle toward the Cambodian border. They got close enough to hear its rear elements, but Kedenburg's team was never in contact with the main body. Air strikes were called in on the NVA unit and RT Nevada was ordered to keep its distance, listening to the powerful explosions. Kedenburg's team was forced to spend an extra day in the field when air assets were diverted to assist another FOB-2 team that had gotten into trouble on a training mission.

Once RT Nevada was safely back at Kontum, Kedenburg secured a new teammate in Specialist Fifth Class Steve Roche, who would serve as his joint one-one and one-two—second-in-charge of the team while also carrying their PRC-25 radio. Roche, who had completed a year and a half of college in Connecticut before enlisting, reached Vietnam in January 1968, serving first at FOB-3 Khe Sanh during the Tet Offensive before being assigned to Kontum. He found Kedenburg to be a serious team leader, training his men constantly before a mission on all different contact scenarios. Recon Team Nevada ran one mission in-country with Kedenburg, Roche, and their mixed team of Montagnards, Nungs, and a Vietnamese interpreter named Trang. During their second mission together, Kedenburg's team had a hot LZ and was shot out before they could land. Through training and hot action, Roche found Kedenburg to be a genuinely nice guy who maintained a good sense of humor. "John was just a natural," he said.[6]

Nevada's next mission commenced on June 12, 1968. The ten-man team—two Americans and eight South Vietnamese—were inserted into southern Laos along Route 110/96 to interdict that portion of the Ho Chi Minh Trail. Kedenburg's recon team was inserted by the 189th Assault Helicopter Company (AHC) with orders to reconnoiter the area, along a known heavily used enemy transport route, report back intelligence, and place motion detectors that could sense enemy troop movements in the area. Kedenburg was to also call in air strikes as appropriate.[7]

Roche believed their insertion method was clever: they were brought in via a three-chopper convoy, although RT Nevada was tightly packed into only the middle bird. As they approached the LZ, the pilots flew just above the treetop level. Upon reaching the insertion point, the team chopper turned on its side and plunged down to just above the jungle floor. The pilot then turned his Huey upright, allowing the team to jump off within about thirty seconds before he pulled his chopper back up to fall into formation with the other two slicks.[8]

Kedenburg immediately fanned out his team in a circular perimeter and maintained absolute silence for thirty minutes. Thin, youthful-looking

One-One Roche was carrying the radio for the mission while also carrying his CAR-15, fourteen magazines of ammo, a half-dozen grenades, two smoke grenades, a canteen, and a rucksack with food, insect repellent, first aid kit, and more. Roche, who weighed a mere 130 pounds, was toting an additional fifty pounds of gear—quite a load on his thin frame. Once he was certain their presence was undetected, Kedenburg moved his ten-man team beyond the tall elephant grass LZ clearing into the surrounding jungle.

Recon Team Nevada proceeded cautiously toward its target area over rough terrain for the remainder of the afternoon. The point man, a South Vietnamese soldier named Dic who carried an M79 grenade launcher, was followed by rifleman Vu, interpreter Trang, Kedenburg, and finally Roche with the balance of their indigenous personnel. There were neither visible signs nor sounds of any NVA all day. About an hour before dark, Kedenburg selected a RON site where his men could mix water and spices into their rice bags to eat. Then they spread out in a circle and got some sleep until first light.

By the afternoon of June 13, they were nearing their objective, the NVA's main supply route, unaware that their position had already been compromised by enemy trackers. Strike Team Nevada was within eighty yards of the road when Roche realized they were in trouble. Point man Dic suddenly spun to his right and opened fire with his M79. Just behind Dic, Vu opened fire on full auto before both indigenous men turned and came racing back toward the team. Roche saw incoming fire pouring in as the entire jungle suddenly came alive with bullets. As all hell broke loose, Kedenburg's men crouched low, returning fire in the direction Dic and Vu had just vacated.[9]

Specialist Fifth Class Steve Roche was the assistant team leader of John Kedenburg's RT Nevada. He clung to an indigenous team member on June 13 as they were battered through the jungle canopy while being extracted on strings. *Joe Parnar*

The recon team was pinned down by an estimated battalion-size NVA force. Against such overwhelming odds, their only option was to break contact and attempt to reach a defensible area until proper air support could be raised. "We took off back the way we had come as fast as we could go," Roche said. "No one had been hit, so we just hauled ass."[10] As Recon Team Nevada gradually outdistanced its pursuers, Kedenburg took the radio to report his situation and to request air cover. Along the way, two of the indigenous team members panicked and started to run. Kedenburg was able to detain one of them but the other disappeared from sight and was presumed to have been killed by the enemy.[11]

With nine of his ten men left, Kedenburg headed for the only defensive spot he had previously seen—several large bomb craters a short distance away. He dropped to the rear of the unit as his team backtracked along their infiltration route, covering their movements by continually harassing the enemy. Kedenburg threw grenades, laid toe popper mines, and blasted NVA with his CAR-15 until RT Nevada arrived at a small clearing with a bomb crater in the center. Roche believed that his one-zero killed at least five opponents in the process of covering the team's escape.

Kedenburg's team had been under heavy fire and in evasion mode for about an hour by the time it reached the bomb crater LZ area. He had put in the call for a prairie fire emergency, and Covey Rider Gerry Denison was en route in an O-1 Bird Dog spotter plane to help coordinate the extraction of RT Nevada. Kedenburg radioed his approximate position, and then marked his team's precise position by throwing a smoke grenade once Denison's forward air control Cessna arrived overhead.

Denison's first passes over the bomb craters drew heavy NVA ground fire toward his little prop plane. He could see that the team was separated, scattered between two large bomb craters. Denison believed that a Huey could get near the ground between the bomb pits, but the enemy was too close for comfort at the moment. He first sent in the fast movers—Navy F-14 jet fighters—to raise hell with the North Vietnamese troops who were converging around the perimeter of the trapped recon team. Further air cover arrived in the form of prop-driven A-1E Skyraiders, who were able to move in slower and lower for effective bombing runs and effective gunfire support. Denison also called in gunships of the 189th AHC and 170th AHC to pinpoint the team's location and to provide covering fire for extraction ships.[12]

The air support was a godsend for RT Nevada, but the view from above was far from optimistic to Covey Rider Denison. One-One Roche was more than a little distressed when Denison relayed to him that his team had apparently stirred up a major NVA battalion.

Great! thought Roche. *We may never get out of this situation alive.*

One of RT Nevada's South Vietnamese team members had become separated during the movement to the LZ. Since that time, while waiting for the first runs made by their air support, another of RT Nevada's indigenous men had been killed as Kedenburg's men fought back hundreds of NVA troops trying to encircle their position.[13]

The stress was felt by all as Roche relayed details to Denison for the air support. At one point, Kedenburg called for the speakerphone. Roche fumbled about in the process, as the radio's cord had become hopelessly tangled. In the midst of enemy gunfire, Kedenburg locked eyes with his one-one as he struggled wildly with untangling the cord. "We both broke into laughter at the absurdity of the whole situation," Roche said. "Somehow that brief shared bit of laughter released the pressure for us."[14]

During the next half hour, the A-1Es made additional passes until Denison relayed word that the extraction choppers were ready to begin moving in. Due to insufficient clearance for the first 189th AHC chopper to land, its pilot, First Lieutenant Uwe Linder, hovered low enough for his crew to drop four rope harnesses. Linder found the surrounding trees and bamboo to be denser than Denison had estimated them to be during his initial passes over the LZ. His slick made it almost to treetop level before intense NVA small-arms fire began finding the range, with bullets ripping through his slick's belly. Linder's chopper was heavily damaged, forcing him to abort the pickup, although he remained on station to offer gun support throughout the extraction attempt.[15]

Kedenburg called for another air strike and requested that it be as close to his team's perimeter as possible. The three remaining slicks were equipped with McGuire rigs, which was now determined to be the only possible way to get RT Nevada out. Following another air strike, the next Huey moved into the area and dropped four 150-foot rappelling ropes, two from each side, onto which the team could connect. This ship was commanded by Warrant Officer Lawrence E. Johnson, who came to a high hover over the landing zone and dropped his ropes under intense enemy fire. Johnson pulled out four indigenous members of Recon Team Nevada as the men snapped their Swiss seats on carabiners attached to their web gear.[16]

A third chopper, piloted by Warrant Officer Joseph W. Winder, moved in over the second LZ, a single bomb crater where separated members of RT Nevada had signaled Denison with smoke grenades. Winder approached under heavy fire and hovered as his crewmen lowered McGuire rigs. He managed to extract another indigenous member of the team before accurate fire forced him away from the LZ.[17]

At the bomb crater LZ, four members of RT Nevada remained under fire: Kedenburg, Roche, interpreter Trang, and a fourth indigenous trooper named Pop. Moments later, Warrant Officer Mike Berry brought his Ghostrider 153 in for a fourth attempt to rescue the balance of RT Nevada. Berry had been flying Avenger gunships in Vietnam for five months with the 189th Assault Helicopter Company. He approached the second LZ, a single bomb crater in the dense jungle, and lowered four McGuire rigs through the triple canopy. Chase medic Joe Parnar looked down into the small opening in the jungle canopy about 350 yards east of Highway 110. He watched the crew chief, Specialist Fourth Class Bill Snow from Mississippi, and the door gunner each lay prone on the floor while dropping two of the sandbag rigs toward the jungle floor as Snow communicated with his pilot over his headset. Unknown to Parnar at that moment, the NVA began closing in on the little LZ as the Huey began its descent.

Snow, fully occupied with working the strings and watching the team below, could see a firefight breaking out and the recon men in their harnesses moving toward the lines. Roche and Trang were first to strap their carabiners onto the lines and secure themselves. Pop and Kedenburg then hurriedly began securing themselves to the last two lines.

At that moment, before Kedenburg could signal to the pilot to pull out, one of the missing indigenous members of Nevada came running across the LZ toward the team. Kedenburg was obviously surprised, as he and his team had written off this last man as dead. From Berry's chopper, Parnar saw the South Vietnamese team member waving a red panel at the chopper to signal that he was friendly. Crew chief Snow could now only make out the canopy cover below and had no vision of the missing man running toward the LZ. His headset thundered with the sounds of hydraulics, transmission, and engine noises. What medic Parnar could see and hear from his vantage point was not welcoming: the NVA was now pouring heavy lead toward his Huey.[18]

The hovering chopper was caught in a perilous spot. Bullets began clanging off the tail section, and Parnar could see machine-gun fire erupting from the jungle a thousand yards to the rear of their slick. Tracer streaks reached for the Huey, making crackling sounds as they passed under the rotor blades about eight feet outside the door. Parnar was more alarmed that chopper pilot Berry and his co-pilot bravely continued to hover under fire as the recon men below finished strapping in.

Roche, still secured to his harness, began firing back at the onrushing NVA. Kedenburg, under a constant hail of fire, jumped from the rig, leaving behind his radio and rucksack. He grabbed his missing man and began tying him in the vacant harness as he signaled the chopper off. Mike

Berry, alarmed by the bullets pinging off his Huey, pulled out abruptly. Bill Snow, still laying prone on the chopper floor, saw numerous NVA right on the LZ as Kedenburg blazed away at them. He could not see below the tall trees, however, to tell how many men were strapped in when his pilot was forced to evade the ground fire pinging off his bird. Steve Roche, dangling from one of the McGuire rigs, was horrified to see his one-zero still on the LZ, firing the last of his ammunition as NVA swarmed his position. By his estimate, Kedenburg killed at least six enemy troops before Roche's vision was obscured by the jungle canopy.[19]

Kedenburg was left with only his emergency URC-10 radio, as Roche was still wearing his PRC-25 field radio when he was pulled free of the scene. Denison later stated, "The chopper lifted out and was returning to Dak To when I got a call from John on his URC-10 that he was still on the ground and what had happened. He told me an indigenous who was missing after the first firefight came in and he gave his seat to him so he could get out. I was on station for about two hours after the exfil of the rest of the team and I was in contact with John for most of that time. He was on the ground, alone. I asked him several times if there was anyone he knew near him or around his location. We were watching NVA search for him. We also killed a bunch of them."[20]

Denison told Kedenburg to attempt to move east, but to keep him advised as to where he was and what he was doing. "He acknowledged this and commenced to tell me where there were bad guys moving around," Denison said. The helicopter gunships expended all their ammunition while he called in additional A-1Es to work over the area. About that time, Denison received word that a second group of choppers was inbound, so he directed Kedenburg to get back into the bomb craters. "He rogered that and that was the last transmission I heard," said Denison.[21]

One-One Roche believed that the abrupt departure of pilot Berry had prevented John Kedenburg from securely strapping himself to a teammate. Roche, interpreter Trang, and the other two indigenous troopers were subjected to a violent and bloody bashing through the canopy as their Huey hauled clear. Instead of going straight up, Berry flew a diagonal path to clear the area. Roche spotted a huge tree coming, grabbed his rope, and managed to kick off the tree. Still, he was dragged through several heavy limbs that smashed his face. Bleeding heavily from his face and hands, he wrapped his arms around his rope and hung on for dear life. He looked around for Trang and spotted him swinging limp in his harness, knocked unconscious as the chopper dragged them through the trees.

Roche somehow managed to swing over, wrap his arms around Trang, and clutch him tightly as they dangled below the departing chopper. Once

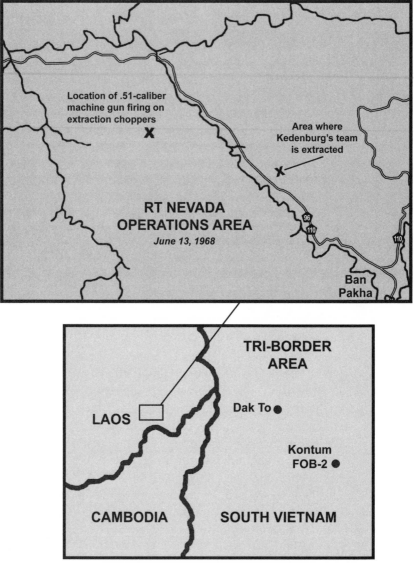

Maps modified based on original work of Joe Parnar

the recon team was clear of the trees, crew chief Snow could only see three men dangling from the lines far below. Berry flew several miles, straight to an old airstrip at the isolated SF camp of Ben Het near the Laotian border. As they were dropped to the ground, medic Parnar jumped from the chopper to offer first aid to them. "I was a sight, with blood all over my face and the entire front of my shirt," said Roche. He had suffered lacerations to his hands and face and a broken nose in the extraction.

Parnar was alarmed by two things: Kedenburg had not made it out, and there were only three men on the four strings. Pop was gone. Roche later believed that Pop may have remained behind to help Kedenburg fight off the enemy, while Parnar believed the fourth, hastily secured indigenous trooper was simply ripped off his rig during the violent bashing through the canopy. In any event, he only had three men to tend to at Ben Het.

Roche approached Berry and asked him why he had not waited long enough for Kedenburg to secure himself to one of the rigs or at least to wrap himself around one of the other four. "He said they were taking too many gunfire hits and pointed to several bullet holes," Roche said. Berry did offer that another chopper pilot, Winder, had managed to pull out one or more South Vietnamese team members. Medic Parnar found the South Vietnamese strapped in by Kedenburg was in fair shape, sporting lacerations similar to those suffered by Roche. Interpreter Trang had unequal pupils, "a sign of intracranial pressure on the brain. We loaded him onto the chopper and headed for the 4th Division medical facility at Dak To."[22]

At Dak To, Trang was carried into the underground medical bunker on a stretcher. Parnar found that the medics at Dak To wanted to know details of what had happened. He instead took Roche and loaded back on their chopper to move away from the medical area. The major in charge threatened Parnar about ever coming into his medical bunker again without offering full disclosure on their mission. When Parnar reached Kontum that evening, he was still shaken by the incident. Sergeant Major Rupert Stratton advised him to give a full report to Lieutenant Colonel Smith, who fully backed up the young chase medic's actions.[23]

Roche, a bloody mess, described to Colonel Smith and his intel men how John Kedenburg had been left behind in the hasty extraction under fire. Smith said he would organize a Bright Light to go after Kedenburg and ordered RT Nevada's one-one to get medical attention. The medic set Roche's nose and stitched up the cut around his left eye and the cuts on his hands. He then went back to his hooch he had shared with Kedenburg, where the day's events hit him all at once. *I'm safe, and poor John is still out there somewhere, by himself and totally surrounded.*[24]

Roche suddenly felt as if his stomach was turning inside out. He raced to the latrine and vomited until his empty, retching stomach ached.

◆◇◆

Denison hovered over the Kedenburg LZ in his Cessna Bird Dog, hoping against all odds that the RT Nevada team leader could be saved. His last radio communication with Kedenburg indicated that the Green Beret was moving back toward the pair of bomb craters where the final team members had been extracted. Before Denison's light plane had to depart the scene for lack of fuel, pilots Johnson and Winder of the 189th AHC had returned, having deposited their survivors at Ben Het. Denison offered his situation analysis to them before departing, but his last impressions of the area were not favorable. Bad weather was closing in, in the form of thunderstorms and rain showers, reducing visibility and generally making the mission more hazardous. Warrant Officer Johnson made another approach on the LZ as gunships worked to suppress the heavy ground fire. This time, there were no recon men visible on the ground, and Johnson was driven off by the accurate fire.

When fuel exhaustion finally forced Denison's plane back to base, his position over the LZ was relieved by another covey rider, Terry Hamric. Choppers continued to offer fire support to keep the searching NVA away from Kedenburg's position until both the FAC and the gunships were forced to abort any further rescue efforts due to deteriorating weather conditions and low fuel supplies. Upon reporting in to Colonel Smith back at Kontum, Denison told him, "Kedenburg is going to get the big one for his actions this day."[25] He felt that the team leader deserved nothing less than a Medal of Honor for sacrificing himself to give up the last rig on the chopper. Denison strongly recommended that forces should be sent back in for Kedenburg early the next morning.

The fact that the eight bodies, living and dead, of RT Nevada had been extracted was due to the valor of many soldiers laying down ordnance and gunfire from the air assets. Eight men of the 189th Assault Helicopter Company were awarded the Air Medal with "V" device for their actions on June 13. Pilot Larry Johnson was awarded the Silver Star, while the other three 189th pilots—Linder, Winder, and Berry—each received the Distinguished Flying Cross, while their four co-pilots were each awarded an Air Medal for their heroism.[26]

✦◇✦

The most troubling issue of the mission was that One-Zero John Kedenburg had been left behind. A Bright Light mission was organized to go in and find him and the indigenous team member, Pop, the following morning.[27]

Specialist Fifth Class Jim Tramel, the newly assigned one-zero of RT Illinois, immediately volunteered his team. His former one-zero, Sherman Batman, was packing to depart for Pleiku at the time the word came in about Kedenburg. Tramel asked Batman to come with him for the mission since he was more experienced. Batman agreed to assist RT Illinois, began gathering his gear, and borrowed a rifle from a Hatchet Force officer.[28]

After a briefing, Tramel and Batman were asked by Lieutenant Colonel Smith to take along a medic just in case they should find Kedenburg alive and badly wounded. The medic selected was young Bryon Loucks, who had been working in the dispensary with John Probart when word came that the survivors from Kedenburg's team were inbound on the ropes. Loucks, a close friend to Kedenburg, soon learned that his mentor was missing on the ground. When he reached Kontum in May, Loucks had often been left at base while his hoochmate, John Barnatowicz, was out with his RT Ohio running targets. One door down, team leader Kedenburg had patiently taken young Loucks under his wing, mentoring him on how to soundproof his equipment, how to pack his armament, and various important field procedures. "The list of things to learn and do was long and John's tutoring went on for many hours and days," Loucks said.[29]

The only way to repay such selfless acts by Kedenburg was for Loucks to volunteer for the Bright Light mission. He was admittedly "as green as they come" but he was accepted due to his medical training and the fact that he was preparing for his own recon missions. Although Loucks hurriedly packed his gear and got his medical bag, One-Zero Tramel was not pleased that he would be taking in the rookie medic. "When you go into a Bright Light, you know you're going to get into a firefight," Tramel said. "That's not the thing you want to do on your first mission."[30]

Team Illinois was flown from Kontum by two Hueys of the 170th AHC, followed by a chase medic Huey. The team went in heavy with nine Montagnards and four Americans—new team leader Tramel, the veteran Batman backing him up, medic Loucks, and a last-minute fourth straphanger, Specialist Fifth Class Tom Cunningham. The latter was another close friend to John Kedenburg who had been through training with him at Fort Bragg. Cunningham was particularly troubled because he had been scheduled to go out with Kedenburg but delays in being extracted from another mission had prevented him from going along.

After stopping at Dak To to top off fuel, the 170th Hueys inserted the team near a large bomb crater close to RT Nevada's extraction point. Covey Rider Gerry Denison helped guide the Bright Light team through the edge of some woods down a peninsula to the spot where he had last seen Kedenburg. Shortly after clearing their LZ, the Green Berets were aware that the NVA had trackers on them.

There were no encounters, so his team commenced searching the area during the early morning of June 14. As they moved into the peninsula, they avoided a nearby clearing before beginning to ascend a hill. Tramel's men moved by two large bomb craters—created by 500-pounders dropped the previous day—at the edge of the clearing before they came upon half of a BAR belt, with a canteen still attached and pockets full of M16 magazines. Batman recognized the belt as the one Kedenburg had worn.

The Bright Light team eased another twenty meters up the hill and found the missing Green Beret, with his back to a log in a position roughly a hundred yards from his team's extraction point. Kedenburg's rucksack had been torn from his lifeless body, his BAR belt was blown apart, and his rifle was mangled from an explosion. "He was leaning against a fallen tree and he had shot himself up with morphine before he died," said Tramel. Although his body did not appear to be booby-trapped, Sherman Batman was still cautious. He used Swiss seat ropes to pull Kedenburg's body away from its position to make sure it had not been rigged with a grenade. The team found his crypto book, mission notes, radio, and codebook buried under leaves within arm's reach of his body. "When we found the codebook we knew the enemy was not aware of John being left on the ground," said Loucks.

Batman and Tramel carried Kedenburg's body to the top of the hill and called Covey Rider Denison shortly before noon to prepare for an extraction. The remainder of the team took up defensive positions while the senior team leaders contemplated how to get a Huey to settle in low enough to load the body. One tall tree near the bomb craters on the hillside stood in the way of an effective landing. Tramel took point while Tom Cunningham and two of his indigenous soldiers went to work setting C-4 plastic explosive charges on the adjacent trees that bordered the bomb crater. Medic Loucks, being new to the recon business, was assigned to a listening post just outside the bomb crater LZ. He instinctively ducked as the C-4 detonated and splintered the tree trunks.

Batman was surprised by the explosion. He knew from Denison that their extraction choppers were just preparing to leave Dak To and would be another twenty minutes in arriving. Cunningham, standing about sixty yards in front of the group, suddenly spotted North Vietnamese soldiers moving swiftly down the peninsula toward him. "I guess our blowing up the trees sparked Charlie's curiosity," he said. Tramel and Batman moved out of the wood line with their Montagnard grenadier to intercept the approaching enemy. They each fired a grenade from their M79s toward the NVA in the style of mortars, hoping the blasts would flush their opponents. At the same instant, however, the North Vietnamese unleashed half a dozen hand grenades toward the American recon team.

"Grenades!" yelled Tramel as he spotted the incoming explosives. One erupted close enough to Cunningham to knock him unconscious. Two indigenous team members, including the team's Vietnamese interpreter, were severely wounded by other grenades. Tramel, who had shouted the warning and sprinted away toward safety, was blown through the air by the blast of another. He was knocked down the side of a hill, his back and right buttocks ripped by shrapnel.

Loucks was lying on his stomach, peering through the limbs and brush when the attack commenced. He heard the thud of something landing in front of him and then he was also knocked unconscious by the explosion of a concussion grenade. When he came to, he found himself lying inside the bomb crater with shrapnel wounds to his face and numerous powder burns. He later learned that Batman had found him in a groggy state and helped drag him back into the crater to save him. Now, Loucks found an intense firefight blazing away all around him.[31]

Cunningham quickly regained his senses and got on the radio to transmit the prairie fire code. His right arm, chest, and the back of his legs were ripped by shrapnel. "One of my calf muscles was bleeding like a son of a bitch," he said. He was only partially conscious of his own injuries due to his plight. Fighting alone, he unleashed a hail of gunfire against five North Vietnamese advancing on his position and killed them all. He continued to lay down defensive fire and man the radio.

One-Zero Mike Tramel realized he was wounded as he picked himself up from the bottom of the hill. He suddenly spotted an enemy squad moving through the nearby wood line, attempting to flank his team. Tramel jumped to his feet and immediately assaulted the NVA soldiers with aggressive fire, killing three of them, wounding a fourth, and sending the fifth man retreating for cover.

Members of the June 14 Bright Light Team.

Left: Sergeant First Class Sherman Batman. *Mike Tramel*

Middle: Specialist Fifth Class Tom Cunningham (*right*), seen with Sergeant Tony Love. *Tom Cunningham via Joe Parnar*

Right: Specialist Fifth Class James "Mike" Tramel had just taken over as one-zero of RT Illinois when his team was called in to search for John Kedenburg. *Joe Parnar*

Sergeant Bryon Loucks was knocked unconscious by a concussion grenade during the Bright Light action. Seen here with his CAR-15 near a Montagnard village, Loucks later became one-zero of RT Washington in 1968. *Bryon Loucks via Joe Parnar*

In the meantime, Batman was firing away at the gathering NVA and shouting curses at them to come and get him. He and his men were fairly safe from gunfire, which could not be directed down into their bomb crater from a distance. Loucks, having recovered some of his senses while lying in the crater, asked Batman what he could do to help.

"Start throwing hand grenades!"

Still weak and groggy from the grenade explosion, Loucks began lobbing grenades toward the enemy. The bomb explosions from the previous day had shattered the sixty-foot tall bamboo in the vicinity and caused much of it to lay at crazy angles. In his dazed state, Loucks lobbed a grenade that failed to clear the bamboo, instead caroming off and ricocheting back toward his own bomb crater.

"Duck!" screamed Batman.

Fortunately, the grenade landed just a few feet shy of the top of the crater and exploded just far enough away to prevent the entire team from being wiped out.

"Take the goddamn grenades away from Loucks and give him a rifle!" Batman shouted.

Losing his new job did not phase the young medic, who was still struggling to figure out why he was so groggy and weak. About fifteen minutes after the action had commenced, Tramel made it back to the larger bomb crater, where he found Batman irritated with Loucks and struggling with his borrowed rifle that continued to jam. Batman finally took the medic's rifle and continued to return fire. Cunningham was still down, in the vicinity of the North Vietnamese, beyond the nearby second bomb crater.

Batman raced forward under fire and dropped into the second crater. Not finding Cunningham, he proceeded to move around collecting extra ammo cartridges before hurrying back to rejoin the rest of the team. Team leader Tramel concerned himself with communicating with Covey Rider Denison via his little emergency radio. His men were in a bad position, totally surrounded with no air support overhead yet. *I don't think we're getting out of this one alive*, he thought to himself.

Two of his indigenous men had been severely wounded in the opening grenade assault and one had expired. Tramel later learned that the other, his Vietnamese interpreter, was screaming in pain. "One of my Montagnards killed him because he was giving away our position," he said. "There was no love lost between the Montagnards and Vietnamese."

Just as Tramel was fearing the worst, things began to turn in his favor. Tom Cunningham, although seriously wounded and bleeding heavily, made it back to their main bomb crater. The first air support arrived on station in the form of fast movers, Air Force F-4 Phantom jets. They were shortly joined by A-1 Skyraiders who proceeded to assault the enemy forces as Tramel called in coordinates. His spirits began to lift. *We might actually survive this.*

In spite of the new air support, the enemy troops continued a relentless assault with automatic fire and grenades against the trapped Americans. Loucks found there were ebbs and flows to the action over the next two hours. He was stunned at one point to hear Denison, their covey rider, announce: "Oh, my God! I can't believe how many forces there are around you!"[32]

Denison later admitted he was merely talking to his covey pilot and was unaware that he had a hot mic. He could see squads of NVA charging up the hill toward the recon team's bomb crater as he called in air strikes to knock them back. "They just kept trying to go up that hill, one squad plus at a time and kept getting killed," he said. "I saw people burning alive after being hit by napalm." Denison had declared a tactical emergency early on in the fight and it was taking all the air support he had. He already had two Spads making runs to drop cluster bombs and napalm. He began calling for a second set of gunships and was surprised to get a reply from a B-52 crew in the area that was carrying a full load of 60,000 pounds of bombs. He asked the pilot to deliver his load nearby right on the Ho Chi Minh trail to blast up the enemy in the area. Denison was later certain that Mike Tramel's Bright Light team was the first outfit to have a B-52 offer close air support.[33]

Attempts to bring in extraction choppers were foiled by the persistence of the massing NVA forces. Bryon Loucks became convinced there was no way he was getting out of his first firefight alive. His team was hopelessly outnumbered, pinned in a bomb crater while their air support struggled to blast back the waves of enemy swarming for hours toward their position. At one point, he was chilled to hear a North Vietnamese voice blaring through a cheap megaphone in broken English: "GI, today you die!"

Even Covey Denison was beginning to have his doubts. *Our guys got back into that area way too easy,* he thought. *The NVA must have let them come in, knowing they could have an easy field day killing a bunch of Americans.*

Tramel's men maintained their composure throughout the early afternoon as the firefight dragged on into a third hour. Every team member still living was suffering from varying degrees of wounds. Halfway through the firefight, Tramel and Cunningham directed their men to accumulate their own wounded and killed in action (KIAs). Throughout the ordeal, air support Spads returned to base to refuel and rearm as replacements arrived overhead. Huey gunships swept in low over the embattled LZ, sweeping the area with deadly mini-gun fire that zipped six inches above the bomb crater inhabited by RT Illinois.

Around 1530, Tramel received word from Denison that three choppers were coming in to make another attempt to extract the besieged team. This time, good fortune was in their favor. The first helicopter, piloted by Chief Warrant Officer Joseph Roger Winterrath of the 170th AHC, landed at the bomb crater. The Bright Light team quickly loaded the bodies of Kedenburg and one of the indigenous fighters, along with the most severely wounded, including Cunningham and medic Loucks, the latter still too dazed to offer much medical assistance.

Loucks was sitting on the floor of the chopper as it lifted off. With his feet on the skids, he blasted away into the surrounding jungle and screamed at the chopper's two gunners to do the same. Both door gunners opened up with their M60 machine guns and pounded the nearby terrain with all they had. Shortly after exiting the site, Loucks felt burning pains in his crotch and assumed he had been shot through his butt. The door gunner could see no blood and had no idea what was wrong with the Green Beret. It took Loucks several moments to realize his pains had been caused by piles of hot M60 brass casings that had piled up in his lap and crotch. Relieved he had not been shot, Loucks collapsed among the body bags of his fallen comrades and slept soundly until the chopper delivered him back to base.

Tramel, Batman, and the remainder of RT Illinois was extracted by a second Huey minutes later and flown to FOB-2. As they lifted out with their feet on the skids, Tramel leaned over to his former team leader and announced, "Batman, I've been hit."

"Where?"

"In my butt!" Tramel shouted.

As Batman began chuckling, Tramel proceeded to drop his fatigues to prove his point. "I nearly dropped out of the chopper laughing," Batman recalled. "I told him it was just like a damned Texan to get shot in the ass!"

Arriving back at the Dak To launch site was a much more sobering experience, however. Tom Cunningham noted that everyone who helped unload Kedenburg's body from the chopper was in tears. "They were tears of sorrow and pride because one of the best had gone," he said.[34]

Steve Roche was sick all over again when Kedenburg's body was returned. "I felt so guilty that I was alive and he wasn't," he said. "I kept replaying the events over and over in my mind. I looked at it from every angle. I prayed about it and finally sleep overtook my exhausted body. I slept for about fourteen hours straight." When he awoke the next morning, he mentally reviewed the events again. Finally, Roche decided that what had happened was beyond his understanding and out of his control.[35]

✦✧✦

The retrieval of John Kedenburg's body had been costly. Several indigenous troopers had been killed and every member of the Bright Light team had been wounded in the process. Still, Loucks felt the mission was successful in that they did retrieve their friend's body and his crypto books. He, Cunningham, Batman, and Tramel would each receive the Bronze Star for the mission.

Kedenburg's sacrifice did not go unnoticed. Lieutenant Colonel Smith recommended his fallen Green Beret to the Awards and Decorations Board for the Medal of Honor and forwarded eyewitness statements from those involved in the mission. "Specialist Kedenburg sacrificed his life for his belief in his country's fight for freedom and so that another man may live to fight another day," wrote Smith.[36] The recommendation moved swiftly through Army command and Kedenburg was later posthumously awarded SOG's third Medal of Honor. In part, his award citation reads: "Specialist Kedenburg's inspiring leadership, consummate courage and willing self-sacrifice permitted his small team to inflict heavy casualties on the enemy and escape almost certain annihilation."[37]

His body was shipped back Stateside, where he was buried with honors in Farmingdale, New York, in the Long Island National Cemetery. The night his body was returned to Kontum, medic Bill Lensch assigned his

newest man the job of cleaning up the body to properly prepare it for shipment home. Silent tears streamed down Joe Parnar's face as he worked, and
he wondered if he would have had the courage to give up his own life for a
teammate as Kedenburg had done. "Washing his body and preparing him
for shipment back to the States is the greatest honor I have ever had," he
recalled.[38]

Parnar joined his fellow Green Berets in the Kontum club that night,
where all the talk involved Kedenburg's sacrifice. In the late hours, after
many a drink had been consumed, the SOG ritual folk song of "Old Blue"
was started. Other fallen heroes were mourned in the singing until the final
verse ended with: "Hey, Kedenburg, you were a good guy, you."[39]

It was the first of many times that Parnar would hear "Old Blue" sung
at the base after one of their own had been killed or had gone missing in
action. "I didn't dare look into anyone else's eyes," he said, "but I suspect
they were as teary as my own."[40]

Chapter Twelve

ENTER THE GLADIATOR

Jack Singlaub's two-year tenure as chief SOG came to a close during May 1968 when he received word of his pending promotion to brigadier general. His handpicked successor was Colonel Steve Cavanaugh, whose career began as a paratrooper in World War II. He was serving in Germany as the 8th Infantry Division's chief of staff when Singlaub called to inform him that he had nominated Cavanaugh to be the new leader of the largest and most secret special ops organization since the OSS.[1]

Cavanaugh was well received by his SOG men, and he put more focus into missions across the border. At FOB-2, there was little time in late June to mourn the loss of John Kedenburg. The new chief SOG was intent on stepping up the missions, and some of the Green Berets elevated into team commands were those involved in the Kedenburg Bright Light. Young medic Bryon Loucks was asked by the recon company first sergeant to organize his own team. Loucks chose to name his new outfit RT Washington in honor of his home state, and his hooch was soon adorned with his state's flag, which he obtained by writing to his state senator. Jim Tramel continued as the one-zero of ST Illinois as Sherman Batman transferred from the base after the Bright Light.

Joe Parnar, who had flown as chase medic on June 13, was still itching to move onto a recon team. He pleaded with Colonel Smith for days to no avail, so Parnar consoled himself in the base club, putting away drinks. He found a willing ear in the form of Sergeant First Class Pappy Webb, the one-zero of RT Texas. In hindsight, Parnar felt that Webb was more willing to listen to the young medic's sob story as long as his comrade was buying the beers. Parnar learned that Webb was sending part of his paychecks to his wife back in the States in addition to covering the apartment rent for a Vietnamese woman he had taken up with named Leiah, who lived just outside the FOB-2 compound with her two small children.[2]

Parnar considered Webb to be one of SOG's finest, a team leader whose courage under fire in the hottest areas was unquestioned. Toward the end of the evening, Webb finally looked him right in the eyes and asked, "Do you really want to get on a recon team?"

Joe assured him that it was something he wanted more than anything, so Webb said he would see what he could do. The next day, Colonel Smith strolled into the dispensary and told Parnar to move his gear into the RT Texas team room. He said that Webb had a medic on his team who wanted off recon for his last three months of duty. Just like that, Joe was on a recon team, and began training with RT Texas as the third American, just behind One-One Paul Morris.[3]

Parnar trained with Webb's team for three weeks into early July before he was moved to a new assignment. He joined ST Ohio under One-Zero Bob Kotin and undertook his first mission during July, a walkout practice mission in which he gained valuable experience in team procedures. Before the month was complete, RT Ohio would be handed off to Staff Sergeant Tommy Carr—Parnar's third recon team leader in little more than a month. Kotin, suffering from a nasty round of malaria contracted in the field, was being shipped out to Pleiku for treatment.

Such was the ever-changing movement of experienced men between teams as enlistments expired, men were injured, or veterans were called to special duties elsewhere. The fluidity of Green Berets was challenging for the Kontum staff to manage but Colonel Smith was fortunate in receiving a welcome old face back into his fold during the summer to ease the burden. Captain Ed Lesesne, badly wounded in February 1967, was back. After recovery in a Japanese hospital, he had returned to Stateside duty until he was fully recovered. Lesesne had enjoyed time with his family at Fort Jackson, but his services in Vietnam were sorely missed.

As the new recon company commander, Lesesne helped Lieutenant Colonel Smith sort through the ample fresh faces that arrived at Kontum in late June 1968. The siege at Khe Sanh had forced the closing of FOB-3 by month's end, and although a new FOB-3 was soon opened at Mai Loc, some of the recon men were shuffled off to other bases in the interim to fill voids.

Among those new arrivals was Staff Sergeant Philip McIntire Brown, a tough Scotch Irish veteran from California who arrived from FOB-3 as RT New York was being reconstituted. One-Zero Robert Kline had completed his tour and his one-one, Dennis Mack, was shifted into RT Colorado. New York was given to Staff Sergeant Jim McGlon, who returned from his brief extension leave to learn of the tragedy that had fallen on his Team Nevada in June.

McGlon took Brown as his one-one and set to work forming his team for upcoming missions. He learned that Phil Brown was a hard-luck kid who had found his calling in the Green Berets. Phil's parents and his siblings were separated at a young age, leaving him to be raised by his mother and stepfather—who was a captain with the Glendale Police Department. Phil joined the Army's 82nd Airborne in 1960 after being kicked out of high school "for drinking too much beer and enjoying myself." His knack for getting into altercations was just beginning. While in the States in 1963, he was charged with assault for kicking a neighbor in the head who had shot Phil in the wrist. He would remain out of the service for a year while his lawyer tried to clear up the court case. Fortunately for him, his accuser was convicted of shooting and killing two other people and Brown was exonerated of the charges against him.

Phil attended Ranger School in 1964, followed by SF training group in 1965. Brown had another altercation at Fayetteville, this time with a group of Bungi Indians. "It was a knife fight and I was the only one without a knife," he said. His face was badly slashed, leaving a long scar that led to a covey rider nicknaming him "Scarface" after he joined SOG. By 1966, Brown had been deployed to Vietnam on an A-team, where he became friends with Jim McGlon. When the two were transferred from FOB-3 to Kontum, it was only natural that the pair formed their own team.

McGlon added a third American to RT New York to carry the radio, Sergeant Bill Bumps. The son of an Air Force pilot, Bumps spent much of his childhood attending school in various states and even in the Philippines and Japan. He enlisted in the Army in 1966 and had served as an A-Team radio operator until volunteering for SOG in the summer of 1968.

The first mission across the fence for Bumps, Brown, and McGlon in late July proved to be a tough initiation. Laos was in the rainy season as early August began. Monsoon season created such foul weather that the team was unable to be extracted for twelve days. "The creeks were turned into rivers," Brown said. "Our Montagnards were forced to find food for us on the barks of trees." McGlon spent several days dodging three elephants that tramped around through the muddy jungle and seemed to follow his team. By the time New York was finally extracted, all three Green Berets had contracted malaria. Scarface Brown would take temporary command of the team for its next two missions while McGlon was hospitalized with a more severe battle with his malaria.

✦◇✦

Spike Team Delaware also had a new team leader by late June. Gene Williams had only one mission under his belt when he took over Delaware from veteran One-Zero Terry Dahling. A former Duke University student who had dropped out to join the Army, Williams was making his second tour in Vietnam. His twin brother Jack had also joined Special Forces six months after him and had been assigned to the Special Forces A camp at Dak Pek—part of a network of camps controlled by a B camp based in Kontum.[4]

Williams made his first trip across the fence within three days of reaching base as one-one for Dahling's RT Delaware, with Specialist Fourth Class Frank Richards as his one-two. The team inserted into the mountains of Cambodia, west of the highway between Kontum and Pleiku due to a recent ambush of a U.S. convoy. Dahling had his men close enough to the roadway that squads of enemy soldiers passed within ten yards of their position. After his first mission, Williams was recommended to take command of the team when Dahling received transfer orders.

A mere five days later, Williams and his new One-One Frank Richards were leading a revamped team, including a new interpreter and several new Montagnards, on his first mission into a mountainous area of Laos north of Ben Het to monitor an NVA infiltration route. Delaware came under enemy fire during its insertion, and Richards sprained his ankle during a ten-foot leap from his chopper. He was medevaced the following day, as was a Montagnard who was accidentally shot by a fellow indigenous team member. Williams kept the balance of his team in for another five days of monitoring the Ho Chi Minh Trail, but found some of his Montagnards to be so mutinous that he fired them upon returning to base. After hiring a loyal group of indigenous men and spending weeks in training, Williams felt ready for his next assignment, an insertion into Laos area X-Ray-3 on July 13, to plant four 26-pound anti-tank mines on Highway 96. His one-two was Specialist Fifth Class Jimmy Marshall, a former pitcher for the Pirates baseball organization who was also part Seminole Indian. The team faced enemy contact the second day across the fence, but Williams managed to shake his pursuers to continue with his original mining mission.

Recon Team Delaware finally holed up on the side of a mountain near Highway 96, where Marshall planted the team's mines in the road during the predawn hours of July 17. Sometime later, as Williams and company waited for their extraction choppers, they heard one of their road mines explode. North Vietnamese soldiers soon had the team pinpointed, and they narrowly survived a McGuire rig extraction under heavy fire. "I was pretty proud of the whole operation," Williams said, "the first successful mining operation by the FOB in two years."

◆◇◆

Pappy Webb was an exception to almost every rule at FOB-2. Unlike newer one-zeros like Gene Williams, Bryon Loucks, and Jim Tramel, he had been in command of his RT Texas for nine months. Although his official code name was "evergreen," he had long since dismissed it in favor of "pappy" whenever he spoke to covey riders over his team radio. Newer team leaders often picked up some of their best survival skills by listening to the advice of veterans like the forty-one-year-old Webb.

Webb, a decorated Korean War veteran, was already something of a Kontum legend. Stories of his bravado across the fence were often the subject of scuttlebutt in the base bar, where Webb could drink most men under the table. His parents had run a busy liquor store back in northwest Texas, at the edge of a wet county that butted up to two dry counties. One of the favorite bar stories involved Webb's destruction of an NVA truck on the Trail. Instead of mining the road, he tossed a Claymore mine in the back of a passing truck, waited until the hundred yards of wire zipped toward its end, blew the charge, and then had his team run like hell before the NVA could react. Webb was also known to go into the field with nonregulation weapons, including a modified M60 machine gun. "Pappy went to the Fifth Special Forces and had it modified by a Filipino weapons specialist," said Sherman Batman. "He lightened it up, cut the barrels down, and transformed it into a usable weapon he could carry into the field."[5]

His courage under fire was never questioned, even if he did run through quite a few junior team members on his team. One of his new assistant team leaders lasted only a few days. "The kid that came in to be Pappy's new replacement brought a green parrot with him that he kept in the Team Texas hooch," Wilson Hunt recalled. "He turned it loose and let it fly all around their hooch." Webb returned to his room from the base club, only to find fresh bird droppings all over his gear, his bunk, and his team maps. "We were standing outside our hooches cooking steaks on the grill," said Hunt. "All of a sudden we heard screaming and cussing, followed by the sound of automatic gunfire." Hunt, Bill Janc, and their comrades ducked for cover around the fire pit until they realized what had happened. "Pappy had grabbed his CAR-15 and dissolved that bird!"[6]

A team parrot was not the only animal casualty at Kontum during the summer of 1968. Covey Rider Gerry Denison felled a cow with his .38-caliber revolver after one late night in the base club. He was in company with RT Maine's Hunt and Bill Janc as they stumbled back toward their hooches. "We were looking down the road to see if any guards were out," said Hunt, "and here's this cow standing down the way in the middle of the road. Denison pulled out his .38, aimed down the road and took one shot. Bang! I guess he got it right in the head, because that cow went down spraddle-legged right in the middle of the road."

Sergeant Billy Waugh, who was training a Montagnard company in their nearby camp across the road, raced out to find out what the gunfire was about. Denison took off, leaving Janc and Hunt to sort out the mess and who would pay for the dead cow. "We tried to cook it on the fire pit by the team rooms," said Hunt. "It didn't work out well. It was tough."[7]

Hunt came to respect the wisdom of one-zeros like Webb as he went through several teammates of his own in the first months of running RT Maine. Webb had dismissed his one-one who brought the ill-fated parrot into his hooch, and his stream of revolving team members seemed never-ending until he took on twenty-two-year-old Specialist Fourth Class Paul Morris in early June. Morris, who lasted more than a half-dozen missions with RT Texas, found the team most often ran light, with himself, Webb, and four Nungs. He learned that Webb generally did not fine his indigenous troopers for screwing up in the field, a reprimand that cost them much-needed funds and caused their families to suffer. "If they screwed up in the field, he would wait for them at the base gates the next morning," said Morris. "Instead of fining them, he would cold-cock them as they came through the gate, and just knocked them on their asses."

When he was not training his team or in the field, Webb spent time with his Vietnamese girlfriend Leiah and her family in the little apartment

Green Berets of ST Texas at the Dak To launch facility in 1968. *Left to right:* Specialist Fourth Class David Gilmer, Sergeant Joe Parnar, and Sergeant First Class Clarence "Pappy" Webb, one-zero of ST Texas. *Jason Hardy*

he had rented just outside the wire on the north edge of the Kontum compound. Bryon Loucks and Joe Parnar were amused with the little banana cat (civet) that Webb kept as a pet in his apartment. Parnar accompanied the RT Texas one-zero on a monthly food ration run to the Army distribution center at Pleiku. "I got my first real taste of Special Forces scrounging while on this trip," Parnar said. Webb quickly occupied the supply soldier with obtaining two cases of string beans. In the soldier's absence, Webb and his men loaded their three-quarter-ton truck with cases of other items stacked nearby. "We must have left with twice as many canned goods as we were allotted," Parnar recalled.[8]

Paul "Slipknot" Morris learned plenty of valuable lessons from Webb when RT Texas was across the fence. He learned how to make a proper RON site by first advancing ninety degrees in one direction into a thicket for a hundred yards before doubling back near their former trail before settling down. "We could see the former path we had made, so if somebody was tracking us they would have to go past where we were hiding," said Morris. Another standard operating procedure that Webb taught him was how to break contact with superior NVA forces by splitting their team into two columns. "Our two front men would engage the bad guys until they were out of ammunition," he said. "Then they would run down the line to reload as the next two guys took over firing. During this process, we were progressing away from the enemy until we were ready to take off and beat feet out of there."

Morris' string of successful missions with Webb came to an end due to an accidental discharge of a Swedish K submachine gun in the Kontum base bar. His buddy Jimmy Marshall was demonstrating to a group of 4th Division soldiers how to properly break down and reassemble the weapon when it discharged a four-round burst. Two men received minor wounds from the ricocheting bullets and another round tore through Morris' ankle. Medic John Hobart patched him up, but Morris was forced to ship out on medical leave for six weeks.

Webb reluctantly relieved Morris, picked up David Gilmer as his new one-one, and continued running RT Texas in his unique style. Webb had little patience for the endless stream of questions that always followed a mission, even though he knew it was the S2's job to ascertain the most minute details about field conditions, terrain, and anything out of the ordinary encountered in the field. Webb reported finding numerous elephant droppings while across the fence but soon tired of the queries regarding the size, volume, amount of moisture in the stool, and other intelligence questions. On his next target, he carried along a little plastic dishpan acquired from a local market and retrieved a fresh pachyderm specimen for intelligence. When the post-mission briefing inevitably led to a quiz session on the freshness of the elephant dung, Webb dumped his artifact on the officer's desk and invited him to examine it himself.

✦◇✦

Although Wilson Hunt admired the hardcore spirit of grizzled team leaders like Webb, he found closer bonds with less experienced SOG men like himself who were similarly earning their stripes as new team leaders.

One of his closest friends at Kontum was Sergeant First Class Wayne Melton, who had become the one-zero of RT Hawaii during April. Like Hunt, Melton was a married man with kids back home; he had been assigned to FOB-2 shortly after the Tet Offensive commenced. Born and raised in Wichita Falls, Texas, Melton had joined the Army right out of high school, was first assigned to an A-team in Vietnam, but then found the rumor of hot action with SOG to be his new focus.

Melton was first assigned to RT Hawaii under One-Zero Mel Trafford, a tall Texan who sported a big handlebar mustache. They served together briefly as a team before Trafford was transferred and Melton was handed the team. He found his first one-one to be below his own standards in the field, so Melton was still trying to meld his unit during late July when he was assigned a new mission across the fence. He had taken on Sergeant First Class Ethyl Duffield, the base first sergeant, to fill in as his assistant team leader. As they prepared to insert from Dak To with their Nung teammates, Melton was joined by a new officer assigned to ride with them for experience.

Melton hurriedly briefed Lieutenant Michael McFall at the launch site on what he expected in the field. On the ground, RT Hawaii executed a long-range patrol deep into Laos that spanned several days. During late morning on July 28, Melton found that Duffield appeared weary from little sleep in their previous evening's RON—that could be a problem when it was time to go to work. The team located a well-worn enemy trail around midday where Melton believed they could successfully take an enemy prisoner. "This place was just a textbook example of how to spring an ambush," he said. He contacted Covey Rider Dallas Longstreath and explained his plans for an ambush. "Negative," came the reply. "There's another team in trouble and we don't have the air assets to help you, also," said Longstreath. But Melton was determined not to pass up the perfect prisoner snatch opportunity.

Longstreath relayed that the Kontum XO was ordering them to stand down from the prisoner snatch. "Tell them to fuck off," snapped Melton.

His CAR-15 automatic weapon always moving with his eyes, Joe Walker, one-zero of Recon Team California, moves cautiously while on patrol in enemy terrain. *Joe Walker*

SOG recon teams were a composite of Green Berets and indigenous members—originally South Vietnamese or Chinese Nungs. By late 1966, FOB-2 teams began using men from local Montagnard villages, as was the case with RT Maine, seen here in June 1968. In the back row (*left to right*) are: Hit, Jeng, Sergeant First Class Wilson Hunt (one-zero), rifleman Chek, Zero-Two Hihn, grenadier Wung, and Staff Sergeant David Warrum (one-two). Kneeling (*left to right*) are: Staff Sergeant Roger Loe (one-one), Y-Yaur, grenadier Munh, and an interpreter Hunt soon removed from the team. Seated in front is Zero-One Kiep, the indigenous team leader. *Wilson Hunt*

Gerald Howland, one-zero of ST Hawaii, after being awarded a Silver Star with Charles Kerns at medal ceremony. *Charles Kerns family via Jason Hardy*

One-Zero Dick Meadows with one of the prisoners he captured in 1966. *Jason Hardy*

J. D. Bath seen on Leghorn in 1966. *Jerry Lee via Jason Hardy*

Right: The recon company patch for FOB-2 Kontum. *Larry Spitler*

Some of FOB-2's Green Berets of the original Kontum Thirty-Three seen during down time in 1966 at Saigon. *Left to right:* Jim Hetrick, Al Fontes, Charlie Humble, Rat Wilson, Lloyd "Snake" Adams, Bob "K9" Brown, Robert "Squirrel" Sprouse, J. D. Bath, and Larry Spitler. *Larry Spitler*

The top-secret radio-relay site called Leghorn was established in January 1967 on a mountaintop in southern Laos. Proposed by Lieutenant Ken Sisler, the site originally known as Heavy Drop was unreachable by NVA forces. *Brian Michael photo via Joe Parnar*

The area of Laos known as "the Bra," seen from the northeast looking southwest. This double curve of the Dak Xou was heavily defended by the NVA and included lethal CCC target locations Hotel-9, India-9, and Juliet-9 near Highway 110, which ran along the river. *Luke Dove photo via Joe Parnar*

THE DISTINGUISHED SERVICE CROSS

Eight Kontum-based Green Berets were awarded the nation's second highest military honor, the Distinguished Service Cross. Six of them are seen here.

Sergeant First Class Morris "Mo" Worley (*left*) was severely wounded in action during his DSC mission on January 20–21, 1967. *Jason Hardy*

First Lieutenant Tom Jaeger received the DSC for his actions on November 15–19, 1968, during the SLAM VII mission. *Tom Jaeger via Jason Hardy*

Sergeant First Class Linwood Dwight Martin was killed in action on March 22, 1968, while leading RT Delaware. *Jason Hardy*

Left: Sergeant First Class Bob Howard (at a 1968 awards ceremony at Kontum) was written up for the Medal of Honor for his actions on November 21, 1967, but the award was later downgraded to the Distinguished Service Cross. *Joe Parnar collection*

Right: Captain James Douglas Birchim was declared Missing in Action after a recon mission with RT New Hampshire on November 15, 1968. *Barbara Birchim*

Left: Staff Sergeant Leonard Tilley was one of the original thirty-three at Kontum. He became one-zero of ST Iowa, whose team sign he stands before. Tilley earned his DSC on February 7, 1967. *Leonard Tilley via Jason Hardy*

Many of the newer Green Berets at FOB-2 started out working the commo bunker at the Dak To launch site. Seen in this 1966 photo are Larry Spitler, the commo boss, and young Al Keller. *Larry Spitler*

A Kontum-based recon team is extracted from the Laos jungle via an aluminum ladder dangling below a Huey chopper. *Edward Wolcoff*

One-Zero Dick Meadows (*center*) with ST Ohio on USS *Intrepid* after their Bright Light. Chuck Kerns (*right*) is bandaged following the crash of his helicopter. *Kerns family via Jason Hardy*

Indian Gal 69, a Navy Sea King chopper, prepares to launch with One-Zero Dick Meadows and his Spike Team Ohio from the deck of the carrier USS *Intrepid* on a Bright Light mission on the morning of October 16, 1966. *U.S. Navy photo*

Indian Gal 69, damaged by gunfire, makes a forced landing in the South China Sea with half of Spike Team Ohio. Destroyer USS *Collett* (DD-730) is seen at the far left. *U.S. Navy photo*

Sea King pilot Dave Murphy masterfully kept his chopper afloat and stabilized while his Navy crew and ST Ohio moved to a rubber raft as destroyer *Collett* approaches. *U.S. Navy photo*

AIRCRAFT USED IN SOG MISSIONS

Sikorsky Kingbee helicopters were flown by South Vietnamese air crews. *Joe Parnar*

Cessna single-engine O-1 Bird Dog observation planes were flown by Covey pilots with rear-seat Covey Riders to assist SOG teams. *Joe Parnar*

UH-1 Huey chopper of the 57th Assault Helicopter Company. *Joe Parnar*

Recon Team Maine boarding a Huey slick at Kontum in 1968. *James "Mike" Tramel*

String extract. Sergeant Wilson Hunt, one-zero of RT Maine, demonstrates a string extraction above FOB-2 in mid-1968. *Wilson Hunt*

Below: McGuire rig extraction. Note the dangling recon men. *Tony Yoakum*

KONTUM RECON TEAMS

One-Zero Willie "Track Shoe" McLeod. *Frank Greco photo via Joe Parnar*

Staff Sergeant Tommy Carr (*left*), one-zero of RT Ohio, seen gearing up with his one-two, Sergeant Joe Parnar, in August 1968. *Bryon Loucks photo via Joe Parnar*

John St. Martin, (*left*) with Ed Wolcoff of RT New York, one day before St. Martin was severely injured across the fence. St. Martin has just finished applying camo paint to Wolcoff's face. The chest pouch on St. Martin carries a claymore mine. *Joe Parnar*

One-Zero Wilson Hunt and his indigenous team leader Kiep stand guard over a wounded NVA lieutenant his Recon Team Maine has just captured in Cambodia on September 25, 1968. *Wilson Hunt*

ACTION ACROSS THE FENCE

Below, left: A Kontum-based Hatchet Force team seen in 1967 advancing along a Ho Chi Minh side trail. *Mecky Schuler*

Below, right: A 57th AHC Huey landing to pick up RT New York in Laos. *Edward Wolcoff*

THE FIRST MEDAL OF HONOR MISSIONS

MACV-SOG's first Medal of Honor recipient was First Lieutenant George Kenton "Ken" Sisler. Seen here in jump gear after exiting a chopper, Ken Sisler (*left*) was killed in action on February 7, 1967. *Larry Spitler*

John Kedenburg, (*center, with gloves*) with radio in the field in May 1968. While leading Spike Team Nevada on June 13, 1968, Specialist Fourth Class Kedenburg was killed in action. He was later post-humously awarded the Medal of Honor. *Wilson Hunt*

Bright Light missions involved both aerial and ground support. *Left:* Chief Warrant Officer Michael D. Berry of the 189th Assault Helicopter Company was pilot of Ghostrider 153 during the Kedenburg extraction. *Joe Parnar. Center:* First Lieutenant Ewe Linder flew another of the extraction choppers. *Joe Parnar. Right:* Gerald "Grommet" Denison, a former one-zero, was flying as the Covey Rider on June 13. *Gerald Denison*

RT California One-Zero Joe Walker (*left*) is seen at Dak To with two of his wounded Montagnard team members following their extraction from the SLAM VII mission in November 1968. Note the medical tag affixed to one man, which informed medical personnel of what medications he had already been administered in the field. *Joe Walker*

An armed A-1 Skyraider (known by the call name Spad) was often the savior of a SOG team in danger of being overrun. *Don Engebretsen*

Above: Taken by Cougar co-pilot Tony Yoakum, this image shows Rick Griffith's broken chopper burning in the Laos jungle after it was shot down while extracting RT Maine on February 19, 1968. *Tony Yoakum*

Left: Sergeant First Class Fred "Zab" Zabitosky receives the Medal of Honor from President Nixon on February 20, 1969. Despite burns, shrapnel wounds, broken ribs, and several crushed vertebrae, Zab rescued men from a burning Huey under heavy NVA gunfire. *Department of Defense*

First Lieutenant Rick Griffith beside his 57th AHC slick in the Kontum compound. He and his co-pilot were pulled from its burning wreckage by Fred Zabitosky, who was later awarded the Medal of Honor. *Courtesy of Richard Griffith*

In this photo taken August 24, 1969, by Green Beret Mike Buckland, his Recon Team Maine is under fire at an LZ in Laos as Cobra gunship rockets pound the jungle around them. Kiep, one of the team's long-standing Montagnards, is seen in the foreground, crouching behind stacked rucksacks. *Mike Buckland*

In December 1968, Sergeant First Class Bob Howard was the fourth Kontum recon man to earn the Medal of Honor. President Nixon drapes the pale blue ribbon around Howard in the White House on March 2, 1971.

Sergeant First Class Louis Maggio and Vietnamese medic To suture a wound on medic Joe Parnar in the CCC operating room on January 8, 1969. Parnar was injured in an explosion while recovering the body of Staff Sergeant Robert Scherdin. *Bryon Loucks photo, courtesy of Joe Parnar*

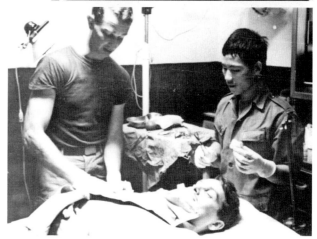

Left: Wilson Hunt, one-zero of RT Maine, seen with face paint and the traditional post-mission beer as he returns to the Kontum helipad following a 1968 recon action across the fence. *Wilson Hunt*

Right: Bob Howard carries a handcuffed wounded POW, captured by David Gilmer's RT Texas, from a chopper through the Kontum compound in July 1969. *Joe Parnar*

Below, right: In this photo taken by One-Zero Ed Wolcoff, black-clad members of his Recon Team New York scramble to board a 57th Assault Helicopter Company slick from a Prairie Fire landing zone in southern Laos. *Edward Wolcoff*

Lieutenant Colonel Fred Abt, base commander of CCC from March 7, 1969 to January 25, 1970. *Kyle Dean photo, courtesy of Joe Parnar*

Franklin Douglas "Doug" Miller, one-zero of RT Vermont, was the fifth Green Beret from Kontum to earn the Medal of Honor. He is seen here (*right*) with fellow One-Zero Ed Wolcoff. *Edward Wolcoff and Don Engebretsen*

Right: Edward Blyth, the one-two of RT Vermont, seen wearing face paint as he is flying in to a target area. *Edward Blyth and Don Engebretsen*

SOG survivors seen recovering at the Pleiku hospital in January 1970. Standing to left is Ed Blyth, who lost part of his left thumb on the mission where One-Zero Doug Miller earned the Medal of Honor. Miller is seated in front. *Edward Blyth and Don Engebretsen*

Staff Sergeant Doug Miller wearing his Medal of Honor following the June 1971 ceremony in Washington. Chief of Staff General William C. Westmoreland is at left. *White House photo*

"I can't tell him that," protested Dallas.

"Yes, you can!" snapped Melton. "Send it in long response. Fox, Uniform, Charlie, Kilo, Yankee, Oscar, Uniform. I want it transmitted just like that!"

A minute later, Melton asked, "Did you send that?"

"They got the message," Longstreath replied. "But it wasn't me that said it. They heard it from you over the radio."[9]

Despite orders to the contrary, Melton spread his eight-man team in an ambush position along the trail. He had his Nungs arrange Claymores in an L-shaped ambush in a big flat area along the trail near a stream. His men were on the uphill side of the flat area, near a little spring while Lieutenant McFall took three Nungs to man the north leg of the ambush, a position that offered little concealment. Melton spread himself out on a large rock near the trail, ready to spring the ambush when a patrol approached. He placed Duffield and another Nung behind him to protect the team from being surprised from the rear. Three hours of silence passed as RT Hawaii lay secured in rocks near the trail. "We were sitting there and Duffield was drifting off to sleep," said Melton. "I gave him one of these pick-me-ups we carried, a Black Beauty [amphetamine]."

Around 1400, McFall signaled that an enemy unit was approaching. Melton spotted a six-man patrol moving up the trail. The point man was followed closely by five other men, all tightly packed behind him. *Well, these are all rookies*, Melton thought. *You don't all bunch up like that. They probably feel safe.* Melton was lying flat on his stomach, with his M16 next to him and the Claymore clapper in his left hand. He watched the point man come across the stream and walk up to within arm's reach of his concealed position. He could see the NVA point man's hat and then his right eye.

At that instant, the enemy soldier made eye contact with the Green Beret. *Shit!* thought Melton. He instantly squeezed the trigger of his M16— which was no more than a foot from the NVA's right eyeball—and also hit the clicker in his left hand to detonate the Claymores.

Recon Team Hawaii took down the entire NVA patrol in one violent burst but suddenly found itself in a world of trouble. Swarms of enemy soldiers suddenly opened up on the team. *Dumbass!* thought Melton. *We've just taken down the point element for an entire company! We're in serious trouble now.*

Heavy automatic weapons fire erupted, along with hand-thrown and rifle-launched grenades from the NVA company. Melton, laying across a rock in an area with other protective rocks around him, was suddenly blown over onto his back by an incoming RPG. The grenade glanced off his head before it struck the rocks behind him and exploded, sending red hot splinters of metal tearing through his left shoulder. As he struggled to regain his senses, he heard Duffield shout: "You're hit in the chest!"

A wave of darkness swept over Melton. He did not feel pain but as he wiped his hand across his face, he saw that it was covered in his own blood. It ran down into his eyes, forcing him to wipe his face again. *Damn!* he thought. *If I'm hit in the chest, how come I've got blood on my face?* He was unaware at the moment that the RPG had glanced off his head before exploding. An eerie calm enveloped Melton for a moment as he lapsed from consciousness and felt an out-of-body experience in which he was looking down at the rock and his inert carcass. Shattered bodies lay around his own near the point where the Claymores had exploded, and enemy soldiers were forming behind that point as the firefight continued.

Duffield and a Nung quickly pulled Melton back up and tended to him as the rest of the team laid down heavy fire into the jungle. Duffield, wounded by another grenade that exploded five yards from his position, called in a prairie fire emergency and soon had air support working over their area to aid in their extraction effort. He ignored his own wounds, directing his team's fire while providing first aid under fire to a wounded Nung. Lieutenant McFall provided covering fire as the wounded men were moved through the jungle to a point deemed a likely extraction site.

Melton regained his senses and managed to retrieve his rucksack from where the patrol men had been killed. He examined the bodies of six NVA point men taken down by his Claymores and gunfire, and quickly confiscated some of their weapons and equipment before returning to his team. Melton's team then broke contact with the NVA company and moved to a small area suitable for extraction by McGuire rigs. He then had his team use composition C-4 explosive to blow down enough jungle cover to create an area for the choppers to drop in strings for them. Melton sent out most of his Nungs on the first choppers until he was finally left on the ground with Duffield, the lieutenant, and one Nung.

The next chopper came in and dropped four lines. Two of the wire rigs landed properly but the man in charge of rigging the other two failed to hook them in, causing the lines to drop to the jungle floor. Melton was furious—such a screwup could easily cost him his life. He sent Duffield and his last Nung up on the two good strings and then was forced to fight out anxious minutes on the ground with Lieutenant McFall until the two good rigs could be dropped back down again to pull him out. McFall assisted his wounded comrade into the McGuire rig before donning his own. Then the two warriors were lifted up through the jungle canopy and out of their little world of hell.

During the mission, Melton had admired the lieutenant's fancy new Seiko watch. Once safely outbound on their chopper, McFall slipped off his watch and handed it to Melton as a showing of gratitude for having survived his first combat. Melton appreciated the gesture, but he was still furious at the chopper crew's snafu with the McGuire rigs. When they landed at the base, men were standing by to offer them their customary can of beer.

Melton brushed right past the proffered brews and sought out the man in charge of preparing the McGuire rigs. "I walked right over there and punched that son of a bitch right in the mouth," he said. He finally cooled down and after the debriefing officer learned of the mistake, nothing further was said about it. Melton, McFall, and Duffield would be awarded Purple Hearts and Bronze Stars for their July 28 firefight.

Wayne Melton was left wishing for more experienced men he could take across the fence with him next time.

✦◇✦

Prior recon experience allowed one Green Beret who arrived at FOB-2 during the summer of 1968 to assume a one-zero role almost immediately. Staff Sergeant Joe Walker was handed the reins to RT California just three days after reaching Kontum.

To the uninformed, Walker certainly did not look the part of a fearless one-zero at first glance. He was a gangly fellow with horn-rimmed glasses who could have passed for a school teacher. But within him burned the spirit of a warrior—a man who loved combat, understood the value of proper tactics, and volunteered for the hottest of combat zones on a regular basis. It was only fitting that his recon code name was "gladiator."

Joe Johnnie Walker came into the world in West Virginia, in 1943. His father, Lawrence Joseph Walker, met his new son in the hospital room in full celebration, with a bottle of Johnnie Walker scotch in his hand. His tough-love wife decided the couple would name their first son Joe Johnnie in honor of his father's preferred name and his favored whiskey.

Young Joe started school in West Virginia but was moved around quite a bit after that as his father worked different jobs. His mother was the dominant force in his youth as he attended school alternately in Delaware, Ohio, and Arizona. He finished high school in West Virginia in 1960 and immediately enlisted in the Army to see the world. During his advanced infantry training, his superiors discovered that he had a knack for spelling and typing. "I typed forty words a minute correctly, so the army was impressed with that," said Walker. "They put me through clerical school."[10]

Once he reached the 25th Infantry Division, however, there were ample clerks and typists at the battle group headquarters. His staff sergeant remarked, "I'm glad you can type. I'll keep that in mind but right now we need infantrymen. I'm sure you being from West Virginia, you've shot a rifle before and you'll get the hang of it." Walker was thus assigned to an infantry company based in Hawaii, where he had the chance to travel to exotic island countries. He took his discharge after three years, returned to the States and began working in Arizona.

Restless, he hitchhiked to Colorado and ended up working with explosive materials for the Climax Molybdenum Corporation. Mining was tough work, but Joe saved enough money to pay cash for a brand new 1964 Ford Galaxy SL 500. By late 1965, he joined the Army again as the Vietnam War was escalating. He was sent to the 82nd Airborne as an ordnance man, but began processing his paperwork to transfer to Special Forces. By 1967, he was stationed at Fort Bragg in SF with three military occupational specialties (MOSs): infantryman, heavy infantry weapons specialist, and military field intelligence.

After arriving in Vietnam as a specialist fourth class, Joe Walker was assigned to Project Delta, where he did long-range reconnaissance patrols near the Fifth Group headquarters. He had heard about SOG through the grapevine but had heard that getting into that elite group required a soldier to be ranked as a sergeant or higher. "I asked the sergeant major about promotion," Walker said. "He said the only way you get promoted here is to take a prisoner. When you get off the helicopter with a prisoner, you'll be promoted to sergeant, E5."

He kept that offer in mind. By his fifth mission, he was the senior adviser in a small patrol when his team captured a Vietnamese prisoner of war and he was promptly promoted, as promised, to sergeant. Six months later, Sergeant Walker's team went into the Ashau Valley on May 11, 1968, to infiltrate a heavily patrolled enemy area about fifty miles from supporting forces. Walker spotted numerous enemy soldiers near a small stream and decided to try for another prisoner, waiting until he had two enemy soldiers by themselves in the stream bed. Joe calmly fired and wounded one and then laid down supporting fire so that his team could nab the injured soldier.

Other NVA began swarming the area as Walker called for extraction choppers. He led his team across the open stream to an LZ, while calling in gunships to suppress his opposition. He waited until his team had secured their prisoner on board before being the last to jump on. "I was promoted to E6 [staff sergeant]," he said of his second POW snatch. "Things were going pretty good with Project Delta."

Things changed for Joe Walker when a tough new sergeant major took over his unit at Nha Trang; Walker felt constrained. *I can do better than this*, he thought. He went to Fifth Group headquarters, applied to MACV-SOG for a new position, and within two hours was on board an airplane into FOB-1 in Da Nang to in-process. Walker stayed there two nights, got on another plane into Kontum, and was assigned to RT California in July of 1968.

Staff Sergeant Walker quickly became the one-zero of RT California based on his experience running recon missions as a senior adviser with Project Delta. His new team was still out in the field when he reached FOB-2. The one-zero, Sergeant First Class Bobby Barnes, was a former football player for the University of Buffalo; he was a husky man who tipped the scales at about 240 pounds. His one-two, Tom Cunningham, recalled: "I probably weighed only 150 pounds at the time. Barnes was a hell of a nice guy but we used to kid him that if anything ever happened to him, we'd have to cut him up to get him out of there."[11]

That was nearly the case on July 14, as Barnes and his team were on long-range patrol when they discovered six NVA soldiers making radio contact with their headquarters. Barnes decided that RT California should attempt a prisoner snatch and withdrew his men to make radio contact with FOB-2 to announce his intentions. During this time, visual contact with the NVA radio crew was lost and Barnes was unaware that an enemy company had moved into his immediate area after his departure.

Upon his return, Barnes advanced alone to the radio site and was within a few feet of it when he was sighted by an NVA sentry. Barnes quickly killed the guard and radio crew before they could open fire on his team but his fire brought the NVA company to full alert. He ordered his team to retreat to higher ground and establish a defensive perimeter on the crest of a nearby hill. Barnes remained behind to delay the assault of the approaching enemy while his one-one, Sergeant Tony Love, made radio contact with their covey. Barnes exposed himself to intensive fire while fighting off the NVA advance before hurrying to the hilltop to join RT California. Love soon noticed enemy soldiers trying to encircle their position, so he moved outside the team's defensive perimeter to plant Claymore mines along their likely advance while under heavy enemy fire. Love then moved from position to position, spotting enemy concentrations so Barnes could call in precise air strikes against them.

Barnes and his team fought back with their rifles and grenades to keep the NVA at bay until they could be extracted. Everyone escaped without injury but it was a rough ride out on strings through the canopy. There was considerable joking for big Bobby Barnes about the strain he had put

Staff Sergeant Joe "Gladiator" Walker, the fearless one-zero of RT California, seen with his pet boa, Georgia, at Kontum. *Joe Walker*

on the chopper that had to lift his massive frame out on a string. But his valor under fire earned him a Silver Star for the heavy losses he, Love, Cunningham, and their indigenous teammates inflicted before their removal.

"He was a big man," Joe Walker said of Barnes. "His Stabo rig wouldn't fit around his legs." Because of his massive frame, Barnes was urged to find another job on the base for his own safety and that of his team. He was a popular man and became even more so when Colonel Smith allowed "Big Bob" to settle in as the club manager for Kontum's base bar. And just like that, Joe Walker found himself in charge of RT California.

His initial orders were simple. "You're the new One-Zero. Be successful and return with your objectives complete." Walker would indeed immediately prove to be one of SOG's most successful one-zeros. Tony Love remained with him during his first days on RT California, helping Walker become oriented to his indigenous teammates and the lay of the land at Kontum. His one-two, Tom Cunningham, was moved to RT Colorado and Love would soon transition into a role flying as a covey rider.

During his first trips across the fence, Walker always returned with his objectives complete. His assignments varied widely. "The mission was whatever they gave you at the moment," he said. "It might be to mine the road for tanks and vehicles, to set up an ambush, to do an area reconnaissance, to take pictures, recon a bridge, recon the Ho Chi Minh Trail, or to attach devices to convoys moving at night with timed M1A pencils that would illuminate the convoy at night so they could bring in an Air Force strike. I had some heavy contact with the enemy on my first missions but succeeded in surviving."

Walker initially ran RT California as a small team, with one other American to carry the radio, and five Sedang Montagnards. Like Webb, he went through a variety of junior Green Beret team members who did not stay on the team long. In August, California was assigned an officer, twenty-two-year-old First Lieutenant James Birchim from Independence, California. Joe Walker was three years his senior in age and had far more years of Army experience. "Officers weren't very pleased to be commanded by an E6," he said. "I always looked kinda young and baby-faced."

Some lieutenants and captains were put off by having a noncommissioned officer serving as their superior in the field, but Lieutenant Birchim was not. Together, they ran several successful missions with Staff Sergeant Walker as the one-zero until Birchim was moved into command of his own recon team in October 1968.

Aside from his willingness to take on the hottest target areas, Walker was also the first Kontum one-zero who kept a python as a pet; he named the snake Georgia. He was at the Dak To launch site when he found several soldiers debating on whether to shoot a snake, toss it back into the jungle, or give it to the Montagnards to eat. The reptile's previous owner had been killed by a rocket. "So, I took it back to camp and let it live in the mortar pit outside my hooch," said Walker. "It was camp entertainment once a week when I would feed her a chicken or some small animal. The only problem was when she would sometimes crawl into my hooch and settle in between me and my poncho liner. Then she would open her rear, make a big deposit of bones and feathers, and then crawl out to leave me with that."

With the exception of his two M79 grenadiers, Walker's team carried CAR-15s in the field. He was open to integrating new weapons into his arsenal, employing anti-tank rocket launchers, a 60-mm mortar, and even sawed-off machine guns at times. On one mission along Highway 110, Walker slipped up close enough to a passing NVA convoy to drop incendiary grenades rigged with delay detonators into the trucks' cargo compartments. His grenades and a follow-up air strike wiped out at least fifteen enemy trucks without his team ever being noticed. Walker also used extraordinary tactics to shake pursuers in the field. When trackers were too close on his team near Highway 110 on one mission, he took his men right onto the road during broad daylight to put a couple of miles between him and his enemy. He knew the NVA trackers could not easily follow their tracks on the hard-packed road surface and would certainly not expect any Americans to be crazy enough to run down their road in the daylight.[12]

Walker trained RT California in between missions to ensure they maintained harmony and control in the field. His men understood to the letter what was expected of them in any situation without him having to say a word. As he explained to a fellow Green Beret, "If you move properly and the NVA see you in a controlled, team formation, they probably won't stay and fight."[13]

Those who did fight Joe Walker—the gladiator—more often than not ended up on the losing side of the match. Within months of reaching FOB-2 in the summer of 1968, Joe Johnnie Walker was already becoming something of a Kontum legend.

Chapter Thirteen

THE WOLFKEIL BRIGHT LIGHT

SOG recon men lived to fight another day in many cases thanks to the top-notch air support they received while operating across the fence. When a chopper or aircraft went down, recon teams went on Bright Light duty to retrieve the downed crewmen or their bodies with the same urgency they used to pull out fellow Green Berets. There was a bond of brotherhood between recon men and their shepherding aviators that generally went unspoken but was felt by all. The August 1968 Bright Light efforts to recover Major Wayne Benjamin Wolfkeil are a testament to this bond.

The thirty-six-year-old Air Force pilot was downed while flying air support in Laos on August 9 for RT Florida. Wolfkeil, a solid man of six feet in height and two hundred pounds, was a native of Wilkes-Barre, Pennsylvania; he who had played football at Penn State. On this date, he was flying his A1-H Skyraider attached to the 6th Special Operations Squadron from Pleiku Air Base. He and his wingman had been dispatched on a Steel Tiger strike into southern Laos. Wolfkeil's hometown sweetheart Anne Marie was at home raising the couple's four children as he and his section leader, Major Bill Constantine, took their Spads in to assault NVA troops near the insertion point of RT Florida.[1]

Recon Team Florida was led by One-Zero Richard Vanderzwalm, who took over the team two months earlier when Bill Hanson was given a special assignment at CCN. Vanderzwalm had been directed to insert his team approximately twenty miles northwest of Dak To. Covey FAC 541, Major Daniel A. Wright, buzzed the area with Covey Rider Gerry Denison on board as the lead chopper settled in. Vanderzwalm jumped from the Huey, followed by several Montagnards.

Major Wayne Benjamin Wolfkeil, pilot of Spad 36, was killed in action supporting Recon Team Florida on August 9, 1968. One-Zero Wilson Hunt's RT Maine would conduct a Bright Light mission to the crash site weeks later. *David Wolfkeil*

In the second chopper, One-One Ralph Rodd prepared to insert with the other half of the team. Rodd had been assigned to RT Florida in April with Sergeant First Class Bill Hanson, a veteran recon man on his third Vietnam tour who had assumed command of the team from outgoing One-Zero Ron Fanning. Rodd served as one-one under Hanson until that NCO left in late June, and Staff Sergeant Vanderzwalm took over RT Florida, retaining Rodd as his assistant team leader.

Vanderzwalm and the first half of the team were taken under fire just as their chopper departed. He immediately opened up on his radio and aggressively waved off the second chopper with Rodd and the rest of his team. For Rodd, it was the first time he had been shot out of an LZ when half of his team was already on the ground. His Huey was just nestling into a hover when it began taking heavy small-arms and automatic-weapons fire from the west side of the LZ from along the river. Rodd was just preparing to jump off when his helicopter began taking fire and the pilot abruptly lifted off.

Major Wright came in low over the area and dropped a smoke grenade to mark the target area. The Huey gunships pulled clear to allow the Spads to do their work. The pilots, Majors Constantine and Wolfkeil, had taken off from Pleiku Air Base at 1358. Spad 35, flown by Constantine, rolled in first to silence an NVA troop emplacement pointed out by the FAC and released his ordnance without incident. Right on his tail came Spad 36, flown by Wolfkeil. Enemy ground fire apparently made a direct hit on his Skyraider as he zoomed in. "As he reached his release point, he appeared to be trying to pull out or break right," reported Gerry Denison, the covey rider flying with FAC Major Wright.[2]

Wolfkeil did not release his napalm or CBU ordnance. "He rolled up on his right wing like he was trying a low-level barrel roll and impacted nose first almost upside down," said Denison.[3] Wolfkeil's plane, carrying its full load of weapons and fully fueled, exploded in a massive ball of flame. Denison did not believe there was any possibility of the pilot surviving the crash. He reported periodic secondary explosions for approximately one hour after Wolfkeil's crash. Vanderzwalm and his Montagnards were finally picked up after surviving more than ninety minutes under fire from heavy enemy resistance. "Fortunately, they weren't very good shots," Vanderzwalm said, as he and his indigenous troops made it out unscathed.[4]

An Army SF team was inserted into the area for an SAR mission but was unable to reach the crash site. Two fresh Spad pilots, Lieutenant Colonel Alexander E. Corey (Spad 37) and Captain Tommy R. Stroud (Spad 38) worked over the area as the team tried to close the scene. The team was unsuccessful, owing to rough terrain, heavy enemy resistance, deteriorating weather, and approaching darkness. The team was pulled out and further attempts to place a Bright Light team in during the ensuing days were frustrated by foul weather and heavy enemy resistance.[5]

Wolfkeil's crash site was still burning by nightfall, six hours after his impact. Since no one witnessed him eject from his Skyraider, he was officially listed as missing in action. Nearly two weeks would pass before another recon team could be inserted into the area. Major Linden Gill, a fellow Spad pilot and close friend of Wolfkeil had the unpleasant duty of inventorying his friend's effects and preparing them for shipment home. He held little hope for his buddy, as Bill Constantine told him there was no real chance of anyone making it out of the crash alive. The efforts to determine the fate of Major Wolfkeil were temporarily sidelined by heavy enemy resistance and weather, but the search would soon continue.

✦◇✦

Sergeant First Class Wilson Hunt had run a number of targets as one-zero of RT Maine. During the summer, his one-one, Roger Loe, was transferred by Sergeant Major Stratton to one-zero school. Hunt felt the move was as much because of Stratton's distaste for Loe's antics, but Loe would in fact return to begin training his own new team, RT Vermont.

Hunt used straphangers to carry his radio on several missions before he was finally assigned a regular one-two when Daniel William Janc reported into the FOB in mid-July 1968 and was assigned to RT Maine. Janc was a large man, six-foot-two inches in height, who hailed from Grand Island, Nebraska; he was new in-country, having just completed the Special Forces Training Group course at Fort Bragg. Although Loe was still in place as RT Maine's one-one when Janc arrived, his position as assistant team leader would quickly be filled by the big Nebraskan.

Wilson, who stood five-ten, commented on Janc's size (four inches taller and some fifty pounds heavier): "If I'm ever wounded, I expect you'll have no trouble carrying me out of there," he laughed. "But, I hate to say it, but if you're ever wounded, I won't be able to return the favor!"[6]

Shortly after Janc joined his team and Loe departed for training, Hunt volunteered to go out on an emergency Bright Light on the afternoon of August 2. Word had reached Kontum that One-Zero Jim Tramel's RT Illinois was surrounded by NVA and was having a rough time being extracted. Many of the Hueys had been shot up, so command decided to put Hunt's team in right before dark via H-34s flown by Vietnamese aircrews. Tony Love volunteered to go along with Hunt, and One-Zero Pappy Webb hopped into another chopper to offer fire support with a .30-caliber machine gun he had borrowed from one of the infantry squads. Hunt brought along his Montagnards from RT Maine, but left his less-experienced one-one, Bill Janc, behind. As their H-34s were refueling at Dak To, Hunt and Love sat listening to the action on the radio while tactical air support made runs to beat down the NVA.

Tramel, inserted into Laos with Sergeant Kent White as his one-one and Bill Mathews as his one-two, had encountered an NVA patrol while moving up a ridgeline. He soon found that the first enemy men he spotted moving down toward him were the point element of a heavy weapons unit. He and Mathews charged forward, killed the three point-element soldiers, and then came under intense counter-fire. Tramel soon spotted the source, an enemy bunker, so Mathews laid down covering fire as his team leader moved to take out the bunker.

Tramel crawled to within ten yards of the bunker and then wiped out the three-man crew with a hand grenade. Assistant team leader White was shot in the leg during the action and was nearly taken prisoner by the NVA before Tramel charged forward to save him. Tramel blazed away as he stood over White and based on the yelps coming from his wounded one-one, Tramel assumed he had been shot again. He soon found that White was just reacting to the hot brass shell casings that were dropping down into his open shirt. Radio operator Mathews continued laying down covering fire while his one-zero retrieved their wounded man.

Tramel picked up White and carried him twenty yards to the safety of RT Illinois' perimeter. He then called for tactical air support and gunships to enable his team to safely withdraw to an LZ area. Darkness was approaching, and the area was ablaze with NVA gunfire. Rescue ships moved in, while the FAC relayed the word to Kontum that additional support for the team might be needed during the night.

Tramel had serious concerns of his men surviving, especially with a wounded man preventing them from running during the overnight hours. Determined to make it out, he guided in the approaching choppers with his strobe light. The North Vietnamese had cut the trees off at about four feet to prevent a chopper from landing, so he stood atop a stump, waving his strobe and calling in air strikes until two slicks finally managed to pull the last of his men to safety while under heavy fire.

Tramel and Mathews each received the Bronze Star with "V" device and White was awarded his first Purple Heart. Love, Hunt, Webb, and the Montagnards of RT Maine standing by at Dak To felt great relief when word was received that Team Illinois had been successfully extracted. Hunt had not relished the thought of fighting it out through the overnight hours against a frenzied NVA force. "If we had spent the night out there, I'm not sure any of us would have made it," he said.

Hunt's team would be called into Bright Light duty again within weeks. In the interim, Kontum's recon company had its share of close calls and tight extractions, including the exfiltration of RT Colorado on August 23. One-Zero Mike Bingo, One-One Tom Cunningham, and their team inserted into Laos to inspect enemy tunnel systems on a mountainside. When the team encountered an approaching North Vietnamese soldier on the trail, Bingo had thoughts of pulling a prisoner snatch. The leading man turned out to be walking about twenty yards in front of a patrol, however, and Bingo's team ended up in a shoot-out during which their potential prisoner was shot.

Recon Team Colorado issued a prairie fire emergency call and their FAC soon had choppers moving in to get them. With darkness approaching, Bingo sent the first half of his team up through the triple canopy using McGuire rigs. The remaining men strapped themselves into their harnesses when rigs were dropped from the second Huey. Several had been wounded in the firefight, including Cunningham with minor shrapnel wounds in his chest and arm. Bingo had to assist one of his seriously wounded indigenous members into his rig.

The NVA assault forced their chopper pilot to pull out abruptly, creating a rough extraction, similar to the one Steve Roche had endured on John Kedenburg's last mission. "Instead of pulling straight up, the pilot put the nose down and tried to clear the area," said Cunningham. "He pulled us through the bamboo and one of the indigenous got knocked out." One-Zero Bingo, clinging to the wounded man he had strapped in, suffered injuries to his own neck and shoulder as his body smashed through bamboo during the extraction. "That bastard almost got pulled out of my arms," Bingo said.[7]

Recon Team Colorado survived the ordeal, but those on the second slick suffered cuts, bruises, and ripped gear during their harrowing ride through the treetops. When their chopper bounced them down on the runway a short while later, one indigenous trooper was still unconscious from his injuries. Mike Bingo's injuries were not serious but he ended up being sidelined for a couple of weeks with a bad case of malaria. When he was well enough to return to Kontum in September, he began training to fly as a covey rider, and his RT Colorado was handed over to Dennis Mack in the fall.

✦◇✦

Major Wayne Wolfkeil had not been forgotten by SOG. His Air Force Spad had been downed on August 9 in Laos, but since that time heavy enemy action and severe weather had prevented any recon teams from reaching the area. There was no belief that Wolfkeil was alive but Colonel Smith's base was still under orders to recover the pilot's body once the action and weather cleared.

On August 25, One-Zero Wilson Hunt and his RT Maine were tapped for the next attempt to go in after Wolfkeil. Hunt was only given the basic facts when he was called before the Kontum S3, First Lieutenant William Mansfield. He was told that a Skyraider supporting RT Florida had been lost earlier in the month. Loaded with ordnance and fuel when it was hit by AA fire, the Spad been seen in a right turn when it slammed into the ground on a heavily wooded hillside and exploded. Those in the air had seen no parachute and had since heard no beeper nor any voice contact from the pilot.

The job of RT Maine was to recover the pilot's body and any parts of the airplane that would identify it beyond all doubt. Hunt was not told the Spad pilot's name but was given the coordinates of where his plane had been seen to crash. Fog and clouds had obscured the mountainside crash area for two weeks, Mansfield continued. Attempts by other recon teams to retrieve the pilot's body shortly after the crash had failed due to weather and heavy NVA resistance. Hunt's team was being called in to search the area because he had spent considerable time training his men on rappelling into tight sites.

Hunt did a map study with the intel group during the late morning.

"Can you be ready to go first thing in the morning?" Mansfield asked.

"Yes, I can be," said Hunt.

"What about Janc, your new One-One? Will he be okay with you?"

Hunt explained that in his limited time with Bill Janc, everything looked good so far. Team Maine would thus be ready to go at first light. He returned to his hooch and informed his new assistant team leader that they would be rappelling into the crash site the following day.

That was when Janc offered some troubling news.

"I haven't rappelled."

"Don't worry about it, Bill," offered Wilson. "It's just like at school at Bragg. It's just like the rappelling tower there, except that you're going to come out and your feet aren't going to hit the side of the tower. It's just a free rappel from the chopper as it hovers over the canopy."

"Hunt, that's not what I mean," Janc protested. "I've never rappelled off anything!"

"You've got to be kidding me!"

In the rush to train new Green Berets at Fort Bragg, Janc had simply not been subjected to rappelling training. Hunt realized he had no time to waste. He had his interpreter Andre round up their Montagnards and explain the situation. The team gathered at the Kontum water tower for practice, some of the Montagnards giggling as the bulky Janc began making his first rappelling attempts. After an hour's practice, Hunt took the team to the helipad to a waiting chopper. The pilot lifted off about seventy-five feet from the ground and Hunt walked his new man through several rappels from the Huey's skid. He spent the rest of the afternoon drawing supplies and ammunition for their Bright Light.

Team Maine was flown up to Dak To the next morning, August 26. Hunt learned from the previous team's attempt to recover the pilot's body that the canopy in the area was particularly high. He managed to find two ropes that would reach a full 150 feet to clear the canopy, and Mike Bingo helped him prepare the ropes for the team by folding the ropes into a sand bag that was weighted with a rock. In theory, the heavy bags seemed like the perfect way to get the lengthy rope mass down through the jungle canopy without becoming tangled. Theory and reality proved to be two different things.

Once the slick went into a hover, crewmen threw the ropes out. Halfway down, the bag came off the ropes, leaving a tangled mess a hundred feet below the chopper. The Air Force was already working over the insertion area to keep down enemy fire, while Hunt, Janc, their Montagnards, and the chopper crew chief struggled with the badly twisted ropes. The team finally reported to Covey Rider Gerry Denison they were forced to cut the ropes off above the tangle. Left with only about one hundred feet length for rappelling in, Hunt and his team pondered their options as the slick pilot made lazy circles while allowing tactical air strikes to continue beating down opposition in their vicinity.

Denison's covey plane did several fly-overs until he spotted a riverbed with gravel bars that looked like an easier insertion point away from the high canopy. He radioed the Bright Light team that he believed they could be landed on one of the sandbars, but it was on the far side of the mountain, far from the Spad crash site. Hunt announced that he was willing to give it a try, so his slick went into a hover above the small river. RT Maine inserted onto the gravel bar of the stream, which was about thirty yards wide with a moderate flow.

They moved to the far bank but found it had steep banks slippery with mud. Precious minutes passed as they moved hundreds of yards along the bank in search of an easier point to ascend. The NVA, in the meantime, realized the American team was coming in from the far side of the mountain. Hunt began hearing signal shots in the distance as his enemy began closing in on their location. He and Montagnard team leader Kiep moved first across the river, chest deep in places, and then scrambled up into the bushes before Hunt motioned back to Bill Janc to follow with the other Montagnards.

The men moved into the undergrowth where they discovered a line of foxholes dug into the soft ground along the river bank. Hunt had Janc set up a perimeter while he moved through the foxholes to place toe popper mines in them. He reckoned that in the event of an air strike the explosives would be a nasty surprise for any NVA troops that tried to use them for shelter. The team then moved swiftly through dense undergrowth toward the base of the mountain they needed to climb. En route, they passed a big bivouac area with bamboo fences. Signal shots continued to ring out in the distance, so Hunt kept Maine moving swiftly past the enemy camp area and on up the base of the mountain.

By the time the team reached the top of the mountain, Hunt was fully aware that enemy soldiers were pursuing them. "We could see the treetops moving below as people were ascending," he said. "It was a natural tendency to grab saplings for support as you climbed, but it allowed us to see movement in the distance." The approaching soldiers appeared to be moving swiftly, so Team Maine responded by doing the same. Hunt moved his men down the other side of the mountain, shifting his line of advance to one side to help evade his pursuers.

The volume of tree movement below indicated a long line of NVA was sweeping up the mountainside behind them. Hunt realized his men still had two-thirds of the distance to cover to reach the crash site, but they had reached the point of no turning back. As his men neared a large gully in the hillside, he decided it was best to hunker down for the night in an RON position, hoping the enemy troops would sweep past them. RT Maine took position in some underbrush near the gully and waited in silence.

Hunt lay so still for some time that he wondered if he was even remembering to breathe. Occasional Vietnamese voices and the soft crunching of dry brush was drawing perilously close to his men. Hunt whispered to Janc and his Montagnards that nobody was to open fire unless he did so first or the NVA directly opened fire on them. Janc, who had been talking to Covey Denison in hushed tones, finally said they were going into radio silence as the enemy patrol moved in close.

Seconds passed like hours as trackers swept through their area. Each man lay motionless, clutching rifles and grenades, expecting the jungle to erupt. The nearest NVA shuffled past them just yards away but appeared to not notice the recon team. Hunt had his men remain still until the scuffling sounds of enemy feet moved on past their place of concealment. Using hand signals, he then motioned for his team to follow, slowly and carefully, down the back side of the mountain toward the crash site.

Moments later, the covey FAC announced that he could see NVA troops beginning to break out into a clearing on the top of the mountain. Denison quickly directed his TAC air to put in heavy strikes to assist RT Maine in its progress. Hunt felt some satisfaction that his trackers were now thoroughly shaken from their task of pursuit as gunships chewed up the mountaintop with cannon fire, napalm, and bombing runs. The canopy was too thick to see the enemy from his position, but Hunt could make out occasional muzzle flashes in the distance.

With the aid of the attacking planes, Maine moved forward swiftly and soon reached the crash site. The area was wide open, as the load of napalm on the A-1H had burned everything in the vicinity when Major Wolfkeil's plane crashed into the side of the mountain. Hunt's team had a body bag for removing the pilot if it proved to be possible. The Skyraider site was a mass of scorched undergrowth and the wreckage was scattered. The front cockpit was open, with no signs of the American pilot. The Bright Light team found no body parts, but did find the pilot's helmet, its nylon straps melted away. Hunt's men also collected parts of the plane, grabbing any metal shards that appeared to have identifying numbers on them.

The scorched hole in the jungle was also littered with CBU bomblets that had been scattered in the jungle. Some were unexploded, looking like oversized grapefruit with fins on them. Hunt had drawn sketches of such CBU with fins to warn his Montagnards about ever picking them up. Still, one of his indigenous troopers picked up some of the bomblets whose fins had snapped off and carried them to the Green Berets. Hunt and Janc immediately instructed their indigenous teammate to carry them away and lay them down carefully.

Once his team had scoured the crash site, Hunt felt that they had done their best to help at least identify the plane. Now it was time to get out alive. Denison called in air strikes to pound the area, hoping to keep enemy pursuit at bay as RT Maine scrambled for an LZ. Various Huey gunships swept over the mountainside, firing Gatling guns and dropping bombs on the NVA patrols that had nearly swept over the team. Hunt used the chaos to his full advantage, moving his men steadily toward a clearing at the bottom of the mountain that Denison had advised them of.

When they reached the area, Hunt realized there were too many saplings for any slick to hover close enough to extract his men. He positioned Janc and his Montagnards to cover him, while he, Zero-One Kiep, and Zero-Two Hihn crawled forward to place charges on the small trees to blow open a wider landing area. Janc remained in contact with covey, who asked him if they were clear enough from the crash site so that he could direct in more air strikes against NVA that could be seen swarming over the crash site. Janc told Denison to proceed but failed to warn his one-zero.

Hunt was still crawling through the elephant grass with Kiep and Hihn, setting charges, when a series of explosions rocked the jungle a short distance from them. "It scared the hell out of me," he said. "I let Janc know that he was never to call in air strikes again without first checking with me." As Janc would later recall, "I got my ass chewed."[8]

Recon Team Maine's one-zero then proceeded to blow his charges, felling enough saplings so that his team could call in the extraction slicks. At least one of the Spad pilots laying down the air strikes on the NVA was only too happy to do so. Major Linden Gill and Wayne Wolfkeil had become close friends in training, and they had come over to Vietnam together. After Wolfkeil had been declared MIA, it was Gill who had inventoried his friend's personal effects. His first real chance at vengeance now came as the circling covey rider directed the Spads to unleash ordnance and napalm loads on the NVA while making low passes over the jungle canopy. "We dropped everything we had on them," Gill said.[9]

Recon Team Maine was extracted from its hellacious Bright Light mission without injury, having spent a long afternoon evading enemy patrols. The recon men had recovered the pilot's helmet and enough aircraft parts for intelligence to hopefully confirm the identity of the missing Skyraider pilot. Wilson Hunt, however, never learned the outcome of this intelligence. Back in his hooch, he agonized over what the family must be thinking. He feared that they would be told their loved one had been declared MIA, leaving them hanging onto hopes that perhaps he had survived and been taken as a POW. Wilson felt certain inside, however, after viewing the horrific crash scene that the pilot had been killed instantly in the explosion. Wondering just who this mystery pilot was and if his family ever learned of his final fate haunted Hunt for decades.

Chapter Fourteen

DOUBLE TAKE

"Parnar, meet Dove. He's our new One-Two." Such simple words from One-Zero Tommy Carr in early September 1968 brought tremendous excitement to Specialist Fourth Class Joe Parnar. The arrival of Staff Sergeant Luke Dove meant that Parnar was graduating to the one-one position and would no longer be carrying RT Ohio's PRC-25 radio in the field. He thus proceeded to the base PX with Carr and drank more beer than he had ever consumed in a 24-hour period, passing out in his bunk long after midnight.[1]

Parnar had little time to nurse his monstrous hangover before Carr had his team back about their business of training for their next missions. Ohio next drew a local recon mission, Parnar's fifth, in which he collected more than a half-dozen leeches embedded in his body while hiking up a mountain stream. Parnar pulled one more camp perimeter recon mission during September before he was taken off recon and moved back into medical duties. "The experience of being in the jungle on recon would serve me well on future operations with the Hatchet Force," he said.[2]

The services of Joe Parnar, Bill Lensch, and the other FOB-2 medics were much appreciated by the recon men, as they often returned from the field wounded or otherwise beaten up from runs through the jungle. One-Zero Wilson Hunt returned banged up from a close call his RT Maine endured in early September. His men had successfully discovered and reported an NVA ammunition cache—including mortars and small arms—located on a mountaintop. Hunt's team moved toward a bomb strike LZ for extraction but came under attack before their exfiltration choppers could pull them free.

"We were down to drinking water out of the bomb crater," said Bill Janc.[3] The team was prepared to go down with a fight, taking enemies with them if they were overrun. Although things looked bleak, close air support finally suppressed the enemy sufficiently for a Huey crew to pull the first half of the team through the canopy on Swiss seats.

The final chopper then dropped its lines to pull out the last three men—One-One Janc, team interpreter Andre, and Hunt. The men had to move fast to strap in while under fire. Andre and Janc had sufficient line to snap into their Swiss seats, but the third line became fouled. Hunt ended up with the short rope, which was dangling nearly fifteen feet above the ground. His only chance to reach it forced him to swiftly scramble up a large tree that had been blown over in the bomb crater.

Hunt snapped into the D-ring and the chopper hauled the men clear. Dangling from their Swiss seats in mid-air while their Huey headed for Ben Het, Hunt had no idea he had been hit by either a grenade or bullet fragment while climbing the tree. "Once we were on the ground, the feeling began coming back to our legs, which had gone numb riding out on the strings," he said. "I noticed a squishing in my right boot. It was full of blood."[4] Hunt removed his boot to find his foot had been slashed severely enough to warrant the award of a Purple Heart, his second.

His debriefing with S3 Bill Mansfield included an exchange that had become familiar to Hunt. He had more than six months duty in the field, qualifying him to take on a less hazardous base job if he so opted.

"Well, Hunt," Mansfield started. "Are you ready to quit and take on a desk job? Was this your last target?"

"No." Hunt paused for a moment and then gave the officer his standard reply. "I think I can run one more."[5]

◆◇◆

The base club at Kontum was often the best source of field intelligence for Green Berets new to FOB-2. The more seasoned veteran recon men—like Pappy Webb, Bob Howard, and Squirrel Sprouse—had their fair share of stories to tell, and each returning team had fresh intelligence regarding what they had encountered across the fence. There was no bragging but there was plenty to learn over a few beers. "If someone did do something heroic, it was one of his teammates who would relate it," said Joe Parnar. "This was typically preceded by an introduction such as, 'You know what that stupid shit did?'"[6]

Just outside the base club, a small theater provided another form of evening entertainment, where the favorites shown included *The Green*

Berets, starring John Wayne, and spaghetti westerns featuring Clint Eastwood. Such little luxuries helped the recon teams unwind between their deadly missions in the field. Bill Janc, for one, did not take too kindly to a comrade who nearly destroyed one of his little luxuries one night.

Janc and Wilson Hunt had acquired a small refrigerator from Kontum City. It was only large enough for them to cool down their beer and sodas but it was a coveted possession in South Vietnam. In mid-September, one of the parties at the base club ended up moving back into the team hooches during the late hours. Phil Brown got into a scuffle with another inebriated Green Beret as they moved into the team rooms. The brawl ended up in RT Maine's room, where Brown took down his opponent, Roger Loe, by ramming his head into the team's mini-fridge.

Hunt and Janc were just making their way back from the bar. As they approached their hooch, another Green Beret hurriedly exited. "Oh, you guys are going to be pissed," he said. "Really sorry. I didn't do it."

Janc eyed their badly dented fridge door and snapped. Brown was still scuffling with his opponent. Sensing Janc's rage, Webb removed a heavy bunk adaptor from the next-door hooch of RT Texas and offered it to his comrade. "Here, Janc, take this and go clear them out."

Janc refused the adaptor and instead charged into the midst of the drunken melee. When he learned that Brown had damaged his fridge with Loe's head, Janc grabbed Brown around the neck and began pounding his head until he broke his own right hand in the process. The excitement was thus ended but Janc would take his share of teasing over breaking his hand on another Green Beret's head. He was still recovering days later, with his hand freshly splinted, when RT Maine was given a new Daniel Boone mission on September 20. Janc's ability to effectively handle a rifle and his radio were restricted, so Captain Ed Lesesne stepped in to run the mission with Sergeant Hunt.

"We were assigned to search for an underwater bridge to have it mined," Hunt said. "The North Vietnamese were crossing a river in the vicinity of our target area, but intelligence couldn't figure out where the bridge was. They suspected that it was built just under the water surface so that it could not be easily spotted from the air."

Lesesne, Hunt, and RT Maine's Montagnards were unable to be inserted, however. Their LZ area proved to be hotly contested by NVA and air support was called in to suppress the enemy. The insertion slicks flew lazy circles around the Sledgehammer mountain relay site while bombers worked over the area, but the heavy fire around the LZ finally forced the day's insertion to be aborted. Back at Kontum, Lesesne was eager to get back on their mission again the next day. As he, Hunt, and their

Montagnards geared up to go, they were surprised to see Bill Janc appear with his field gear—his broken hand still in a splint.

"The hell with it," Janc announced. "I'm going with you. I can recuperate in the field just as well as I can sitting around the base."

Recon Team Maine was inserted into Cambodia on September 21, and the team spent two days searching along the river for the rumored underwater bridge without luck. Janc made contact with covey in the late afternoon of September 22 and passed the word to base that the team wanted to be extracted after first light the following day. Hunt had his Montagnards prepare their RON site per their team custom, emplacing Claymores around its perimeter. He then took up his customary position, preparing to sleep beside his radio operator Janc. "Bill had a bad habit of snoring," said Hunt. "It scared the hell out of our Yards. So, I always slept beside him so I could nudge him if he started snoring."

Before it was completely dark, the recon team began hearing noises in their vicinity. There were some rifle shots, and voices of people talking could be heard. The members of RT Maine soon made out the forms of NVA soldiers moving across the side of a nearby dry rice paddy, and they decided the enemy was possibly in the process of hunting birds. Huddling in quiet conference, Hunt, Lesesne, and Janc decided they would attempt to pull a prisoner snatch—something that had not been accomplished by any SOG team in months—the following morning. From what they could see before dark, there were never more than two or three NVA moving about at one time, offering them decent odds of capturing an enemy soldier if they moved in against one of these small groups. After first light on September 23, Janc raised covey and passed the news in the form of a coded message. Recon Team Maine was not coming out after all: the team had the opportunity to snatch a prisoner.

Hunt and Lesesne believed they were dealing with nothing more than an NVA squad, perhaps numbering only as many as five or six

Captain Ed Lesesne (*right*) with Sergeant First Class Bill Kendall at FOB-2 in 1968. Lesesne joined Wilson Hunt's RT Maine for two successful prisoner snatch missions in September. *Joe Parnar*

soldiers. They informed command through their covey that they intended to observe the enemy through the day and would be ready to make their prisoner snatch the following morning. "We sat out there and watched them all day," said Hunt. "We never saw more than two or three NVA at a time." The Green Berets assumed they were seeing the same small group of people all the time, all of whom appeared to be as happy-go-lucky as they could be. The NVA continued to hunt birds, and the smell of their campfire smoke drifted over to the concealed team. "We could hear them talking but our Yards that could speak Vietnamese couldn't make out their words because of the distance," said Hunt.

He and Lesesne discussed their options for taking a prisoner, as they watched the NVA men periodically moving through the fields of waist-high rice in small numbers. They decided it should be possible to slip in close, wait for a lone soldier to pass by, shoot him in the leg, and drag him out while the rest of their team provided covering fire for any opposition. With their plan in place, the mission now became a waiting game.

Hunt consumed some of his rations as they continued observing the enemy. Among his indigenous rations were foot-long tubes about a third of which was filled with rice. Each morning, he topped off one of the tubes with water from his canteen. The rice slowly absorbed the water and caused the bag to swell. He could then munch on handfuls of rice through the day, along with some of his other indigenous rations. After more than a dozen missions across the fence, he had long since found that he did not have the stomach for the freeze-dried fish and shrimp that were a common feature of the indigenous rations. He always looked for the ration with rice and blood sausage, and his routine had become eating half of the blood sausage and half of the rice in the morning. At noon, he ate a little canned jelly ration, spooning it on top of peanut butter. In the evening, before they went into RON, Hunt would finish off the other half of his rice tube and blood sausage.

Recon Team Maine found their opponents uncooperative in terms of walking into their ambush. They spent the entire next day, September 24, lying in wait only to be frustrated. The NVA men simply did not advance far enough across the field for them to initiate their attack, as they were reluctant to drag a wounded man all the way across the vast open field. Janc made his usual late afternoon contact with covey again, and he passed the word to base that action would come the next morning, hell or high water. The team was getting antsy. Doubt had begun to creep in as to how much longer they could hold out while remaining undetected. They prepared themselves for action the following morning, determined to crawl in close to the wood line on the far side of the field to initiate the action. Janc asked covey to have air support standing by the next morning, ready for immediate assistance once their ambush had been sprung.

Three nights of sleeping within a stone's throw of the enemy was more than enough for Ed Lesesne and Wilson Hunt. It was do-or-die time.

✦◇✦

Hunt peered toward the far wood line once dawn's first light began to creep across the rice paddy on September 25.

It looks like just another day for them, he thought. *They're going about their business, the same as usual. Good. We should be able to surprise them.*

Recon Team Maine secured their RON and Hunt quietly briefed his Montagnards on their exact roles in the prisoner snatch. He and Captain Lesesne would crawl across the rice field and take positions with two of their Montagnards, ready to shoot the first unsuspecting North Vietnamese soldier that came close to them. Hunt instructed them to use automatic fire and grenade launchers to make their enemy believe they were being attacked by a much larger force than a mere recon team. Janc took position with his radio and positioned the five remaining Montagnards—interpreter Andre, Check, Hep, and grenadiers Munh and Wung—to prepare to lay down covering fire for the four who were to spring the ambush.

Lesesne crawled forward with Zero-Zero Kiep while Hunt moved forward with Zero-One Hinh. As the two pairs crawled forward, the smell of campfire smoke drifted across the field. Hunt could hear people talking as they approached the distant wood line. As he eased into the far undergrowth, his stomach was not prepared for what he saw. In the edge of the woods, he spotted a large area that had been cleared beneath the trees. Instead of a single campfire, he now saw several campfires and numerous hammocks strung out between the trees.

Oh, hell! he thought. *There's way more people here than we've been seeing. We've just crawled right up into the middle of an NVA platoon! We're outnumbered three to one.*

Lesesne and Hunt crawled close together to converse in whispers and hand gestures.

"What the hell do we do now?"

"Do we turn around and try to crawl back out of here?" Hunt asked.

"If we start crawling out of here and one of them sees us, they're going to kill us all," said Lesesne. "If they make first contact, they'll kill us."

"We might as well go ahead and run the prisoner snatch. We're right here in the middle of them and they have no idea. Let's just fire first, take one of them down, and then open up with everything."

The Green Berets then pushed forward to carry out their plan. Lesesne and Kiep crawled a little further alongside a little foot trail near the enemy platoon's camp to get a little closer for their shot. Hunt and Hihn took position to lay down covering fire once the enemy soldier had been wounded. Behind them, Janc and the youngest Montagnard, Check, were prepared to coordinate the radio with the nearby covey. Lesesne and Kiep eased along another fifteen yards on their bellies without being compromised until a lone enemy soldier suddenly ventured out on a nearby trail. Lesesne carefully eased off a shot with his M16, hitting the NVA in the leg. He then handed his gun to Kiep, pounced on the screaming soldier, and secured him with tie wraps that served as handcuffs.

As soon as Lesesne fired his shot, Sergeant Hunt and Hihn opened up with a blaze of fire into the NVA camp. The startled North Vietnamese soldiers panicked and began running across the dry paddy. Some carried rifles while others were caught unarmed as the first bursts of automatic fire opened up. Some unwittingly ran straight into the recon team's ambush. Hunt and the other Montagnards nearest him mowed down the soldiers as they raced for cover. "We really decimated that platoon," said Hunt. He used only short bursts to gun down several soldiers that ran as close as thirty feet from him—point-blank range. The surviving NVA regained their composure and began firing back.

Hunt noted the excitement of his Montagnards firing on full automatic as they cut down several advancing NVA. "We see VC!" they shouted. Invariably, the Montagnards called every opponent VC, whether they were North Vietnamese regulars or guerillas. After unleashing bursts of automatic fire, they excitedly proclaimed, "No VC now!" Once the mad bedlam of firing subsided, Hunt used considerable effort to advise his Montagnards to start conserving their ammunition.

The heaviest return fire came from the far-left side of the field about thirty yards from Lesesne. With his NVA prisoner secured with tie wraps, the recon captain hoisted the wounded man over his shoulder and began running toward the rest of his team. "We hadn't gone very far when we came under fire from a machine-gun nest that I hadn't seen," Lesesne said. "We dove behind a termite mound that was about five feet tall and I immediately tossed a grenade in the direction of the enemy fire."

The instant the grenade exploded, Lesesne jumped up and spotted the NVA machine gunners while they were off balance. He immediately lobbed a second grenade into their midst and wiped out the threat. Lesesne and Kiep hauled their prisoner toward the far end of the field where Janc was communicating with their air support. Hunt, still near the point of ambush, suddenly realized that no one else was rushing toward him. The strange feeling hit him that it would be a good idea to hide some of the bodies. *Somebody's going to see all these bodies,* he thought. *We've got to get them out of the way.*

Hunt began dragging some of the NVA corpses off the trail into the undergrowth. In the back of his mind, he thought the team might find one still living and could even pull a second prisoner. As he moved about, Janc had already directed RT Maine's air support to begin shooting up the countryside while they retreated toward their LZ with the prisoner. Lesesne administered morphine to his bound POW and tied a tight tourniquet around his thigh. Hunt hurried back toward the LZ, having abandoned his thoughts of hiding the NVA bodies. Now, he took his little camera and snapped pictures of his teammates with their prisoner while they waited for the chase ship to come in.

The prisoner was making considerable noise, shouting angrily.

"What the hell is he yelling about?" Hunt asked his interpreter Andre. "He say he come from an important North Vietnamese town where all the great NVA soldiers came from," replied Andre. "He shouts for his comrades to come kill the Americans."

"Shut him up!" Hunt yelled. "Hit him with another morphine!"

Janc jabbed the prisoner with another morphine syrette and he soon became groggy. All the while, gunships made runs against the enemy encampment to blast the countryside. The entire action had consumed less than ten minutes by the time the chase ship hovered over the team to extract their prisoner. The team shoved their POW on board, and Lesesne jumped in with several Montagnards, intent on guarding his prisoner back to American hands.

The next slick that landed collected Janc, Sergeant Hunt, and the remaining Montagnards. There was a tremendous adrenaline high among the team as their Huey flew from Cambodia toward Dak To. Lesesne boarded another chopper at Dak To with his prisoner and flew with him to Pleiku. There, the prisoner was given medical treatment to stabilize him while intelligence interrogated him. They found that RT Maine had grabbed not only SOG's first prisoner in nine months, but an officer to boot.

Word of the prisoner snatch effort received plenty of attention back at Kontum and at headquarters. By the time the returning team landed at Kontum, they were greeted by Colonel Jack Warren, the CCN base commander, who had flown down from Da Nang. For Hunt, it was a proud moment when the beaming colonel congratulated them with welcomed cold beers.

◆◇◆

Staff Sergeant Bill Janc (*right*), RT Maine's radio operator, with the team's first captured NVA soldier. One-Zero Wilson Hunt and Montagnard team leader Kiep are at left. *Wilson Hunt*

Team Maine's captured NVA officer provided plenty of good intelligence. From him, headquarter interrogators learned that Hunt's team had actually crept up on an enemy platoon that was guarding an ammunition dump on September 25. Command further sorted through the details the following day before passing the word that a return mission was in order to destroy the ammo cache. Colonel Smith's recon base was ordered to send in a Hatchet Force company loaded with explosives to destroy the dump.

When Captain Lesesne returned from Pleiku, he was armed with intelligence that SOG interrogators had pumped out of their captured officer. Lesesne gathered Hunt and Janc, informing them that command wanted their team to serve as point men for the Hatchet Force that would be landed to destroy the ammo dump. The regular Montagnards of Hunt's RT Maine would be left behind this time, replaced by the indigenous members of the reaction battalion. The NVA undoubtedly expected the Americans to use the same LZ when they returned, so the new force would land in a different place to avoid landing in a possibly booby-trapped LZ. The three Green Berets knew the local Cambodian terrain intimately from having spent three days surveying the area. They would be invaluable in leading in the new force.

Lesesne outlined his plans for the mission. Hunt was to serve as the point man, leading the reaction force from the LZ toward the NVA dump. Janc, carrying the radio, was to bring up the rear and remain in communication with covey and the air support. Hunt and Janc were immediately disturbed by two details. First, they would be separated from each other by a great distance and, second, they were not being allowed to bring their own familiar Montagnard team members. Janc suggested that he and his one-zero could remain in contact with each other by wearing little squad radios attached to their heads. Janc visited supply sergeant Bob Howard to draw two short-range radios that would allow the pair to talk as long as they were within two hundred yards of each other.

The next morning, September 27, Hunt, Lesesne, and Janc loaded onto choppers at Kontum and picked up a thirty-man Hatchet Force company. It was led by a young lieutenant, John Hart, whose team was supplied with ample rations and mosquito repellent. As the slicks refueled at Dak To, Hunt fully expected the Hatchet Force team to distribute their extra rations but found that this was not the case. Instead, Lieutenant Hart and Captain Lesesne boarded one chopper while Hunt and Janc climbed into another, along with a number of Hart's Montagnards.

The reaction force headed back to the site of the prisoner snatch from two days prior. The first of a half-dozen slicks hovered over the new LZ while gunships and a chase slick circled nearby. The first ships tossed boxes of supplies and weapons out as Hart and Lesesne hit the ground. Hunt and Janc came in on one of the last choppers, talking to each other on their head-mounted short-range radios.

"When you hit the LZ, run for it," Hunt ordered. "Break to our right front and get into the brush as fast as you can. Go right front."

Hunt and Janc dropped onto the LZ and sprinted forward for cover. Behind them, Hart, Lesesne, and the Montagnard platoon worked swiftly to break down the ration boxes on the LZ. Hunt was not impressed with the plan. He felt certain the NVA would take the opportunity to attack the large American force as the Hatchet Force Montagnards casually hollered back and forth to each other as they broke down the rations and mosquito repellent in the middle of the drop zone.

"We're going to get hit," he radioed Janc. "As soon as we do, you and I are going to E&E east toward South Vietnam just as hard as we can go."

Escape and evasion on foot was a remote option, but Hunt did not relish remaining near the scene of the noisy, clumsy ration distribution process that was unfolding. He remained under cover in the brush, silently amazed that no enemy attack had materialized by the time the Montagnard company was finally organized, lined up, and was ready to move. Lieutenant Hart then detailed three of his Montagnards to remain with Janc to bring up the rear, pulled another three indigenous troopers to accompany Hunt as the point team, and then sent the point out to begin the mission.

Hunt took careful note of the terrain as he moved forward from the LZ. To his right was a gently sloping mountainside with a well-worn trail running up it. He moved swiftly along the bottom of the hill. Intelligence gleaned from RT Maine's prisoner indicated that the NVA supply dump was only a short distance away. Hunt moved swiftly with his trio of Hatchet Force Montagnards and had covered little more than fifty-five yards when they stumbled on a clearing.

Hunt pushed aside the overhanging vines and brush to step through the cover into the clearing. To his shock, he suddenly found himself staring at a North Vietnamese soldier in the edge of the bushes on the other side. What happened next was pure instinct.

Hunt opened with a burst from his CAR-15 as he dropped toward the ground. The enemy soldier unloaded a burst at the same instant. Hunt hit the ground, uninjured, and fired another few rounds toward the soldier's position. He lost complete track of the NVA for at that moment, the entire mountainside suddenly erupted into a tremendous volume of machine-gun fire.

They were waiting for us! Hunt realized. *The whole time our party was screwing around on the LZ, these guys were just setting an ambush for us near this trail! They must have known we would come after their ammo dump.*

He could tell instantly from the amount of fire raining down through the underbrush that his Hatchet Force team had stumbled into a sizable enemy force—at least the same size as their own. The NVA had apparently place an L-shaped ambush into the cover, with the long axis of the L running along the base of the hillside. The short axis of the L lay perpendicular to the trail. Hunt had unwittingly rushed right into their midst and triggered the NVA ambush before the rest of the American force had closed the area. Now, he and his Montagnards were pinned in the midst of a hellacious firefight.

Hunt and his three indigenous comrades commenced the fastest low crawl they had ever performed. Fortunately for them, the gentle rise in the hill was causing most of the fire from the ambush force to sail just high enough to clear their heads. "Somehow, I didn't get a scratch from all the fire I took," he said. "But it was just raining leaves, branches, and twigs like a hailstorm of crap falling out of the trees. Their fire was going high, through the tops of the bushes, cutting limbs and leaves as we crawled back as fast as we could."

Hunt's point team scurried back to the LZ, where they found that the Hatchet Force team had formed a perimeter. He crawled in next to Lieutenant Hart, who was laying with his back stretched out and his head against a tree.

"Oh, my God," hollered the lieutenant. "I've got seventeen days left. Seventeen days! Oh, my God!"

Hunt realized that the officer was out of sorts and would be of no help for the moment in the midst of the firefight. Nearby, he found Ed Lesesne thoroughly irate as he hollered for the team radio.

"Where's the radio?" Lesesne yelled. "Where is the radio?"

Janc, who normally carried the PRC-25 for RT Maine, was without his usual equipment for this mission. One of the Hatchet Force Montagnards had instead assumed the duty. Janc crawled back into the perimeter to check on his fellow Green Berets and found a livid Captain Lesesne demanding the radio. Janc spotted the indigenous radioman, who had also crawled back into the perimeter to take cover from the automatic fire.

"Where is the fucking radio!" Lesesne screamed again.

Jungle confetti continued to rain down on the prone Americans as the NVA force blasted through the LZ. Janc, a powerful man twice the size of most Montagnards, realized that the radioman had frozen. He partially stood, then scurried to the Montagnard and seized him by his web gear. With one violent motion, Janc lifted the indigenous radioman from the ground and hurled his body in the direction of the ranting recon captain.

"There's your fucking radio!" he snapped.

The Hatchet Force company firing with a vengeance as Lesesne snatched the radio away from the indigenous RTO and raised the covey. He transmitted the prairie fire code and called for tactical air support to begin blasting the entrenched NVA. He then turned back to Sergeant Hunt.

"What the hell happened?" Lesesne shouted.

"I don't know," Hunt explained. "I think we triggered their ambush. I hit a little clearing and on this other side was an NVA soldier. He came up to fire at me and I fired. We both fired and then the whole damn hillside just exploded."

Lesesne's next command was not one Hunt expected or cared to hear.

"Well, crawl back out there and see if you hit him!"

An order was an order, so Hunt took several Montagnards and began crawling back toward the edge of the clearing where he had exchanged fire with the enemy soldier. By this time, some of the heaviest firing had died down as TAC air moved in to bomb and machine-gun the hillside. When Hunt reached the little clearing by crawling around its edges, he could not see a body. He did spot expended AK47 cartridge casings littering the ground near the scene of his shoot-out.

He continued to ease forward and finally found blood spatters on the ground. He radioed back to Janc that he had a blood trail, a sign that one or more of his shots must have at least wounded his opponent. Janc relayed the word to Captain Lesesne, who passed the word for Hunt to continue searching. He continued crawling forward with his CAR-15 ready.

After passing through the blood trail, he came upon an NVA fatigue shirt soaked with blood that someone had discarded. Clearly, he had wounded his man. Continuing forward on his belly, Hunt found the soldier's rifle. Just beyond the discarded weapon was a dried-up washout. Hunt carefully crawled to the edge of the ditch and spotted a North Vietnamese soldier laying shirtless. The NVA was on his back, moaning and clutching his bloodied belly. Hunt saw that his head was also bleeding profusely. He quickly fumbled for his radio.

"I've found the guy I shot," he told Janc. "He's breathing. His chest is moving, but I don't think he's going to live very long."

Lesesne then passed the word to Janc. "Get him back here quick! We're going to bring in choppers and we'll try to get him to a hospital."

For the second time in three days, Hunt's mission had turned into a prisoner snatch, although this one was completely unplanned. He worried for a moment on how to proceed. The enemy soldier was cupping his belly. *What if he's clutching a grenade in his hands?* he wondered. *He may have pulled the pin and he's just waiting on us to come down there with him. He knows he's dying, so he's just waiting to take us with him.*

Hunt found the Montagnards unwilling to crawl down and pull the soldier's hands apart to see if he was holding anything. He called back to Janc: "Bill, I need help. The Yards won't go close to him. Come help me, Bill."

Janc appeared within moments, low-crawling out to the clearing by the little ditch. Hunt's radio operator was less than pleased with the assignment. "I was the low-ranking guy," said Janc. "So I was the one who had to go up there and see if he had a grenade." He used a long tree branch to ease up to the soldier, forcing the man's hands far enough apart to see that he was not holding a grenade. Moving swiftly, Janc and Hunt grabbed the soldier and dragged him from the ditch onto flat ground. Hunt could now see that the NVA had a serious side wound and a nasty gunshot wound that had creased the side of his skull. His hair was matted down with blood and his upper body was drenched.

The two Green Berets half carried and half-dragged the wounded soldier back toward the landing zone as their Montagnards continued to return sporadic enemy rifle fire. By the time they entered the Hatchet Force's perimeter, they found that Lesesne had already called in the chase ship to retrieve their latest prisoner. As the Huey went into a hover over their position, Lesesne called in the dogs to work over the enemy. Gunships roared in low, their mini-guns chewing up the hillside full of NVA.

The chase slick moved in behind the gunships and had barely settled into its hover before the Green Berets heaved their latest prisoner into the chopper. Lesesne, as the ranking member of the party, jumped on to guard the prisoner and ordered the pilot to make speed for Pleiku in order to have medics save their man for intelligence purposes. Lieutenant Hart remained in charge of the balance of the Hatchet Force as extraction choppers began moving in to recover the balance of the Americans and Montagnards. The area was too hotly contested to put men in to find the ammunition dump, so gunships and bombers took over the operation, raining down cluster bomb units (CBUs) and napalm over the entire area to either chase out or exterminate the remaining NVA ambush force.

Hunt and Janc had been on the ground less than ninety minutes, but they had managed to pull their second prisoner and make it out alive once again. Intelligence would soon find that once again, they had lucked into snatching an NVA officer. "We learned that the guy I shot was their company commander," Hunt said. "The previous guy we had captured was a lieutenant but this guy was the commander in charge of setting the L-ambush for us. When Lesesne returned from Pleiku, he said our latest prisoner was the equivalent of a captain in the North Vietnamese Army."

By the time the two Americans from RT Maine reached the helicopter pad at Kontum that afternoon, they found a large greeting party which once again included Colonel Warren from CCN. As Janc and Hunt climbed from their chopper, the colonel was again grinning with delight as he pressed cold beers into the grimy hands of the weary Green Berets. "He was just ecstatic," said Hunt. "Our base had gone a long time without pulling a prisoner alive and here we had just snatched two in three days."

Lesesne felt proud that his Green Berets were held in high esteem, while Hunt was quick to remind his buddy Joe Walker of the beer bet they had made about who would return with the first live prisoner snatched from across the fence. Lesesne and Hunt would each receive the Silver Star, while Janc was given two Army Commendation Medals with "V" device, one for each successful prisoner snatch.[7]

The recon company had a long-standing tradition of issuing a cash reward for the indigenous team members and special R&R for the Green Berets for each prisoner snatched. In Hunt's case, his remaining time before his "date eligible for return from overseas" (DEROS) was so short that he would never enjoy both liberties, but he and his two companions did enjoy one ten-day leave together, drinking and living it up in Taiwan.

Chapter Fifteen

CLOSE SHAVES

One-Zero Phil Brown nearly lost his radio operator during the same week that Lesesne, Hunt, and Janc were busy snatching prisoners. Brown had taken acting command of RT New York while team leader Jim McGlon was recovering from malaria. Inserted into Laos, the team was preparing to move from its RON position on the morning of September 23 when it was assaulted by an NVA patrol. Sergeant Bill Bumps was checking his radio gear when he noticed one of his Montagnards staring intently into the jungle. He elbowed the man and asked him in sign language, "What the hell?"[1]

The Montagnard cupped his ear to indicate he had heard something in the jungle. *Okay, don't start anything here*, Bumps thought. His indigenous teammate then silently lifted his M16 and began slowly swinging it as if he was following a target in the distant undergrowth. Bumps silently pleaded, *Don't start something we can't finish!*

The Montagnard suddenly emptied the entire clip of his M16 on a target Bumps could not make out. Men grabbed their weapons and gear as the jungle erupted with gunfire between the unseen NVA company and the surprised American recon team. Brown was standing beside a large tree with his CAR-15 when the terrific explosion of an RPG knocked him to the ground. His body was perforated in several places by hot shrapnel but the tree fortunately shielded him from taking life-threatening injuries.

Bumps was less fortunate: he was blown off his feet and thrown back into the jungle by a slam of pressure that felt as if someone had kicked him in the lower back. He rolled back to his feet and saw his one-zero and indigenous personnel scrambling for cover. Bumps' immediate objective was to stay with Phil Brown, but as he charged forward, he felt a strange tugging on his gear. His radio gear was fouled in the Laotian jungle. Bumps, known on air by his code name "close shave," cursed his luck as he fumbled with freeing his radio. His RTO predecessor had rigged his radio set with a piece of coat hanger to allow the receiver to be hung from his fatigues, but the hook had snagged enough thick vines to hold him securely to the jungle. He thought briefly about ditching the entire set as he watched the rest of RT New York disappear into the jungle.

I have to have that handset! he thought.

Bumps knelt and fumbled furiously, tearing away the tangled mess. When he looked up, he noticed the figures of three men moving toward him. *It's the team,* he thought. *They've come back!* Bill's optimism drained as he noted their uniforms, blanched wooden stock rifles, and the RPG tube hung over one man's shoulder. They were NVA, and the RPG was the one that had nearly killed him.

The NVA spotted Bumps just as he freed his radio gear. The Green Beret left his gear and ran toward the cover of a nearby large tree as his opponents spread out behind other trees. Bumps raced around the right side of the tree and surprised one of the NVA—who was aiming his rifle the other direction in search of the lone American. He pushed his CAR-15 forward, let loose with a quick burst, and saw his first opponent crumple as he swung his weapon toward the next NVA. Bumps emptied his clip and pushed the magazine release to reload. He scurried back to his gear, slamming in a fresh magazine.

Staff Sergeant Phil "Scarface" Brown, one-zero of RT New York. *Jason Hardy*

Sergeant Bill "Close Shave" Bumps became separated from Brown's team on September 23, 1968, during heavy enemy contact. *Jason Hardy*

Bumps snatched a fragmentation grenade from his web gear, pulled the pin, and hurled it in the direction of the third NVA soldier. He pulled on his gear, tossed a smoke grenade to cover his exit, and raced up over a small ridge. As he dropped down to scan for his teammates, his mind raced with activity. *Should I go back in the direction of the firefight? Surely, Phil will bring the team back to search for me. No, that's stupid. They're not coming back. Phil said we're going to go west to get to an LZ for the choppers. That's where I should go.*

The words to a popular Bob Dylan song filtered through his mind as his pulse raced. *How does it feel? To be on your own, with no direction home, like a rolling stone.* He checked his wrist compass to determine which direction was west and surged stealthily forward. His rifle was on full automatic—his finger touching the trigger—as he trained it in each direction with the movements of his head. He moved a considerable distance before he decided to crouch and use his radio. He was greatly relieved when the Leghorn relay site responded: "Go ahead."

"This is close shave," Bill replied. "Team split due to enemy contact."

"How many casualties? How many enemy?"

Bumps reported that he was alone and wounded. Leghorn told him to stay quiet while they contacted Kontum to apprise them of the tactical emergency. Bumps took cover in thick vegetation, content to hide himself until air cover could reach his position.

In the meantime, Phil Brown and his four Montagnards had cleared the area of the first firefight. He was able to make contact with air support and similarly update them on his team's emergency. Brown returned to the area where the NVA had attacked his team, but his men found only blood where Bumps had been hit. The covey directed in an A1-A Spad to suppress the NVA while coaching Brown to a safer extraction point. Brown and his Montagnards were soon lifted out by chopper but Bumps was nowhere to be found, leaving the one-zero with the sinking realization that he would have to report his only American team member to be MIA.

By afternoon, Bumps was still in contact with Leghorn. His spirits soared when the first A1 Skyraider thundered over his position. Bill was vectored toward a nearby clearing where his air support believed he could be extracted. His tactical emergency had diverted air cover to his vicinity to offer him a fighting chance of making it out alive. He was directed toward a very steep hill, where his covey believed it was clear enough to land a chopper.

As Bumps ascended the hill, he found his path impeded by a tall thicket too dense to push through. Covey informed him that the circling slick would be unable to drop him a line until he reached the hilltop, so

Bumps resorted to crawling through the hedges on his hands and knees and finally his belly. Halfway through on his stomach, he realized he was dragging his CAR-15 behind him, still set on full automatic. *Any little twig could set that thing off!* he realized. *Wouldn't this be piss poor? This close to the end, and I blow myself away.*

He carefully slid his carbine forward and set it on safe—the first time he had done so since the shooting began hours earlier. He continued crawling through the thicket, trying to ignore his painful wounds. To his dismay, he was forced to penetrate a second dense mass of undergrowth before he finally reached the LZ area. As the chopper set down, he did not even have the strength to clamber aboard.

Bumps could only manage to put one knee on the skid as the chopper began lifting away. The Huey door gunner—noticing the pitiful look in the eyes of the wounded Green Beret—leaned out, grabbed Bumps by the harness, and swung him forcefully into the chopper as the pilot pulled clear. He collapsed in pain and exhaustion on the floor of the Huey, unable to even carry his own gear when they finally landed at the Kontum heliport. One-Zero Phil Brown was standing by.

"I thought you were dead!"

"No, not me," Bumps muttered through clenched teeth.

Brown and Bumps were immediately summoned to see FOB-2 commander Smith at the base bar. Smith pushed stiff drinks into their hands before they even had time to mention their injuries. Brown proceeded to relate the mission's events until Smith finally noted the pools of blood gathering beneath the wounded Green Berets. They were dismissed to the dispensary, where medics cut away Bumps' bloody uniform. Upon removing the webbing Bumps had stuffed into his wound, the medics were alarmed at how close his laceration was to his spine.

The wound was repacked and Bumps was flown out on a stretcher to Pleiku, where doctors tended to him for two days before transporting him on to Japan for more extensive medical attention. Recon Team New York had not seen the last of Bill Bumps, who soon rejoined Brown for more missions across the fence.

✦◇✦

Sergeant First Class Bill Kendall's first mission was another close shave. The native of Jefferson, Iowa, had been assigned to Kontum for a mere three days before he made his first Daniel Boone operation as the junior American member of RT Hawaii. Kendall, who weighed 135 pounds and stood just five-foot-five, had been forced to grow up tough. He admittedly had an attitude problem and had been suspended from school twice before graduating in 1954. After reaching Fort Bragg, his hopes of becoming Special Forces qualified were threatened when he was told his weight was insufficient for jump school (all Green Berets must be airborne qualified). Kendall managed to bulk up enough to make it through jump school three months later, and by late 1965 he had already completed his first tour with SOG.

He had escaped death during that first tour when a truck he was riding in hit a land mine, killing the driver and ejecting Kendall with such force that he suffered a concussion. When he returned to Vietnam in the fall of 1968, he was eager to get back into recon work on a team. Kendall drew all of his equipment from supply sergeant Bob Howard on October 1 and reported to first sergeant Ethyl Duffield for assignment. "Duff says I'll go in with one of the teams today or tomorrow," Kendall wrote in his secret, forbidden diary. "Sure will be glad to get first mission over with."[2]

Kendall flew a visual reconnaissance on October 3 in preparation for inserting as part of RT Delaware but foul weather foiled the plans this day. When he reported back to Sergeant Duffield, Kendall was told he would instead insert the following day as part of One-Zero Bill Hanson's RT Hawaii. Hanson, who had arrived at Kontum in April 1968, led RT Florida on several missions before leaving that team to tackle a special assignment. Hanson had a solid reputation for running teams, and soon found himself installed as the team leader for RT Hawaii with a Kontum newbie, Sergeant First Class Bill Delima, as his one-one.

On the morning of October 4, Hanson, Delima, One-Two Bill Kendall, and RT Hawaii's indigenous recon men gathered at the airfield for the chopper flight into their launch site. Kendall had been advised by Captain Frank Jaks that his first operation in Cambodia was expected to be routine. From the start, however, the members of RT Hawaii found the AO to be anything from routine. "We were shot at going in," rookie Kendall noted in his diary. "Received fire from south of LZ." [3]

Hanson leaped from the chopper and began returning the fire while the remainder of his team dismounted and sought temporary cover. Once RT Hawaii was set, he led the men in a southerly direction toward their assigned recon area to avoid further contact. Along the way, Kendall occasionally heard Vietnamese voices in the jungle, and Hanson wisely changed directions every hour to help throw off any possible trackers. One-One Delima brought up the rear of the file, sterilizing their back trail to help erase any visible signs of the team's passage. He remained in radio contact with their covey to keep air support apprised of their situation.

Hanson knew the LZ ground fire aimed at his team was reason enough to call in the gunships and then have his team pulled out. "But I thought I could get away with staying in because it started raining," he said.[4] In their jungle environment, the noise of the rain was a golden opportunity to keep moving. The damp undergrowth and forest floor foliage allowed him to move two miles while making almost no noise.

It was not blind luck that teams run by Bill Hanson had thus far returned from every mission without a team member lost or wounded. His team communicated via well-rehearsed hand and arm signals, with the one-zero being the only one to talk if necessary. Any spoken words he felt were necessary were executed by pressing his mouth very close to the other man's ear. They were given in a gentle whisper while trying not to use words with the letter "s" that generally made more noise.

In spite of such careful methods, RT Hawaii picked up an NVA tracker that afternoon. Enemy trackers had the advantage of being more aware of their surroundings, forcing Hanson to remain alert for trail crossings where the NVA could already have a team lying in wait to ambush them. Kendall heard dogs barking in the distance and two shots from the trackers rang out that afternoon, and he realized his first mission was going to be as exciting as he had hoped it would be.

Hanson moved only a short distance from the LZ in the late afternoon before he decided it was time for his team to go into their RON. He had learned many valuable lessons from wise former Vietnamese team members on how to successfully go into his chosen "remain overnight" positions. He never shared his secrets, figuring that the more teams that employed his strategies would only lead to the NVA figuring them out.

Recon Team Hawaii moved early on the morning of October 5, crossing fresh trails that were well worn from both enemy soldiers and water buffalo. The NVA trackers remained close at hand, firing a half-dozen shots during the day. Hanson did not allow his men to be steered by the enemy shots, but they still very nearly ran afoul of a twenty-man North Vietnamese patrol.

The men of RT Hawaii took cover in the dense jungle, waiting anxiously as the NVA patrol slowly advanced through the area without spotting them. Bill Kendall silently hoped his luck would hold out.

✦✧✦

Another nearby recon team was less successful in their RON position during the early morning of October 5.

They were hit by an NVA element and the ensuing firefight caused some of the team members to become scattered, so Covey Rider Gerry Denison was sent up to assist the team. Although he normally flew with

Air Force O-1 pilots, he was dispatched that morning with a pilot from the U.S. Army's 219th Aviation Company—known both as the "Headhunters" and as "Sneaky Pete Air Force" or SPAF. The SPAF aircraft he flew in was a U.S. Army O-1 Bird Dog, configured with half a dozen 2.75-inch rockets under each wing. Denison was to offer training for a new covey rider, Terry Hamric, who was flying in an Air Force O-2 launched first from the Kontum airstrip. Hamric had joined the covey ranks of other previous one-zeros like Dallas Longstreath and Jim Tramel, who were currently part of the FOB-2 covey rotation. While Hamric was waiting for his ride, Denison took off with SPAF-4 to the AO to search for the separated team members.

Denison, with more than four months of experience as a covey rider, was greatly respected by his recon teammates on the ground. Soon after his O-1 pilot had them over the team's RON area, Denison spotted some of the men on the ground and called in air support to work the area. His little Skymaster had just turned to make a pass up the little valley when it came under fire from a North Vietnamese 51-mm antiaircraft emplacement. Denison felt the light craft lurch as shells began ripping apart the tender two-seater, forcing his pilot to crash-land their SPAF-4 in the top of a massive teak tree.

The AA fire and crash of the Cessna caused little harm to the pilot, but Denison was in agony. His left hand was gashed, ripping the tendons in three of his fingers. A bullet or a piece of one of the enemy shells tore through his face from left to right, knocking out teeth and shattering his upper jaw in three places and his lower jaw in five places. Denison was further scraped and battered as he emerged from the rear cockpit and ricocheted off numerous branches as he fell down to the ground. "I immediately got on my Perk-10 radio and called Hillsboro, the airborne controller of all TAC air over Laos and North Vietnam," said Denison. His speech badly slurred from his wounds, he identified himself by his call name, grommet, and was immediately advised that he was calling from a radio frequency reserved only for the ground forces.

"Grommet, you're not supposed to be on this frequency!"

"Hillsboro from Grommet," Denison replied. "We are on the ground."

The shocked voice on the radio could only reply: "Oh, shit!"[5]

Denison was prepared for the worst. He was only ten days shy of completing his service period at Kontum and he now faced the possibility of fighting for his life while badly wounded. Fortunately, he was armed with a German 9-mm submachine gun and a Swedish K magazine vest holding nine magazines for his weapon. He and his SPAF pilot were recovered within hours by an extraction force, but Denison would spend months in hospitals recovering from the wound that shattered his jaws.

✦◇✦

Bill Kendall could hear the enemy moving about in his vicinity during the night of October 5–6. The trackers fired off two shots, and Kendall also heard the distant sound of chopping.

Recon Team Hawaii was on the move again the next morning, their third day across the fence. One-Zero Bill Hanson was experienced enough to know they would not shake their trackers. He continued his E&E maneuver but his luck ran out on October 6, when the North Vietnamese methodically penned in RT Hawaii. Hanson had his new one-two raise their covey, and Kendall asked that the team be pulled. While the request was passed along to Captain Jaks, Hanson organized his team into a defensive perimeter and prepared for an assault. He could hear enemy soldiers nearby, talking among themselves. Then he received an update from Jaks via their covey rider.

"Are you under fire?" he was asked.

Hanson explained that they were not but their mission had been compromised by the NVA tracking team that now had his men surrounded. Covey then relayed back that command had denied RT Hawaii's extraction request. Hanson was furious that his experience was being called into question.

"They're not going to pull us out?" he radioed.

"Negative," the covey rider said. "Not unless your team is under enemy fire."

Hanson's reply was short: "Give me a minute."

Switching his CAR-15 to fully automatic, he aimed toward the nearby sound of enemy troops moving toward him and began firing. Instantly, the jungle erupted into a vicious firefight. North Vietnamese soldiers charged toward Team Hawaii's perimeter with guns blazing. The recon team stayed low as they fired back.

"You hear it now?" Hanson hollered over the radio. "Now bring them ships in here!"

Hanson expertly deployed his team in such a tight perimeter that the NVA could not penetrate their ring. As gunships and tactical air support arrived overhead, he directed their fire to punish the enemy troops. The first choppers attempted to extract RT Hawaii with McGuire rigs but they were driven off by heavy enemy fire and a simultaneous NVA charge. Bill Delima exposed himself to enemy fire while calling in napalm strikes to within fifty-five yards of his team's perimeter, and he had the gunships strafe to within twenty-eight yards of his men. Hanson led the counter-offensive to push back the advancing enemy, and in the process, Kendall shot down at least two NVA soldiers that came within five yards of his team's perimeter.

The NVA withdrew temporarily and Hanson urgently called in gunships to work them over. Additional Hueys then settled in low to attempt to pull the recon team from the jungle. The team did not have the luxury of McGuire rigs on the ends of the dropped lines, forcing them to fashion their own Swiss seats out of the rope they carried for the purpose. Kendall and three of the team's indigenous fighters strapped themselves into the lines while Delima laid down covering fire and continued calling in air strikes over the radio.

Delima, Hanson, and two of their indigenous teammates were the last to strap in on the second chopper. The men were forced to endure an excruciating ride for an hour and twenty-five minutes suspended in their Swiss seats as the choppers flew back to the Dak To launch site. "We couldn't even move our legs after swinging below the choppers for that long," said Hanson. "We had to be helped on our feet after they got us out of those Swiss seats."[6] All three Americans were later awarded the Bronze Star for their valor under fire.

Hanson was less than amused when his team returned to Kontum. He sought out Ed Lesesne, the recon company commander, and announced that his team's hastily rigged Swiss seats had been unacceptable. "This is bullshit!" he announced. "Let's come up with something different."

Hanson experimented with various options of how to improve the Swiss seat extraction rigs, and ultimately came up with a solution that Captain Lesesne believed would work. The new creation, concocted from an A7A nylon cargo strap, was tested and deemed a more worthy method for helicopter extraction.

Bill Hanson's extraction harness soon became known by SOG men as the "Hanson rig." Although the inventor himself would never have an occasion to use it, the new device proved to be priceless to future recon teams in need of a hasty extraction or as a means of hoisting out a wounded team member.

◆◇◆

Bill Kendall was quick to return to action. He was assigned by recon sergeant Ethyl Duffield to serve on One-Zero Ralph Rodd's RT Florida for bomb damage assessment missions just days later. During his first BDA mission from October 9–13, Kendall's new team met little resistance while reconnoitering enemy areas. Rodd's team was inserted again on October 14 to perform yet another BDA. One of his indigenous men, who had dropped below the ground to inspect an NVA tunnel area, suddenly announced that he had found a wire running through the tunnel.[7]

"Booby trap!" Kendall and Rodd shouted simultaneously.

It was too late. The careless Montagnard pulled on the wire and set off the booby trap with a resounding explosion. The enclosed area created a devastating effect, slicing Rodd, Kendall, and two others with frags. The Montagnard who had tugged on the wire was hit in an eye and had both feet blown off. Recon Team Florida, including its severely injured indigenous teammate, was extracted less than two hours later. Kendall was flown to Nha Trang three days later to have shrapnel removed from his arm, only to be diagnosed with malaria that would sideline him from further action for two weeks.

By late October, several teams were in transition as senior men were scheduled for DEROS. Three one-zeros—Gene Williams, Wayne Melton, and Wilson Hunt—handed over their men to new team leaders. Melton worked on base after handing RT Hawaii off weeks earlier to veteran Bill Hanson. Williams turned RT Delaware over to Staff Sergeant Luke Dove, who spent the latter part of October training with the team.

Hunt was the last of the three to step down from team command. He gave a few personal items to his former teammate Bill Janc, the new one-zero of RT Maine. To his respected interpreter Andre, he handed off his personal Browning .25-caliber automatic pistol. Hunt had also placed a special catalog order to Montgomery Wards as his DEROS approached. "I went through the kids' department and ordered a pair of Levis blue jeans for every one of my Montagnards," he said. "When they arrived and I handed them out the week before I left, the Montagnards just went wild. They put them on and ran through the compound, yelling and showing everyone their jeans from the United States."[8]

Content that he was leaving his men in good hands, Hunt prepared to depart the following morning, October 27. As the day progressed, word made the rounds that RT Colorado was in trouble. The team had been hit by an NVA attack days before and split. One American, a black sergeant, was missing and presumed dead after a grenade attack, while the rest of the team was fighting its way toward an extraction.

One-Zero Dennis Mack had been sent in with his team to locate a man believed to be cooperating with the NVA by helping to call in artillery strikes. Mack's RT Colorado was attacked on the afternoon of October 24 as they prepared their RON site. Mack instantly set off the Claymores his team had placed and the whole area erupted into a nasty firefight. His men scattered down the hill as automatic fire chewed up their campsite. "One bullet went through my pant leg," said Mack. "Then it went through my rifle magazine, hit the bolt, and froze the weapon. Another went into the radio."[9]

Recon Team Colorado crossed the river and took cover as the NVA used grenade launchers to pound the area. Mack was unable to raise a covey, as night had fallen. He was left with five Montagnards and one other American, Staff Sergeant James D. Lewis. Mack had been wounded in the head and face by shrapnel, while Lewis had been badly hit in both hands.[10]

Once they had evaded the enemy, Mack moved RT Colorado onward for the next two days. In the midst of the grenade attack, Sergeant Floyd Bryant had gone missing, presumed to have been killed by the enemy. With the team radio out of commission, Mack was unable to raise a covey except with his small emergency radio, which had a very limited transmission distance. On October 26, he managed to attract the attention of a pair of low-flying Spads returning from a bombing run. The A-1Es buzzed the recon team and extraction choppers were called in.[11]

The plight of RT Colorado was soon making the rounds back at Kontum. Wilson Hunt and Wayne Melton were preparing to leave FOB-2 the following morning when they heard the news that one of their fellow teams had been hit two days before and that a Green Beret was missing and presumed dead. The other Americans, Mack and Lewis, were wounded but were in the process of being rescued by choppers, along with their five Montagnards. Melton and Hunt scurried over to the Kontum launch area to listen in on the extraction efforts over the radio. The group grew larger as they listened to the energetic exchanges between the team, their covey, and the air support pilots. Captain Lesesne joined the group and finally reported that all had been extracted except one American Green Beret, the man who was believed to be killed in action (KIA).

Lesesne announced that he was taking Lieutenant Bill Groves in on a Bright Light to recover the body. The area was overrun with NVA, so he wanted to take in a larger than normal number of additional Americans. Groves and Lesesne asked for volunteers to join the force. Knowing they had turned in their gear and were departing in the morning, Hunt and Melton waited to see who would volunteer. After a silent moment, Lesesne cursed, barked that he would go out by himself if he had to, and slammed the door to the radio bunker on his way out.

"Well, if he's going by himself, I'll go with him," Hunt said, racing after the captain.

"If you're going, I'm going too!" called Melton.[12]

They ran to the compound to borrow indigenous rucksacks, blankets, weapons, and ammunition. Hunt had already shipped his civilian clothes home and had turned in his CAR-15 and other gear. By the time they reached the airstrip, they found Lesesne and Groves loading up. They had been joined by Joel "Ranger" Haynes and One-Zero Phil Brown, who volunteered the Montagnards from his company to join those of Groves' platoon. Brown had just returned to base after struggling through a nasty bout of malaria.

The ad hoc force that flew to the Dak To staging area numbered about three dozen Americans and Montagnards. The Bright Light team, ferried in by nine choppers, was landed without enemy attack near the area where the recon team had first been overrun. Lesesne moved his men on a thorough search of the action area for hours with no success. "Once we got to the end of the day, we got on the radio and relayed to Covey and to headquarters that we had been unable to find Bryant," Hunt said. "We told them we would RON and continue the search in the morning."[13]

The team huddled in tight, squeezing into their RON in the cool mountain air. Most were eager to get moving and warm up after daybreak on October 27. During the morning, various noises were heard in the jungle. Although no contact was made, the recon team realized that NVA troops were moving near them. Lesesne made radio contact with his covey, announcing the search had been fruitless so far and halted to allow his men to eat as the Montagnards formed a perimeter. As they were finishing their meal, one of the Montagnards suddenly beckoned with frantic gestures that movement had been detected on the hillside below. Hunt gazed in the direction and saw the tops of trees quivering as though someone was using them for support to move up the mountainside.

Phil Brown was prepared to mow down the first NVA that stepped from the jungle. He was stunned by what he saw, however. From out the trees emerged a tattered African American Green Beret, dragging himself along with his weapon. "We had done our best, but we had given up on finding his body," said Hunt. "No one expected to find him alive."

Several Montagnards scurried forward to help Bryant make his way to the team's perimeter. He did not even have time to relate his tale before Lesesne's point men picked up more movement in the trees below from the direction in which Bryant had appeared. A pair of NVA point men were spotted for a split second before they ducked back down the mountainside.

They're following him, Hunt realized. *They must have used him for bait to find us and now they've gone back to gather their main body. There's probably a whole NVA battalion ready to sweep us off this mountain.*

Groves opened up on the radio, reporting that his team had successfully secured their target and were in need of extraction. Captain Lesesne ordered his men in motion to head for an acceptable LZ that covey had spotted, a little clearing near a stream a short distance away. As the platoon moved quiet but steady in the prescribed direction, they realized they were on the verge of a firefight. Signal shots erupted in the distance as the NVA trackers called in their reinforcements. Lesesne strung out his team near the edge of the clearing as a string of extraction Hueys approached.

As the first bird settled down, Lesesne and Brown jumped on board with Sergeant Bryant and three Montagnards. It lifted clear, followed by two more that continued lifting out the recon men. *This is almost too easy to believe*, thought Hunt. *We know they're out there tracking us and we're getting out without a shot being fired.*

He and Melton scrambled aboard the fourth Huey along with a group of their indigenous teammates. The pilot lifted up and powered forward, gaining speed as he climbed with his heavy iron bird. The jungle below suddenly erupted into a hailstorm of automatic fire, and bullets ripped through and pinged off the Huey like hail. The pilot maintained control of his crippled bird and made it into Dak To without incident.

Lieutenant Groves, Joel Haynes, and their last four Montagnards had been anxiously awaiting the final chopper when all hell broke loose. Groves was already on edge. Haynes was pushing to go ahead and blow their Claymores before the last chopper landed to keep the NVA from charging them. *If we blow them too early, the NVA will be all over us*, Groves thought. Haynes kept prompting the lieutenant to go ahead and blow them until Groves snapped, "I'll do it when I'm ready!"[14]

Two RPGs erupted nearby as the last chopper approached. Automatic AK fire and more RPGs roared to life all around the area as the NVA blasted away at the chopper departing with Hunt and Melton. Groves and Haynes remained on the LZ firing as the chopper slid in. They urged their Montagnards aboard, followed by Haynes. Groves jumped in last as the chopper pilot began sliding away, but the Huey was slammed by gunfire as Groves rattled away with his CAR-15. The pilot had his shoulder strap and mic boom shot away by charging NVA who were firing directly into his cockpit. One of the Montagnards sitting by the open door was hit by a round and he fell out of the chopper to the ground. Groves leaped from the Huey and helped the man back on board. In the process, the NVA opened fire with a vengeance, wounding another Montagnard and knocking him from the chopper.[15]

Once again, Groves jumped out to help his indigenous team member back into the bird. Haynes also jumped out to offer assistance to the downed Montagnard while Groves returned fire. Realizing the chopper would likely be downed if it remained hovering any longer, Groves signaled the pilot away. The pilot narrowly cleared the tall jungle trees as he moved out with a badly riddled Huey.

First Lieutenant Bill Groves (*right*) narrowly escaped his October 1968 Bright Light mission. He is seen here at FOB-2 with Master Sergeant Bill Boyle in 1968. *Joe Parnar*

Haynes lifted the wounded Montagnard to his shoulder and raced to a nearby wood line while Groves remained on the LZ to cover them. Once Haynes had his man on the edge of the woods, Groves sprinted across the LZ to join them. Bullets filled the air, and several tore through his rucksack with such force that Groves was spun around and knocked to the ground. His rescue chopper was long gone, his radio was hit, and he found himself with a badly wrenched back and a throbbing left shoulder. He lay on the LZ, unable to control the left side of his body. He rolled away and fumbled about with his unresponsive left arm, trying to change out the magazine in his CAR-15.

Enemy rounds kicked up soil and undergrowth all around him, connected with his radio and slammed him into the ground again as he called for another extraction chopper. Bullets engulfed him, wounding him and ripping the emergency radio from his hand. He rolled over into a shallow irrigation ditch near the landing zone, a rice paddy filled with water, forcing his CAR-15 down into three feet of water as he struggled to pull it free. Enemy soldiers came around to the other side of the rice paddy and started firing as Groves struggled to pull his weapon from the muck.

Haynes continued to fire back while helping the wounded Montagnard near the tree line. It would be another twenty minutes before the chase ship came back in with the gunships to attempt to rescue Haynes and Groves. During that time, Groves thought of what had happened to John Kedenburg when he remained behind months before. He kept shooting until he had nearly exhausted all of his ammunition. Groves was still struggling with loss of feeling in the left side of his body, but he managed to make his way from the ditch to Haynes and the Montagnard.

They used their radio to call in air strikes against the massing NVA soldiers and finally saw the welcome sight of an extraction chopper. It had been twenty minutes since they had been forced from their first ride, and the incoming pilot, First Lieutenant Craig Collier, assumed the two Green

Berets had been killed. Then he heard a whispering on the guard frequency from a portable emergency radio: "We're still alive and just pretending to be dead."[16]

Collier brought his slick in quickly as gunships blasted away at the NVA massing around the LZ's perimeter. Haynes jumped to his feet, exposing himself to automatic fire as he helped lift the wounded Montagnard on board Collier's slick. Haynes then helped Groves struggle to safety. Both were pulled on board by the chopper's door gunner, who then spotted an NVA sniper in a tree just alongside their exit flight path. Pilot Collier was proud that his gunner continued to secure the wounded recon men with one hand while coolly machine-gunning the enemy sniper out of the tree at short range.[17]

Hunt and Melton, having cheated death once again, were written up for Army Commendation Medals and were on the Kontum chopper pad at first light the next day for their flight to CCN headquarters at Da Nang for their final debriefing. Lieutenant Groves ultimately received both the Purple Heart and a Silver Star, while Haynes was awarded the Bronze Star with "V" device. The return of Floyd Bryant from the dead was the source of much talk around the recon base.

✦✧✦

Joe Walker had his own close shave with NVA on October 26. He was operating across the fence with Terry Brents as his new one-one for RT California, following the shift of Jim Birchim to start a new team, RT New Hampshire. Walker's team was taking a rest at 0830 when they were assaulted by six soldiers firing AK-47s. Pinned down by heavy fire, the recon team was organized into a defensive position, intent on breaking contact before the NVA squad could be reinforced. Walker braved the enemy fire as he picked off one of the enemy. During the next chaotic five minutes, the other five enemy soldiers advanced within ten yards of the Kontum team as Walker unleashed a fusillade of ten grenades, killing four more NVA and wounding the last man. The lone NVA fled, RT California cleared the area unharmed, and Walker was later pinned with a Bronze Star for his quick thinking and heroic actions in saving his comrades.

Not all of Walker's October missions went as planned. A case in point was another venture across the fence into Laos where Walker attempted a prisoner snatch. His team set up near a bend in a jungle trail and soon found an NVA soldier coming around the bend. He was promptly shot in the leg with a silenced weapon, but a second NVA appeared before the wounded soldier could be subdued. Walker's Montagnards then panicked and opened fire, killing both soldiers in the process. RT California was extracted and flown back to Dak To, where Walker proceeded to chew out his indigenous charges for fouling up the snatch attempt.[18]

Joe brought back the M16 rifles the NVA had been carrying, along with every stitch of clothing the enemy soldiers had been wearing. He was tired of the endless debriefing questions he knew he would face. As he explained to medic Joe Parnar that day, "If they want to know how many buttons were on the NVAs' shirts, they can count them themselves."[19]

Chapter Sixteen

SLAM VII: "SHOT ALL TO HELL"

SOG hunters sometimes found themselves to be the hunted. American recon teams inserting into Cambodia and Laos faced an ever-increasing danger of being tracked by professional kill teams. North Vietnamese counter-recon forces and tactics had steadily advanced since SOG's earliest Shining Brass days, when NVA and Vietcong units had suffered heavy losses at the hands of Green Berets. By 1967, the Hanoi high command was employing route protection battalions and rear security units along the Ho Chi Minh Trail to specifically patrol against SOG forces. In March 1967, the first class of an organization of "Special Operations Forces in the Vietnamese people's war" graduated, in a ceremony attended by North Vietnamese Premier Ho Chi Minh himself.[1]

Members of the NVA's elite 305th Airborne Brigade were converted into "sappers"—night infiltrators who raided U.S. base camps—and into special counter-recon units charged with hunting down and killing SOG teams. This defensive system had matured during 1968 into a layered program with both trackers and reaction forces, in addition to fixed security at major installations. The counter-recon teams communicated efficiently by radios and phones, using an expanded LZ watch force to report when and where a SOG team landed. When a helicopter insertion was spotted, regional commanders often dispatched such companies of elite killers, sometimes accompanied by dog teams, to scour the jungle trails and surround the SOG teams.[2]

One-Zero Joe Walker's Recon Team California encountered one of these counter-recon patrols in November, and his team's mission quickly

231

mushroomed into a ten-day offensive that included a full SLAM platoon on the ground. Walker had inserted with the intention of snatching a live NVA soldier, a feat that had eluded most Green Berets at FOB-2 during 1968. The only team to successfully do so during the year was that of Hunt, Lesesne, and Janc. Walker had twice been promoted for hauling in a live POW prior to his arrival at Kontum, but since taking over RT California in July, his attempts to bring in another had not panned out.

Walker had higher hopes of achieving this goal by November and adopted a new style of "running heavy" with his team. In his first months at FOB-2, he had run light, taking only one other American with him in the field. When RT California inserted into Laos on November 8, he took six Montagnards and two newer Green Berets with him: his one-one, Sergeant Terry Brents, and a new radio operator, Staff Sergeant Rudolph "Mike" Machata. They were deposited by three choppers during the late afternoon into an area near the Bra known as Juliet-9.

Juliet-9 was densely populated with NVA and was known to be especially dangerous. No enemy troops were encountered the first day, so Walker moved his men into the vicinity of Highway 96 to set up a simple, linear roadside ambush. As events unfolded, the affair turned out to be anything but "simple." By 0500 on November 10, the team lay in position, observing the road. The next four hours passed quietly, but at 0900, four North Vietnamese soldiers were spotted approaching their kill zone. "I was going to initiate the ambush if the traffic came from my direction," Walker said. "But the NVA traffic came from my new guy's end of the ambush site, so the opportunity to fire would be given to him."

Terry Brents waited until the NVA soldiers were perilously close before he attempted to initiate the ambush. When he pulled the trigger, his CAR-15 malfunctioned. Walker realized instantly that his whole operation had been exposed to the enemy when they heard the misfiring American Colt. He noted that the first soldier carried a Soviet-made RPD 7.62-mm light machine gun, while the other two men had wooden panels strapped to their chests. "These wooden panels had six F1 hand grenades attached by the operating pull pins," Walker said. "The last enemy soldier carried another RPD machine gun, covering their rear field of fire."[3]

The four NVA soldiers dropped into kneeling positions to assault the American team. The two RPD gunners let loose with continuous, full bursts of machine-gun bullets until their ammo belts were expended, while the two grenadiers lobbed their twelve grenades in an underhanded sling fashion into RT California's ambush area. Walker's men lobbed hand grenades in return and laid down heavy automatic fire on the kneeling soldiers before Walker led an assault into the kill zone. The firefight had been so intense that the four M18 Claymore mines Walker's team had planted had their wires severed by NVA grenade fragments.

The NVA quartet disappeared into the jungle, leaving only blood trails on the road. Walker doubted his team had scored any kills, but they had certainly maimed some of their opponents.

These guys are good, he thought. *We're not dealing with regular NVA. This is a counter-ambush team sent out to get us!*

Walker and others had long suspected a Vietnamese Army officer in their camp to be acting as a double-agent. He now believed his mission had been compromised from the get-go: he felt his team's plans had been shared with the enemy. Realizing his only hope was to get the hell out of the hot zone, Walker took a quick inventory of his team. Three of the Montagnards had been wounded but were still able to move. His count came up one short on the American side, however.

"Where's Brents? Where the hell is he?" he asked Machata.

Recon Team California quickly swept back through the light brush where they had lain concealed near the road and found Sergeant Brents stretched out on the ground with a bullet wound to his head and grenade shrapnel in his head and chest.

"What happened?" Brents murmured as Walker bent to check him out.

After being seriously wounded, Brents had corrected his jammed weapon and then tried to assist his team as best he could until he passed out from loss of blood. Walker found that Brents' skull had been sliced open like a cantaloupe, leaving his brain exposed. "Every time his heart beat, you could watch his brain pulse," he said. "The bullet had flicked off a slice of his skull but had not penetrated the brain. It was amazing and it was cleanly done. A surgeon couldn't have done any better."

Walker tried to reassure his severely wounded one-one. "Hang in there, Brents. We're going to get you some help."[4]

Recon Team California raised their base via a relay from covey, but the news was not encouraging. They were advised that another team in the area had encountered a large enemy force and was in the midst of hot action. All available air assets and ground forces were committed to extracting the other team. Walker's men took cover and administered first aid to Brents and the three wounded Montagnards in the meantime. Although Kontum sent word that help would be on its way as soon as possible, Walker knew they would have to sweat it out for at least a few hours. He prayed that his wounded one-one could last that long.

◆◇◆

"Gladiator's team is in trouble!" The word spread like wildfire through the base at Kontum. Joe Walker was one of the most well-respected one-zeros, so there was no shortage of volunteers to go save him.

Lieutenant Lee Swain had been on standby at Dak To since Walker's team had been inserted. Swain hailed from Iowa, where he had grown up fishing on lazy streams in his spare time. He joined the Army in the spring of 1966 after graduating from Northeast Missouri State, and was now a veteran of six months of commanding Hatchet Force platoons from Kontum. Swain's Hatchet Force numbered around thirty-five Montagnards plus two sergeants first class, Ratchford Haynes and Richard W. Girard. They boarded a group of choppers and headed in on November 10 to help evacuate the wounded from Walker's team.

It was mid-afternoon when Walker finally heard the welcome news that rescue birds were en route to his position. Brents was still stable in spite of his horrific-looking head wound when the Bright Light team appeared, hovering over their LZ. Lieutenant Swain's Hatchet Force team quickly secured the area and then called for the medevac choppers to come in and get Walker's wounded men out.

Medic Joe Parnar was riding the first chase ship that came in to land. He was greeted by a Green Beret and several Montagnards, who quickly led him to where Brents was laying. Parnar found RT California's new one-one to have a strong pulse despite his head injuries. Brents and three of Walker's wounded Montagnards were hauled back to the waiting chopper and flown back to the 4th Division medical facility at Dak To. Walker and Swain, however, were directed to remain on the ground and continue looking for enemy targets.[5]

Lieutenant Swain carried the PRC-25 radio and walked point behind a Montagnard, while the rest of his Americans were dispersed among the Hatchet Force. The forty-man platoon avoided contact on November 11, but Sergeant Haynes sprained his knee during the operation. By the following morning, November 12, his knee was swollen and painful, making his progress difficult. The team made contact with NVA and got into a firefight, during which one of their Montagnards was shot in the arm. Swain radioed in for an extraction. When the medevac landed to extract Haynes and the wounded soldier, Swain received two reinforcements: Bill Kendall, recently recovered from shrapnel wounds and a round of malaria, and Sergeant Floyd Bryant, the NCO recovered weeks before during the Bright Light mission that nearly cost Bill Groves his life.

Swain's platoon continued moving as directed throughout the day on November 13 without further contact. That evening, they prepared their RON site; they established a perimeter with one edge near a tree line, with a river down the bank beyond the tree line. The rest of the Hatchet Force formed a circle around a clump of bamboo and dug foxholes, lining their perimeter with Claymores and toe poppers. "The one and only M60 machine gun was placed to cover the open area," said Swain. "I made contact with Leghorn and gave them our position."[6]

Swain, Walker, and the three RT California Montagnards took shelter next to the bamboo in the center of the perimeter without digging foxholes. During the early morning hours of November 14, their RON site came under assault by a skilled NVA force that ripped into the platoon with mortars, rifle grenades, and automatic weapons fire. One of the North Vietnamese troops employed either a bugle or a megaphone to unnerve the SOG force. "I don't know what they used, but it made you shiver," said Swain.[7]

Swain radioed the Leghorn relay site to report they were under attack as he lay side by side with Walker during the initial gunfire. Suddenly a grenade exploded near them, peppering Walker with four shrapnel wounds. One piece of fragmentation ripped across his eyebrow, shattering his glasses, and slitting open a large flap of skin right on his eyebrow. He was also shot in the left leg by a bullet that remained embedded. He lay immobile for some time. Lieutenant Swain noted that Walker could talk but could not move, and that several of his Montagnards had also been wounded. Then another explosion sent shrapnel ripping through Sergeant Girard's legs.

Bill Kendall, who kept a secret journal documenting his missions, made note of the Green Beret casualties: "Walker, Brents, Machata, Bryant, and myself got shot all to hell. Walker four times with shrapnel. Bryant is really messed up. Brents is bad also plus Girard is wounded in both legs. Mine only in leg."[8]

The intensity of the attack increased and the perimeter started to collapse as Swain's Montagnards began retreating toward the tree line. Walker had recovered sufficiently to move before their position was overrun. Swain grabbed Girard and dragged him with them as they moved partially into the tree line, where the lieutenant was able to administer morphine to Girard. In the course of the firefight, Sergeant Bryant and five Montagnards, all wounded, became separated from the rest of the group and took shelter in foxholes up on a hillside. In the meantime, Walker, Swain, and the other thirty-plus men moved toward the river.

Swain raised his covey and alerted command to their desperate situation. Air cover, contacted by the Leghorn relay site, soon arrived, but the pilots could do little to tell friend from foe in the darkness. Swain asked them to dive and shoot anyway, hoping that his team would not be further shot up in the process. He and Walker then moved toward the river, dragging Girard with them as they went. They moved across the water and set up a perimeter on the far bank with the wounded men in the middle. The overrun and badly scattered Hatchet Force had no recourse but to wait out the night.

◆◇◆

Laos was a hotbed of activity during the night of November 13–14. Even before the NVA hit Walker and Swain's unit again, another SOG team was being overrun by counter-recon forces.

RT Vermont, led by One-Zero Roger Loe, was inserted on a SLAM VII mission with ten days of food and ammunition. They were dropped into rolling, forested mountains twenty-nine miles west of Dak To in the Laotian province of Attapeu. Loe's new one-one and radio operator was Specialist Fourth Class William Michael Copley, whom his family called Mike but was better known to his recon buddies as Bill. Nineteen-year-old Copley graduated from Chatsworth High School in Southern California's San Fernando Valley, and enlisted in the Army, where he graduated in the top five percent of his military class.[9]

After about four days on the ground, Loe, Copley, and their eight Montagnards were advised to hole up, as other recon teams on the ground were in trouble and there would be no air support available. RT Vermont utilized a different RON site each night for the next six days within close proximity of their reported location. Early on the morning of November 13, Loe was given another mission and had to move again. His team was in desperate need of water at this point and struck out toward a river shown on his map to the northeast. He found signs that an estimated company-size NVA force had bivouacked about four hundred yards from Vermont's RON site.[10]

Loe's men were preparing to set up their RON that evening when they were ambushed. He heard NVA voices shouting in English, "American die now" and "pray to your Buddha." During the initial burst of automatic gunfire, Bill Copley was hit by a round that penetrated his upper left shoulder and exited his back.

"Help me! I'm hit!" he cried.

Sergeant First Class Loe scrambled to apply a pressure bandage to his young teammate, who appeared weak from heavy blood loss. Calling for his Montagnards to cover him, Loe hoisted Copley onto his back and ran toward their defensive perimeter as the NVA lobbed concussion grenades. As he tried to run with his cumbersome load, he lost his footing on the uneven terrain and fell. Ignoring the raging firefight, he began working to save Copley again until he could see the color and life fade from the teenage Green Beret's face.

Recon Team Vermont was in danger of being overrun, forcing Loe to abandon Copley's body for the time being in order to save others. The massing NVA forced the recon team to fight its way backward, in retreat from their advancing opponents. During the scramble, Loe crashed down a steep hill through the undergrowth with only two of his Montagnards, Bying and Theiu, still with him. They ran full-out for a half-hour before stopping to fill their canteens near the base of a waterfall. "I had hardly had a drink when we heard hollering again behind us and then from the west of us was more hollering and rifle fire," said Loe.

The trio ran for their lives for another half-hour before reaching a steep, rocky wall. They climbed a hundred feet up and took cover for the night on a little ledge surrounded by trees. Loe lost his emergency radio in the flight and now had no way to call for an extraction. Unknown to him, a Bright Light extraction team was inserted into Laos that evening to search for RT Vermont and attempt to have them extracted.

A twelve-man team, RT New Hampshire, was ordered to conduct a long-range reconnaissance patrol into Laos west of Ben Het to find and rescue Roger Loe's men. The one-zero was Lieutenant Jim Birchim, who was caught with his regular one-one on temporary leave when RT New Hampshire was tapped for the Bright Light. He quickly found a willing volunteer in the form of Specialist Fourth Class Frank Belletire, a recent arrival to Kontum who was not yet regularly assigned to a team. Belletire, who quit school at Northern Illinois University before his senior year in 1967 to join the Army, agreed to join Birchim to carry the radio and act as the team's acting one-one. The remainder of RT New Hampshire were Montagnards: interpreter Nam, Zero-Zero Sergeant Ngo van Chien, and riflemen Hlur, Phier, Mion, Miang, Bang, Tok, Teo, and Beng.[11]

On the morning of November 14, Birchim's team began searching for RT Vermont, which was still trying to evade the enemy. Recon Team New Hampshire moved farther west through the dense jungle on November 15 until team members began hearing voices in the jungle and a bamboo signaling device to the north of their position. Birchim steadily moved his men back to where the ambush had occurred and spent the next two days searching in vain for Bill Copley. Since he was last seen barely alive, he was officially listed as MIA. Loe and his two Montagnards, Bying and Theiu, were still very much alive. They waited until daylight on November 14 before departing their rocky bluff to head northeast down-slope toward a nearby stream.[12]

When they came under enemy fire again this day, Loe became entangled in a vine trap and lost sight of team member Theiu in the process. By the time he had cut himself free from the vines, he was left with only Bying. The two charged across the top of a slope under fire by NVA and crashed through thick trees on the back side of the slope. They waited out the night and began moving again the next afternoon, but Loe and his Montagnard ran afoul of yet another NVA patrol. After Loe emptied his magazine, he moved down a path, thinking that Bying was right behind him. When he stopped to reload, he spotted his indigenous companion up on a hill with his signal mirror out.

Before Loe could get to him, Bying was cut down by enemy fire. Loe emptied another magazine and ran for his life once again, fighting through quicksand-like mud at the bottom of the hill. He headed for the primary LZ his team had come in on, still pursued by the NVA. He found the heavy bamboo in his area made it difficult to move without making a lot of noise, so he holed up for a while to rest and bandaged himself. "I had lost quite a lot of blood," he said. "I prayed for strength, for rain, and lots of wind."

As if in answer to his supplication, a heavy rainstorm with strong winds commenced. He used the welcome cover to move swiftly out of the bamboo to a wide valley with elephant grass. The next morning, he was able to signal an aircraft with his emergency mirror. Although unsure that he had been seen, Loe was finally extracted from the jungle three days later by a Vietnamese H-35 helicopter crew.

Loe had been declared MIA for three days before he was recovered. Four days after arriving at the Pleiku hospital, he was informed that four Montagnards from RT Vermont had been picked up. "They had walked out and I had been so sure that they were all dead," he said. "The only reason I figure I didn't get shot before I did, or worse, was they wanted to take me alive as a prisoner. Maybe someone upstairs was taking care of me."

◆◇◆

The Hatchet Force platoon under Lee Swain and Joe Walker was in rough shape as the sun began to break through the Laotian jungle on the morning of November 14. Girard, Machata, Kendall, and several Montagnards were wounded, while Sergeant Bryant and five other Montagnards had not been seen since the NVA overran their RON hours before. Walker was suffering with shrapnel wounds and a bullet in his left leg. The laceration through his eyebrow had allowed a large hunk of skin to droop over his eye, where blood and flesh had dried like an eye patch. "I thought I had lost my eye and was blind," he said.

Lieutenant Swain's emergency calls into Leghorn had been relayed to Kontum, where base commander Colonel Smith wasted no time. Walker's team had been overrun for the second time in four days, so this time, he opted to send in heavy forces on the morning of November 14 to help the platoon. Captain Lolly Sciriaev, a relative newcomer to the base, was in charge of the company-sized unit—about 115 men, including Green Berets and Montagnards. Lieutenant Tom Jaeger was second in command, and his own platoon included Bright Light veterans Bob Howard and Steve Roche. Howard, never one to miss a good fight, would serve as Jaeger's first sergeant for the mission.

The other three platoon leaders were lieutenants Walter Huczko, Robert Price, and Bill Groves. The latter was only recently recovered from the late October Bright Light in which he had been badly wounded rescuing Sergeant Bryant—who was now missing in action once again. Huczko, a fiery redhead, had three other Americans in his platoon: Sergeant First Class Lloyd "OD" O'Daniel, Staff Sergeant Bob Gron, and Sergeant Alan Farrell. It took two trips of eight choppers—four Kingbees and four Huey slicks—to ferry all of the reaction battalion to Dak To. Medic Joe Parnar, assigned to the chase ship, waited around for an hour for the second half of the group to reach the staging base. Then, the first birds lifted off for Juliet-9, eight slicks carrying about fifty men, escorted by four gunships.

Before they arrived, Lieutenant Swain had already been in contact with the Cessna Bird Dog overhead. He, Walker, and the largest contingent of their platoon were on the bank of the river, just opposite the RON site where they had been overrun. Swain, hoping to cross back to search for other surviving members of his platoon, called for an air strike between the waterline and the top of the far bank. The Cessna swooped in low to drop a willy peter smoke round to mark the spot, followed by a gunship that began chewing up that area. Screams suddenly erupted from the area and Walker saw two of his Montagnards who had gotten separated during the night action. Walker ran to the middle of the river to meet them as the Bird Dog swooped in low to reconnoiter the RON site.

The covey then directed two H-34 Kingbees to land on the sandbar that was a little over twenty yards wide to begin taking out the wounded from the Hatchet Force. Captain Sciriaev and his men jumped out and quickly sized up the situation. The chopper carrying Lieutenant Tom Jaeger also deposited most of its platoon, including First Sergeant Bob Howard. Jaeger opted to remain in the chopper for the moment to take a covey rider type aerial view of the battlefield. As the last of the platoons were inserted, the last two choppers began taking 37-mm AA fire from a distance to the southwest.

Medic Parnar moved quickly to help tend the wounded. Joe Walker was much relieved to see Bob Howard and the reaction battalion moving in. He and his men were disorganized, low on weapons and ammunition, having spent several hours lying low near the river, trying to keep Sergeant Girard's moans of pain from giving them away to the enemy. Walker tried to refuse any medical attention for himself, although one lens of his glasses had been blown out. Parnar ignored the protests, quickly suturing the flap of skin over Walker's eye to improve his vision. He then turned his attention to helping move Girard and the other wounded men toward the sandbar for extraction.[13]

Texan Tony Dorff, who had arrived at Kontum a month prior, was flying as the second chase-slick medic to help with the wounded. As his Huey settled onto the narrow sandbar, he could see Howard and others helping the wounded Montagnards across the stream. Dorff helped Walker load three of his wounded Montagnards onto the chopper as it settled onto the sandbar. Joe Parnar, in talking to Walker, mentioned that if anyone was still alive up on their RON site they would need medical attention immediately. The choppers were preparing to lift off with Walker and his wounded teammates, but the one-zero agreed with Parnar and added, "I'm going up there."[14]

Dorff was stunned. *This is the damnedest thing I've ever seen in my life,* he thought. *When most people get into a firefight and get shot up, they're happy to get on a helicopter and get out of there. He's going right back in.* As Walker turned to head with Parnar and others for the RON site, Dorff was further shocked to see Walker's three wounded Montagnards instinctively jump off the chopper to remain with their team leader.

Walker went to Captain Sciriaev, the Hatchet Force commander, and announced that he was heading back to the RON site. He was joined by Bob Howard, Sergeant Lloyd O'Daniel, medic Parnar, and several others. The water was quite deep in places, forcing Howard to hold up some of the shorter Montagnards as they bobbed across. The group climbed up the hillside and found a massacre site: five Montagnards and Floyd Bryant were laying in their foxholes that had been dug the previous night, each man having been shot in the head and left for dead.

Howard was cautiously moving past Bryant's body when something caught his attention. He was looking at the NCO's face as he crept past when he noticed one of Bryant's eyeballs following his movement.

"Damn! This one's alive!" Howard shouted.[15]

O'Daniel found that the NVA's head shot had only grazed Bryant's forehead. "He had other shrapnel wounds but his biggest concern was for his manhood," said O'Daniel. "He had been shot in the crotch also."[16] Alan

Staff Sergeant Rudolph "Mike" Machata, wounded during SLAM VII, was later killed in action during 1969. *Jon Davidson photo via Joe Parnar*

Sergeant Alan Farrell, seen atop Leghorn in 1968, was another of the fifty-plus SOG men who were killed or wounded during the SLAM VII mission. *Alan Farrell via Joe Parnar*

Farrell was amazed that Bryant had survived. "The round had not penetrated the skull. It had gone around under the skin, under the head and came out under the temple."[17]

Walker noticed a puddle of coagulated blood, seemingly quart-sized, beside where Bryant lay curled up, facing uphill. Parnar rushed up the hill, began assessing Bryant's wounds, and opened his shirt to start an IV. He estimated the Green Beret had nineteen wounds over his body. As Parnar worked on him, Bryant stammered out a chilling tale to his rescuers. He said the NVA had moved through their RON site shortly after sunrise, firing shots into the dead and wounded to make sure they were finished off. The bullet fired into Bryant's forehead left a secondary wound where it had bounced off his skull and exited. Other men rigged a makeshift stretcher while Bryant spoke, and then he was carried down toward the river sandbar while Parnar shuffled alongside holding the IV bottle.[18]

Bryant was taken out on one of the choppers, along with the dead indigenous soldiers, the wounded Joe Walker, and his three wounded Montagnards. Medics were unable to extract the bullet from Walker's left leg, leaving him with a lifelong souvenir from Vietnam. Bill Kendall, also medevaced out with minor wounds, would record in his contraband journal: "Four KIA, 8 MIA, 23 WIA. I think we took a hell of a beating on this operation."[19]

The extraction was not without incident. One of the Hueys was hit by enemy fire and made a forced landing in the vicinity. In the ensuing crash,

Staff Sergeant Mike Machata was pinned in the wreckage. He had survived two assaults on Walker's team but now found himself in grave peril. Machata extracted himself, helped the badly shaken chopper crew set up a perimeter, and then used demolitions to blow up the downed bird. Amid heavy NVA gunfire, Machata and his comrades were finally extracted.

Once the dead and wounded were cleared from the river area, Lieutenant Swain was left on the ground with the remainder of his indigenous platoon. Captain Sciriaev, in charge of the SLAM VII force as senior officer present, was directed to continue the mission, with Lieutenant Tom Jaeger as his second in command. Joe Parnar assumed incorrectly that the reaction battalion would be heading out. "We received instructions to proceed in the direction of the 37mm guns that had been shooting at the choppers," he said. "I realized I had screwed up royally as my chase medic pack contained only medical supplies and no food."[20]

More than a hundred men strong, the SLAM company moved south, following the river. Sciriaev, Jaeger, Swain, Howard, Huczko, Groves, and Price moved their men back across the river at another point where the water was chest deep and flowing fast. A couple of hundred yards farther, the company prepared their RON position. The men could hear truck engines moving down Highway 96 during the night hours but they escaped enemy attack at least for this night.

After daybreak on November 15, the SLAM company had its breakfast and then moved out. For most of the battalion, it was their second day across the fence in a very hostile region. Lee Swain, who had inserted on November 10 to support Walker's team, was already marking his sixth day in Juliet-9.

◆◇◆

Recon Team New Hampshire was still trying to find Roger Loe's RT Vermont on November 15. Jim Birchim's team had lunch and then proceeded westward, staying on the north side of a hill in the afternoon. He then decided to change direction and headed north, moving into a dry streambed and then up the other side. As they reached the top of the hill about 1430, they were ambushed by NVA soldiers with grenades and automatic weapons. Sergeant Chien used hand signals to tell Birchim that interpreter Nam had been hit in the chest and was killed. The rest of the team retreated down the hill back to the streambed.

As they reached the bottom of the gully, Birchim slipped and fell, breaking his ankle. With the aid of Belletire and some of the Montagnards, Birchim and the others climbed back up the hill they had just descended.

Halfway up, Belletire made contact with the FAC circling overhead. He apprised them of their situation and estimated that New Hampshire was surrounded by approximately twenty-five NVA. Belletire requested air strikes to suppress the NVA action and an emergency extraction.

Fighter aircraft arrived overhead about 1500 to provide close air support and began making runs on identified targets. Birchim's team, soon under NVA fire once again, was forced to split up to escape and evade toward a designated area for extraction. At about 1600, Birchim and Belletire moved together toward a small LZ some 550 yards to the east. Birchim, suffering from shrapnel in his back and his ankle injury, was supported by Belletire en route. As they hobbled forward, they first found Beng, one of their Montagnards who had ran off earlier, and then Sergeant Chien. The foursome was assaulted once again by NVA grenades and small-arms fire, compelling Belletire to radio in for another air strike. The enemy force was no more than fifty-five yards away and rapidly closing, so he called for the explosives to be put right onto their team. The resulting strike was successful in either killing or driving away the NVA.

By 1800, a light rain was falling as night approached. There would be time for only one desperate extraction attempt, and the FAC quickly coached in a 57th AHC Gladiator slick toward the designated LZ. Gladiator 26, piloted by First Lieutenant Craig Collier, circled as four Montagnards from RT New Hampshire—Miang, Bang, Tok, and Teo—prepared their extraction gear. Collier dropped his chopper to a hundred feet above the trees and hovered as his crewmen tossed out the sandbags to drop the four strings in the gathering darkness. Two strings hung up in the trees, requiring the four indigenous personnel to attach themselves to only two ropes.[21]

Once the four Montagnards were attached to the two good lines, Collier began lifting up directly. He found that his Huey did not have sufficient lift in the mountainous altitudes and nearly stalled out. His struggle to attain power resulted in New Hampshire's indigenous troops being dragged through the canopy at about twenty-five miles per hour for a few long seconds until the aircraft could rise through transition to flight. Collier fought his way through a violent storm en route to base, his SF men swinging wildly on their lines the entire way as ice formed on their clothing in the storm. The pilot was forced to fly the twisting Plei Trap valley by memory until he finally emerged from the storm and the mountain valley with less than five minutes of reserve fuel to fly another ten miles.[22]

Collier made it to Kontum's runway with no reserve fuel and lowered the four recon men on their 150-foot strings to waiting hands. His four extracted Montagnards survived their icy ordeal, but the rest of RT

New Hampshire suffered even more. Four recon men—Birchim, Belletire, Chien, and Beng—remained on the ground some distance from the first LZ after Collier's departure.

Rather than wait on them to reach the LZ, Warrant Officer First Class Carl Hoeck, pilot of Gladiator 342, hovered his second Huey at an altitude of a hundred to 120 feet over a small hole in the jungle canopy above them. Hoeck's crew chief and door gunner dropped McGuire extraction rigs through the canopy for the four men, but one of the four rigs hung up in the canopy. Birchim ensured that Chien and Beng, each wounded by grenade frags during the running gun battle, were secured into their rigs. The two Americans were not seriously wounded so they climbed into the third rig dangling from the other side and secured themselves. Pilot Hoeck heard from his crew that one of the men below had signaled for them to take off, so he lifted off, dragging Team New Hampshire through the trees and nearly dislodging all of them.

Hoeck battled the same mountainous elements and lift challenges that his comrade Collier had faced moments before. His only means of obtaining sufficient power to lift the men was to at first move forward while lifting up. Birchim's team was pounded by the canopy until Gladiator 342 cleared the jungle. Immediately after climbing for altitude, Hoeck realized they were in clouds and he had to fly by instruments alone. He fought to control his aircraft due to the weight of the four men swinging below. It took some thirty to forty minutes to battle through the storm, and when he reached Kontum airfield, his crew found that only three of the four men remained on the rigs.

The extraction had been pure hell for Frank Belletire. As they smacked through the canopy, he and Birchim became unseated, leaving Belletire hanging in the McGuire rig with his head down and Birchim on his back. Due to the darkness and cloud cover, the Huey crew was unable to see their predicament. The two Green Berets clung to each other desperately for a half hour, both in extreme pain and Belletire only semiconscious as they endured a violent, heavy tropical storm in pitch-black darkness. Lieutenant Birchim began slipping during the flight and he slowly slid down Belletire's body. "He was down to my foot, and then gone," Belletire said. He attempted to hang onto the lieutenant, but the rigging wrapped around his arm and neck until Belletire blacked out.[23]

Upon landing, Belletire and the two remaining Montagnards were shivering and their clothes were laden with ice. Belletire was unconscious, with rope burns cut deep into his hands where he had tried to hang onto his one-zero. Intelligence officers who reviewed the information believe that Birchim slipped from the rig and fell from a height of fifteen hundred to two thousand feet into jungle-covered mountains just north of Highway QL 14, approximately six miles north-northwest of Dak To. Hoeck's chopper flew a total of forty-eight miles from the point of extraction to Kontum Airfield. Due to uncertainty of the loss point and the complete darkness, no additional search effort was mounted to find Lieutenant Birchim. He was declared MIA and his body remains unrecovered.

Jim Birchim was posthumously awarded the Distinguished Service Cross, on January 21, 1972, for "extraordinary heroism and devotion to duty." He was the eighth recon man running from Kontum to earn the nation's second highest military award.

✦◇✦

The tragedy involving Birchim and RT New Hampshire was unknown to the SLAM VII company still on the ground.

Medic Joe Parnar had accepted half of an unfinished spaghetti ration that morning but had no idea what he would eat for the rest of the mission. Captain Sciriaev moved his SLAM company without contact on November 15. As darkness approached, they prepared to RON on a small hilltop and the Montagnards began digging foxholes. The Americans opted not to dig in, but merely picked spots on which to lay on the open ground.[24]

Parnar picked a sleeping position near Specialist Fifth Class Steve Roche and Sergeant Bob Howard. He felt secure being near Howard, who had already received a Distinguished Service Cross. Parnar was happy to accept a can of C rations from Roche before he lay down to share a poncho liner with Roche for the night's rest.

Around 0400 on November 16, mortar explosions and rifle grenades suddenly rained down on the SLAM company in the darkness. Red-hot shrapnel chewed up the hillside and tore through rucksacks, fatigues, and flesh. Lieutenant Bill Groves was hit, along with Jon Davidson, Bob Van Hall, and Staff Sergeant Fred Hubel. *What a hell of a way to spend my twenty-sixth birthday!* thought Lee Swain as his platoon fired back.

Parnar, Roche, and Howard began crawling toward a rotten tree stump and fallen log as explosions rocked their vicinity. Howard and Parnar, the last to reach the meager cover, were wounded in their backs by shrapnel as they moved. Ignoring his injuries, Howard crawled from position to position directing his Montagnards' return fire, ordering them to fire only their M79 grenade launchers, to avoid muzzle flashes from their rifles becoming the enemy's aiming point.

Lieutenant Tom Jaeger raised Leghorn via radio that his force was under a heavy RPG attack. Lloyd O'Daniel hustled about, moving the wounded into the center of the company's perimeter and assisting medics Dorff and Parnar, both wounded, with offering first aid. With the dawn on November 16 came welcomed air strikes from Skyraider pilots, who pounded the enemy position with CBU bomblets, bullets, and explosives. The SLAM company was surrounded by NVA and had an estimated eleven men already wounded badly enough to warrant extraction.

Captain Sciriaev, relaying the thoughts shared by his platoon commanders, asked Kontum command that their company be extracted. The orders that came back were disconcerting: "Break out of your encirclement and continue your mission!"[25]

Further requests to have the SLAM company extracted were met with harsh replies from base. The radio crackled with orders that the wounded were to be medevaced out, along with Sciriaev, and that the second-in-command, Lieutenant Jaeger, was to assume command of the operation. When the extraction choppers began settling on the LZ, platoon leader Bill Groves, Jon Davidson, Tony Dorff, and more than a dozen other wounded were taken out. As a medic, Dorff—lightly wounded by shrapnel—expressed his desires to stay in but was denied. "The company commander said that anybody that was wounded was going out, and he was serious about that," said Dorff.

Sciriaev boarded one of the extraction Hueys, and he would be reassigned from Kontum elsewhere within days. First Lieutenant Craig Collier of the 57th AHC was awarded a Distinguished Flying Cross for pulling out fourteen wounded SLAM men while under fire, far over the acceptable load for a UH-1H in the mountains. When he landed his Huey at Dak To, there were numerous blood streaks from the passenger compartment all the way back to the end of the tail boom.[26]

Bill Kendall, already wounded on November 14, received an Air Medal for taking part in three resupply flights in support of the SLAM company. He was wounded by shrapnel two more times in the process. Kendall noted in his journal entry for November 17 the toll that had already been inflicted on the men of SLAM VII: "So far, 18 Americans WIA, 2 KIA [Copley, Birchim]. 36 SCU [indigenous personnel] WIA, six MIA, 4 KIA. Seven days of action so far."[27]

And the mission was far from over.

✦◇✦

"We were too large a group to be able to go unnoticed," said Tom Jaeger.[28] The lieutenant, placed in command after his captain had been ordered out, realized that the NVA knew exactly where his Hatchet Force company established their RON site each night. Jaeger moved his company down Highway 96, zigzagging in the general direction of where the enemy's 37-mm guns were suspected to be located. He made his next RON site deep in the jungle in an area so rocky that Steve Roche and Joe Parnar could scarcely scrape depressions deep enough in which to rest. Jaeger called for a resupply on the morning of November 17, as his men were running short of food and supplies. The first plane came in low, but Lieutenant Lee Swain watched in disgust as the parachute supply bundle drifted far from their LZ and landed near a far tree line occupied by the NVA.[29]

It was deemed too dangerous to attempt to retrieve. Fortunately, the second bundle landed only about a hundred yards from their perimeter and the men were able to retrieve it. The wooden case, although marked as "mortar ammunition," was found to contain numerous cartons of cigarettes. "I got five full packs of Marlboros," said Parnar. "I remember how the first cigarette I lit up made me dizzy from not having smoked for so long."[30]

Jaeger moved the SLAM company another quarter-mile to a new clearing and called for another chopper drop of food and plastic bottles of water. As his recon men hurried to move the goods back to the new perimeter, gunfire broke out on the LZ and a Montagnard was hit in the elbow by an AK round. Bob Howard charged forward down the hill, with medic Parnar close behind, both firing at the NVA until they could pull the Montagnard to safety and apply first aid.

An estimated two squads of NVA were responsible for the intense small-arms fire that swept through the small security element left to guard the supplies. Lieutenant Walt Huczko led his platoon back to the LZ and directed their fire until the supplies were moved to a safer position. Lloyd O'Daniel was credited with killing three VC and wounding several others before the aggressors were forced to break contact. During the night, Parnar became worried enough about his noisy wounded Montagnard that he administered morphine to prevent the wounded man's groans from drawing more NVA fire. Shortly after daybreak on November 18, Jaeger was able to get the Montagnard extracted. The company continued to make progress toward its target area, split into two columns sixteen yards apart to give them opportunity to return fire to their left or right flanks.[31]

By mid-afternoon, the SLAM company had emerged from the dense jungle to a point near Highway 96 with a large clearing and an intersecting, well-worn secondary road. "We were told to move across the clearing to a tree line," said Lee Swain.[32] Lieutenant Jaeger, sensing something was wrong, called Leghorn to request a Dak To–based FAC to be placed overhead as they crossed the exposed area.

Once the air cover arrived, Jaeger ordered his company to move on. Bob Howard and Lieutenant Swain took point and began walking together across the tall grass of the clearing, lined with thickets of trees on each side. They were side by side, with various Montagnards spread out behind them, abreast rather than in a file. About three-quarters of the way across, Howard suddenly paused and motioned to Swain.

"There's NVA up ahead, in the tree line. What should we do?"

"Well, they know we're here," Swain whispered. "Let's just spring the ambush first."

The pair opened up with their CAR-15s on the NVA concealed ahead of them. As the enemy responded with rifle grenades and automatic fire, Jaeger realized his company had nearly walked right into the kill zone of a large NVA force. "They had us surrounded," he said. "Howard and Swain had tripped the ambush before we walked into the kill zone. Then all hell broke loose."[33] He found himself in the center of the initial barrage of fire about thirty yards behind his point men.

Swain and Howard dropped to the ground near a small bush and returned the fire coming from the tree line. Shortly into the fight, an RPG round screamed in and exploded with terrific force beside Swain. He looked back and saw that his left foot was at an odd angle, but he could not immediately comprehend how severe his injuries were.

He poked Howard: "I'm wounded!"

The recon sergeant glanced quickly at the lieutenant and reassured him, "You're okay." He continued firing into the tree line.

"Look again," Swain pleaded. "It's my foot."

Howard could see that the lieutenant's wounds were life threatening but for the moment they had no choice but to continue firing back at the NVA. Swain's right calf was gone, blown away by the RPG, and the smaller bone in his leg was snapped. "The tail end of the rocket slid underneath my ankle and took everything out except my Achilles tendon," Swain said. "My foot was just hanging by a tendon." He knew if Howard tried to stand to carry him out, he would be shot and killed.

"I can't move," Swain said. "If you have to leave me, kill me first."

Lieutenant Jaeger was on the radio, calling for air support as soon as the enemy attack commenced. He spotted a wounded Vietnamese Hatchet Force man lying some twenty yards away, so he raced without hesitation through a hail of bullets to help administer life-saving aid. Jaeger was then notified that his subordinate Lee Swain had been badly hit. He ran more than forty yards across the field under heavy fire to check his condition and found that Swain's right leg was hanging only by tendons. The left leg was also torn by shrapnel and was bleeding profusely. Jaeger removed his

First Lieutenant Lee Swain (*right*) lost one of his legs due to severe injuries from an RPG explosion on the SLAM VII mission. *Lee Swain via Jason Hardy*

Green Beret medic Joe Parnar (*right*) has just been pinned with a Purple Heart by CCC base commander Colonel Roy Bahr at a January 1969 awards ceremony. Parnar helped save Swain and many others during this mission. *Joe Parnar*

belt, fashioned a tourniquet around Swain's left leg, and called back for a medic.

Joe Parnar advanced on the double with his buddy Steve Roche, noting many Montagnards firing into the surrounding jungle as explosions went off all around them. Parnar spotted Howard lying on the ground, helping to administer to Lieutenant Swain. "His foot was blown off cleanly at the ankle and attached to his leg only by the Achilles tendon," Parnar said. "The other leg looked as if a giant hand had ripped out a chunk of his calf, exposing the tibia and fibula bones." Parnar was equally shocked at the site of the exposed white bones as he was with the fortitude Swain was maintaining under such incredible duress. "He was lying on his stomach with his chin resting on his crossed wrists and saying to Bob Howard that this would take care of his pheasant hunting."[34]

Parnar tried to reassure the officer. "Don't worry, sir, you're going to do a lot of pheasant hunting."

"What do you mean?" Swain snapped. "My foot's blown off!"

Parnar put a tourniquet on Swain's right leg as the officer was given morphine. Jaeger immediately got on the radio and called for a medevac chopper. He then crawled to a position close to Howard and lay there calling in air strikes against the NVA massing to their south, east, and west. The enemy was strongest on their southern perimeter, so Jaeger called for one of the A-1Es to lay down ordnance particularly close. "He got it within twenty-five yards of our southern perimeter and really took out a lot of bad guys," Jaeger said.[35]

The bomb cluster fragments that stripped branches from trees tore through the flesh of several Hatchet Force men as well. Howard and Parnar were both hit as they continued to work on Lieutenant Swain. Parnar attempted to brush a burning fragment off his right calf but found that the metal had penetrated into the muscle. One of the indigenous troops from Lloyd O'Daniel's Montagnard camp platoon cried out for a doctor in Vietnamese as blood poured from his head wound.

Parnar finished putting a large combat dressing around Swain's nearly severed ankle, then used another to tie around Swain's boot, running up his calf, to help hold the dangling foot in place. As he completed his make-shift medical treatment, O'Daniel's wounded Montagnard was escorted to him, trying to clutch a large flap of skin hanging from the right side of his face off his jaw. As Parnar applied a combat dressing to hold the man's face together, another Montagnard summoned him to where an American lay wounded. Parnar directed an indigenous trooper to help his wounded friend maintain pressure to the dressing on his face before grabbing his M16 to head into the jungle where Sergeant Lee Dickerson lay in a small grove of bamboo.

"I can't see," Dickerson cried. "I can't see!"

Dickerson had been hit by enemy fire as he and his platoon leader, First Lieutenant Bob Price, were advancing across the field a short distance from Swain and Howard. Price had also been wounded, but he managed to help treat Dickerson and help drag him closer to safety. Parnar found that the sergeant was still lying exposed out beyond the company's defensive perimeter. He, the Montagnard, and Price grabbed Dickerson and carefully dragged him back to the perimeter as machine-gun bullets thumped into the jungle floor all around them. Parnar administered first aid and dressings to Dickerson's chest wound before moving back to attend to other wounded men.

Lieutenant Jaeger called for a medevac chopper to remove the most seriously wounded but his SLAM company remained under enemy attack during the ninety minutes it took for help to arrive. Sergeant O'Daniel, finding his platoon pinned down at one point by an NVA machine gun, picked up a light anti-tank weapon, charged toward the bunker, and killed all four North Vietnamese within. Joe Parnar spent that time treating the wounded, giving Lieutenant Swain another shot of morphine as his level of pain spiked.

The medevac choppers could not come soon enough for Swain or Parnar.

✦✧✦

Tony Dorff was flying chase medic on one of the inbound Hueys on the late afternoon of November 18. Feeling remorse for having been extracted with minor shrapnel wounds two days prior, he offered to go back in when he heard the company had been hit again.

One of the 57th AHC pilots making this extraction attempt was First Lieutenant Craig Collier. His Gladiator Huey had already been shot up during his actions on previous days to resupply the SLAM company and to pull out the most seriously wounded men. Collier now found the LZ area to be highly contested by NVA, who unleashed a fury of ground fire toward the American choppers. "Attempts to just recon drew such intense fire that you couldn't hear the radio's talk," he said.[36]

The senior pilot leading the flight of four UH-1H Huey Gladiators from Dak To was twenty-year-old Warrant Officer Carl M. Hoeck. When his flight arrived over Juliet-9, he found the covey rider to be former recon man Mike Bingo—call sign "cheetah"—flying in an O-2 Cessna Skymaster. Hoeck's co-pilot was Lieutenant Fred Ledfors, who outranked him but had less experience, thus putting him in the right seat. Bingo asked the four Hueys to orbit at nine thousand feet a few miles to the southeast while he sorted out the mess below. Hoeck began communicating with the SF on the ground while he hovered. "He told me about his wounded that weren't going to make it unless we got them out soon," Hoeck said. "His voice had the sharp edge of desperation."[37] Forty-five minutes ticked away as the chopper pilots waited on sufficient TAC air to go in.

At length, Hoeck advised Bingo he could make only one try to get a bird into the hot LZ without TAC air before their fuel situation became desperate. Hoeck communicated with fellow pilot Collier that they would pretend to leave the area, then double back at low altitude and move in at treetop level, with his chopper making the first attempt. Hoeck directed the other choppers to remain at altitude some distance away.

Medic Dorff, flying in the rear compartment of Hoeck's Gladiator 167, felt a sudden drop as his pilot went in low from north to south at tree-top level. Hoeck slowly lowered his collective pitch, added an excessive amount of left pedal, and rolled into a tight, descending left spiral. The jungle flashed by as cheetah called out headings for the Huey pilot. All of a sudden, the jungle ahead of Hoeck's slick thinned out as he reached a more open area. His chopper was immediately greeted by the popping sound of AK small-arms fire, so Hoeck's door gunner and crew chief opened up with their M60s in return.[38]

"Gladiator 167 receiving fire," he called over the radio.

Hoeck slouched down in his seat to get entirely behind the sliding chest armor ("chicken plate"), peering over the top as he flashed past the LZ on his first run with his gunners blazing through their ammunition. Hoeck called to Bingo for vectors for a second run to the LZ, this time moving from west to east to avoid the heaviest gunfire.

The ground fire was lighter due to Gladiator 167 moving in over thicker jungle cover. As Bingo called out one kilometer to the LZ, Hoeck began slowing his bird.

"Two hundred meters out," called Bingo. "One hundred meters out. Now, look to your one o'clock!"

As Hoeck slowed his Huey down through forty-five knots, door gunner Wayne Gilmore suddenly cried out, "Sir, there's a tank!"

As the chopper settled into a hover, a .51-caliber (12.7-mm heavy machine gun) antiaircraft gun on tracks suddenly commenced fire on it. On the ground, Bob Howard suspected it was a half-tracked vehicle he had heard rumbling in the nearby cover. Hoeck felt rounds slamming into his chopper's right side like someone pounding away with a sledgehammer. He opened up on his mic and announced again, "Gladiator 167 receiving fire!" As his Huey drifted laterally away from the impacting rounds, Hoeck's master caution light was flashing and a glance at the caution panel showed he had lost his engine, hydraulics, and everything vital to remaining airborne.

"167's hit!" Hoeck called. "We're on fire. We're going in!"

Below, Tom Jaeger saw that the chopper was almost above his Hatchet Force company when the anti-aircraft gun crew scored a direct hit. More rounds punched through the floor of Gladiator 167, one of the blasts violent enough to slam the chopper's crew chief off the ceiling and leave him with a painfully jammed neck.

Hoeck, hoping to avoid crashing into the SF men below, scanned desperately for a suitable landing spot as he slid his mortally wounded ship a little farther along his existing trajectory. Spotting a thinner patch of jungle, he made a smooth, quick pull to full pitch to avoid splattering hard in the jungle. As he neared impact, the trees around him blurred with the dropping speed. "The rotor system took a full bite of air, and you could feel the deceleration," he said. "Then we hit."[39]

Gladiator 167 smashed hard and bounced up more than ten feet. Hoeck floated out of his seat and hit his helmet on the greenhouse window above. He tried to keep his chopper centered as it smashed hard again into the soft jungle soil, blasting dirt and grass across the opening created by the impact. Hoeck was stunned as he noticed the red-orange flames licking at his right elbow. He struggled to free himself from his shoulder harness release and found that his door was stuck firmly. A momentary flash of panic seized the pilot. *I'm going to burn to death here in my seat!*

The other occupants were equally shaken. Tony Dorff injured his knee, back, and neck in the crash, dislocated his shoulder, and suffered broken ribs. Miraculously, no one on board was killed or more seriously injured. Fellow medic Parnar, tending to the wounded Hatchet Force men on the ground, watched the crippled Huey slam into the jungle a hundred meters beyond his position. *Oh, no*, he thought. *I don't need any more wounded.*[40]

Jaeger, suffering from painful grenade shrapnel wounds and carrying the company radio on his back, had little time to worry about his own pain as he suddenly noticed NVA soldiers moving toward the downed chopper some seventy-five feet away. Without hesitating, he and Bob Howard began yelling and jumped up to run to their aid. Pilot Hoeck was still fumbling with his harness release when a Green Beret helped pull him through the door window, depositing him on the ripe, earthy-smelling jungle floor.

Howard and Jaeger charged forward, followed by Bob Price—the latter already wounded twice—all shooting down enemy soldiers as they approached the blazing chopper. Pilot Hoeck and Fred Ledfors moved away from their burning chopper armed with a .357 Magnum revolver, an M16, and a bag of Claymores between them. Howard, Price, and Jaeger urgently waved at the downed aviators to move their way, but door gunner Gilmore was screaming in pain and unable to walk. The .51-caliber AA gun had ripped his upper leg and right hip with fragments. Sergeant Howard, spotting a North Vietnamese soldier attempting to climb into the back side of the downed Huey, gunned him down and joined Jaeger in shooting another trying to get into the door of the chopper.

Lieuteant Jaeger and pilot Hoeck struggled to help support the badly wounded Gilmore, who made it only fifteen feet before he collapsed, screaming in pain. Hoeck shouted encouragements to his crewman as he and the lieutenant helped drag him to his feet and toward the safety of the SLAM company's perimeter. Bob Howard vigorously fired at the enemy as he assisted the Huey's crew into the perimeter.

Tom Jaeger noted that the downed chopper beyond them was still burning furiously, with its ammunition beginning to cook off from the heat. He opened up on the radio, calling for a second medevac chopper to help extract his growing collection of wounded men. Pilot Hoeck was met on the LZ by a smiling Montagnard who handed him two M26 hand grenades. "I had a sinking feeling," he said. "I had fled to this LZ thinking these guys might save me."[41]

Several wounded Montagnards lay under a big tree, where medics Parnar and Dorff worked feverishly to patch them up. They struggled to

254 | Chapter Sixteen

get an IV started in Sergeant Dickerson, and then cut away the flight pants of Gilmore to evaluate his serious wounds. Hoeck reported in to cheetah that his men were alive but in need of extraction. The covey rider acknowledged but announced that the birds needed to return to Dak To to refuel first. Hoeck decided to pass the time digging in with his crew chief with an entrenching tool to give them something to do during the ongoing firefight. Aggressive Skyraider pilots helped buy time for the trapped SF men by continuing to pound the nearby enemy troops.

As an RPG exploded perilously close to the SLAM team, Howard suddenly began jumping around in violent contortions. *What the hell is he doing?* Jaeger thought. Shrapnel from the RPG had cut into the inside of Howard's thigh and other hot pieces of steel had torn into the flesh of his buttocks. Jaeger could not help being momentarily amused as he watched the sergeant jumping about in pain before resuming his defense of their perimeter.

◆◇◆

Craig Collier figured it was now or never. His Gladiator 26 was deep in Laos, low on fuel, and without any gun support. He had just watched the Huey of his senior pilot get blown apart by the NVA half-track antiaircraft guns. Below, he could see a mad scramble of men on the ground and he could hear their desperate cries for assistance. Once the A-1s had laid down another round of ordnance against the NVA, Collier figured he would make one final extraction attempt before his fuel was exhausted.

Pilot Carl Hoeck, still stunned from his chopper's crash, was relieved when he finally heard the wonderful sound of rotors approaching as his buddy Collier masterfully eased his Huey down on the LZ under fire. The Green Berets knew that every second counted, and they moved swiftly to load the most seriously wounded on board Gladiator 26, Sergeant Dickerson and Lieutenant Swain being top priorities. It was late afternoon on November 18 and dusk was approaching.

By the time medic Parnar reached the chopper with others who were helping him carry Lieutenant Swain, it was already filled with wounded Montagnards. "We had to pile Swain on the laps of some people already on the ship," said Parnar. "Swain was screaming in pain as the chopper rose with his foot hanging over the side and dangling by the Achilles tendon."[42]

An alert door gunner sprawled on his stomach and helped secure the flopping foot to ease Swain's agony. Pilots Hoeck and Fred Ledfors stayed behind to give up their seats to those who had been injured. A second Huey soon returned and extracted most of the downed chopper crew, others who were wounded to varying degrees, and medic Tony Dorff, who would be awarded his second Purple Heart in a matter of three days—both while working on the same SLAM mission.

Collier's first ship pulled clear by hovering straight up while under heavy fire. He was burning the last of his fuel when he reached Dak To, but he had picked up fifteen of the most severely wounded, which again exceeded the usual ability of his chopper to lift them. When Collier's medevac chopper landed at Dak To, Swain handed over his map to one of the waiting officers, along with the watches he was carrying, collected from the wounded men. He was only semiconscious as medics hustled him away to tend to his horribly shredded legs.

✦◇✦

Darkness began to settle over the besieged Hatchet Force team after the sound of the last choppers faded away. Tom Jaeger had Bob Howard move around to survey their men's ammunition status. "About one magazine per man, plus some grenades," was the grim report the sergeant came back with. Many had varying degrees of injuries including Jaeger, who had shrapnel in his back. His Montagnards had been busy during the last bit of daylight, digging foxholes and forming an oval perimeter to defend during the night.

We need a resupply of ammunition desperately, Jaeger thought. He had already been told by Kontum command that his men would have to fight through another night. When he insisted that his men would not make it without a resupply, he was assured that more ammo was en route. The resupply bird arrived about forty-five minutes later and began settling into the meadow to offload more ammo.

Howard suddenly announced, "The track is headed back!"

The mechanized antiaircraft piece that had downed the first medevac chopper was rumbling again in the jungle. Jaeger pondered the possibilities for only a moment before he called off the resupply. His concern was that by doing so, he had sacrificed his entire company. He had little hope of his men surviving the night but he knew the AA crew would certainly bring down the ammo chopper and kill more Americans in the process of resupplying him. With a heavy heart, Jaeger radioed that his men would have to try and make it until dawn without the resupply.

Medic Parnar was armed with an M16 and fifteen full magazines he had secured before Tony Dorff departed, but he had little time to use it. He passed out ten of his magazines to others, along with three grenades, and collected extra combat dressings from other men in the process. The survivors numbered close to a hundred men, some wounded. Alan Farrell had been hit by shrapnel in the right shoulder, and platoon leader Bob Price had been hit four times by bullets and shrapnel. Lieutenant Walt Huczko moved about for hours, exposing himself to enemy fire while helping to treat the wounded and direct the defensive fire of his platoon. Steve Roche was one of the few who had thus far escaped injury on the SLAM mission—even though he had spent hours moving about during the firefight helping the wounded and directing his Montagnards' return fire.

Jaeger's men dug in for the night and prepared to make their last stand. Many lay on their backs on the rear edges of their foxholes, hoping that the NVA would not initiate an overnight assault. Jets swept in around their vicinity, dropping payloads of bombs and expending their ordnance. Jaeger remained on the radio with the FAC all night, calling in air strikes. Their engines would then fade away, only to be replaced in short order by the welcome sound of another group of air support aircraft.

Hours later, a Douglas AC-47 "Spooky" gunship (also nicknamed "Puff, the Magic Dragon") arrived with a heavy load of firepower—its three 7.62-mm mini-guns could selectively fire either fifty or a hundred rounds per second. Jaeger had his company outline their perimeter with strobe lights to avoid being hit. Joe Parnar was particularly impressed with the devastation caused by the Spooky strike. "The shredding of the leaves from the mini-gun rounds ripping through the trees sounded like a summer hailstorm in a forest."[43]

Lieutenant Jaeger was thankful for the heavy gun support but felt a little unnerved that his company's strobes also pointed out their exact position to the North Vietnamese. Around midnight, one of the jets making bomb and napalm strikes apparently touched off an enemy ammunition dump up on a ridgeline near where the NVA's 37-mm guns were located. The entire ridgeline to the south was aglow with secondary explosions as the ammo cache continued to cook off all night long.

To Parnar, the small-arms ammunition cooking off sounded like a popcorn popper for the next hour. Periodic explosions and brilliant flashes continued for hours. He remained hunched low in his foxhole, wary of unexploded CBU clusters lying just outside his protective den. "I tried to make my peace with God," Parnar recalled. "I promised to try to be a better person if we were permitted to survive this night."[44]

✦◇✦

At daybreak on November 19, the sun began to rise over a burning, smoky battlefield. A heavy fog hung eerily about the vicinity until the sun

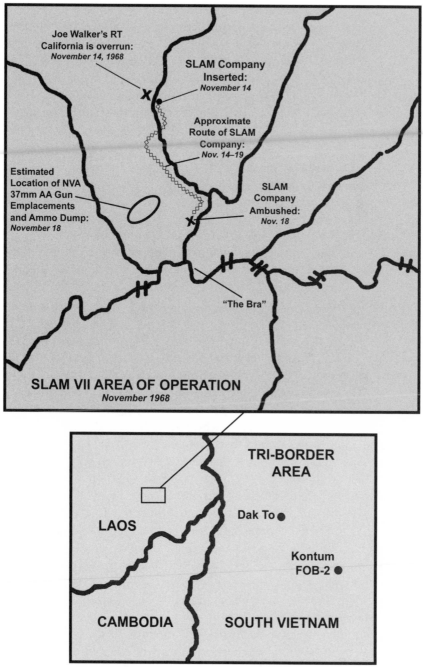

Joe Walker's RT
California is overrun:
November 14, 1968

SLAM Company
Inserted:
November 14

Approximate
Route of SLAM
Company:
Nov. 14–19

Estimated
Location of NVA
37mm AA Gun
Emplacements
and Ammo Dump:
November 18

SLAM
Company
Ambushed:
Nov. 18

"The Bra"

SLAM VII AREA OF OPERATION
November 1968

TRI-BORDER
AREA

LAOS

Dak To ●

Kontum
FOB-2 ●

CAMBODIA

SOUTH VIETNAM

Maps modified based on original work of Joe Parnar

began burning it off. Tom Jaeger fully expected the enemy to make a strong attack after daybreak. He had men set Claymores around their perimeter and communicated to the FAC to prepare to extract his men after daybreak. Right at daybreak, the lieutenant was surprised to see two North Vietnamese soldiers moving swiftly toward their perimeter with their hands up. Hatchet Force member Bob Gron saw that the NVA were holding their AKs above their heads, yelling "Chu hoi!" to signal their intentions to surrender. "Before we could stop them, the Montagnards ripped them," said Gron.[45]

The North Vietnamese soldiers were killed near the perimeter in spite of frantic pleas from several Green Berets for them to hold their fire. A short time later, another NVA approached the northern side with his hands up. "He walked right up on our perimeter," Steve Roche said. "We had a hell of a time keeping our Montagnards from opening fire."[46]

This time, Jaeger ordered everyone to hold their fire, as he sensed the man wanted to surrender. Bob Gron could see that this soldier had no weapon, and Sergeant First Class Howard moved toward the man before the Montagnards could dispose of this enemy soldier. He jumped on his opponent, subdued him, and slung him over his shoulder like a sack of potatoes. To the despair of Lieutenant Jaeger, Howard hauled his POW right into the American perimeter. Squad leader Gron was equally nervous, fearful that the NVA soldier might snatch one of Howard's own grenades. The Hatchet Force interpreter learned from the prisoner that the SLAM company had been fighting two full companies of NVA, but that their spirits were waning. Many of them were wounded. In spite of this reassuring intel, Jaeger knew that his men were not provisioned well enough to hold out any longer. It was time to get his men out of Laos.

The first of the extraction choppers began arriving about an hour after Howard had secured the prisoner. Jaeger was exhausted. He had been wounded and he had spent fourteen hours directing air strikes, rescuing men from the downed chopper, and helping to direct first aid efforts. As each chopper came in, he had his company detonate one of their Claymores to keep the enemy at bay. Alan Farrell, nursing a wounded right shoulder and relieved to be heading back, watched men firing away as the chopper lifted. "I'm not sure if they were shooting at known targets or just shooting because they were pissed off," said Farrell.[47]

Craig Collier, leading the extraction force of slicks, gunships, and A-1Es, was terrified to be braving such a level of enemy fire again. Still, he was determined to go in first to help get the SLAM team out. "The fear stopped abruptly during the approach and a great calm came over me. I knew at that point I was in God's hands," said Collier.[48]

The pilot was shocked when his Huey landed without enemy fire, the silence broken only by the continuous air strikes against the AA positions. Joe Parnar boarded the last bird with Lieutenant Jaeger, three other Americans, and Bob Howard—who made sure his NVA prisoner was hauled out as well. Base intelligence interrogated the prisoner, who told them the reason they did not attack the company during that last night was because of all the heavy air cover that had lasted until dawn.

Jaeger's men detonated their last Claymores just before the final slick hauled them clear. SLAM VII was one for the books. The men were physically and mentally spent. Parnar felt like the entire world was being lifted from his shoulders as the Huey gained altitude. Sitting on the edge of the helicopter, he could not stop the tears that suddenly began streaming down his face, so he stuck his face into the wind stream to hide them.[49]

"If Howard or any of the other Americans saw me, I wanted them to think the wind was just making my eyes water and I wasn't a candy ass."

◆◇◆

By the time SLAM VII officially ceased operation in early December, thirteen recon teams, four platoons, and four companies had been utilized. Some 112 tactical air strikes and 42 helicopter gunship sorties had been launched in support of the missions against the NVA. From Kontum, five indigenous members of the sustained action in Laos had been killed on November 14. From that time moving forward during the next six days, no participating members of SLAM VII had been killed, although more than forty-five had been wounded.[50]

Bob Howard's prisoner, the only one taken during Prairie Fire operations in 1968, proved to be quite valuable. He shed much light on operations in the area and led to the targeting of nine successful Arc Light bombing missions in that area of Laos.[51]

The awards board was busy for days writing up recommendations for the Kontum recon men who had participated in the November SLAM. Colonel Smith approved a long list of awards: aside from numerous Purple Hearts, the Distinguished Service Cross went to Tom Jaeger (the seventh award of the medal to a Kontum recon man); Silver Stars went to Swain, Price, and O'Daniel; Bronze Stars were pinned on Parnar, Roche, and Brents; Kendall and Delima received Air Medals; and Army Commendation Medals were conferred upon Walker, Machata, Huczko, and Dorff. Bob Howard was written up for the Medal of Honor for the second time in a year. The first had been downgraded to a DSC; this recommendation would eventually result in a Silver Star.

Lee Swain, the lieutenant whose legs had been mangled by an RPG, was first flown to Dak To. Medics worked on him through the night before rushing him to the more advanced hospital at Pleiku. He was moved to a hospital in Japan, and then flown back Stateside, where he endured numerous rounds of operations trying to fuse his right leg. In January 1969, doctors in Colorado finally amputated his left leg below the knee. The resilient officer fought through his rehabilitation, began regaining strength, and by spring, he managed to attempt skiing with special crutches. In time, Swain would take up flight training, earning his commercial license and later a crop dusting license.

As with all such major actions, many valiant deeds went without official recognition. Others felt slighted by the politics of the process. One-Zero Joe Walker, written up for a Silver Star, saw it downgraded to an Army Commendation Medal and was so disgusted with the system he expressed the fact that he had no further use for any such honors. The only thing that mattered to him was what his team accomplished in the field.[52]

Chapter Seventeen

HOWARD'S MIRACLE MISSION

Joe Walker was out of action for weeks following the SLAM mission. During his recuperation, he moved in with a Montagnard lady from the village who cared for him. His bullet wound led to a serious infection days later, causing Walker to run a high fever that left him sweating profusely, throwing up, and suffering convulsions. The stout Montagnard woman finally put the lanky one-zero over her shoulder during the night and hauled him in to the camp medics for treatment. Walker would soon fully recover and return to training new men for his RT California.

SLAM VII had taken a toll on FOB-2's recon company, but on November 23 Phil Brown witnessed that violent encounters in Vietnam were not limited to trips across the fence. He and Jim McGlon ran into an old friend that morning, Staff Sergeant James Richard Golding, the one-zero of RT Cobra from FOB-4. Due to the location of his target, Golding's team was staged to launch from Kontum but foul weather caused the mission to be postponed. After the team stood down from their mission, Golding met up with Brown and McGlon, and the three went off base with some of their indigenous teammates to enjoy breakfast in downtown Kontum.[1]

Thanks to FOB-2 policy, the off-base group was unarmed. As the group dined, Golding's indigenous zero-one suddenly appeared, his face bloody and appearing beaten, with an ARVN artillery lieutenant and his platoon in hot pursuit. Golding, who spoke fluent Vietnamese, quickly intervened and got into a heated exchange with the ARVN officer. "The lieutenant shoved McGlon first and then slapped Golding," said Brown. "Golding cold-cocked the lieutenant, and they began to fight."[2] A brawl ensued in the restaurant, involving the ARVN artillery unit, the Americans, and their Montagnards. Brown was bloodied, struck in the head by several folding chairs, as the melee spilled out into the street.

The lieutenant took a beating until he reached for his gun, and the unarmed Americans were unable to stop him before he began firing. One of his bullets hit McGlon almost point blank in the chest near his collarbone, blowing him backwards off his feet. The Vietnamese officer then jumped into the passenger side of a deuce-and-a-half truck and ordered the driver to run over the wounded American. Brown and Golding jumped onto the back of the truck as the driver was trying to crank it up. Brown grabbed the driver and pulled him from the vehicle while Golding ran around to the front.

The lieutenant then shot Golding in the chest and fled with his unit. Brown was not severely injured so he tried to administer first aid to both McGlon and Golding. "You'll be okay," he told Golding as he examined the wound in the left side of his stomach. To his surprise, Golding replied, "No, they killed me. I'm dying."

The wounded Americans were transported to the CCC dispensary, where medic Joe Parnar went to work on Golding's gunshot wound. He found the one-zero's blood pressure to be so low that the medics were unable to get a needle into a vein to start an IV. Both men were stabilized and medevaced to Pleiku, but Golding passed away from his wounds en route. McGlon was eventually medevaced back to the United States and was medically retired from the Army.[3]

The aftermath of the incident was ugly. Lieutenant Colonel Sam Sanford, deputy commander of CCC, issued orders to halt a heavily armed group of his Green Berets from rushing into Kontum to seek revenge on the ARVN lieutenant. A U.S. Army military police investigation unit at first tried to charge the three Americans with inciting the fight, but the MPs quickly retreated from that action after the Kontum Province police chief who had witnessed the event verified the story of the Green Berets. The policy of the Americans having to leave base unarmed was soon changed.[4]

Other new policies were instated to protect the men of FOB-2 as command of the recon base passed on December 1 to a new man, Lieutenant Colonel Roy Bahr. Born in Jacksonville, Florida, in 1930, Bahr joined the Naval Air Reserve on his seventeenth birthday and served as an aviation ordnanceman for three years. He joined the Army in 1950, attended and graduated from Infantry Officer Candidate School (OCS) at Fort Benning, Georgia, and deployed to Korea as an infantry platoon leader. He was also a SOG veteran, having commanded FOB-3 during the height of the siege at Khe Sanh earlier in the year and then FOB-1 in Phu Bai.

Roy Bahr brought two of his senior officers with him to Kontum: Major Clyde Sincere and Captain Frank Jaks. The latter had been with Bahr since he lost his former XO, Major George Quamo—who was posthumously awarded the Distinguished Service Cross for his actions during the Khe Sanh siege. Sent by Colonel Jack Warren to assist, Jaks remained with Bahr from FOB-3 to FOB-1 before making his return to his familiar base at FOB-2. The new trio of officers arriving at Kontum were as close as brothers and their command style was rock solid.

Wisconsin native Clyde Sincere had served at Pleiku during 1966 and 1967 with the Mobile Strike Force Command, or Mike Force, a quick reaction force active under MACV. Sincere was also a Korean War veteran who had served nine years as an enlisted man before being sent to OCS. He had already been awarded the Distinguished Service Cross for his valor on November 11, 1966, when he was wounded while leading the rescue of a besieged Special Forces company. Under Bahr's direction, Sincere had commanded the forward launch base at Mai Lok until its closure the previous month.

Lieutenant Colonel Bahr stepped in as MACV-SOG was continuing Daniel Boone recon operations as deep as eighteen miles into Cambodia to gather intelligence on enemy troops and bases. By late 1968, SOG was conducting an average of forty-six Daniel Boone missions per month in addition to its Prairie Fire missions into Laos. The name Daniel Boone would be changed to Salem House in the spring of 1969 after a *Newsweek* magazine article compromised the SOG code name.[5]

Roy Bahr found no shortage of worthy men among his recon company. Sergeant First Class Bob Howard seemed bulletproof in December. A reluctant hero, Howard had already been twice written up for the Medal of Honor for missions that could have ended his life, and he had been awarded the DSC for his November 1967 mission. When the medal was finally pinned on the husky supply sergeant during an awards ceremony at Kontum in late 1968, his fellow recon men threw a celebration in his honor that night. "The Vietnamese had a party for him and he got drunk," said Gene McCarley.[6] Colonel Bahr finally asked McCarley and the bar sergeant, Bobby Barnes, to put Howard to bed. "Howard didn't drink much, but when he did, he was hard to handle," said McCarley. Both were large men: McCarley weighed about two hundred pounds and Barnes tipped the scales at around 250. But instead of dragging their comrade, Barnes and McCarley found that physical fitness guru Howard grabbed each of them under one arm and carried them along.

Just weeks after being lacerated by shrapnel in fifty places during the heated November SLAM VII mission, Sergeant Howard volunteered for a prisoner-snatch operation into the Bra region of Laos on December 8. He would straphang as the acting one-one for a nameless composite team led by One-Zero Larry White, who had originally cut his teeth at Kontum in 1967 carrying the radio for Johnny Arvai's RT Maine. The rugged Arkansas native had since moved into a team command position, extended for a second Vietnam tour, and had spent the first half of 1968 commanding an Omega team from SOG's southern Ban Me Thuot base. Staff Sergeant White could not have been more pleased to have Howard as his assistant team leader; he had run missions with Howard in 1967. "He was ready to go all the time," said White.[7] The balance of the new Kontum composite team was filled out by Specialist Fourth Class Robert Clough as one-two, an ARVN officer, and six Montagnards.

The mission was red-hot from the start. White's primary LZ was so consumed with enemy ground fire that the chopper pilots were forced to shift to a secondary LZ. Once again, volumes of bullets stymied the Hueys until the recon team was forced to fly another mile to a backup insertion point. As the slick flared out to insert the team, small-arms fire began ripping into the chopper from all directions. White, the first man out, was wounded in the leg immediately. Bullets chewed through the chopper, hitting the pilot, co-pilot, and both gunners, leaving the door gunner slumped over his M60. The Huey shook violently and then slammed three feet down into the ground. Other bullets struck the team's ARVN officer and tore into radio operator Clough and one of the team's indigenous fighters as they exited the chopper.[8]

The force of the slugs ripping into Clough's side and arm knocked him back into the Huey. Without regard to his own wounds, he immediately dragged the limp door gunner back into the chopper and took over the M60. Clough blazed away with the machine gun, putting such deadly fire into the advancing NVA company that he forced their temporary retreat.[9]

In the same instant, Bob Howard leapt from the Huey to lay down a heavy volume of suppressive firepower. Noting the wounded Larry White, he helped direct the team's fire as the North Vietnamese soldiers surged forward again to within ten feet of the grounded helicopter. White and Howard then moved swiftly to help load their wounded comrades back onto the Huey.

The bloodied pilot attempted to lift off, gained several feet of altitude momentarily, and then was forced to set down again when the power failed. The determined enemy launched another vicious assault, which was repelled by the suppressive fire being laid down by Howard with his automatic carbine and Clough on the M60. As the enemy fell back once again, the remaining men on the ground jumped into the open door.[10]

As White struggled aboard, the NVA company surged forward, wounding the American one-zero a second time in the arm. White whirled around and fired, killing three North Vietnamese soldiers and wounding a fourth in a deadly burst of automatic fire. As the last enemy soldier fell, he shot White again. The bullet ripped through his CAR-15's trigger housing, went through White's hand, and finally buried itself in his chest. Although shot three times, White managed to fire another burst to finish off his opponent before he fell to the ground unconscious. Howard, having seen that all other wounded men were loaded aboard the Huey, opened up another vicious barrage of counter-fire to suppress the advancing enemy before he raced out and dragged his fallen team leader back on board, collecting a bullet wound in the process. To add insult to injury, White was wounded a fourth time by one of the bullets that ripped through the Huey's underside during takeoff.

Clough continued his deadly M60 fire as the wounded pilot built up the needed RPMs to finally lift off. The extensively damaged helicopter limped back toward its staging area as Howard moved from one wounded man to another to administer first aid. White regained consciousness during the outbound flight but refused any medical attention for himself until all of the more critically wounded had been tended to. For their deadly firepower to hold off the enemy and save eight wounded comrades, Clough and Howard would receive the Air Medal for heroism and the Purple Heart.

Larry White, seriously wounded by four bullets, received the Bronze Star for the December 8 mission but spent months recovering in military hospitals in Vietnam, Japan, and the United States. He returned to duty at Fort Bragg, but in 1970 he volunteered to return to the service he loved and would see action again as the one-zero of RT Hawaii.[11]

◆◇◆

Joe Parnar more often than not found himself in the thick of the action as a chase medic. His service was called on once again on December 19 for a downed Cobra gunship crew of the 361st Aviation Company Escort (ACE), known as the "Pink Panthers."

The 361st Cobras were engaged this day attacking an underwater bridge reported by a covey pilot in the Bra region. One of the pilots, First Lieutenant Paul Renner, began taking heavy enemy fire while attacking the bridge, and was shot down. Renner struggled out of his downed ship but his co-pilot, Chief Warrant Officer 2 Ben Hervey Ide, was severely wounded. Parnar was flying nearby in Bikini 29, one of the slicks providing escort for the 170th AHC. He and Renner lifted Ide from the wreckage and began applying tourniquets as Bikini 29 lifted off. Parnar performed CPR during the flight back to the 4th Division medical facility at Dak To, but Ide died soon after arrival.[12]

At first, Parnar felt a sense of guilt about not being been able to save Ide, but those feelings were soon replaced by anger at CCC officers who had opted to use gunships to take out a bridge that could have been safely destroyed by a B-52 bomb strike.

As the 1968 holiday season approached, new faces joined the Kontum recon company to replace those recently transferred and men who had stepped up to other duties. Veteran One-Zero Bill Hanson turned over RT Hawaii to Lonnie Pulliam so he could begin flying covey in rotation with former team leaders Terry Hamric and Jim Tramel. Colonel Bahr's newest assignees arrived at the Kontum city airport on Christmas Eve and rode a flatbed truck down Highway 14 into the FOB-2 compound. After an initial in-briefing, the trio of Green Berets were ushered to the recon company office to receive assignments from the first sergeant, Lionel Pinn.

Pinn assigned the most experienced of the trio, Staff Sergeant Reinald Pope, to a recon team. The second newbie, Sergeant Glenn Uemura, was soon taken in by RT Hawaii, leaving the third fresh Green Beret, Minnesota native John Plaster, to draw field gear and await an assignment. Plaster joined the Army at age eighteen directly out of high school and advanced through Special Forces training during the next year. He was eager to see action but spent his first days at FOB-2 adapting to the Central Highlands heat and the concussions of distant 175-mm artillery firing until his coveted recon billet finally arrived. Sergeant Pinn and Captain Ed Lesesne assigned young Plaster to Recon Team New Mexico, led by Specialist Fifth Class Larry Stephens.[13]

He would hold the team's third American slot, and as the one-two he would carry the heavy PRC-25 radio. Standing in formation in the Kontum compound the next morning as a member of RT New Mexico, Plaster considered this to be his proudest moment thus far in Special Forces. The hazards of combat across the fence in Cambodia or Laos beckoned, and he intended to prove his worth. Plaster knew that each day of training further prepared him for his inevitable ultimate test against enemy forces.

He listened carefully to the advice of the base training NCO, Bob Howard, the most impressive Green Beret he had yet encountered. "Physically imposing, he stood just six feet, but every ounce of his 170 pounds was solid muscle, backed up by an attitude that didn't take much lightly," said Plaster.[14] The fact that Howard had already been written up twice for the Medal of Honor resonated within Plaster.

"If y'all screw off, don't worry 'bout Bob Howard catching you," the training sergeant warned his newer Green Berets. Squinching his face into a sardonic grin like a Clint Eastwood character, Howard growled, "No, sir, the NVA's gonna kill you. Then you'll know you should'a trained harder."[15]

Team New Mexico's newest member took his mentor's advice to heart. Within days of arriving at SOG's Kontum forward operating base, Plaster would learn why Howard was an SF trooper with few equals.

◆◇◆

Missing in action. These three words had a profound effect on the recon company. The dreaded phrase made the rounds quickly on the afternoon of December 29, 1968: a CCN-based recon team was hit and one of the Americans was lost. The survivors returned with a harrowing tale. The ten-man team, consisting of two Green Berets and eight Montagnards, had been inserted four miles inside of Cambodia, west of the Dak To launch site. Shortly after the one-zero broke his team into two sections, both groups came under heavy attack by NVA troops. Staff Sergeant Robert Francis Scherdin, heading the rear element, was badly wounded in the right side by automatic weapons fire and was unable to walk. One of his Montagnards, Nguang, tried to assist him but Scherdin could not move. Nguang was then wounded and was forced to flee with the other three Montagnards of the rear element.[16]

In two separate extractions, choppers were finally able to pull nine of the ten recon men, leaving only Bob Scherdin behind badly wounded. Hours later, shortly before sunset, an Air Force FAC plane overflew the battle zone and heard Scherdin's emergency beeper. There was no voice contact, leaving plenty of speculation as to whether the Green Beret was too badly injured to respond or whether the NVA were attempting to set a deadly trap with his body.[17]

There was only one way to find out. That night, Lieutenant Colonel Bahr called a meeting of his senior officers, including First Sergeant Pinn and training NCO Bob Howard. He explained the situation, the firefight, and how Scherdin had been wounded and left behind. Howard recalled how he had talked with Scherdin at Dak To before the mission, letting him know that he did not need to go out. Scherdin had only recently recovered from malaria, but he had insisted to Howard that he was physically fit and wanted to go with his team.[18]

When Bahr explained that a Hatchet Force platoon would be sent in on a Bright Light mission to recover either Scherdin or his body, Howard did not hesitate.

"I'll go," he said.[19]

Bahr consented and put First Lieutenant Jim Jerson, a twenty-one-year old with a wife back in New Orleans, in charge of the mission. Sergeant First Class Howard would serve as his second-in-command, the senior noncommissioned officer of Platoon C. Under his charge were two other Green Berets, Sergeant Jerome Griffin and Staff Sergeant Bob Gron, the latter a veteran of the SLAM VII mission in which Howard had also participated. The four Americans were accompanied by one ARVN officer and twenty-nine Vietnamese personnel. "We didn't have time to really prepare for the mission or go through immediate action drills," said Howard. "We had to go in immediately."[20]

Kontum's airfield was buzzing with choppers at first light on December 30. Lieutenant Jerson's thirty-four-man Bright Light platoon boarded the waiting Vietnamese Kingbee choppers, supported by 170th AHC gunships. Howard displayed the serious demeanor of a veteran Green Beret intent on bringing back one of his own. His platoon was shuttled to Dak To, where last-minute planning consumed the balance of the morning. Once the Bright Light Kingbees reached Scherdin's last known coordinates, Howard could see from the air that the NVA had reinforced the area heavily. Menacing small-arms fire clawed up toward the choppers from the dense green jungle below. The mountainous terrain was heavily pocketed with vines, bushes, and bamboo that served to limit visibility but did not form enough of a canopy to prevent Lieutenant Jerson's platoon from safely inserting around 1515. He signaled his men to begin moving west through the dense growth, whose copious volumes of dried, decaying vegetation made silent movement all but impossible.[21]

Bob Gron, leader of the second squad located in the center of the platoon's file formation, could tell right away that troops had been in the area by the slashed vegetation in their vicinity. After moving in single file for around fifty yards, Jerson signaled for a security halt. Enemy troops could be heard moving parallel to the platoon's direction of movement some eighty to a hundred yards away. Gron sensed that the NVA were converging on both of their flanks.

It was approximately 1600—just three-quarters of an hour after insertion—when Jerson decided to move his platoon toward a RON position. With luck, maybe they could shake their trackers and resume their Bright Light mission unimpeded after first light. But after moving fewer than 165 yards, the Green Berets could still hear North Vietnamese soldiers on both sides of their platoon.

The enemy appeared to be little more than 50 yards away, signaling to each other, trying to move into position to attack the small platoon. "We heard banging, like people slapping two sticks together or knocking sticks against tree trunks," said Gron.[22]

About two hundred yards from their LZ, the platoon crossed a recently used trail as they moved uphill toward the position where Scherdin's beeper had been transmitting. Once Sergeant Griffin's rear security was across the trail, Jerson stopped his platoon to listen again. Howard, Jerson, their point man, and several Vietnamese team members formed the front line moving up the hill, while Gron advanced with his second squad near the center of the platoon's file formation, and Griffin's first squad brought up the rear.

The noisy jungle floor let the Americans know that NVA soldiers appeared to now be within thirty to fifty yards, and on both sides of the platoon. Jerson signaled for his men to continue up onto higher ground to form a perimeter before it started getting dark. Gron noted that the terrain leveled out a bit as they neared the crest of the hill, forming a little depression in the side of the hill just before the ground climbed up steeper. The inset was only about fifty yards ahead, and Gron's squad had just reached it when an enemy ambush erupted and sent him ducking for cover.

Hellacious volumes of semiautomatic and full-automatic weapons fire made confetti of the foliage as an estimated two companies of NVA soldiers opened up on the Kontum recon platoon. Jerson's men instinctively returned fire with their automatic weapons and M79s. Howard caught sight of four enemy infantrymen and he cut them down in a swift barrage as he hit the ground. The platoon's Vietnamese point man, just ahead of Howard, was hit by bullets in the initial contact. Three more members of the platoon were seriously wounded, one fatally, while trying to assist the suffering point man. An estimated seven or eight NVA were wounded or killed in the same exchange.

Howard and Jerson were pinned down near each other, about fifteen yards in advance of Sergeant Gron's second squad. A large tree between Jerson and Howard afforded them some cover as gunfire ripped through the air around them. They began firing back but several enemy soldiers raced to within ten or fifteen yards of their position to throw hand grenades. Shouting to each other over the barrage, Jerson and his senior noncom agreed that they should move on, over the crest of the hill. In the midst of making that decision, their world suddenly went black with a violent flash and roar as an NVA grenade detonated only yards away.[23]

The force of the blast blew Howard about ten feet back, flipped him upside down, and crumpled him into a heap on the ground. Gron had to duck his head for several seconds because of the intensity of enemy fire. He saw Sergeant First Class Howard lying motionless and assumed that he

Staff Sergeant Robert Scherdin (*left*), was killed in action December 29, 1968. Bob Howard would earn his Medal of Honor during a Bright Light to retrieve Scherdin's body, during which First Lieutenant James Jerson (*center*) was mortally wounded. Scherdin and Jerson are seen with Staff Sergeant Cecil Davis. *Craig Davis photo, via Joe Parnar*

Staff Sergeant Bob Gron earned a Bronze Star Medal with Valor for actions with Bob Howard on the December 30, 1968, Scherdin Bright Light mission. *Robert Gron*

was dead. Howard was unconscious for a moment before his groggy senses began to return. Blood was pouring down into his face obscuring his vision. Panic set in for a brief moment. *God, please help me see!* he thought.

The concussion of the close grenade blast had caught his head with tremendous force. Gradually, his eyes began to regain focus. He found that much of his web gear had been blown off and that his weapon had absorbed a great deal of the impact. It was blown all to hell and rendered useless. Howard was hurting all over, as shrapnel had ripped his hands, groin, and lower legs. Other red-hot metal shards had torn up his ankle, leaving him unable to walk. "And then I smelled the most awful smell I've ever smelled in my whole life," he said.[24]

Howard pulled himself up to look around. There, just a short distance from him, was a North Vietnamese soldier with a flamethrower. He was moving about the kill zone, burning four of the wounded indigenous members of the Hatchet Force platoon to death. Jim Jerson was laying wounded, just to the left of the soldier with the flamethrower. Howard struggled to retrieve an M33 hand grenade he kept strapped in place on his left side. *I'm about to be blown up and burnt up, but I can at least take him out with me,* he thought. He struggled in considerable pain to remove the pin with fingers that were badly slashed by shrapnel. The NVA soldier spotted the Green Beret struggling for his hand grenade and moved within yards of Howard.

The opponents made direct eye contact, acknowledging in an instant the finality of the standoff. "I could tell by looking at him that he was a well-trained North Vietnamese soldier," said Howard. "He had a look of determination and hate on his face. He had an evil look in his eye, like 'I'm going to kill you.'"[25]

Howard stared down his opponent with a sly smirk. He found dark humor in the minutes-old battle as he faced death; he thought to himself, *I've got you! Not matter how bad I'm blown up, I've got you and you know it.*

No words were exchanged but the North Vietnamese soldier ceased using the flamethrower on the downed indigenous men. He began backing away from the American while shouting commands in Vietnamese. Howard somehow did not have the heart to kill the enemy who had chosen not to douse him with the flamethrower. He merely lobbed his grenade toward the soldier, knowing the blast would at least momentarily chase him off, as well as the other NVA the man was calling in.

Howard's attention then turned to Lieutenant Jerson, whom he could hear crying out in agony. He found that the grenade blast had thrown the lieutenant into an exposed area, where enemy machine gunners were shooting at the helpless officer. Howard was unable to walk, so he began crawling toward Jerson's crumpled body, oblivious to his own pain and the hail of gunfire.

When he reached him, Howard found the officer had been hit by grenade fragments and small-arms fire and was unable to move. Howard's fingers were too badly mangled to drag Jerson, so he finally wedged the lieutenant's feet between his elbows and awkwardly dragged him back down the hill toward other members of his platoon.[26]

The NVA commenced a frontal attack again as Howard slowly pulled his unconscious team leader down the hill. Jerson, unable to assist their progress, was struck by more rounds of small-arms fire in the process. Three NVA charged forward, apparently hoping to take the two Americans as prisoners. Fortunately for Howard, Bob Gron came to his defense at this moment. "As I crawled to him, he started laying down a base of fire and killed those enemy soldiers that were attacking me," Howard said.[27] As soon as he reached Gron's position in the little depression, Howard began administering emergency first aid to Lieutenant Jerson. "He used my morphine to help ease the lieutenant's pain, never once caring for his own wounds," said Gron.[28] He began stripping the PRC-25 radio and web gear from Jerson's body. As he did so, enemy fire suddenly struck the web gear and detonated several rounds of ammunition. The exploding ammo lifted Howard off the ground and blew him several yards away from the others as Gron dove for cover.

Howard felt intense pressure in his stomach and was unable to breathe as he once again lay crumpled on the ground. As he regained his breath and his senses, he realized that he was pretty badly wounded and that Lieutenant Jerson was left lying exposed to enemy fire with no ability to move on his own. Gron was some distance away where he had dived for cover as the ammunition belt exploded. Howard noted in anger that his platoon's remaining indigenous had long since fled downhill for better cover. He and Gron were the only two remaining on the upper slope to fight off the surging NVA and to help Jerson. In a split second, the thought raced through Howard's mind: *I've got to do what's right. I don't want to go back and get hit again, but there's nobody else nearby that can help the lieutenant. I guess if I die, they can look back at me and say, "That guy died the way he wanted to die."*

Under a withering hail of enemy fire, he crawled to his platoon leader and began dragging him back while Gron lay down defensive fire. Gron had donned Jerson's PRC-25 and was calling for air support as Jerson was retrieved. Gron fired his M16 with one hand, operated the radio with the other, and periodically passed his weapon to Sergeant Howard so he could fire a few bursts while Gron was manning the radio. Howard then swapped with Gron and took over the radio to call in to their FAC.

They moved about a dozen yards to a lower position where they joined Jerome Griffin, the remaining American. Griffin had been some sixty-five yards to the rear of the main action, working the radio as the platoon came under assault. He had used his interpreter to order his men to fire two magazines on full automatic to sweep the area. As Griffin tried moving forward, he was met by about eight of their Vietnamese platoon members who were fleeing downhill, away from the firefight.

Howard's teammates helped position him where he could give commands and make decisions on the use of firepower. After learning that the remaining platoon members had retreated, he got on the radio to advise command and his FAC of their situation. Howard then took a .45-caliber pistol from Griffin and began leading the way toward the LZ though he could only crawl. He struggled as he painfully dragged himself over the ground, trying to keep the gun in his hand ready for firing. Howard had scarcely managed to get his tattered finger to the trigger when several NVA came charging toward him. He turned and shot one in the chest, then dropped the other two with the Colt. His mind could not absorb the fact that he was somehow still alive in the midst of the constantly charging enemy. *God is performing miracles for me!*[29]

Along the way, Howard collected four of his Vietnamese platoon members, rallied them to his support, and continued crawling toward the

LZ while under fire. A short distance down the hill, he found the ARVN officer who had accompanied his platoon in the field. The Vietnamese man was badly wounded, so Howard stopped to administer first aid before instructing the officer to follow his squad toward the LZ. En route, he stopped again to give aid to another Vietnamese platoon member who had been shot twice in the leg.

This time, Howard ordered Gron and Griffin to set up a small defensive perimeter for a short rest before moving on toward the nearby LZ with their Vietnamese interpreter. He told them to wait several minutes while he cleared the LZ and set out crawling forward, armed only with a pistol with a half-empty magazine. His intention was to continue regrouping the platoon, secure the LZ, and then establish a main defensive position. The enemy, however, was not about to give up. They sensed that victory was close at hand and closed in on all sides while raining down heavy fire on the besieged recon platoon.

Howard continued to crawl through the fire toward the previously used insertion point, where he found the remaining Vietnamese members of his platoon. Seeing the bloodied recon sergeant continuing to advance fearlessly, most of them regained their composure and rallied to support Howard. He led them in a low crawl through continued gunfire until they were able to set up a proper defensive perimeter near the LZ. An aerial observer was overhead through the action, but his fuel supply was beginning to run low. He put in an emergency call to Dak To for a replacement FAC to come take station over the platoon.

In the meantime, Sergeant Gron called for additional support from Griffin to help move Lieutenant Jerson to the LZ. "We were killing him by moving him," said Gron.[30] He remained with the lieutenant and their interpreter while Griffin moved on ahead to inform Howard of their situation. Griffin was given two additional men by Howard and they crawled back to help provide covering fire for those moving the lieutenant to the LZ.

Once the lieutenant was moved into the new perimeter, Howard had him placed nearby where he could personally care for Jerson while he directed his men. He kept one of the American squad leaders with him to keep a close watch on Jerson. Howard refused all efforts by his comrades to help treat his own wounds, saying that others needed attention far more than he did. It was now 1900, three hours into the bloody firefight. He directed his men to lay their Claymores in the most critical areas surrounding their perimeter and to save them for last-ditch use.

"We had three strobe lights and it was just getting dark," Howard said.[31] He had one of the sergeants put one of the strobes on him and prop him up against a rucksack to serve as a beacon for the FAC overhead. Howard

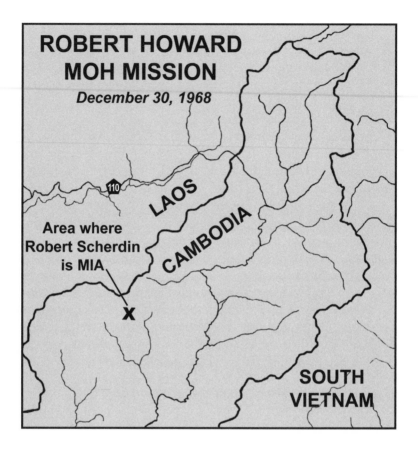

ROBERT HOWARD
MOH MISSION
December 30, 1968

110

LAOS

Area where
Robert Scherdin
is MIA

CAMBODIA

X

SOUTH
VIETNAM

sat with a blinking strobe light on him, holding a weapon in one shredded hand while talking to the FAC over the radio. He directed the other two strobes to be situated to mark the extremes of their perimeter for the aviators.

Good news finally arrived over the radio at this time. A new FAC had arrived overhead to help defend the men: Captain Lyle R. Hill of the 219th Recon Airplane Company, with First Lieutenant Terry Hamric flying in his O-1 as covey rider. Hill was informed by Howard that four of his Vietnamese paramilitary personnel had been killed, seven more were wounded, and that he and Lieutenant Jerson were also wounded. Hamric immediately called back to Dak To to request helicopter gunships.[32]

Until they could arrive, Hill's little O-1 was the entire cavalry element charged with defending Jim Jerson's platoon. Hill reported that he had four rockets on his plane, so Howard directed him to fire all four, one on each side of his perimeter to within fifty-five yards of his men. Howard had carefully marked his platoon's defensive position with strobe lights as reference points for the O-1's suppressive assaults. Unfortunately, one of the rockets exploded close enough to wound two of the Vietnamese team members with fragments of white-hot phosphorous. The rocket explosions succeeded in stopping the advancing enemy for a few minutes, but Howard came back over the radio, reporting that the enemy was now moving in against his western perimeter.

Captain Hill dived in low to allow Hamric to toss hand grenades out his rear window toward the areas as Howard directed him. The little O-1 then made continued low passes as Hamric blazed away with his M16 rifle into enemy positions until he had exhausted all twenty-eight of his magazines, slowing the enemy advance in the process. Hill observed muzzle flashes during each pass and later estimated that the recon platoon was surrounded by at least two full NVA companies.

Darkness had begun to settle over the battleground. Hamric announced that TAC air was en route, but the enemy was not about to give them a break in the action. The North Vietnamese began advancing on the small perimeter from a creek bed. Howard gathered his M79 grenadiers together, moved to a portion of the perimeter, and then directed their fire toward the advancing NVA splashing through the creek. Their firepower was effective in knocking down some of the soldiers and forcing the balance to retreat back to the creek bed. Howard wondered how much longer they could possibly hold out without better air support.

In answer to his silent prayers, Huey gunships finally arrived overhead even as Covey Rider Hamric was putting in a call for a flare ship to help light up the area. Howard directed the first gunship strikes into the streambed, where he could hear the NVA sloshing through the water. Once they had been gunned down, he directed more strikes in a full 360-degrees around their defensive circle. The determined enemy did not retreat, however; they had instead closed to within fifty-five yards of the battered recon platoon. Howard crawled about the circle, effectively directing various members in suppressing each new advance from various directions. As their ammunition supply began running low, Howard ordered his men to begin setting off all their protective Claymore mines along the outsides of their perimeter.

Every minute counted now, and the frightening roar of the Claymores bought them additional time in holding off the enemy. Darkness had long since enveloped the jungle as the ferocious battle raged into the night hours. The next ray of hope to shine upon them came in the form of the flare ship arriving overhead with additional gunships. It was a Moonbeam, a C-119 armed with 20-mm cannons and flares. Howard continued directing multiple gunship strikes against his enemy while he prepared his men to be extracted. Throughout the fight, he made sure that Griffin remained with Lieutenant Jerson to continue administering first aid and what little comfort he could offer.

At one point, he directed one of the planes to drop a bomb close to their perimeter. He called in the 250-pound bomb perilously close to his position, close enough that the force of the blast peppered him with several more pieces of shrapnel. At about 2030, Griffin crawled over to check on Lieutenant Jerson. He hollered to Howard, "He's stopped breathing!"

He immediately ordered Griffin to administer mouth-to-mouth resuscitation and external heart massage to their fallen leader, but Griffin's attempts proved unsuccessful. Howard turned back to the fight, continuing to crawl around and direct his men's efforts.

Hamric, hearing that the platoon leader had expired, called back with new hope for them: Vietnamese-manned Kingbee extraction choppers of the 219th Squadron were on their way from Dak To. The fight had raged for four-and-a-half hours by the time the welcomed Sikorsky CH-34s began settling onto the hot LZ. Howard supervised the loading of Jerson's body and the most critically wounded Vietnamese team members into the first chopper. He sent more of his men out on the next ones, until only he, Gron, and Griffin remained on the ground along with several of their indigenous troopers.

The last bird in was a Huey. The pilot did not settle all the way down, so the shorter Montagnards had a tough time climbing in. Sergeant Gron helped push them up to safety as the Huey bounced up and down about to his chest height. Once the indigenous men were loaded, Gron reached up and was able to grab a handle behind the pilot's seat. He put one knee and one foot on the skid, slung his rifle up, and held on with one hand. The door gunners were blazing away as Gron turned to offer a helping hand to Griffin and Howard.

He instead heard Howard yelling, "No! No!"[33]

Howard and Griffin were still on the ground, motioning toward something unseen. *They know something I don't know*, Gron thought. Howard finally motioned toward an object in the weeds and had the pilot switch on his spotlight. There was Lieutenant Jerson's body, apparently shoved out of the first chopper to lighten the load. "Howard had seen them push it off," Gron said. "The first chopper had a Vietnamese crew on it and no Americans. If there had been an American on that bird, the guy that did it would have had a gun upside his head!"

There was a cardinal rule among SF soldiers to leave no man behind, so Gron jumped down off the skid to assist Griffin and Howard in retrieving Jerson's body. Gron scrambled back on board and then helped Howard up.

Having fought for hours through intense pain, Howard passed out, awakening later in a field hospital with his hands and his many other wounds freshly dressed. He had given his all. While Lieutenant Jerson's wounds proved mortal, Howard had saved two other Americans and many of his Vietnamese team members.

In return, his small platoon killed twenty-five enemy soldiers who could be counted, had slain an estimated twenty-five more, and had wounded at least fifteen of the NVA fighters. After-action reports estimated that at least fifty more enemy soldiers were likely killed in the ongoing firefight and aerial assaults upon them. Bob Howard's men had suffered greatly, but they had dished out an estimated four times as many casualties in the process. Captain Lesesne, the recon company commander, wrote Howard up for the Medal of Honor for the third time. Roy Bahr, who considered Howard to be "a super soldier who stood out" from the pack, readily endorsed the recommendation.

The nation's highest military honor would still be a long time in coming, but the paperwork process was set in motion to honor the man who was destined to become SOG's most decorated warrior.

Chapter Eighteen

"NO LONGER A CHERRY"

Joe Parnar lay quietly in a mass of heavy vegetation, trying to get some sleep in the relative security of a dense bamboo thicket. Nearby, Staff Sergeant Ken Worthley listened to the events going down on his PRC-25 radio into the evening hours as Bob Howard was fighting the battle of his life. The action in Cambodia was close enough that Parnar and Worthley could hear faint battle sounds in the distance.[1]

Parnar had volunteered as a straphanger for RT Florida, under One-Zero Ralph Rodd. Rodd had gone in heavy, with eleven men: himself, One-One Worthley, straphangers Parnar, Specialist Fourth Class Craig Davis, and Sergeant Dan Harvey, plus his indigenous team members. Their mission was to snatch an NVA prisoner, using their medic to keep their captive alive after wounding him, but Rodd's team was advised to hold off on their prisoner snatch until Howard and his Hatchet Force platoon were extracted the next day. Word finally reached RT Florida on New Year's Day 1969 that they were cleared to attempt their mission.

When the time came to capture a prisoner, however, Rodd's team found itself in an area with a large number of NVA approaching. RT Florida spent the next two days falling back, attempting to distance itself from an alerted enemy force. During the morning of January 3, their fifth day across the fence, Rodd's team was approached by three NVA trackers and a dog that soon pointed out their position. Chin, one of Rodd's indigenous troops, dropped the three trackers with a burst of his machine gun and a firefight ensued with other trackers.[2]

Rodd called for an extraction as enemy troops closed on his team's front and rear. The first extraction chopper to arrive found that RT Florida would have to be pulled out through twenty-foot-tall bamboo that even made the use of McGuire rigs risky. The chopper crew dropped a rope ladder made of aluminum rungs and cable, first pulling out three indigenous men, plus Parnar and Harvey. The first four scrambled up the ladder to safety but the pilot pulled out abruptly as .30-caliber machine-gun fire began chewing up the bamboo. Parnar had his indigenous team members hold his legs and lower him head first over the side of the chopper to assist Harvey, who was whipping toward the rear of the Huey as it gathered altitude.

The prisoner snatch mission was a bust but all had made it out safely. Parnar's luck was not as good three days later when he was back flying chase medic on January 8 to retrieve a recon team that had been inserted to retrieve the body of Staff Sergeant Bob Scherdin—the same MIA that Bob Howard had gone in after. The team was led by Staff Sergeant Gerald Frank Apperson, with Specialist Fourth Class Bill Fred Williams Jr. and four Montagnards of Scherdin's original team. Apperson's men were unable to find Scherdin's body and further tragedy occurred when their extraction chopper was downed after taking hits. The entire crew of the 170th AHC Huey—First Lieutenant Alan Clark Gilles (pilot), Warrant Officer 1 Jon Patrick Roche (co-pilot), Specialist Fourth Class Robert Don Case (crew chief), and Specialist Fourth Class Steven Douglas Bartman (door gunner) —was killed when their slick went down two-and-a-half miles short of a Special Forces camp at Ben Het.

Parnar bravely rappelled in solo through dense bamboo with only a PRC-25 radio that the aircrew lowered to him. He found another American on the ground, Sergeant First Class Bobby J. Dunham from a Ben Het patrol, and the two tried to approach the burning Huey after enemy gunfire eased. They found the bodies of downed recon man Bill Williams and one of the Montagnards, but in the process of recovering them, Parnar and Dunham were hit by another enemy attack. Dunham was severely wounded and Parnar took shrapnel in his shoulder. Dunham was extracted by a Bright Light team alive, although he would succumb to his wounds the following day. Parnar was flown back to Kontum, where the head medic, Sergeant First Class Lou Maggio, determined during surgery to leave the shrapnel in Parnar's chest rather than risk further tissue trauma by removing it.[3]

Parnar would remain on light duty for a week, but he considered himself fortunate. The chopper crash had taken the lives of three specialists—Williams, Dunham, and Apperson—plus four Montagnards from the CCC recon company, and four pilots and crewmen of the slick sent to extract them. Counting Lieutenant Jerson, eight Americans and a number of indigenous personnel had perished in the week-plus effort to recover the body of Sergeant Scherdin. A Bright Light team composed of Bill Janc's RT Maine and medic Bryon Loucks was landed to remove the bodies from the chopper crash site. Loucks returned the following day with a Hatchet Force platoon led by First Lieutenant Frank Longaker to police up additional remains and weapons. Bob Scherdin's remains have never been recovered and he is officially listed as MIA.

◆◇◆

In mid-January 1969 FOB-2 received a new identity. Lieutenant Colonel Roy Bahr, base commander for only six weeks, was notified on January 15 that his base was being renamed Command and Control Central (CCC) answering directly to SOG headquarters in Saigon. Da Nang became Command and Control North (CCN) and Ban Me Thuot was now Command and Control South (CCS). "It had a big effect," said Bahr. "Previously, FOB-2 came under the command of CCN, but as of 15 January I started reporting directly to the Chief SOG in Saigon, which gave me more flexibility."[4] Missions into southern Laos and northern Cambodia proceeded as usual, but signs from the mess hall to jeep bumpers were switched from FOB-2 to CCC overnight. Recon man John Plaster reflected, "As innocuous a name as the Studies and Observations Group, Command and Control Central intentionally inspired yawns and kept the curious at bay."[5]

Bahr was fortunate to retain many able officers; Captain Frank Jaks remained as his deputy commanding officer (DCO), and Major Clyde Sincere as his base XO. Captain Ed Lesesne, commander of the recon company, was another able assistant. FOB-2 Kontum, now officially known as CCC, was nearing three years in operation in January 1969. Five new recon teams—RT New Hampshire, RT New Mexico, RT South Carolina, RT Vermont, and RT Washington—had come into operation since mid-1968, bringing Kontum's total to twenty-one recon teams, an all-time high for the base. The other teams, in various states of operation or training, were: RT Arkansas under Larry Williams; Darrell Redman's RT Arizona; Joe Walker's RT California; Dennis Mack's RT Colorado; Luke Dove's RT Delaware; Ralph Rodd's RT Florida; Lonnie Pulliam's RT Hawaii; Ken Snyder's RT Iowa; Ben Thompson's RT Illinois; Floyd Ambrose's RT Kentucky; Marvin Montgomery's RT Maine; Barry Keefer's RT Nevada; Phil Brown's RT New York; Thomas Stanton's RT Ohio; Pappy Webb's RT Texas; and RT Wyoming under Squirrel Sprouse.

The action in Laos was heating up, and counter-recon teams were vigilant. Staff Sergeant Ambrose, leading RT Kentucky across the fence from January 23–25, had his hands full by the third day. Three of his team members had fallen ill, and NVA trackers with dogs were trailing them. Ambrose was forced to call for an extract, during which he valiantly remained behind, killing three enemy soldiers and laying down heavy fire until all of his men were successfully loaded. Recon Team Kentucky made it back to base without injury but the next CCC team inserted that day would not be as fortunate.

✦◇✦

RT New Mexico was a tight team. The unit had been formed at Kontum in September 1968 with the core of One-Zero Larry Stephens, One-One Tom Templin, and One-Two Billy Joe Simmons. All three had come into Kontum together yearning for action but each had at first been assigned to duty at the commo bunker. "We wanted to be the action guys," said Templin.[6] As casualties decreased the operational men, the trio jumped at the chance to form their own recon team.

Templin and Simmons were particularly close, having gone through their entire training, from Airborne School through Special Forces training. Billy Simmons was a full-blooded Cherokee who hailed from Phoenix, where Templin had visited and gotten to know his buddy's mother, father, sister, and extended family. With Specialist Fifth Class Larry Stephens running the team, RT New Mexico had pulled three missions across the fence by late December 1968 and had come out without injury from each.

Templin was then sent to the Recon Team Leaders Course (also known as "One-Zero School") at Camp Long Thanh (B-53) to prepare him for taking on his own team in the future. His position was temporarily filled by a new recon man at Kontum, John Plaster. Upon Templin's return in January, he was sent to Da Nang to take care of some administrative issues. During his absence, Stephens was informed that his team was targeted for a mission into southeast Laos. Newcomer Plaster was all ears as he listened to Captain Jaks explain how RT New Mexico was to execute an area recon and report any enemy presence near Highway 110. His morale was further boosted that day upon seeing a bandaged and exhausted-looking Bob Howard report back in to Captain Lesesne. Fearing that Army doctors might ship him to Japan for recovery, Howard had gone AWOL from the hospital and hitched a ride on a Huey back to Kontum, where he was content to allow senior medic Lou Maggio pull his stitches and remove dead tissue from around his wounds.[7]

Left: Larry Stephens, one-zero of RT New Mexico, was killed when his team was overrun in their RON site in January 1969. *Paul Stephens via Jason Hardy*

Right: Another casualty of the team was Staff Sergeant Charles Bullard. *Bullard family via Jason Hardy*

Stephens flew a visual recon of his team's target area aboard an O-1 Bird Dog reconnaissance plane the next day and returned to prepare his team for their insertion. On the morning of January 28, RT New Mexico climbed aboard Pleiku-based 189th AHC slicks for the twenty-five-minute flight into Dak To. One-Two Plaster was rechecking his gear for the tenth time when another Huey landed with Billy Simmons and one of his good friends, Staff Sergeant Charles Dorian Bullard. They had just gone through One-Zero School together and Simmons now requested that Bullard be allowed to join the team as a straphanger for experience.[8]

The extra man created too much weight for the insertion slicks, and Plaster found himself left behind when New Mexico lifted off for Laos. The less experienced Green Beret flew back to Kontum that afternoon with camouflage stick still on his face, feeling like the last unchosen kid for a ball game. His dejection turned to a hollow feeling the next morning when he was called into the recon company room before Bob Howard, Captain Lesesne, and Staff Sergeant Pinn. Lesesne informed Plaster that his team had failed to report via radio that morning, January 29. New Mexico's last transmission had been Bullard reporting at dusk that the team was going into its RON position.

Lieutenant Tom Jaeger led the Bright Light team sent in to retrieve Stephens and his team. Following his participation in the big November SLAM mission, Jaeger had gone Stateside on leave, where he was delayed extra days in the hospital while fighting off a bout of malaria. He had just returned to Kontum when RT New Mexico went silent. His men were infiltrated near the RON site One-Two Bullard had reported the previous evening. The only other intel passed on to Jaeger was that the team had radioed the Leghorn relay station during the night to report movement outside their RON position.

The Bright Light team found a location littered with food wrappers, cigarette butts, and other refuse—certainly not the discards of a SOG team.

A short distance away, they found evidence of an ambush with expended ammunition and blood, the trails leading Jaeger's team to the bodies of Bullard, Simmons, and Stephens. Their indigenous members had apparently eluded the NVA and escaped, leaving the Bright Light team with the somber duty of bagging the remains of their fallen Green Beret brothers to be flown out.

During the Vietnam War, ten SOG recon teams would disappear entirely deep in enemy territory. Recon Team New Mexico became one of the other fourteen teams whose American team members were completely wiped out—lost either to being overrun by enemy forces or in a helicopter crash. Further tragedy struck Kontum on January 29, when another Green Beret, Private First Class Jerrald Joseph Bulin, was shot and killed by a lone Vietcong while serving on compound security duty. The loss of Bulin and RT New Mexico brought the losses to six Americans from Kontum killed during the month, in addition to the indigenous team members lost and the four helicopter crew casualties.

Tom Templin was devastated by the deaths of his two close friends on RT New Mexico. He visited some of his wounded Montagnard teammates who had escaped the ambush and then found himself straphanging with other teams until a busted ankle suffered on one mission took him out of action for months. His replacement on the team, John Plaster, found himself in limbo, waiting for his next chance to be pulled onto a recon team. Recon Team New Mexico would be out of commission temporarily, as such losses were not easy to replace. Eighty percent of the Army's Special Forces–qualified personnel worldwide had already served in Vietnam by 1968. Beginning in early 1969, added pressure from the Pentagon to maintain special ops programs like MACV-SOG at full strength resulted in only ten percent of the men reporting at Nha Trang having battlefield experience and one-quarter of them not even being SF qualified.[9]

General Creighton W. Abrams, the MACV-SOG commander, had MACV analyze SOG casualties for the first two months of 1969. Sixty-eight men had been wounded, fifteen Americans were killed or MIA, and ten helicopters had been destroyed. SOG estimated that in its missions during January and February, its teams had destroyed 13 trucks, killed 1,400 enemy soldiers, and called in air strikes that created 455 secondary explosions and 100 sustained fires. The kill ratio was nearly one hundred NVA killed for each SOG man lost, far greater than the conventional unit kill ratio of about 15 to 1.[10] SOG records showed that 108 NVA had been killed during 1968 for each Green Beret lost. At its peak efficiency in 1970, the ratio would jump to 153 to 1, likely one of the highest combat efficiency ratings in U.S. history.[11]

✦◇✦

These ratios were accomplished in spite of the North Vietnamese Army growing wiser in it ways of handling SOG's recon teams. Watch teams were deployed near the most promising LZs, while other sentries manned tree platforms to scan general areas, and such scouts used predetermined signals to warn other troops when an American recon team had landed. Specially trained PAVN regulars were called in to track the SOG men with bloodhounds, and financial incentives were offered for the killing of members of a recon team.[12]

Such NVA tactics forced team leaders to adapt. One-Zero Jon Davidson, who had taken over RT Wyoming when Squirrel Spouse went on leave, soon realized that familiarity could lead to death. His and Joe Walker's teams went in after artillery strikes during early 1969 but found that there was a spy among them that often led to their team being compromised almost as soon as they hit the ground in enemy territory. Davidson resorted to putting his team in on three different possible LZs, but did not decide until it was time to land which one he would pick. "I'd use two false ones and one real one," he said. "That way, I always just barely managed to avoid the enemy's traps." Some of Davidson's evasion techniques included moving up creeks and putting CS powder across their trail to throw off the efforts of the NVA's tracker dogs.

Tom Jaeger, promoted to captain by mid-February and moved from Hatchet Force to command RT Kentucky, was similarly challenged by aggressive enemy tracking. On his first recon mission, he led a ten-man team including Second Lieutenant Jim Young and Specialist Fourth Class Daniel Lindblom. The team successfully eluded trackers for three days while conducting reconnaissance along the Ho Chi Minh Trail. On the afternoon of February 18, Jaeger moved his team to a ridgeline, where they soon spotted a twenty-man team that appeared to be searching for them. He put RT Kentucky on the run to clear the area but his team was soon completely surrounded. Jaeger formed a perimeter and prepared for the enemy assault. He had Lindblom call for an extraction but the slicks were driven off by heavy enemy fire.

As soon as the choppers pulled away, a vicious enemy attack commenced. Jaeger was hit by shrapnel in his right leg and Lieutenant Young was also wounded. Lindblom, who remained exposed to coach in air strikes, had his TAC air drop napalm within fifty-five yards of his team's perimeter and called in gunship strikes to within twenty-five yards. Lindblom and Jaeger continued directing air strikes in as the first chopper lifted out many of the team's indigenous troopers by string because of the high canopy. Although pretty beat-up, RT Kentucky made it out without loss of life and returned with fresh stories of an overly alert enemy tracking system.

Roy Bahr and his command staff continued blending in the newbies to supplement the loss of the wounded recon men and the inevitable leaves and transfers. Two veteran one-zeros, Joe Walker and Phil Brown, left Kontum in February for a forty-five-day leave in Australia. They lived it up at the Oceanic Hotel in Sydney, where the top floor was reserved for Special Forces men on leave. Brown's grandfather, Henry Albert "Harry" Burland, was the assistant mayor for the South Sydney Municipality, so he helped Brown find the strongest beer in the region.

John Plaster, stranded after his temporary assignment to the now-decimated RT New Mexico, soon got his next chance on a team when Bob Howard called him in for a meeting. There, he was introduced to two black NCOs: One-Zero Ben Thompson and his one-one, Jim Stevenson, the latter slated to rotate back home. Plaster became a member of RT Illinois, stepping up to one-one after Stevenson's departure. Thompson added a third Green Beret, Sergeant George Bacon, and commenced training his team in earnest along with their Vietnamese counterparts. Plaster learned that along with his coveted CAR-15—still scarce enough at Kontum that few beyond one-zeros had them—Thompson preferred carrying the radio himself while across the fence and held high hopes of pulling off a prisoner snatch.[13]

As one-one, Plaster did not have access to a CAR-15 so he opted for a suppressed Swedish K. In late February, he took part in his first mission across the fence into Laos with Thompson, Bacon, and the five indigenous teammates of RT Illinois. The team gathered intelligence on enemy positions, called in air strikes, and was extracted without loss days later. As their Huey settled onto the CCC chopper pad that afternoon, Plaster was surprised to see forty or more members of the Kontum recon company gathered. In addition to Lionel Pinn, Bob Howard, and Ed Lesesne, Green Berets from a dozen teams were there to press cold beers into the hands of the returning successful team. Plaster had never felt such a bond.[14] He thought, *We may be on different teams, but we're all in this together.*

✦◇✦

Half a world away and more than a year after the actions that resulted in his recommendation for the Medal of Honor, former Kontum One-Zero Fred Zabitosky was finally being recognized by his country. Beneath his uniform, his skin still held the burns and scars from February 1968, when he had pulled two pilots from their burning chopper while struggling with a crushed back, shrapnel wounds, and broken ribs. His back was healed and Zabitosky had returned to Kontum to help train other teams. Once word made the rounds that he was up for the Medal of Honor, he was unable to participate in any further mission across the fence.

By February 1969, Zabitosky had been returned to the States and was serving at Fort Bragg when the word came for him to report to the White House to be presented with his medal. On March 7, Sergeant First Class Zabitosky sat in the Red Room with his wife and child awaiting President Richard Nixon. Captain Bud Williams, a former straphanger on Zabitosky's team, was also present to witness the presentation. General Westmoreland arrived and explained to Zabitosky that his citation, due to security reasons, would list his actions as having taken place in Vietnam rather than Laos. Nixon came into the room and added that the classified nature of the ongoing recon work forbid the disclosure of the true location. "But, I have had engraved on the back of your medal: FOB 2, C&C Detachment, 5th Special Forces," Nixon added.[15]

Zabitosky stood proudly in the White House as President Nixon read the citations for his valor and also those for two other recipients, Sergeant Joe Ronnie Hooper and Specialist Fifth Class Clarence Eugene Sasser. Reflecting back on the mission, Zabitosky would say that at the time of his actions, heroism was not on his mind. "You think strictly about the people you are with, and what you can do for each other," he said. "I wear the medal, but it was earned by Doug Glover, my indigenous team members, and all the Special Forces enlisted men who served on special projects. All the guys who wore that beret in combat have done just as much as I have, even though they may not have received the Medal of Honor."[16]

◆◇◆

Just two days into March 1969, Command and Control Central was attacked. Many of the men had enjoyed a late night at the base club, and some were still playing poker into the predawn hours. Medic Joe Parnar's first notion of trouble came when he was awakened by a loud bang at 0400. As he heard sand tinkling down on the tin roof of his building, he shouted to roommate Bryon Loucks, "It's incoming! Get under your bunk!"[17]

As the pair scrambled under their bunks, the Kontum warning siren began to wail. The recon base was under a sapper attack. Suddenly, a loud explosion and flash ripped through their room as a B-40 RPG round hit, ripping both Parnar and Loucks with shrapnel. The rocket had impacted their door, punched a hole through their room into the adjacent team rooms, and exited by making an eight-inch hole through the outer cement wall. The third new Kontum medic, John Walton (son of the WalMart founder), was still playing poker at the time and thus escaped serious injury. Loucks was taken to the dispensary, suffering from a chest wound and shrapnel in a knee that would soon see him med-evaced to Pleiku for treatment. The RPG attack on CCC—the first to create casualties within the compound—put a new emphasis on security patrols outside the perimeter to prevent other insurgents from slipping in close enough to launch their rocket-propelled grenades.

Early March also saw a change in command as Roy Bahr was rotated home and turned over command of CCC to a new CO. Ironically, he passed the torch to Lieutenant Colonel Frederick T. Abt, whom Bahr had not seen since 1951 when young First Lieutenant Abt had served as his tactical officer at OCS. A former enlisted man in the U.S. Marines during World War II and a Korean War veteran, Fred Abt was gray-haired with blue-grey eyes; he proved to be easily accessible to his recon company. He and right-hand man Clyde Sincere noted that Bob Howard was still eager for action but they kept him occupied with training their men, as his Medal of Honor was still pending.

During his second week of command at Kontum, Abt had his hands full with teams caught in hot action. John Plaster would witness plenty of it, as his team under Ben Thompson was deployed to Dak To to relieve One-Zero Marvin Montgomery's RT Maine of Bright Light duty. Upon arriving at Dak To, Plaster learned that six teams were on the ground in southern Laos, the maximum number deemed prudent to operate across the fence at once. Plaster found that his buddy Glenn Uemura was on one of those six teams, RT Hawaii, serving as one-two under One-Zero Bill Delima and a new one-one, First Lieutenant Greg Glashauser.[18]

By mid-afternoon on March 14, before RT Illinois could take over from Montgomery's RT Maine for Bright Light rotation, RT New Hampshire transmitted a prairie fire call. Montgomery, his one-one, Specialist Fourth Class Dave Baker, and three Montagnards lifted off in a Huey to assist the overrun team. RT New Hampshire was fighting for its life just twenty-five miles away in Laos in area Juliet-9, near the Leghorn relay site. The team leader, First Lieutenant Jim Ripanti, had been trying to outma-neuver tracker teams and platoons of searchers for three days before his luck ran out. His team got into a firefight and Ripanti was hit in the chest by an AK round, while his one-one, Staff Sergeant George Fails, was badly shot through both legs.

Ripanti refused first aid and attempted to direct the team's defense, even though he was mortally wounded. One of his Montagnards was too badly wounded to walk. Fails, also unable to walk, took over the radio from his one-two, Sergeant Mike Kinnear, allowing the latter to crawl about and fire on the NVA each time they assaulted. Heavy enemy gunfire winged and drove away the Bright Light chopper carrying Montgomery's RT Maine men around 1300, until Fails was able to radio in sufficient Cobras and A-1s to pound back the opposition.

Montgomery, Baker, and three Montagnards rappelled into the hostile zone under heavy fire. Kinnear and his Montagnards continued to hold off the enemy while Montgomery and Baker rendered first aid to Fails and their badly injured Montagnard. Montgomery called in an extraction Huey, which dropped ropes to pull out the badly wounded Montagnard, Fails, and team leader Ripanti, whose body had been rigged into a jungle extraction harness.[19]

After the dead and wounded had been extracted, the remnants of the two teams reformed and broke through the ring of advancing enemy, while Baker remained behind to direct fire and lay mines in order to retard the NVA advance. Despite problems of difficult terrain and weather, the team reached a clearing suitable for exfiltration and was extracted at 1830 with no additional casualties. The next morning, RT Kentucky, under One-Zero Tom Jaeger, One-One Ron Gravett (making his third combat mission), and One-Two Dave Kirschbaum, was inserted to take over the mission.

Recon Team Kentucky was hit by NVA during its second day and became split in the ensuing firefight—Jaeger with some of the Montagnards and Gravett and Kirschbaum with the rest. The new one-two began calling in Cobra gunships to lay their ordnance on the NVA. One enemy round exploded close enough that Gravett received a nasty shrapnel wound to the head that soaked his ERC-10 survival radio in blood. Kirschbaum called in a prairie fire emergency, bringing in rocket-armed choppers to chew up the enemy while extraction choppers moved in to pull Jaeger's team from the hot LZ on McGuire rigs.

◆◇◆

Recon missions from CCC were all carried out with determined vigor to disrupt the NVA, but Operation Nightcap was groundbreaking.

The first big offensive launched under new CCC commander Fred Abt's reign took place in March 1969, aimed at shutting down NVA convoys along Routes 96 and 110 at a point shortly before the joint roads divided in Laos. The troubles began on March 3, when NVA forces attacked the isolated Special Forces Camp at Ben Het. They used Russian PT-76 tanks and BMP-40 armored personnel carriers to attack the SF camp, located about eight miles east of the Laotian border and nine miles west of the MACV-SOG launch site at Dak To—which itself would remain under siege for the next four months.[20]

Saigon sent orders to CCC to disrupt the supply lines to the NVA troops conducting the siege by carrying out SLAM IX. Abt's men were to restrict material moving down Routes 96/110 in Laos by interdicting a section of highway about twenty-one miles from Ben Het and less than one mile from the point where 96 and 110 divided. At that point, 96 continued into Cambodia and 110 made its way north then east into Vietnam in the tri-border area.

The S3 group put together a SLAM mission to handle the highway blocking task, led by Hatchet Force Company A under Captain Barre R. McClelland. His men were inserted via choppers on March 15, and they were supported by RT Arizona, which was to supply recon capabilities and serve as the eyes and ears of the SLAM operation. The Americans of RT Arizona were: one-zero, First Lieutenant Darrell Redman; one-one, Specialist Fourth Class Joe McCammond (a straphanger); and one-two, Specialist Fourth Class Kyle Dean.

Their target area was in Hotel-6, so the troops made their way to within a few hundred yards of Highway 96/110 onto a small hill across a river to the west of the road. Captain McClelland had two platoons, one led by First Lieutenant Frank Longaker, while First Lieutenant James McCauley was in charge of a 60-mm mortar crew.

It was the first cross-border operation for Kyle Dean, freshly arrived in Vietnam and married less than one year. His first ever helicopter ride had been the one going into Dak To that morning. Now, his second was riding a Kingbee that was banking for the final insertion run into enemy territory; Dean's stomach dropping as Cobra gunships ahead of him chewed up the LZ. "I prayed for a cool LZ, although I didn't even know what a hot LZ was like," Dean wrote. "I found myself in a daze as I jumped from the chopper into the most hot and humid spot I think I have ever been."[21]

Lieutenant Redman ordered Dean to switch packs with him so he could carry the one-two's radio for communications. Dean cursed his luck as he donned his one-zero's heavily loaded pack of rations and sweated through the afternoon while RT Arizona clawed its way up a hill and dug in to a defensive position. His team worked on improving their foxholes the next day, March 16, until the SLAM team called in A1-E Skyraider strikes against NVA troops that had been discovered. Dean, dug into a foxhole near the middle of the SOG force, heard one of the officers order everyone to take cover as the strike force came in. "The sound of that aircraft coming in so low made it sound like the end of the world," Dean said.

"It almost was for me. The napalm hit in a tree above my foxhole, burst, and engulfed the next two foxholes in its line of flight."[22]

Joe McCammond of RT Arizona was pushed down into his foxhole and his body was selflessly shielded by an indigenous team member who spared him from serious injury. Eight Montagnards of Company A were burned in the mishap, and four would perish, two instantly. The heat of the flash set off grenades and left the survivors in the area feeling as if they had been badly sunburned by the flashes. One-Zero Darrell Redman and medic Tony Dorff moved swiftly to administer assistance to the five surviving Montagnards. "I was slapping my face because I thought I was on fire," Dean said. "I literally thought I was in hell. Getting the bodies out of the foxholes was tough because the skin just peeled off of the bones as if it was cooked."

Chase medic Joe Parnar arrived on a Huey that successfully pulled the five burned Montagnards. To reinforce the roadblock team, Major Sam Sanford inserted with additional personnel and equipment that afternoon and assumed command of the SLAM IX mission. The following day, Sanford directed the clearing of the jungle to help shore up the company's defensive perimeter and to gain greater exposure to the nearby highway. A new LZ was built within the camp's perimeter and the bodies of the deceased Montagnards were dragged onto it for extraction at a later time.

In this photo taken by Kyle Dean, Montagnards of Company A are seen firing at NVA troops during March 1969's roadblock operation, code name Nightcap. *Joe Parnar*

Sanford's company continued calling in strikes by attack jets during the ensuing days, and their bombs helped crater the nearby NVA road. At night, a strobe light placed in the center of the perimeter kept the SLAM team pinpointed so that Shadow and Spectre aircraft did not mistakenly unload their ordnance too close again.

Lieutenant McCauley's 60-mm mortar team fired more than six hundred rounds in defense of the company's hilltop position during the next few days. Each night, the NVA responded with mortar and rocket attacks directed against the SLAM company. Enemy troops made attempts to scale the hill on various nights to assault the CCC men, but were greeted each time by well-placed Claymores, machine-gun fire, and aerial assaults. One Vietnamese member of the SLAM company was killed during a firefight by mistake when a Montagnard saw him stick his head up near their bunker and heard him speaking in Vietnamese.

The Americans sent out at night to perform listening duties near the hilltop did so at great personal risk. Staff Sergeant Peter Tandy braved a hail of NVA small-arms fire and shrapnel to direct his troops in repulsing an enemy advance, and Tandy was wounded in the process. Staff Sergeant Earl Savage was also wounded by fragments from a grenade blast that night, but First Lieutenant Redman helped pull him safely back into the perimeter. Others were wounded in the relentless battles each night. Sergeant First Class Tyrone Massey, manning the SLAM company's 90-mm recoilless rifle, was wounded by grenade shrapnel and suffered a dislocated shoulder when a shattered tree branch fell on him.

Massey's place on the 90-mm rifle was taken on March 19 by First Lieutenant Tom Waskovich, whose Bright Light team came in during an extraction of the wounded men. During that night, the fifth of Operation Nightcap, Kyle Dean was also wounded. "Problem was, the attackers were between me and the camp. Bad feeling!" he wrote. Having detected enemy movement outside the perimeter, he began blowing the planted Claymores. The next explosion he felt slammed him into some bamboo, where Dean slowly regained his senses and realized he was bleeding from his right leg, right lower back, and shoulder. He managed to make his way back within the company's perimeter to suffer through his sixth night on the hilltop, but Dean was evacuated on a supply chopper on March 21. His place was filled for the next three days of the mission by Staff Sergeant Phil Rice, the one-one of RT Iowa. "That night, I got drunk but still couldn't sleep," Dean said. "I had been initiated! I was no longer a cherry."[23]

Operation Nightcap was proving to be quite costly in terms of men killed and wounded, but steady resupply runs from choppers bringing ammunition and water ensured that the SLAM efforts would continue.

Mortar attacks continued during the next three nights, exposing the men to further injury from shrapnel. Enemy trucks attempted to run the company's roadblock area, but accurate firing from American recon men disabled one vehicle that was left destroyed on the road. Additional trucks were destroyed that tried to make it around the disabled vehicle.

Major Sanford and Captain McClelland kept their troops focused on their mission of road interdiction with success. Lieutenant Colonel Abt was kept apprised of the ongoing operation through relays from Leghorn and he even flew over the company's position twice to discuss the situation on secure FM radio. The SLAM company was finally extracted from the hilltop on the morning of March 24. Sam Sanford was last to board a chopper, pulling the igniter on a long fuse to a bunker loaded with excess ammunition and explosives as he did.[24]

His company had successfully disrupted traffic on Route 96/110 for more than a week, during which time four Montagnards had perished and four Green Berets received Purple Hearts. Five CCC men were awarded the Bronze Star Medal with "V" device and eleven would receive the Army Commendation Medal with "V" device. SOG command was pleased enough with the results of SLAM IX to order two more roadblock insertions within the next year to further stress NVA supply lines.

Chapter Nineteen

"IN THE FRYING PAN"

Master Sergeant Lionel Pinn, knowing he was in the waning days of his military career, received permission from base XO Clyde Sincere to run one last target during April. He was inserted with a Mike Force, three Green Berets, and a dozen Montagnards, into southeastern Laos to recover electronic devices planted near the Ho Chi Minh Trail. Pinn's group had scarcely cleared the LZ to take cover in a nearby brush line when enemy gunfire erupted. More NVA forces joined the battle, and Pinn soon found himself helping to patch up two wounded Montagnards.[1]

The enemy set fire to the tall grass covering the recon team, forcing them to fire while retreating backward toward shorter grass. Pinn called in a prairie fire emergency and fought it out while his team moved toward an emergency LZ. Every other survivor of the platoon—including Pinn and straphanger Jon Davidson—was wounded to some degree by bullets and shrapnel by the time they were finally extracted. Davidson noted Pinn hanging limp in his harness as they were pulled on strings up through heavy tree cover, but he could tell the old warrior was still alive. Pinn was awarded his eighth Purple Heart on this mission, his first having been received decades earlier in 1944. It was his last trip across the fence and his position as first sergeant of the Kontum recon company was taken over by Master Sergeant Bob Howard, who was still forbidden from running combat missions due to the pending award of his Medal of Honor.

Howard assumed the never-ending task of bringing the latest Kontum recruits up to speed on operations and blending them into teams needing a new man. Among those reporting to him in late April were

Specialist Fourth Class Frank Greco and Staff Sergeant Ron Gravett. Greco and a buddy from SF Training Group had encountered Gravett at Nha Trang shortly after being processed through Saigon. Gravett, a veteran of missions with RT Kentucky, told them they should ask for CCC because "that's where the action is at." They did, and the trio was soon on board a C-130 bound for Lieutenant Colonel Abt's base at Kontum.[2]

Greco reported in to Howard, was issued weapons and gear, and was told to report to RT Colorado. The longstanding Kontum team was led by One-Zero Willie McLeod and included One-One Sergeant Charles Erickson and One-Two Sergeant Ruben Angeles. The latter was slated to return home soon, so Greco would be assuming his spot and learning the ropes. "I was the proverbial 'fucking new guy' [FNG] and as such had to run two or three missions across the fence before being even remotely accepted, or even spoken to, by the rest of those who ran recon," Greco said.[3]

Within weeks, Greco was on his first Prairie Fire mission into Laos. He dutifully humped the radio and took in the details from his comrades of how to conduct himself in the field. One-Zero McLeod had RT Colorado attempt a prisoner snatch near a well-used trail but the ambush ended in a firefight and a hasty E&E for the team. "We ran like hell, were able to make radio contact, and were extracted later that day," said Greco.[4] He had gotten his first taste of action and had come out alive. In short order, Frank Greco would become an experienced recon man with multiple trips across the fence under his belt.

✦✧✦

Specialist Fourth Class Kyle Dean's second trip across the fence was as a straphanger with One-Zero Carlos Parker's RT South Carolina. He spent the first night in his RON slapping his face and body to rid what he assumed to be mosquitoes. "The next morning I awoke and saw that my rucksack was covered with ants," he said. "I had slept next to an ant hill. I managed to salvage breakfast but never slept next to small hills or mounds again."[5]

Parker's team became aware of NVA trackers stalking them the next two days until he was finally forced to call for an extraction. Their LZ soon proved to be in an area infested with enemy bunkers, necessitating close firing runs from Cobra gunships to cover South Carolina's extraction Hueys. Dean was pulled out in a Hanson rig, dangling in numbness from ninety feet of rope thousands of feet above the jungle for forty minutes until the choppers could reach the safety of Ben Het's SF camp. He was fortunate to escape with only a small frag wound to the neck.

Joe Walker was back at Kontum by mid-April after his extended leave in Australia with buddy Phil Brown. Walker had enlisted for another tour of duty but found partying in Sydney to be more of a priority than his pending return to combat until he was confronted by a sergeant major sent to reel him back in.

"Did you forget to come back to Vietnam, or what the hell's going on?" the sergeant major demanded.

"Well, I just kinda let time slide by, I guess," said Walker.

"I strongly suggest you get on the next airplane. Desertion charges are blooming!"[6]

Fortunately for Walker, his reputation in the field as a fierce warrior helped him negate any AWOL charges, even if he did stall his return to CCC by a few more days with extra escapades in Saigon. He was then rewarded with orders to take his team into Juliet-9, one of the hottest target areas that had produced a number of recent recon casualties.

A former CCC recon man, Jerry Shriver, had gone missing from CCS on a bomb damage assessment mission into Cambodia on April 24. Into his third year of running recon with SOG, Shriver was well known among both his comrades and even Radio Hanoi, which had dubbed him a "mad dog" and placed a bounty on his head—which is how he acquired the nickname of "Mad Dog." His Hatchet Force company was ambushed upon insertion, suffering numerous casualties, and Shriver was last seen rushing into the jungle with several Montagnards to silence a machine-gun bunker that had pinned his Hatchet Force down.[7]

Sergeant First Class Jerry "Mad Dog" Shriver served from FOB-2 in 1967. The legendary Green Beret had accumulated two Silver Stars, seven Bronze Stars, three Army Commendation Medals, a Purple Heart, and other medals by April 24, 1969, when he was listed as missing in action in Cambodia following a severe firefight. *Joe Parnar*

In the first few months of 1969, Fred Abt's sixty-man recon company at Kontum had endured six Americans killed and another twenty-two wounded. Just days after the loss of Shriver from CCS, Joe Walker's RT California was ordered into Juliet-9 on April 28 with Private First Class Harry Williams serving as his one-one and Specialist Fourth Class Bill Stubbs as his one-two.[8]

Walker's team struggled with bad weather, pushing through dense mountainous terrain while discovering abandoned enemy gun positions and material. Recon Team California had an uneventful RON that night, and then began moving along a small access road on April 29 that lay just off a major NVA infiltration and resupply route. Walker's point man suddenly spotted two enemy soldiers running, so he gained the element of surprise by doing the unthinkable: his team raced right down the highway in broad daylight to a more secure area. There, Stubbs contacted their FAC with the alert that RT California was facing imminent enemy contact.[9]

Walker broke his team into two elements, leaving assistant team leader Williams in charge of a 60-mm mortar team set to provide cover. Walker moved forward with Stubbs and their remaining Montagnards toward the spot where the enemy had been seen, hoping to lay down their possible ambush plan. Walker soon spotted an NVA soldier who revealed his position and was dropped by a quick burst. Walker's Montagnards then opened fire, killing two more enemy soldiers and wounding an unknown additional number. Stubbs laid down heavy support fire over the heads of his comrades as they pulled back, and then lobbed hand grenades while directing the fire of a Montagnard grenadier.[10]

Walker boldly moved forward to search the bodies of the dead NVA for key documents, despite movement and continued fire from the regrouped enemy force. He then fell back, regrouped RT California, and reported in to headquarters of their actions. His alert actions, coupled with deadly mortar assaults from Harry Williams' group, saved the team from being ambushed and prevented them from incurring any casualties. Walker's successful return from such a hot area may have surprised some of his superiors, who proceeded to write him up for a Bronze Star.

◆◇◆

Soon after the triumphant return of RT California, Ben Thompson led his RT Illinois into a hot area of northeast Cambodia that had been freshly pounded by more than ten thousand B-52 bombs. The objective was to neutralize NVA 27th Infantry Regiment units besieging the Ben Het Special Forces Camp and Thompson's team was charged with conducting a bomb damage assessment into the stirred-up bomb zone with hopes of snatching a prisoner.

Distant smoke and rising dust from the bombs were still plainly visible as Kingbee choppers inserted RT Illinois that morning. Less than an hour on the ground, Thompson's team was still slinking forward through the splintered trees and freshly powdered soil when it was engaged by an NVA squad. One-One John Plaster found his first big gunfight to be an adrenaline rush that called for endurance as he tossed grenades and laid down fire with his suppressed Swedish K. Thompson kept his team on the move toward an LZ, heavily engaged by the enemy as Cougar gunships moved in to light up the area with their mini-guns and 2.75-inch rockets.[11]

By the time Vietnamese Kingbees lifted his team from the Cambodian canopy, Plaster had exhausted all of his ammunition and grenades. Two of his Montagnard teammates had been wounded in the action and his jungle fatigues had been sprayed with their blood. After returning to Kontum that evening, Plaster complained to new base commander Fred Abt that his 9-mm Swedish K did not have the necessary stopping power to keep his opponents down. His request to be issued a more desirable—and lethal—CAR-15 was granted the following morning. "After five months in recon, I finally had my own CAR-15, a weapon whose bullet generated four times the ballistic lethality of a Swedish K's 9-mm," said Plaster.

Colonel Abt's SOG teams continued their relentless mission pace, often disrupting convoy traffic along Laotian Highway 110 with anti-truck mines. Prisoner snatching continued to be a key goal among the teams, although CCC's luck for achieving this goal had dried up since the double-snatch efforts of Wilson Hunt and Ed Lesesne during the previous September and Bob Howard's SLAM VII prisoner. Extracting a live enemy prisoner was so rare that SOG teams pulled fewer than fifty POWs from Laos and Cambodia during the entire Vietnam War.[12]

Master Sergeant Norm Doney, one-zero of RT Florida, nearly accomplished the feat on May 11. Having disabled a lone NVA with a suppressed .22 pistol, he was preparing to hog-tie his victim when a large NVA unit attacked and he was ripped by RPG shrapnel. Doney's prisoner leaped for his AK, but the wounded Green Beret was quick enough to save his own skin by dispatching his prisoner.[13]

The first CCC-based team to successfully pull off a prisoner snatch in 1969 was RT Texas, marking the first live capture in eight months for any Kontum recon unit. The team's able one-zero was David Gilmer, an unassuming country boy from Mississippi who had spent enough time in the woods hunting and fishing that he felt it well prepared him for his new job. Gilmer had absorbed tactics during his time on Joe Walker's RT California and on Luke Dove's RT Delaware before he was moved up to one-zero. His men—One-One Dick Nowack and One-Two Clarence Long—were a tight unit that willingly put in the hours for training on immediate action drills, weapons training, and even special emphasis on pulling off a prisoner snatch.

"That was a goal we really worked hard on," said Nowack, a twenty-two-year old Ohio native who had originally been drafted into the Army. After completing Airborne School, Nowack had gone through full medic training before he was finally shipped over to Vietnam and assigned to Kontum. He had been seasoned by two missions carrying radio for RT Nevada and RT Ohio before Bob Howard assigned him as Gilmer's new assistant team leader for RT Texas.

Gilmer's team had previously tried unsuccessfully to grab a prisoner but overwhelming numbers of NVA had forced RT Texas to run for their lives. His relentless training on prisoner snatch tactics finally paid off in mid-July 1969. As fate would have it, One-Two Long was temporarily out of action due to a training mission injury, so he recruited Sergeant John Peterson to carry the radio for the team's insertion into Laos. Their area near Highway 110 was a hot one the team had frequented on numerous prior insertions, which had often ended with them being shot out from a hot LZ. Gilmer moved his two Green Berets and their Montagnard contingent through a valley near a river, where they crossed the stream to set up their RON near a well-traveled road.

Recon Team Texas was on the move early, with the men eating a quick breakfast before establishing their ambush site near the trail. Gilmer's team undertook the unorthodox maneuver of donning gas masks, preparing to surprise any NVA element with teargas grenades to help achieve the necessary element of surprise. A short time later, as Nowack crouched to the right of his team with his Montagnard tail gunner, he caught sight of a seven-man NVA patrol moving down the road. Recon Team Texas struck with lightning precision, lobbing in a grenade to cripple the patrol while simultaneously hitting their left and right flanks with teargas grenades fired from the grenadier's M79.

The recon team swept over their downed opponents, where they found a young NVA soldier trying to play possum. The man had only a minor shrapnel wound to his leg, so RT Texas overpowered him, handcuffed him, gagged him, and hustled him toward their nearby LZ. Gilmer used his CAR-15 to dispatch several soldiers who reached for their weapons, but he knew the dead men on the trail would be discovered quickly. Peterson immediately contacted his covey to announce they had one "in the frying pan"—SOG code for an enemy prisoner successfully snatched.

To his dismay, Gilmer was informed that it might be hours before an extraction effort could be made for them. Three others teams—Glenn Uemura's RT Hawaii, Bill Delima's RT Florida, and Floyd Ambrose's RT Washington—had each suffered wounded and were in heated situations. The RT Texas one-zero, having finally achieved the incredible feat, had little patience as he grabbed the team radio.

"I'll tell you what," Gilmer said. "You'd better get here in about half an hour or you're not going to have a prisoner anymore!"[14]

The sounds of extraction Hueys could be heard in short order, and Gilmer's triumphant team was pulled from the Laotian jungle with its prize. They had achieved what no other CCC recon team had done since November 1968. Stepping from their choppers to the waiting cold beers, Dick Nowack and his comrades felt like rock stars. First Sergeant Bob Howard wrapped his powerful arms around the small, wounded North Vietnamese soldier and carried him like a child across the Kontum compound to have shrapnel pulled from his leg. Gilmer later escorted his prisoner on to Saigon to hand off to the intelligence division.

Recon Team Texas was showered with praise. Colonel Abt promised a Silver Star to Gilmer, although he was rotated back home to Mississippi weeks later without seeing the commendation go through. Even better than the momentary fame for Nowack was the $250 cash bonus for each Green Beret and a lengthy R&R in Taiwan—a worthy payoff for the months of hard training his team had put in.

◆◇◆

Kontum's recon company saw more than its fair share of personnel changes during the spring and summer of 1969.

Major Clyde Sincere and Captain Frank Jaks were the highest ranking CCC officers to be rotated to new duties during May. On the night of their exchange, the pair happened to meet an old friend at the Ghost Club in Nha Trang, Major Bobby Leites, who had done two previous brief stints during Kontum's early formation under Charlie Norton and Jerry Kilburn. Knowing that Leites was scheduled to replace him as second-in-command at Kontum, Sincere took great pleasure in getting his comrade completely inebriated.

The next morning, he took Leites to the airport after cutting every bit of rank and insignia from his uniform, leaving him with little more than his beret and his boots. Turning to the Vietnamese pilot, Sincere instructed, "You will not land with Colonel Leites anywhere except when he reports to Colonel Abt. Do you understand?"

Sincere then placed a call to Fred Abt, telling him not to blame his new XO for his startling first appearance. Puzzled, Abt was left to wait for the arrival of his badly hung-over new executive officer. "Don't blame him," Sincere warned with a chuckle.[15]

Abt and Leites would have their hands full coordinating the personnel shuffle among their twenty active recon teams. Leites, with far more Special Forces experience than his new boss, took it upon himself to make sure that his new commander was properly respected by their men. One of his first challenges was the temporary loss of Bob Howard, who rotated back to the States in June. The popular sergeant, still pending Medal of Honor paperwork that would linger for many more months, would return later in 1969 but in the interim his position as Recon Company first sergeant would be filled by Norm Doney, the former one-zero of RT Florida. His new men found him to be a big believer in the sharing of field knowledge by distributing mimeographed "Think" sheets about recon team and NVA intelligence. Doney also handed out "Tips of the Trade" sheets with useful info on properly running recon.[16]

Doney's recon teams soon sported a rising class of newer one-zeros. Men like Pappy Webb, Squirrel Sprouse, Bryon Loucks, Phil Brown, Bill Janc, Joe Parnar, and Luke Dove had rotated on during the first half of the year. These losses were compounded by many other old-timers being rotated during the ensuing months, including Joe Walker, David Gilmer, Bill Delima, Joe Messer, and Ralph Rodd, the latter being wounded and evacuated after a July mission.

The departing veterans left their teams with hand-picked replacements deemed fully capable of carrying on the work. Still, first missions for some new one-zeros were anything but easy. Case in point was the first across the fence insertion for Glenn Uemura, a seven-month veteran now the new team leader of RT Hawaii. His team was deposited into heavily enemy infested Juliet-9 on July 16 with three other Americans, including Bill Delima. Scheduled to rotate home, Delima agreed to go along as an adviser and assistant team leader to lend Uemura a hand.[17]

The following morning, Recon Team Hawaii mixed it up with the enemy and was forced to beat a hasty retreat back to their insertion LZ. Uemura's covey rider soon informed him that they would have to avoid contact until RT Florida and RT Washington could be extracted from their own troubles.

When the first chopper finally approached their LZ more than four hours later, Uemura sent the first four men of his team forward. The jungle suddenly erupted with enemy fire and RT Hawaii's Montagnard point man was fatally wounded. By the time Delima and three Montagnards were finally extracted, radio operator Specialist Fourth Class Dennis Bingham had also been mortally wounded by shrapnel.

Uemura called in more air strikes to suppress the NVA assault until another chopper could pull him, One-Two Joe Morris, the remaining two Montagnards, and the bodies of their fallen teammates from the murderous ground fire. In the Kontum club that night, Delima led his fellow Green Berets in singing an emotional version of "Old Blue," to honor Bingham, but RT Hawaii was a shaken team. Delima rotated home, Morris transferred to the commo bunker, and Uemura chose to ride out his CCC rotation serving as either a one-one or a straphanger for other teams.[18]

◆◇◆

Sergeant Kyle Dean was surprised that his third trip across the fence in late July turned out to be "the perfect mission." It started on a cautionary note, as his RT Arizona was inserted into Hotel-9 at the very LZ where Sergeant Phil Rice's RT Iowa was being extracted. Rice reported lots of enemy movement and signal shots from the far side of the LZ, yet Dean's team somehow managed to catch their enemy off guard with the quick insertion.[19]

Dean went in as RT Arizona's one-two, with his new one-zero, Lieutenant Jim Young; one-one, Sergeant Mike Wilson; and six Montagnards. Signal shots kept them on alert through most of the night. After contacting base on the morning on July 21, Young's team learned that astronaut Neil

Recon Team Arizona seen on Bright Light duty at Dak To in the summer of 1969. Sergeant Kyle Dean, second from left, standing, is carrying the team radio. Lieutenant Jim Young, fourth from left, was the team one-zero. Fourth from left, kneeling, is One-One Sergeant Mike Wilson. *Kyle Dean*

Armstrong had made history overnight by becoming the first man to step on the moon. "We celebrated by passing among the team two small whiskey bottles (airline size) that we had smuggled along," Dean wrote. "This was unheard of and it was the first and only time something like that was done in a combat situation that I was involved with."[20]

Young's team accomplished its objective without a firefight, successfully tapping into an NVA communications wire to collect eight hours of taped intelligence. "Something had to go wrong, but it didn't," Dean recalled. "I got the greatest satisfaction of my life from what we had accomplished," he recalled after Colonel Abt met his team at the Kontum airstrip with the traditional case of beer.[21]

Phil Rice's RT Iowa was back in action within weeks of their trip into Hotel-9. This time, the seasoned one-zero inserted into a wide-open, grassy plain northeast of Dak To known as "the Golf Course," just across the border in southern Laos. A pathway that was part of the Ho Chi Minh Trail ran right through the open plain and NVA were often seen moving south across it en route to the Central Highlands of South Vietnam.

Rice's team of Montagnards, One-One Ray Harris, and One-Two Tom Lois inserted for a road watch mission to monitor the traffic on the Trail by planting radio-operated vibration sensors. Recon Team Iowa set up a point just in the wood line where it could watch traffic along the Golf Course trail. The sensors, intended to detect enemy movement at night, proved to be too sensitive. "Either the wind vibrating waves of grass during the day or rain coming in at night made them constantly sound their alarm," said Harris. "After a day or so of this, we went out at dusk and removed them."[22]

On their fifth day near the Golf Course, RT Iowa attempted to snatch a prisoner when a lone soldier suddenly appeared, moving across the field toward some ponds. Rice moved forward, followed by Dominque and Kehn, two of his Montagnards. Rice tried to shoot his legs but his first shot missed. Adjusting his M16, he squeezed off another round that hit the soldier's lower buttocks and blew out his lower bowels.[23]

Unfortunately, before Rice and his companions could reach the wounded soldier, one of the Montagnards opened up on automatic and hit the enemy soldier in the neck. Rice grabbed the man's rucksack and searched him, finding a captured U.S. .45-caliber automatic pistol. The rest of the team's indigenous members helped haul the dying prisoner's body to the wood line, where he expired. Back at the FOB, his gear was inspected and he was found to be the executive officer of a VC engineering battalion. He was also of Montagnard heritage—surprising to the team that the Vietnamese would have taken him into their ranks and made him an officer.

✦◇✦

Green Berets possessing the guts to grit it out often found themselves advancing from RTOs to capable one-zeros in a matter of months. Such was the experience of Staff Sergeant Ed Wolcoff, a twenty-one-year-old Virginian who inherited his own team by mid-August and would eventually complete twenty-five recon missions.

Wolcoff's desire to join SOG was born during his SF training Stateside, where his instructors included several former CCC veterans, including Johnny Arvai. He had learned enough about the clandestine force through confidential sources that he put in a request to Billye Alexander in the Pentagon to request the assignment after he had joined the 6th SF Group. Ed's wish came true soon enough: in March 1969, he was riding a Blackbird from Nha Trang into Kontum. The first American he encountered as he set foot on the base was an old buddy from training group, Sergeant John St. Martin—a powerfully built All-American with classic good looks and strong physique. Sergeant St. Martin, the one-one for RT New York, explained that his team had an opening for another Green Beret to serve in the one-two position. Recon Team New York's new one-zero, Mike Kinnear, had recently inherited the team after its previous commander, Lieutenant Ripanti, was killed.

Wolcoff leaned heavily on St. Martin to teach him the ropes: how to pack for missions, how to set up his web gear, how to encrypt messages—and everything else he needed to know. Ed found his new one-zero to be egotistical and less interested in training a rookie. The team's Montagnards seemed to worship St. Martin for the respect he showed them, as opposed to the treatment they received from their one-zero.

Other concerning issues with Kinnear compelled Wolcoff and St. Martin to approach recon sergeant Bob Howard after their first week of assigned Bright Light duty. Howard respected the judgment of the men and soon reassigned New York's team leader, but his replacement, Captain Michael Potter, proved to be even less personable with the team's indigenous troops than Kinnear had been. Potter garnered neither the confidence of his team nor another officer who served as a straphanger with RT New York. His team was gearing up at Dak To for a mission across the fence in July when Wolcoff was surprised to see Lieutenant Colonel Abt arrive.

Abt relieved Potter on the spot. He turned to John St. Martin, inquiring, "Can you take the team?"

St. Martin agreed, moving his buddy Wolcoff into the assistant team leader position and adding Sergeant John Blaauw as their new radio operator. Under its new one-zero, New York became a solid unit, with St. Martin leading his men on two July missions into the tri-border area of Hotel-9. On the first, they picked up trackers before settling into their RON site. Coming out of RON the next morning, their Montagnard point man gunned down an NVA soldier he had spotted approaching their position. Another Montagnard hastily detonated one of RT New York's planted Claymores without giving proper warning; St. Martin was flung backwards by the force of the blast but escaped serious injury.

The team attempted to perform wiretap operations during the next few days near well-worn trails. When RT New York was inserted into Hotel-9 again for its next mission, St. Martin led his men on an area recon. Near the busiest trails, they found trees with stepladders that were obviously being used by NVA spotters. They managed to evade an enemy patrol and locate a communications wire before being extracted. Their replacement team came in with proper wiretapping equipment to gather intelligence.

Wolcoff, with more than half a dozen missions under his belt, had developed strong preferences in gear and attire. He wore black jungle fatigues to help blend in with the jungle floor and tree trunks of the same color. He also hoped that his Caucasian appearance in black gear might make an NVA ponder for a split second whether he was a Russian adviser working their side. He preferred firing the RPD machine gun with 500 rounds in drum magazines after twice suffering jams in the field with his CAR-15. He had also abandoned his issued rucksack in favor of lighter gear that allowed him to carry a Claymore mine in his chest pouch.

On August 12, RT New York was next inserted into a hot target area known as Tango-7 to reconnoiter Laotian Highway 110, part of the Ho Chi Minh Trail. St. Martin took in eight men, including Wolcoff, Blaauw, and five Montagnards; they inserted less than two miles from where Dennis Bingham of RT Hawaii had been killed the previous month. St. Martin's recon mission went undetected into its third day before they emerged from a bamboo forest to make a significant discovery.

Wolcoff could hear Vietnamese voices ahead. He crept forward near his team leader's position to get a better view. "There were four heavy buildings made of logs in a cleared encampment that was sheltered by the overhead canopy," he said. "Even regiments camped in flimsy bamboo structures, so we knew this had to be a major NVA headquarters."[24] He would later learn that this was the likely base for the 66th NVA Regiment, one of the elite units better trained to handle SOG interventions.

The Green Berets pulled back into the jungle to discuss their options. St. Martin wanted to assault the log buildings to try and seize important documents and hopefully haul out a senior NVA prisoner or two. Wolcoff attempted to dissuade him, hoping to first call in air strikes before RT New York made its attack. St. Martin agreed and contacted Covey Rider Karate Davis to offer his plan. Kontum's S3 ordered the team via relay to hold off until air strikes could weaken the enemy position. The team waited anxiously while Davis and his FAC pilot, Captain Donald F. Fulton of the 20th Tactical Air Support Squadron from Pleiku, called in air support to hit the area.

It was already late afternoon and the approach of dusk made Wolcoff all the more anxious. He believed the team could wait it out until morning before making their assault but he found St. Martin was fixated on pulling off their prisoner snatch before dark. "We were reluctant to mark our position with smoke grenades for the aircraft because we knew this would also give us away to the enemy," Wolcoff said. "So, we directed in the bombing attacks by hearing."

Fulton was able to coach in strike aircraft returning from another mission. Their ordnance—CBU bomblets and 500-pound bombs—was not ideal for such close proximity to a team on the ground, but there was little choice. St. Martin could only indicate his team's position via signal mirror as they tried to pull back far enough to avoid the deadly blasts of the 500-pounders dropped by Air Force A-1s. Some of the concussions were dangerously close. Once Karate Davis radioed that the last bomb was being dropped, St. Martin readied his team to move forward. He and One-One Wolcoff eased up to a fallen log, ahead of their other six men as they prepared to attack. With the two team leaders was their point man and a second indigenous trooper. A short distance behind them in the second rank was radio operator John Blaauw, two M79 grenadiers, and a Montagnard tail gunner.

Everyone was ready, so St. Martin signaled that he would lead the assault on the log structures that remained undamaged by the air strikes. He and Wolcoff each pulled the pins on a grenade and began stepping over the fallen log, with St. Martin in the lead. Their eyes were set on the largest log structure in the compound, seemingly the one most worthy of attack. Suddenly, Wolcoff spotted a trio of armed NVA moving across the compound toward a bunker in the direction of RT New York.

St. Martin was just crossing over the log when his body began convulsing as NVA machine-gun bullets ripped through his right thigh, ankle, and stomach. Somehow, he managed to unload his ready grenade on the other side of the log to escape further injury from its blast, but the one-zero was gravely injured by the enemy's bullets. Wolcoff quickly lobbed his grenade and sprang to St. Martin's aid. Ed saw that one of the bullets had opened up his team leader's abdomen, causing his intestines to spill out.

St. Martin writhed in pain as his team's Montagnards blasted away with automatic weapons and their M79s. Wolcoff struggled to administer morphine to his team leader as Blaauw called for emergency assistance over the radio. Ed was unable to do much for St. Martin's belly wound, so he simply stuffed his intestines back into his stomach, tucked St. Martin's jungle undershirt over them, and tightened his belt down to help hold the stomach wound together. Small-arms fire ripped through the area as he dragged his leader back into their perimeter for Blaauw to assist him with emergency first aid. "St. Martin was a stocky, muscular guy of more than 200 pounds," said Wolcoff. "He outweighed me by 35 pounds but we needed to move him back into the dead bamboo to an LZ."

He distributed St. Martin's rucksack, gear, and weapon to three of the team's Montagnards while he struggled to drag his one-zero back toward an acceptable extraction point. St. Martin screamed in agony as his shattered ankle flopped around while he was being hauled clear under enemy fire. Several of the Montagnards darted into the jungle to use an old trick of rattling the bamboo, thus throwing off some of the enemy onto false trails. Blaauw kept up a steady communication with Covey Rider Davis in Captain Fulton's circling O-2. From above, the FAC team could see enemy tracers as RT New York hauled their fallen leader some seventy-five yards to the LZ. Fulton had only fourteen rockets, so he tried to use them wisely. Some of his treetop level passes were just hoaxes to save a couple of rockets while Davis fired out the window with his CAR-15. Half an hour after St. Martin was hit, the O-2 aviators could see large numbers of enemy troops, estimated at division size, massing as darkness began settling over the area.

Fulton had exhausted the last of his rockets when TAC air in the form of A-1 Spads finally arrived on the scene. Rainfall set in after darkness to further complicate the emergency extraction that was needed. Finally, UH-1D extraction choppers arrived and lit up the area with spotlights while another moved in to drop strings to the team. Wolcoff ordered three Montagnards onto the first three strings while he fashioned a Swiss seat out of nylon rope for St. Martin. He then had another knot tied off on one of the strings to rig in another Montagnard, sending out five men on the first chopper.

When the second bird arrived, Blaauw, the remaining Montagnard, and Wolcoff snapped in with Hanson rigs. Ed found that his string had not been properly prepared for the Hanson rig, so he hurriedly fashioned a field-expedient Swiss seat by looping the rope around his waist and between his legs, then tying off the balance to the strap around his waist. He ended up hooking on a lower loop and attaching the radio on the lower loop of another rope, just as the chopper lifted off. He could see orange tracers below as they cleared the area at ninety miles per hour in an increasing rain storm. All the while, the radio attached to the other string swung around like a pendulum, striking Wolcoff each time it swung back. He grabbed the radio on one of its backswings and begged the pilot to set them down somewhere to alleviate the hellacious pain he felt from his hastily-rigged seat cutting into his legs. The pilot ignored him until Wolcoff finally released the radio and let it return to swinging around and smacking him periodically as he suffered in silence for the rest of the trip.

Don Fulton made it back to Pleiku with only two gallons remaining in his little O-2. His Cessna was "shot to shit,"[25] but he had hung on valiantly until RT New York was pulled to safety. Wolcoff had a harrowing landing when his chopper came into Dak To. The pilot dragged him down the concrete strip with sparks flying until he finally settled in and dropped the recon men like sacks of potatoes at the landing point. The pilot later apologized for his lack of depth perception that caused him to drag Wolcoff. Ed later realized the sparks from his gear had been caused by one of his Claymore mines dragging on the strip. "It shaved off most of the plastic from the cap wells and I had dual-primed my Claymores, so the caps were about to explode," he said. "If he had dragged me much further, it would have been all over for me and that chopper."

St. Martin was quickly moved to Pleiku for emergency treatment, including transfusions of seven pints of blood, where his life was spared by the selfless actions of his teammates. Wolcoff put St. Martin in for a Bronze Star, but it was downgraded to an Army Commendation Medal with "V" device, while Wolcoff and Blaauw were each awarded Bronze Stars for saving their team leader. Karate Davis was awarded an Air Medal, while Captain Fulton received his second Distinguished Flying Cross.[26]

Ed Wolcoff assumed command of RT New York and began training his team in earnest, with Blaauw as his new one-one. As with all SOG teams, there was little time to mourn casualties: their team would be across the fence on another perilous mission within two weeks.

Chapter Twenty

CASUALTIES OF THE FALL

Nineteen-year-old Specialist Fourth Class Mike Buckland was one of the youngest recon men at Kontum when he arrived in April 1969. Within months, he was a veteran of several missions with A Company of the Hatchet Force. Only a year out of high school in Alaska, Buckland pushed for a transfer to a recon team until he was shifted into RT Maine, under One-Zero Dave Kirschbaum and One-One Dave Baker. By late summer, Baker had taken over as team leader and Buckland had experienced his first over the fence mission into the hot Juliet-9 target area. RT Maine performed recon on the Ho Chi Minh Trail for eight days undetected, an unusual success in such a heavily patrolled area.

Buckland's next mission into Laos on August 24 was anything but easy. The lead Kingbee deposited Dave Baker, veteran team point man Kiep, a grenadier, and interpreter Andre—who had been with RT Maine for more than a year. The second H-34 settled into the LZ, depositing radio operator Buckland, two more Montagnards, and the team one-one, a Cajun specialist fourth class from Louisiana named Sherman Miller. The second half of the team was still clearing the chopper as Baker headed his lead element from the open LZ area toward a wood line. What they found there stopped them dead in their tracks: a series of log and earth bunkers swarming with NVA soldiers.[1]

The NVA did not open fire at once, but instead seemed to be verifying that the camouflaged recon team was indeed American. A command element of officers approached the edge of the wood line to inspect Baker, Buckland, and Kiep before the SOG trio finally ripped through them at close range. Miller and the remainder of RT Maine joined the firing in earnest, piling on the casualties in the seconds of advantage they enjoyed before their confused enemy returned a nasty barrage.

Miller defiantly stood in the open LZ, raining accurate fire down on the NVA while Buckland and two Montagnards scrambled for defensive positions. During the early minutes of the fight, Buckland called in a pair of A-1 Skyraiders to take down an assaulting NVA squad with their 20-mm cannons and cluster bombs. Baker hustled his team into a knee-deep depression, allowing them to lie belly-down as angry fire crisscrossed above them from the enemy shelters. Baker took over his one-two's radio to call in more gunship strikes as heavy small-arms fire, RPGs, and occasional mortar rounds flung soil and greenery in all directions. A pair of 12.7-mm guns chewed up their perimeter, but Baker noted with satisfaction that the enemy emplacement was armed with antiaircraft guns whose deadly muzzles could not be depressed low enough to hit RT Maine's men.[2]

Buckland took the lead position and began lobbing grenades into the enemy ranks. During a momentary lull in the action, he used his camera to snap combat photos of his team in action. The NVA soon massed for another assault but the recon men cut them down with their CAR-15s. Baker refused an offered extract attempt until his enemy could be pushed back but the gunfight was becoming overwhelming. Bullets thumped into the team's stacked rucksacks and one round ripped a URC-10 radio from the one-zero's hand. More human assault waves swept toward the recon team and NVA bodies began piling up ever closer to RT Maine's perimeter.

Baker finally called for the Skyraiders to douse the area in napalm as another fifteen NVA surged toward his position. One of the 750-pound napalm canisters nearly spelled the end for RT Maine as its petroleum contents spattered onto the team's rucksacks and weapons. Buckland furiously wiped away napalm globs from his shirt and hands as he watched the surging NVA soldiers collapse in flames. Miller rushed through enemy fire and pulled two team members, stunned by the explosion, to safety. He also smothered out the flames on one of the team's weapons that had become engulfed in napalm, thus preventing its rounds from cooking off and further wounding his teammates.

One-Zero Baker received a head wound in the heavy fighting when a grenade exploded nearby, but he valiantly remained on the ground as a chopper nestled into the LZ to extract Buckland and half of RT Maine. The napalm strike had beaten back the enemy sufficiently enough to continue the team's extraction but the respite was only fleeting. A second Kingbee settled low and began loading the remainder of Baker's men. Another barrage of heavy enemy fire began landing shots on the chopper, forcing its pilot to abruptly pull away, leaving Baker and Miller on the ground in the process.

The stranded Green Berets took cover, calling in additional air strikes as they lobbed more grenades and blazed away with their CAR-15s until a third Kingbee snatched them from the jaws of death. All three Green Berets were written up for Army Commendation Medals for their actions in the harrowing firefight. RT Maine had only been on the ground for forty-two minutes, but the team had expended some fifty grenades and nearly four thousand rounds of small-arms ammunition. Intelligence estimates put NVA dead and wounded at more than a hundred, a heavy loss traded for no losses from a small recon team whose lives had been spared largely through the shrewd mission planning and tactical skills of team leader Dave Baker.[3]

One day later, on August 25, RT Florida experienced less good fortune. Staff Sergeant Ken Worthley's seven-man team inserted into northeastern Cambodia and was picked up by a pair of NVA trackers within two hours. An indigenous team member dropped one of the two enemy soldiers, but a nearby NVA company fanned out to encircle the recon team. Worthley's men fought back and ran for protection throughout the afternoon. One-Two Dale Hanson lost his left middle finger in the blistering firefights, suffering silently through the night after the team finally settled into a gulley for its RON position.[4]

Tracker dogs sniffing out the American-led team during the night were diverted thanks to liberal doses of teargas powder Worthley's men applied to their back trail. RT Florida was several hours into its silent escape through the jungle on August 26 before recon men encountered another two NVA soldiers. Worthley and his point man cut down the pair in a brief exchange of fire, and then moved forward to search the bodies. One of the newly deceased proved to be a high-ranking intelligence officer carrying a thick leather satchel of documents. Worthley scooped up the satchel and led his team on another run to clear the area.

Once the NVA discovered the two bodies, the members of RT Florida could hear excited voices and heavy crashing of brush as a company moved in to cut off their flight. Worthley's team took cover in a heavy bamboo grove, hiding for half an hour while Hanson called their FAC for an extract. The first Huey was taken under fire, so A-1s rolled in to pound back the NVA with mini-guns and 500-pound bombs. A second Huey then dropped four ropes through the treetops.

One-One Bob Garcia saw three indigenous men snap in to the strings. Before Worthley could help a fourth snap in, he was killed instantly by a bullet that struck his neck. His teammates harnessed his body to the rope and the chopper lifted away under resumed NVA fire. A second Huey moved in under gunfire to extract Garcia, Hanson, and their wounded point man, but enemy bullets cut one line. Another rope became snared in the trees, threatening to tether the Huey to the ground. The three men snapped into the two remaining good lines as murderous gunfire reached for the chopper. Hanson and his point man frantically hacked away at the snared rope as the Huey pulled it to the snapping point.

By the time Hanson had sawed through it, his head had been creased by another bullet. RT Florida had scarcely been returned to Kontum with its wounded and deceased one-zero when a SOG C-130 Blackbird rushed Worthley's captured documents to Saigon. Analysts found that the satchel contained a partial roster of enemy double agents and spies operating within South Vietnam, a windfall of enemy intelligence for the CIA and the South Vietnamese Central Intelligence Organization.[5]

Master Sergeant Norm Doney, who had recently handed off RT Florida to Ken Worthley, was among the many who joined in singing "Old Blue" at the bar that night. Just two days later, on August 28, CCC would mourn the loss of another recon man, Specialist Fourth Class Richard Joecken. He was fatally wounded while on a Hatchet Force mission into Laos with another dozen Americans and a hundred Montagnards led by Captain Barre McClelland. By the time choppers could lift the Hatchet Force team away from the heavy ground fire, many Montagnards had been hit, along with a pair of lieutenants (Frank Longaker and Ken Snyder), several sergeants—Pete Tandy, Robert Wallace, and Terry Minnihan—and Specialist Joecken.

Ken Worthley was posthumously awarded the Silver Star; his remains were shipped back to the States, where Bob Howard was still on leave and en route to his home in Alabama. He delayed his return by three days to thoughtfully escort Worthley's body to his parents' home in Sherburne, Minnesota.[6]

◆◇◆

In early September, John Plaster led his first mission into Cambodia as a one-zero. He became suspicious of his Vietnamese interpreter's loyalty, as the man had stirred the team's point man into opening fire on a false contact. Recon Team Illinois survived a fast run to outpace a nearby NVA company but Plaster wisely fired his interpreter and the entire Vietnamese team upon returning to Kontum.

Ed Wolcoff's first mission as a new one-zero was equally challenging. He had taken command only weeks before when John St. Martin was severely wounded in their assault on the NVA headquarters. Now, Ed was inserted into the Tango-7 area with One-One John Blaauw and their Montagnards to conduct a BDA following a B-52 strike. The standard procedure had been to land a team before daylight en route to the beaten zone, have them RON, and then perform their bomb damage assessment after first light. Wolcoff, quick to absorb lessons from each prior mission, informed his S3 that he had other ideas. "I told him I wanted to land on the main bomb zone, take my photographs, do my intelligence gathering, maybe try to snatch a prisoner, and then be extracted that same day before dark," he said.

The operations officer agreed, so Wolcoff's RT New York was inserted into the bomb area as soon as the dust had settled. In the process of inspecting the bomb craters on a hilltop, he discovered a major NVA underground tunnel system. His Montagnard point man refused to crawl into the tunnels to inspect, so Wolcoff dropped in with a pen light and a .45 to do it himself. He crawled as far as he dared before fears of the bomb-weakened tunnel collapsing on him compelled him to back out.

Ed found his Montagnards to be excited, saying that had seen an NVA patrol crossing the bomb area about three hundred yards away, moving up a slope. Wolcoff called for an extraction but his FAC warned him that they would have to move to an LZ with more clearance for the large CH-34s that were available to get them. As they moved toward an appropriate LZ, they transited a wooded area that had not been damaged by the B-52 strike. Ed was infuriated when Jerong, his Montagnard point man, suddenly took off running toward their new LZ. He took over as point man and led his men to where the choppers were able to extract them.

He quizzed his Montagnards once they were safely extracted. "While passing through the wooded verge, another Yard observed the enemy ambush. He took no action, fearing to initiate enemy fire while we were still in the kill zone," Wolcoff said. "The only reason the enemy hadn't fire on us was because of the Cobra gunships doing orbits above the treetops as we moved toward the LZ." In the wake of the mission, Wolcoff fired his frightened point man. "There was one of my nine lives used up," he said.[7]

During twenty-five months with RT New York, Wolcoff would have more than his fair share of close escapes. His team once had trackers on them immediately after being inserted into Tango-7. He did three daylight, high-risk river crossings in hopes of throwing off the NVA counter-recon team, whose trackers had the advantage of concealed high-speed trails. After two days of being pursued, RT New York managed to turn the tables on their opponents and attacked the NVA kill team as it came up behind them on a ridge, after passing through an elephant grass clearing.

Wolcoff and his tail gunner killed the NVA squad leader, a B-40 rocket man, and several more enemy fighters along one leg of an L-shaped assault their opponents were executing. Ed's team then raced downhill and along a stream toward an extraction LZ while A-1 Skyraiders dropped cluster bombs and strafed with their 20-mm cannons. As Wolcoff and his team were finally hoisted into the sky from a bomb crater with an aluminum rope ladder, he caught sight of a heavily concealed enemy main supply route (MSR) only ten yards away that he had not previously detected due to heavy vegetation. "I discovered some very interesting targets such as a concealed road and a high-speed trail network toward Cambodia that should have been of primary interest," said Wolcoff. "Only later did I find out that the 7th Air Force called the shots on which targets should be exploited, some of which were never revisited by recon teams."

Wolcoff's use of black fatigues helped his men survive another mission in Laos in which they literally passed right through an NVA kill zone. RT New York was reconnoitering a new enemy road that was well hidden by lashed-together treetops that formed a solid canopy above it. Several yards along the western side of the NVA road, Ed's men found coaxial communications cables, 55-gallon fuel drums, and other evidence that they were in the presence of a major NVA headquarters or large unit facility.

Wolcoff hoped to surprise the enemy facility with his team's unexpected presence, but he was unable to find it before dusk set in. As

Left: One-Zero Ed Wolcoff at launch site preparing for a mission into Laos. *Right:* Wolcoff snapped this photo of RT New York being extracted from a Laos LZ. *Edward Wolcoff*

he directed his team back toward the road the following morning, he felt one of his Montagnards tugging at his sleeve. "Through our interpreter, he told me that we had just walked through the kill zone of an enemy ambush," said Wolcoff. "I could only assume they did not fire because our uniforms and some of our equipment were of enemy material."[8]

With only one LZ in the target area, Wolcoff called in air strikes against the enemy location and arranged for an emergency extraction. As Huey slicks from the 57th Assault Helicopter Company dropped into the elephant grass LZ to extract RT New York, Wolcoff remained concealed while snapping photos of the exfiltration operation with his recon camera. "The pilot was quite angry as I paused to take photos," he said.[9]

◆◇◆

The next personnel loss suffered by Fred Abt's CCC came in late September, when Captain Ron Goulet led a Hatchet Force mission that was taken under ground fire upon insertion. After one of the Kingbees was knocked down on the LZ, Goulet fearlessly raced forward to rescue Staff Sergeant Mike Sheppard from the burning chopper. The Hatchet Force skirmished with NVA squads for the next two days before Goulet's luck ran out on September 26. His men had just captured an enemy ammunition stockpile and was redeploying for a counterattack when Goulet was killed by an exploding RPG.[10]

Less than a month later, Kontum's recon company lost a seasoned one-zero. Sergeant First Class Dick "Moose" Gross, a veteran of a previous tour of duty at CCN, had taken over RT California in late summer when Joe Walker began a new special assignment for a year in northern Laos. Gross retained Walker's one-one, Bill Stubbs, and brought in Bob Mohs as his one-two. Gross and his team were pulling their third consecutive cross-border Laos mission in a short period of time by mid-October. Stubbs, feeling an ominous premonition as he turned his personal effects in to Norm Doney before the latest mission, instructed the first sergeant to turn over his cash to the base bar should he fail to return.[11]

On the morning of October 20, RT California was assaulted by an NVA unit that surged forward as a North Vietnamese officer shouted, "Take prisoners!" Stubbs was killed by gunfire in the initial assault, and three of his Montagnards were wounded by AK fire. Dick Gross, hit in the neck by RPG shrapnel, spent the rest of the day evading and hiding with his survivors until A-1 Skyraiders helped cover the extraction choppers that pulled RT California from an LZ at dusk. John Blaauw and RT New York, sent in on a Bright Light the next morning to attempt to recover Stubbs' body, found that the NVA had sterilized the battle area and were chattering on Stubbs' survival radio. Bill Stubbs' remains were never recovered and he officially became yet another of the nearly six hundred Americans missing in action in Laos during the Vietnam War.[12]

Just days after the loss of Stubbs, a forty-five-man CCC Hatchet Force platoon under Captain Joseph Whelan was ambushed in Laos on October 25. Hit from all sides and outnumbered at least three to one, the American-led platoon took heavy casualties. Whelan was killed by exploding grenades and RPGs, and several Montagnards and Green Berets were wounded in the NVA assault. Frank Belletire was rushing to help Whelan when another RPG exploded close enough to shatter Belletire's skull. "They chewed us up," Belletire said.[13]

Dazed, he was initially dumped into a pile of the dead for extraction. But Belletire was among the survivors pulled out by Hueys the next morning; he was barely clinging to life. Staff Sergeant Ron Bozikis had been less fortunate; his body was among those hauled out of Laos when the Hatchet Force was extracted.[14]

✦◇✦

Some of the newer faces joining the CCC recon team during 1969 wasted little time in moving up the ranks to command their own teams.

One such notable leader was Sergeant Franklin Douglas "Doug" Miller, who had been on the ground in Vietnam since March 1966. Although Special Forces qualified, Miller had been assigned to the 1st Air Cavalry Division to serve in recon platoons. Born in North Carolina and raised in New Mexico, he was lean, stood six-foot-three, was darkly tanned, and had hair bleached blond from more than three years of jungle sun. Fellow CCC one-zero John Plaster found Miller to be "bold almost to the brink of recklessness. Miller sounded and acted more like a California surfer than an Army NCO and preferred an old French paratrooper jacket over an American one."[15]

Miller was in Vietnam for four months before he killed his first man during a skirmish between his twenty-eight-man platoon and seven enemy soldiers. His comrades slapped him on the back and offered congratulations after he cut down a VC soldier with his M16 on automatic fire mode, but Miller realized he had simply acted more quickly than his enemy. He soon learned to carry no unnecessary weight into the field and he became physically fit from all the jungle patrols. By the time he entered his second tour of duty in Vietnam, Miller had been promoted to specialist fourth class and was in charge of a recon element with his platoon.[16]

His valor in the field did not go unnoticed. During the fall of 1967 Miller was awarded the Bronze Star with "V" device for helping save two wounded team members by charging an enemy position and killing three VC. His most harrowing patrol occurred in late 1967, when two members of his patrol were killed in a firefight in a rugged, mountainous region of the Central Highlands. As Miller and his recon team moved to retrieve their bodies near a stream, they were hit by a violent ambush that killed six more platoon members. Waves of VC soldiers swept the pinned-down team with automatic fire and mortars as Miller fired his M60 machine gun until the barrel was red hot. By the time the survivors were extracted the next day with the assist of artillery and infantry support, nineteen American soldiers had been killed. Miller was awarded the Silver Star for his help in covering the withdrawal of his platoon.[17]

Miller spent time in a Japanese hospital in late 1967 due to a thigh wound, one of six different occasions he would be wounded in Vietnam and Laos. He suffered considerable pain when a punji stick jabbed through his calf on one mission but fought through with his platoon until they were extracted the following day. Following more than two years of infantry recon duty, he applied for a position within MACV-SOG, and spent eight weeks at an A Camp outside Nha Trang before being sent to CCC at Kontum in August 1969.[18]

Doug Miller was assigned to RT Vermont as the radio operator for One-Zero David Wieprecht and One-One Donald Bemis. Across the fence, Miller found his team to be less aggressive in firefights than was his personal preference. Wieprecht was scheduled for rotation home, and Miller was advanced to command of RT Vermont during the fall of 1969. As team leader, Miller picked his Montagnards carefully, based on their skills with weapons, physical strength to help carry wounded, and their abilities in the field. His RT Vermont was aggressive, whether it was tasked with photographing enemy troops moving down the Trail or attempting a prisoner snatch by attacking a truck convoy. His first such effort ended in failure, after blowing a Claymore on the last truck only to find that his overzealous indigenous teammates killed the driver while riddling the cab.[19]

Miller was unafraid of any situation, including hitching rides from Kontum to Pleiku to party during his down times. He simply walked the open road with his comrades, almost tempting the VC to come after him. When he was not testing various ordnance on the range or drinking with friends in the base bar, Miller was known to enjoy rat hunting. He used meat or peanut butter to bait out a rice supply warehouse, waiting in the dark for the sound of scurrying varmints before he and his buddies flipped on the lights to open fire.[20]

Miller killed more than rats in the field, and he took some knocks, too. Even when he received a wound significant enough to justify a Purple Heart, he would be back in the field running missions in short order. His combat and survival skills coupled with his aggressive nature brought him back from some missions that might not have played out so favorably for others.

◆◇◆

Colonel Steve Cavanaugh's MACV-SOG accomplished much in 1969 in spite of its small size. By year's end, his covert command had only 394 total officers and enlisted men to cover all of its operations.

A total of 443 Salem House missions were run across the border into Cambodia, generating 607 intelligence information reports, a 45 percent increase from the previous year. In addition, 901 target areas were developed by the SOG teams, who also attempted three wiretap operations, located 939 enemy trails in Cambodia, and captured 4 POWs. In its other main operational area of Laos, SOG ran 458 total Prairie Fire missions. The teams generated 766 intelligence reports—doubling the previous year's Prairie Fire reports on enemy activities and compounds—while also developing 864 targets, attempting 7 wiretap operations, locating 665 enemy trails, and finding 25 weapons caches.[21]

Kontum's CCC base maintained an indigenous personnel ratio during 1969 of six to one in favor of Montagnards being used versus Vietnamese and Chinese team members. SOG casualties for the year amounted to 287 U.S. personnel killed, wounded, or MIA during Salem House and Prairie Fire operations. In return, the recon teams claimed 2,239 enemy soldiers killed in these two areas of operation.[22]

Death lurked around every corner for Kontum's recon teams. Aside from the obvious perils of running missions across the fence, a Green Beret could just as easily be killed by enemy sniper fire or by attacks made on their staging areas. Command and Control Central lost recon man Specialist Fifth Class Randy Rhea on November 12 when the NVA made a brief mortar attack with 82-mm shells on the isolated Dak Pek runway. The Huey and Kingbee pilots scrambled to get their birds airborne as explosions erupted on their hilltop dirt strip. As Rhea ran into the open to assist a pilot, he was killed by a tiny piece of shrapnel that penetrated his heart.[23]

The CCC base dirge, "Old Blue," would sadly add another verse just weeks later on December 3. Following the loss of his Hatchet Force buddy Ron Bozikis in late October, Sergeant Wayne Anderson had pledged to kill ten NVA in revenge. He fought valiantly when his platoon was hit by a full

NVA company in Laos, assaulting their position and repelling them, but Anderson was mortally wounded in the process.[24]

The remaining weeks of 1969 were equally taxing on the Kontum recon company. One Green Beret who would miss some of this action was RT Illinois One-Zero John Plaster, only twenty years old but already a veteran of a dozen Special Forces missions against the enemy. His tour of duty officially ended in December, but Plaster opted to extend his service for another six months and was given a thirty-day extension leave. He traveled a bit with his buddy Glenn Uemura before heading back to Minnesota to share the holidays with his family.

When Plaster returned to Kontum in mid-January 1970, he found that his beloved RT Illinois was largely nonexistent. His former one-one and acting team leader during his absence, Bill Spencer, had not been able to stand the down time. Eager for action, Spencer had joined a Mike Force unit deployed to Bu Dop on the Cambodian border. Inserted to help save a besieged Special Forces camp, Spencer was killed instantly by an RPG only minutes after jumping off his chopper. To compound its losses, several Montagnards of RT Illinois had accompanied a truck-monitoring mission along Laotian Highway 110 in which two of them had been killed in action and a third had been badly shot up and hospitalized.[25]

Team Illinois would take some time to reform and in the interim, Plaster would be asked to take command of RT Washington. The news of his lost teammates was a bitter pill to swallow but it was not the only tough news he heard upon returning in January. One of his respected one-zero comrades, Doug Miller, had been subjected to a hellacious mission in early January.

As Plaster heard the details of the astonishing engagement, it became apparent that Miller's men had endured a mission as legendary as those of some of CCC's most respected forerunners—those who had earned top honors for SOG service: Ken Sisler, John Kedenburg, Fred Zabitosky, and Bob Howard.

Chapter Twenty-One

"VIETNAMESE ALAMO"

The first rays of sunlight were still sweeping over the dirt strip at Kontum as four Gladiator slicks applied throttle and began lifting off from the base. Aside from their regular gunners, co-pilots, and pilots, the veteran 57th AHC Gladiator Hueys were moving out with the three American Green Berets and four Montagnards of RT Vermont, which would be using the call sign "wolf girl" this day, January 5, 1970.

Staff Sergeant Ed Blyth, the team's radio operator, made a last check of his face paint, his gear, and his trusted CAR-15. He glanced out from his speeding slick and was comforted by the presence of four AH-1G Cobras from the 361st Aerial Weapons Company flying escort as they moved from Kontum toward the Dak To forward launch site. Based at Camp Holloway in Pleiku, the "Pink Panthers" gunship company was always a welcomed support arm for insertions across the fence. Four recon teams were on patrol across the border this day and three more were scheduled for insertion. For Blyth, it would be his first mission so deep into enemy territory.[1]

Blyth was young and confident, originally from Tulsa, Oklahoma, and a member of the CCC recon base since August 1969. His early months there had been spent in training and running local missions before he was assigned to Doug Miller's RT Vermont in December as the one-two. He considered his new team leader to be well experienced, possessing great instincts in the field. Blyth had run one ambush mission outside the compound that month but the enemy he could hear moving through the jungle never came close enough for a firefight. The other American on his new team, Staff Sergeant Robert C. Brown, was trained as a staff medic but had only been Miller's one-one for the same prior mission.

Miller's team was scheduled for insertion into the tri-border area of northeastern Cambodia's Ratanakiri Province, which was dubbed Base Area 609 by U.S. intelligence. It was a known hot area that typically contained at least two NVA regiments of about a thousand men each. Recon Team Vermont was to search for enemy base camps and the team had additionally been briefed the previous evening about the possibility of a downed jet in their area. Miller had briefed base commander Fred Abt on his mission plans the night before and had been given the green light. After early morning briefings at the FOB compound, the day's mission was now in motion.[2]

Having nestled into Dak To, the Gladiator Hueys and Pink Panther Cobras were quickly refueled. Miller used the minutes to offer the duty Bright Light team some of his plans. His team included One-One Brown, One-Two Blyth, Prap as his zero-one Montagnard team leader, point man Hyuk, interpreter Gai, and fourteen-year-old James Yu-B as his tail gunner.[3]

The Gladiator slicks moved RT Vermont to a final staging area across the border. Kontum's Hatchet Force was gearing up for another roadblock mission near the borders of Laos and Cambodia, where Colonel Abt had been charged with evaluating enemy movement and stopping any convoy movements. Captain Richard Todd's three platoons, each consisting of three Green Berets and thirty-two Montagnards, were still being inserted about ten miles from Dak To into Laos on a hilltop. "We could see the Ho Chi Minh Trail from our high vantage point," said Second Lieutenant Terry Cadenbach, one of the Hatchet Force squad leaders.[4]

After landing among the Hatchet Force roadblock team, One-Zero Doug Miller met with the officers of the platoons while Blyth, Brown, and their Montagnards sat with their gear. The final debriefing took about twenty minutes on high ground perched atop a tapering valley below. Blyth felt some reassurance that his team was not going into Indian country alone: Captain Todd's reaction force platoon was nearby and could be called upon if the team encountered heavy action. In an unorthodox move, Colonel Abt himself landed at the roadblock site with some of Todd's Hatchet Force company to coordinate the efforts of his men this day.

Miller soon returned and told his men it was time to head out. January 5 would be a busy day across the fence. Four recon units were already on the ground, including the Hatchet Force operating under the call sign "on side," plus three teams, code-named "shirttail," "sugarcoat," and "track shoe." A covey rider, Master Sergeant Charles A. Septer (call sign "putter"), was monitoring their actions throughout the day from an O-2 plane flown by Richard I. "Rick" Felker. Three additional teams were also being inserted, using the call signs wolf girl (RT Vermont), spindown (RT Delaware), and stardust.

Doug Miller's team walked into their operation area by moving down the mountain from the reaction battalion, crossing from Laos into the edge of Cambodia. They began moving southwest through extremely steep terrain interspersed with frequent small streams. Radio operator Blyth cursed himself for being so unprepared for the hilly terrain he faced. He was carrying roughly a hundred pounds of gear, far more weight than was comfortable for his first mission so deep into enemy territory. Blyth felt some relief as Vermont began moving across a fairly level valley after descending the higher ground.

The team had covered more than 550 yards from their insertion point when Miller quietly announced that he and indigenous leader Prap would scout ahead for a short while. Brown, Blyth, Gai, and their other two Montagnards positioned themselves and waited quietly. When Miller returned, he announced that they had found a crash site farther ahead in the jungle that was heavily infested with NVA. The team backtracked from the site and then continued on until it reached a stream that forked into two branches, one cutting away into the jungle and the other branch going up a small valley. The ground here had risen about forty feet from the lower valley, and Miller moved his men upstream through dense brush until they crossed the Y-junction to head for the valley entrance.[5]

Hyuk moved on point up a slight incline along the narrow stream. Close behind him, Miller paused at around 1120 to make an entry in his notebook after hearing a shot about 650 yards off in the distance. The balance of the team was following a short distance behind when Hyuk suddenly pointed out an apparent booby trap, a clear plastic line lying just two inches below the surface of the stream. He carefully grasped the line, stepped over it, and handed it to Miller. The one-zero in turn cleared the line, handed it to his gunner, and moved forward as the Montagnard passed it to radioman Blyth.

Ed cautiously stepped over the plastic-covered wire, and handed it to Yu-B, who was followed by Gai, Brown, and Prap. Unbeknownst to Blyth, one of the Montagnards a mere 11 yards behind him apparently decided the NVA certainly would not mine an area so heavily traveled by their own men. Grabbing the plastic line, he gave it a tug.

The jungle beside the stream suddenly erupted with such force that Blyth and several others were knocked to the ground. Searing shrapnel slashed into Blyth, Brown, Gai, Yu-B, and Prap. Farther ahead, Miller immediately hit the ground as leaves, branches, dirt, and stones rained down amid a gray cloud of residue from the explosion. He scurried back to check on his team. Yu-B appeared to have a concussion and was seriously injured with multiple frag wounds in his chest, legs, and arms. But Montagnard leader Prap had taken the brunt of the blast, deemed by Blyth to have been from a booby-trapped grenade. Prap was riddled with shrapnel wounds, his clothing in shreds, and his pack blown away.

Blyth was bleeding in several places but a quick check assured him that he was not disabled. Medic Brown, ignoring his own injuries, hurriedly inspected the various wounds suffered by Prap, Yu-B, and Gai. Miller then cautioned that the blast would certainly bring an NVA patrol down on them quickly. Just minutes after the explosion, he spotted the point element of what he estimated to be a platoon-sized enemy force moving slowly through the brush, crossing a nearby ridge directly toward their location. Miller did not hesitate. He instructed the team that they were to withdraw up the steep hillside to their rear across the stream.

Brown and Blyth helped deploy the Montagnards to the more secure location, hauling all of their equipment while assisting the more badly wounded men. Miller waited alone by the creek bed, peering through the vegetation for the unseen enemy he could hear moving closer. And then he could see two NVA point men advancing toward his position of concealment. He waited until they were perilously close before he opened up with his automatic rifle and killed them both.

Blyth wasted no time in establishing communication with Covey 580, an O-2 team flown by Lieutenant John Arthur LeHecka with veteran recon man Sergeant First Class James Henry "Sam" Zumbrun (call sign "haymaker") as his covey rider.

"Prairie fire emergency!" Blyth called.[6] He was outlining RT Vermont's tactical emergency to Zumbrun when the sudden chattering of machine-gun fire and screams shattered the silence. The abrupt eruption of violence startled the wounded recon men momentarily as they realized how close the enemy was to them. They heard the unmistakable sounds of One-Zero Miller's weapon as he single-handedly dealt destruction to the NVA squad, hoping to buy time for his men. They had moved halfway up the slope above the creek when other enemy troops could be heard moving about on the hilltop above.

Brown and Blyth realized they were falling into a hopeless situation. RT Vermont was being surrounded, with troops approaching from above as Miller engaged another platoon element on the lower ground across the stream. Blyth, Gai, and Hyuk deployed themselves in defensive positions as Brown administered to Yu-B and Prap's wounds. Miller continued to lay down a heavy base of suppressive fire that finally caused the enemy platoon to fall back and attempt to regroup. He then scrambled back across the stream to rejoin his team halfway up the hill to his rear.

Miller quickly briefed them on the situation below and called in additional details to the FAC, Lieutenant LeHecka, circling above. It was a grim site. Brown was working as best he could to save lives but as they retreated, the American team had left a heavy blood trail that would be easy for the NVA to follow. Miller helped effect a tighter defensive perimeter on the slope to help protect his four wounded men before he moved out solo once again. He moved to a vantage point near the small creek, concealed himself, and waited with a clear view of any enemy that might attempt to cross over. He did not have long to wait.[7]

Minutes later, he spotted NVA point men moving stealthily through the brush toward his position. Miller drew a careful bead on the first man, anxiously waiting as he came closer and closer, before shooting him dead. He then unleashed devastating automatic fire on the approaching platoon and a machine gun the enemy had set up near the creek. They returned fire on Miller with a blistering barrage the likes of which he had never experienced. Numerous rounds chewed through the vegetation all around his prone form but all somehow missed their mark. Miller then returned fire so aggressively that he once again forced the platoon to retreat and regroup.[8] He knew his respite would be brief.

◆◇◆

The sound of A-1 Skyraiders arriving overhead was like an answered prayer. The Da Nang-based OLAA (Operating Location Alpha Alpha) Spads were already in the immediate area after being scrambled to respond to a prairie fire emergency call from spindown (RT Delaware). They were working with Covey 566 and had not yet been asked to drop their ordnance, when they departed to assist Covey 580's new call for help with a prairie fire situation. After a short hop of several minutes, the two pilots of USAF 56th Special Operations Wing (SOW) unit arrived as the scattered members of RT Vermont fought for their lives.

First Lieutenant Don Engebretsen was flying wing on First Lieutenant James F. Seith, a qualified pilot who had recently been upgraded to flight lead. When they arrived over RT Vermont's area, Engebretsen could hear RTO Ed Blyth calling over the radio for assistance in an animated fashion. Covey Rider Zumbrun, noting the colored panels being flashed by the Green Berets, advised the Spad pilots that the recon team had just crossed a large creek to the east but that they were slightly scattered from each other.[9]

Spad pilot First Lieutenant Don Engebretsen standing before his A-1 Skyraider. On January 5, 1970, he ignored orders from his section leader and made bombing runs over RT Vermont that ultimately saved lives. *Don Engebretsen*

One-Zero Doug Miller knew he needed to carefully mark his team's position for the Spads to help point out where they should bomb the enemy troops. Crawling to within eyesight of his RT Vermont, he called to Blyth— situated about thirty yards uphill—for a willie peter smoke grenade. Ed duly pulled an M34 from his web gear, careful to not remove the pin, and hollered to his one-zero, "Here it comes." Miller, having turned his attention elsewhere momentarily, was badly startled as the chemical grenade splashed in the edge of the narrow stream. He cursed back at his one-two as he scurried over to retrieve it, pulling the pin, and heaving the smoke grenade a little farther upstream from their position to precisely mark where the Spads should deliver their ordnance. Blyth called Covey Rider Zumbrun to announce that the Spads should begin delivering their CBU where the willie pete had erupted.

Apparently, Engebretsen was the only aerial observer who saw the small wafting smoke rising from the high, dense foliage in the defining "V" that marked the unseen river bed. Seith headed in well to the west of the mark, with Engebretsen's A-1 lined up behind and to the left (east) of his leader. Seith unloaded CBU-25 bomblets and proceeded to jink his aircraft to avoid AA fire. As he pulled another hard left, he caught a momentary sight of Engebretsen preparing to dump his own load of bomblets much closer to the SOG team. He opened up on the radio to order his wingman, "Don't drop! Pull off! Do not drop!"

Engebretsen, however, was roaring in only twenty feet above the tree-tops which reached nearly a hundred feet into the Cambodian air. The shouts of Blyth to "put it right on us!" were still ringing in his ears as his section leader shouted at him to abort his run. Engebretsen had less than a second to decide which way to react, and he opted to risk his career to answer the frantic pleas of the Green Berets below. He dumped a partial load of CBU bomblets right over the treetops where the smoke was rising from. Covey pilot John LeHecka noted intense enemy gunfire exploding from several hillside locations as the propeller-driven fighter zoomed through.

As he pulled out, Engebretsen heard shouting and screams from various men over the team's radio, which must have been left open. His head began swimming with apprehension momentarily as he feared that his ordnance had landed directly on the Green Beret team he was hoping to save. *I'm screwed!* he thought. *I hit them!*

But the next radio call from RTO Blyth reassured him of his decision. "Do it again! Do it again!"

Engebretsen's delivery had hit the NVA solidly and inflicted heavy loss. Blyth continued hollering for the Spads to hit the enemy again. Tail gunner James Yu-B later related to Engebretsen that his ordnance had erupted a scant twenty feet from his position and no more than a hundred from that of Blyth. But the devastation to the NVA was severe enough that the recon men asked for more of the same. Blyth estimated that the Spad's ordnance drop reduced the enemy's ground fire by two-thirds.

The next pass by the Skyraiders was a release of napalm. Engebretsen and Seith returned for six more passes, unloading more cluster bombs that bracketed the team while expending the bulk of their ammunition during their next runs. Blyth noted that the enemy counter-fire was reduced significantly after the first two offensive runs.

During this time, FAC LeHecka advised Miller over the PRC-25 that his men had ensconced themselves about 165 yards from a bomb crater that appeared suitable for helicopters to lower ropes for extracting the men in their jungle harnesses. Miller realized that moving his wounded men might very well lead them into an ambush as they made their way to the bomb crater, so he decided to first check the situation out alone.

The Spads had done their best to pound the NVA platoon with nearly everything they had for the past quarter-hour. Miller used the break in the enemy attacks to once again move ahead of his team to recon a path through the enemy soldiers. Miller's trip to the bomb crater proved to be uneventful, as the hilly terrain was fairly easy to traverse in a ten-minute period. As he moved, he noted that the skies had cleared considerably, allowing him occasional glimpses of the FAC's Cessna O-2 as it circled above. He carefully flashed his recognition mirror until Covey Rider

Zumbrun keyed his radio twice to acknowledge that he had spotted the American near the edge of the bomb hole. Miller then made his way back through the jungle to his team to prepare them to advance to the new LZ.[10]

Ever mindful of the NVA setting ambushes, he organized the team and instructed them to follow him at intervals of about thirty yards as he walked point for the team. Prap, the most severely wounded man, was assisted by another Montagnard but everyone was still able to keep moving at this point. They knew that the enemy was somewhere close at hand and searching for them but were not in sight. Miller continued to guide his men into the bomb crater that was to serve as a landing zone. He positioned those still capable of firing their weapons—Brown, Blyth, Hyuk, and Yu-B—where they could best lay down defensive fire. Shortly after taking their spots, the men of RT Vermont were assaulted again by a sizable NVA force.

Automatic fire lit up the surrounding jungle as the exchange erupted in force. In the midst of the heated gunfight, an extraction Huey suddenly dropped down within five yards of the rim of the canyon, catching Miller completely by surprise. He was thrilled to see an American door gunner scanning the area with his M60, but he had no time to enjoy this view of his would-be rescuers. The jungle surrounding the crater exploded in a terrifying display of firepower—mortar, anti-tank, and 7.62-mm rounds—intent on bringing down the chopper.

The rescue choppers were slicks of the 57th AHC, whose pilots had deposited Sergeant Dan Ster's RT Delaware into the extreme northeastern corner of Cambodia. Captain Vaughn "Bobby" Ross was flying co-pilot in Chief Warrant Officer Carter Higginbotham's leading Huey and was pleased that RT Delaware had been inserted cold—the team was on the ground undetected and moving. En route back to Dak To to refuel, Ross heard a prairie fire call being transmitted from wolf girl, Miller's RT Vermont. The Gladiator slicks immediately rerouted to come to the team's aid, only to hear a second prairie fire call come in from spindown (RT Delaware) as that team also came under attack.[11]

As the Gladiator slicks approached the bomb crater, they were joined by Huey Cobra gunships from their unit's Cougar gun platoon led by Joe Sottile. Bobby Ross became aware of the close enemy fire as his slick headed in toward the LZ. An RPG round exploded just beneath his chopper's tail boom, shoving it skyward with such force that Higginbotham aborted their run.

On the ground, the noise was deafening as tracers ripped through trees, B-40 rockets crisscrossed toward the bomb crater, and bullets chewed through rock, soil, trees, and metal. Miller hugged the ground, hoping to ride out the whirlwind of destruction until it calmed a bit. He noted 7.62-mm rounds beginning to stitch through the Huey's metal skin as its door gunners returned fire.[12]

Miller was caught fairly exposed—crouching near a twenty-foot dead tree—as a Cobra gunship swept in low with its guns blazing. Powerful 20-mm rounds slammed into the trunk, sending wood chips flying like a blizzard. Miller cursed loudly enough for his comrades to hear as the Cobra's rounds reduced the tree to a three-foot stump.

Ed Blyth blazed away at a group of NVA attempting to swarm the LZ, and he saw his bullets knock down three of them. The chopper was still trying to settle in a short distant from him and the badly wounded indigenous leader, Prap. Blyth had just cut down the advancing troops when an RPG streaked in and exploded between Prap and the Huey. Shrapnel tore through RT Vermont, and poor Prap caught the brunt of it with devastating effect—removing most of his lower jaw and shredding his throat. Farther away, Blyth was seriously injured by red hot metal that punctured his body in numerous places, perforating his spleen and sheering off the end of his left thumb.

The 57th AHC slick sustained multiple small-arms hits before it was driven away by the exploding B-40s. The Gladiators, already seriously low on fuel, scurried back to Dak To to refuel for another extraction attempt. Doug Miller's RT Vermont would be on its own in the interim.

✦◇✦

During this time, Captain Todd's Hatchet Force platoons had heard some of the action going on with Team Vermont from their mountaintop roadblock position.

First Lieutenant Jerry Pool, commanding one of the platoons, listened to the action over the radio between the team and their FAC. He heard Miller's M16 over the radio at different points as he fought off enemy attacks. Colonel Abt was also listening to emergency calls in a bomb crater with his Hatchet Force radioman. Sergeant First Class Andrew Brown, a Brooklyn-born medic who worked in the Kontum dispensary, was nearby and overhead Abt issue orders to Todd, "Get every man you can and go relieve Miller. His team is being overrun."[13]

Captain Todd gathered Jerry Pool and about twenty American and indigenous troops to head for the bomb crater where Miller's team was sending out its prairie fire call. His team moved swiftly, heading off from their higher vantage point in Laos down into the valley of Cambodia below where the sounds of gunfire could be heard in the distance. En route, they encountered a trail that led across the valley toward the distant hillside where RT Vermont was under siege. Todd halted his men and shuffled back to medic Andy Brown with new orders.

"Brown," he said. "I want you to take these four Montagnards, take that trail, and move across that valley. See if you can get to Miller. We'll be coming."

Brown acknowledged the order and moved into the lead with four Montagnards completely unknown to him from the Hatchet Force company. His assignment was not one that he coveted. The trail ahead broke from the jungle thicket into an open field roughly fifty-five yards long that contained only knee-high weed tangles and trampled elephant grass.

What a perfect kill zone for the NVA, Brown thought. Anger flashed through his mind as he pictured Captain Todd leading the balance of the men around the trail through thicker cover. *I guess a black NCO leading four indigenous soldiers is expendable!*[14]

Brown halted his little group at the edge of the clearing, scanning the perimeter as they held their weapons at the ready. In the distance, he could hear the unmistakable sound of Doug Miller's M16, which was easily distinguishable from the report made be the weapons used by the NVA. Wary of enemy attack, he ordered one of his Montagnards to proceed across the clearing while the balance took position to counter any ambush. Seconds passed like days as the Montagnard point man advanced through the weeds and finally reached a timber line on the far side of the field unscathed. Brown then motioned to his three remaining Montagnards to follow and set out across the 55-yard clearing.

Halfway across, the ambush feared by Brown commenced. Two RPGs screamed in from a distant wood line and exploded perilously close to his men as they hit the ground. Before the dirt and debris finished plummeting back to earth, Brown had his men on their feet racing for the distant tree line. Unseen NVA soldiers unleashed a deadly stream of automatic fire that mowed down the three Montagnards nearest Brown as he charged ahead. As he reached the thicket and took cover, two more violent explosions from NVA-launched ordnance ripped up the edge of the trees in his wake. Andy Brown was on his own.

Three of his Montagnard comrades lay bleeding out in the field and the Montagnard that had scurried ahead of them was now nowhere to be found. He fired back bursts in the direction of his NVA opponents, oblivious to the stinging pain of frag wounds that had ripped through his lower legs. Brown simply clutched his weapon and charged forward toward the hillside where Miller's besieged recon team needed any help he could offer them.

✦◇✦

Recon Team Vermont was in desperate condition. Its Montagnard zero-one, Prap, had sustained mortal wounds during the attempted extraction. James Yu-B, the teenage tail gunner, was in critical condition with a concussion and multiple frag wounds to his legs and chest. Interpreter Gai had been hit by frags in his upper body and Hyuk has sustained serious wounds to his left upper back. One-One Robert Brown was bleeding from shrapnel wounds to his left leg and buttock, while radio operator Ed Blyth was suffering with fresh frag wounds that had ripped his legs and left side and removed part of his left thumb. Brown expertly fashioned a tourniquet around Blyth's left wrist to help stem the blood loss.

Even One-Zero Doug Miller's good luck was running out. During the fierce firefight on the LZ, he was ripped by B-40 shrapnel that tore into his left arm, chest, and leg, yet his fighting drive remained unchecked. He continued firing back until his beleaguered team managed to push the enemy back. There was a brief lull in the heavy action once the sounds of the choppers faded away. Miller quickly assessed his situation: his team had sustained a 100 percent casualty rate, two of his men were unable to walk, and he knew the NVA would not wait long before attempting to surge over them.

Miller moved over to Blyth and took over the PRC-25 team radio due to his RTO's serious wounds. He then positioned his team twenty yards to the rear while he advanced across the bomb crater to meet the next enemy assault alone, having secured additional ammunition from Prap and Hyuk. Miller eased out of the bomb crater and crawled to the edge of the jungle cover. He realized there was one most likely avenue of approach through the jungle, so he positioned himself there, some thirty yards from the crater, and waited for the NVA platoon to close with him. The FAC reassured him over the radio that a friendly reaction battalion was approaching his position.

Miller prepared for battle, taking cover behind a large rock with plenty of vegetation for concealment. He readied his spare magazines, his final frag, and last two CS grenades as he heard the sounds of troops massing to his front. *In the next few minutes, a whole bunch of people are going to come along*, he thought. *There's going to be a lot of kickass, and everything I can do still won't be enough.*[15]

A large group of enemy soldiers slowly materialized from its concealed position and stalked in his direction. Fortunately, they were somewhat massed, offering Miller an advantage. He opened fire when they were a little over a dozen yards from his position, catching them off guard. Several

NVA crumpled under his first rounds, but the remainder hit him with a heavy barrage. An anti-tank round slammed into the rock he was hiding behind and then the enemy surged forward. Miller threw his frag, the blast from which knocked down more enemy and caused the rest to scatter. He then picked off the cripples but had only a brief respite before the balance of the platoon mounted another assault.

Realizing his position was no longer defensible, he popped the two CS grenades and threw them in front of the advancing wave. During the momentary confusion as their charge was halted, Miller retreated back to the crater. He had just cleared the rim of the hole and gotten into a fighting posture when the NVA came rushing through the gas. He fired into them, joined by several other members of RT Vermont. Blyth, weak from blood loss, tried to concentrate on where the next targets would appear as he fought back with his CAR-15. His biggest challenge was keeping the blood from his left hand from causing dirt and debris to stick to his magazines and foul them.

The NVA platoon persisted in its advance. Miller was just shifting his sights to another target when a bullet ripped through his left forearm, the impact sending him tumbling toward the center of the bomb crater. Around him, other team members were either dead or in serious condition. Glancing at his own bloody lower arm, Miller thought, *We are doomed.*

He wrapped a rag around his arm and returned to the radio. Unbeknownst to him, two saving factors were working in his favor: members of the reaction battalion were fast approaching his bomb crater and Gladiators slicks from the 57th AHC were inbound from the launch site. Co-pilot Bobby Ross was shocked to hear the RT Vermont one-zero begin singing, in almost humorous fashion, the lyrics to a well-known Beatles tune over and over: "Help! I neeeeed somebody. Help!"[16]

Doug Miller was running low on ammunition and optimism. He tossed another fragmentation grenade over the rim of the crater and prepared for the final wave that he knew would overrun his recon team by moving further on up the hill by himself once again. He took cover near a large boulder and began stacking his remaining ammunition, intent on making a last stand against his enemy. The situation had become so desperate that Miller would later refer to this mission as his "Vietnamese Alamo."[17]

It was at this bleak moment that the first form of reinforcement reached RT Vermont's perimeter. Medic Andy Brown, having been hit by shrapnel while losing all four of his Montagnards in the clearing far below, had completed his solo charge up the hillside. He quickly tended to two badly wounded Montagnards of RT Vermont before he spotted Staff Sergeant Robert Brown leaning up against a tree.

"Brownie, how you doing?" called Andy. "Where are you hit?"

Recon Team Vermont's one-one announced that he had been hit in the legs, so Andy Brown went to work, quickly cutting open his fatigues. He saw the sergeant's darkened thighs and obvious entry wounds where the shrapnel frags had sliced through him.

"Andy, I can fix that. Miller's up on the hill by himself," the wounded one-one said.

As Medic Brown worked on assistant team leader Brown, a severely wounded Montagnard dragged himself closer. Andy could see that the poor man's groin and lower extremities had been shredded, leaving him with only a faint chance of survival. He passed his medical bag to the one-one and asked him to look after the Montagnard and himself before he scurried up the hillside with the other medical provisions he had packed into his gear. Automatic fire cut the air above Brown's head as he moved forward, but he noted that the rounds seemed to be aiming at something higher. As he neared a slight trail, he called ahead for Miller. No answer.

Brown called again, and then heard a reply. "Over here!"

Brown charged forward and finally spotted Doug Miller propped against a boulder, appearing to be nursing injuries beneath his tucked arms. Miller's M16 lay beside him, along with his remaining spare magazines. The scene was reminiscent of Custer's Last Stand: a valiant leader trying to hold off a final enemy charge while his wounded comrades lay below in an area that they could not hold much longer.

Unbeknownst to Andy Brown, Lieutenant Jerry Pool and his Montagnard battalion swept up over the rim of RT Vermont's bomb crater just as he was trying to evaluate One-Zero Miller. Pool's separate bunch had been guided in by the sounds of the fighting and the sight of Miller's smoke grenades. As he jumped into the hole with the battered remnant of RT Vermont, Pool sent a six-man Montagnard team forward to engage the massing NVA.[18]

The NVA were mounting yet another charge, even as Pool's Montagnards pushed forward to fight and Miller and Brown tried to avoid the automatic fire sweeping their vicinity. But the lifesaving Spads flown by First Lieutenants Engebretsen and Seith were still orbiting overhead, having spent two-and-a-half hours covering Miller's men. A large pocket of enemy soldiers was laying down intense gunfire from a gorge twenty-two yards from RT Vermont's wounded men and the Hatchet Force platoon. Engebretsen knew that any error in his delivery would be disastrous but he rolled his Skyraider down to treetop level and unloaded his ordnance precisely on target. The densely massed NVA formation was shredded, allowing Pool's Hatchet Force men to finish beating back the opposition.

Covey Rider Sam Zumbrun called in the Gladiator slicks once again to make a fresh evacuation attempt.[19]

As the air strikes rocked the hillside, Andy Brown noted a dramatic shift in the action. The NVA appeared to be pulling back as ordnance pounded them. Brown used the lull to assist Miller to his feet and they shuffled down the hill toward the bomb crater as the welcome sound of thumping chopper rotors approached.

Ed Blyth was weak from blood loss but exhilarated to see the first slick settle low just above the bomb crater. As the door gunner swung his gun side to side to track any charging NVA, the most severely injured members of RT Vermont and Prap's body were hastily loaded. Blyth clambered into the second chopper, noting that his badly wounded one-zero refused to leave until everyone was brought out. The next flight of Hueys lifted out the majority of Pool's reaction force men, until Doug Miller finally was the last man to board an extraction chopper.[20]

The salvation of RT Vermont was truly a group effort. Team leader Miller had given his all in holding off an overwhelming enemy force that had made him feel something like Lieutenant Colonel William Barret Travis at the Alamo, encouraging wounded men against a vastly superior opposing force that was overrunning the besieged mission. In the case of Miller's team, there was a different ending to the story thanks to the efforts of a dedicated covey rider team, a swift-moving reaction battalion already on the ground in the vicinity, repeated assaults made by A-1 Spad pilots, the valiant extraction work of the 57th Assault Helicopter Company, and other aerial support.

Bobby Ross, co-pilot of one of the extraction Gladiators was greatly relieved as the Hueys pulled the last men of the reaction force and team leader Miller from the hot LZ. His return flight out of the deadly valley would rival his later flight back home from Vietnam as the most exhilarating flight of his life.[21]

◆◇◆

Ed Wolcoff, one-zero of RT New York, was on Bright Light duty that afternoon when the survivors from RT Vermont were rescued from their personal hell. He had followed the action over the radio for hours, and fully expected to be called in to recover bodies when it was all over. Instead, Wolcoff and others hurried to assist the first slicks as they settled in at Ben Het to unload their blood-splattered casualties. His friend and fellow team leader Doug Miller had survived, but he looked thoroughly exhausted from the ordeal.

By the time his last chopper landed, Miller found that medics had already stretched out members of his team on the ground to administer first aid. He felt a wave of emotions sweep over him as medevac choppers were summoned to move them to the Pleiku AFB's 71st Medical Evaluation Hospital for surgery and other emergency treatment. "Emotionally, I was devastated," said Miller. "Tears welled up into my eyes, triggered partly by joy at our rescue, but mostly by sadness." Lieutenant Colonel Abt, his commander at Kontum, arrived to check on his men, and he offered a reassuring hand on Miller's shoulder to let him know that he understood what they had endured.[22]

When the medevac choppers finally landed at Pleiku, medical teams were standing by to wheel the recon men into surgery. Miller watched young Yu-B being carted away first, and he refused to accept treatment once again until all of his RT Vermont had been tended to first. When he awoke later after his own surgery, Miller found that his chest was heavily bandaged, his various shrapnel wounds had been patched, and his left arm was suspended in a plaster cast. He, Yu-B, and Ed Blyth would spend the next few days at Pleiku in intensive care.[23]

Six days after reaching Pleiku, Ed Blyth was medevaced to Japan for another two weeks of hospitalization. When he was finally flown back Stateside, he would spend two weeks in a California hospital before being sent on to Fort Bragg. Blyth, Robert Brown, and numerous other members of both the ground personnel and their air support would receive the Bronze Star for their performances against the enemy on January 5. Medic Andy Brown, who had been wounded and had lost most of his Montagnard team while fighting his way in to help rescue RT Vermont, was given an Army Commendation Medal—although it was later bumped up to a Bronze Star as well. The shock and stress of the action had prevented him from even noting his own shrapnel wounds until he reached the security of his Hatchet Force company atop the hill, where a fellow medic cut open his fatigues, blood-soaked from his thighs to his feet.

Don Engebretsen and Jim Seith, the A-1 pilots who had used their slow-moving prop planes to safeguard RT Vermont for hours, were each written up for the Silver Star. "Our awards were later downgraded to Distinguished Flying Crosses, likely because the NVA had not managed to put any holes in our planes," Engebretsen noted.[24] Some of the other heroes who had helped save Doug Miller's team were soon lost in other action.

Hatchet Force leader Jerry Pool went on to serve as a recon one-zero at Kontum, but he was killed two months later on March 24, 1970, when the 170th AHC Bikini chopper extracting his RT Pennsylvania from Cambodia was shot down with no survivors. Two of RT Vermont's aerial saviors—

the covey pilot, John LeHecka, and his covey rider, Sam Zumbrun—would also be killed in action just five days after the January 5 Miller mission.

Before his departure from Pleiku, Doug Miller was informed that Colonel Abt and his awards board had submitted him for the nation's second-highest award, the Distinguished Service Cross. Within weeks, SOG brass and Army officials who reviewed his actions determined that Staff Sergeant Miller was worthy of the Medal of Honor and revised and resubmitted his award recommendation. By that time, Miller had returned from rehabilitation in Japan and resumed command of his RT Vermont with Glenn Uemura as his one-one. It would be another couple of months before his MOH paperwork had snaked through the process far enough to warrant pulling him from the field.

The official paperwork from Kontum XO Major Bobby Leites was dated March 11, 1970, and the approval for Miller's receipt of the Medal of Honor was officially announced on June 6. He was cited for his "gallantry, intrepidity in action, and selfless devotion to the welfare of his comrades" in single-handedly repulsing hostile attackers while seriously wounded. Staff Sergeant Miller would thus become the fifth recon man from Command and Control Central to receive the nation's highest military award for valor and selfless devotion to their comrades.

The war in Vietnam, Laos, and Cambodia was far from over, but Kontum's SOG men had already set the bar for their performance under fire. Known during its first years of operation as FOB-2 and then CCC, this forward operating base was allotted a sixty-man recon company, although the unit was understrength during its formative months. Never in American history had such a small military unit included eight members who received the Distinguished Service Cross and five recipients of the Medal of Honor. In a war whose veterans were not received back home with the adulation and victory parades bestowed on heroes of former conflicts, the Green Berets of SOG's Kontum base compiled a combat record that might never be equaled. Their valor, their sacrifices, and their selfless service are the lifeblood upon which our cherished national freedom was founded.

Epilogue

"A COLLECTION OF HEROES"

The CCC base at Kontum was deactivated in March 1971, but continued operation under the new name Task Force 2 Advisory Element (TF2AE) until the SOG organization was officially terminated in March 1972—although several covert missions were made across the fence after that time. Between the summer of 1966 and January 1970, there were hundreds of awards for valor earned by the Green Berets of the Kontum recon company: Purple Hearts, Army Commendation Medals, Air Medals, Bronze Stars, and Silver Stars. Additionally, eight CCC veterans were awarded the nation's second-highest military honor, the Distinguished Service Cross.

During its eight-year existence, SOG logged a roster of 7,800 men and its members received more than two thousand individual awards for heroism, including ten of the nation's highest form of recognition, the Medal of Honor, for actions of "conspicuous gallantry … above and beyond the call of duty"[1]—that's twice as many as the 82nd Division received in two world wars. Studies and Observations Group veterans also received twenty-three awards of the Distinguished Service Cross. During it service period, ten teams went missing, fourteen teams were overrun or destroyed, and fifty SOG men remain listed as MIA.

Since first being awarded to six Union Army soldiers during the Civil War on March 25, 1863, the Medal of Honor has only been presented 3,515 times as of July 2016—including nineteen men who received the medal twice. Many of those receiving the Medal of Honor did not survive the action for which it was awarded. It is the only military medal worn suspended from a ribbon around the neck (though it can also be represented by a ribbon bar) and as a matter of custom, its recipients are the only individuals the Commander-in-Chief salutes.[2]

In its early history, the Medal of Honor was presented en masse to 310 members of the 27th Maine Volunteer Infantry Regiment and to 29 men who served as honor guard for Abraham Lincoln's body when it was sent home to Springfield for burial. More than 15 medals were awarded for actions during the Civil War, 126 for World War I, 471 for World War II, 145 for Korea, and 258 for the Vietnam War (for actions between 1955 and 1975). Since the Civil War, no single company has boasted as many Medal of Honor recipients as SOG's forward operating base at Kontum. The fact that five men were recognized—two posthumously—from such a small Special Forces unit in less than three years' time is an outstanding feat.

Bob Howard, nominated three times for the Medal of Honor while serving in SOG, extended his tours in Vietnam until the lengthy award process finally caught up with him in late February 1971. At that time, he was a captain in charge of a 218-man Special Forces company that was under heavy ground assault near Kontum City during the night. More than two years had passed since the December 1968 mission for which his valor was finally being recognized. That thought was farthest from his mind as Howard directed his men against the enemy. As he ran to a mortar pit and jumped over the sandbags to take cover, a bullet slammed into his right foot.[3]

Another captain from the unit's tactical operations center reached him in the mortar pit, lugging a military TA-312 field telephone.

"I've got the Chief of Staff of the Army on the telephone," he panted. "He's calling all the way from Washington, DC."

"Does he want to talk about the battle or what?" asked Howard.

"No," said the operations officer. "He wants to talk to you."

As he picked up the receiver, Westmoreland said, "Bob, how you doing?"

"Sir, the situation is pretty damn bad here," said Howard. He added that he was in pain from a gunshot wound to his foot.

"Well, congratulations, Bob," the general continued. "Our nation has just awarded you the Medal of Honor."[4]

Howard thanked Westmoreland but added that it would be hard for the Army to extract him from his present conflict to receive any military award. Westmoreland assured him that he would contact the 4th Infantry Division to provide security to extract him. With an extra infantry brigade added to their ranks, Captain Howard's company was able to suppress the North Vietnamese enough after daybreak to allow a Beechcraft C-12 twin-engine turboprop aircraft that had been sent from Saigon under orders of General Creighton W. Abrams, the MACV-SOG commander, to land in the midst of the action. The enemy was still firing as the wounded captain was spirited out of Kontum City to the airfield on the back of a machine-gun armed deuce-and-a-half truck. He limped to the aircraft with the support of a lieutenant colonel. "We took about four hits on take-off," said Howard.[5]

In Saigon, Howard's wound was treated and he was given a new uniform for his flight back to Washington. He returned to a nation in a state of unrest, where protestors delayed the originally scheduled February 27 presentation. A radical group called the Weather Underground was protesting the ongoing U.S.-supported invasion of Laos, and claimed credit for a bomb that exploded in the Capitol building on March 1. In the midst of such unrest, Captain Howard's ceremony was conducted on March 2, 1971, as he stood in the White House wearing his Special Forces uniform.

He tried to present the appearance of a brave warrior, solid as stone, but his nerves took over as President Richard Nixon draped the pale blue ribbon around his neck.

"Are you okay?" Nixon asked. "You're mighty pale."

Bob Howard, seen wearing his Medal of Honor in 1971, served in the U.S. military for thirty-six years and was among the most decorated of all servicemen. *Congressional Medal of Honor Society*

Howard fought off the urge to faint, mumbling, "I'm fine, sir. Thank you so much."[6]

Nixon then asked the new Medal of Honor recipient what he planned to do in Washington that day. Howard relayed his appreciation for the award and said he wanted to visit the Tomb of the Unknown Soldier at Arlington National Cemetery. With his family in tow, he did just that, reflecting quietly on those who had paid the ultimate price in combat—including the father and three uncles he had lost in World War II. When his young daughter Melissa asked what the memorial stood for, Howard quietly explained it, adding that the lost men all had families they had left behind while serving their country.[7]

As they walked away from the tomb, Howard patted Melissa on the shoulder, asking softly, "You get it?"

"I do get it," she said.[8]

Doug Miller, the fifth recon man from Kontum to receive the Medal of Honor, similarly returned to Washington for his own ceremony just three months later. After the action that resulted in the award, Miller had continued to serve his country from Kontum for another year before his presence was requested in Washington, DC. Donning a new class A uniform, he was flown from Vietnam first class and was met at the airport by his mother, stepfather, and brother Walter. Days later, on June 15, 1971, he stood with one other soldier to receive the nation's highest award. Five of the men receiving the Medal of Honor from President Nixon that day did so posthumously. Miller felt an incredible rush of joy and sorrow intermixed as he glanced at the medal laying against his chest.[9]

When asked by the president what he would like to do next, Miller requested to be returned to service in Vietnam with his unit. Upon his return in-country, Miller assumed a staff assignment in the S2 section, which he filled until completing his tour of duty in Vietnam in November 1972. He retired from the Army in 1992 as a command sergeant major and continued to advocate for his comrades as a benefits counselor for the Veterans Administration. During his four years of Vietnam combat, Miller was also the recipient of the Silver Star, two Bronze Stars, the Air Medal, and six Purple Hearts.

Miller attended the 57th Assault Helicopter Company's reunion in 1997, where he was presented with a plaque by former Huey pilot Bobby Ross, whose crew had extracted RT Vermont in January 1970. Miller's final battle was with cancer and he passed away on June 30, 2000.

Ken Sisler, MACV-SOG's first Medal of Honor recipient, was buried in his hometown of Dexter, Missouri. On February 28, 1998, his widow, Jane, christened a large medium-speed, roll-on/roll-off (LMSR) the *Sisler* (T-AKR-311) in San Diego. In 2002, Jane Sisler was also on hand with her sons David and Jim for the unveiling of a statue of her late husband that now stands on the grounds of the Keller Public Library in Dexter.

John Kedenburg, the third man from Kontum to receive the Medal of Honor, is buried in the Long Island National Cemetery, and has a street named in his honor at Fort Bragg. The base's Zabitosky Road similarly honors Medal of Honor recipient Fred Zabitosky. The action that resulted in Zabitosky's award occurred only a few months before that of Kedenburg. Zabitosky retired from the Army with the rank of master sergeant after thirty years of service; he succumbed to a brain aneurism on January 18, 1996, at the age of fifty-three and is buried in Lumbee Memorial Park in Lumberton, North Carolina.

Fred Zabitosky was the featured speaker at a reunion of the 57th AHC in October 1995. There, he finally had the chance to reunite with Rick Griffith, one of the pilots he had rescued in 1968 from their burning Huey.

Two of the eight Kontum recon men who received the Distinguished Service Cross, Linwood Martin and Jim Birchim, were killed during the actions for which they were decorated. Billy Evans has since passed away, and Steven Comerford, who retired as a command sergeant major, died in 2004 in Rhode Island. Leonard Tilley retired as a captain after twenty years of service and continues to be active within the annual Special Operations Association Reunion (SOAR) conventions. Lieutenant Colonel Tom Jaeger retired from the Army in 1986; his last billet found him at the Pentagon serving in the Office of the Deputy Chief of Staff for Logistics for the U.S. Army Headquarters.

Morris Worley, who nearly lost his right arm in the action that resulted in his being awarded the Distinguished Service Cross in early 1967, served more than twenty years and retired in October 1977 as a command sergeant major. He returned to North Carolina and taught junior ROTC for fourteen years, two of those as a senior Army instructor. Worley then transferred to the University of North Carolina, School of Dentistry, where he worked until his retirement designing computer software to support periodontal research.

Bob Howard, who received the DSC before being awarded the Medal of Honor proudly served thirty-six years, eight months, and eight days in uniform. His post-Vietnam assignments included: training officer at the Army Airborne School; company commander in the 2nd Ranger Battalion at Ft. Lewis, Washington; officer in charge of SF training at Camp Mackall in North Carolina; mountain training officer at the U.S. Army Ranger's Camp Frank D. Merrill at Dahlonega, Georgia; and commander of the Special Forces Detachment, Korea. He earned a bachelor's degree in police administration from Texas Christian University in 1973 and two master's degrees from Central Michigan University by 1981. Howard retired as a full colonel, spending another twenty years with the Department of Veteran Affairs.

During his career, he participated in the filming of two John Wayne movies, *The Longest Day* and *The Green Berets*. His courage, stout leadership, humble personality, and athleticism would long be remembered by the thousands of soldiers he commanded during that time. His legacy was carried forward by his son, Robert Lewis Howard Jr., who opted to follow in his father's footsteps by completing Army airborne training—and Bob senior was there to proudly speak at his son's graduation. Robert Howard Jr.'s service to his country included a fifteen-month tour in Afghanistan.[10]

Colonel Howard made frequent trips overseas to visit soldiers in remote battle areas in Iraq and Afghanistan, offering his message of service and sacrifice to their country. He believed that many other men also deserved the Medal of Honor, but they had not been fortunate enough to have surviving witnesses to nominate them for their courage. On March 25, 2009, Bob Howard visited the Arlington National Cemetery wearing his Medal of Honor in the company of President Barack Obama and fellow Medal of Honor recipients. Near the Tomb of the Unknown Soldier, Howard stated, "They made the ultimate sacrifice. There's not many left of those that were in the battles I was in. A lot of them were killed. I wear it for them."[11]

He was diagnosed with terminal pancreatic cancer that year and passed away on December 23, 2009. Bob Howard left two daughters from his first marriage, a son and daughter from his second marriage, and four grandchildren at the time of his death. One of America's most decorated warriors, Colonel Robert Lewis Howard was laid to rest in Arlington National Cemetery in 2010. A partial list of his awards includes: the Medal of Honor, the Distinguished Service Cross, the Silver Star, four Bronze Stars with "V" device, three Air Medals with "V" device, four Army Commendation Medals with "V" device, the Defense Superior Service Medal, three Army Meritorious Service Medals, four awards of the Legion of Merit, the Joint Service Commendation Medal, the Army Achievement Medal, eight Purple Hearts, the Vietnamese Cross of Gallantry with Silver Star, and the Vietnamese Cross of Gallantry with Bronze Star.

Several buildings have been named after Colonel Howard, including the 5th Special Forces Group headquarters building at Ft. Campbell,

Kentucky, a state veterans home in Pell City, Alabama, and the Pathfinder School at Ft. Benning, Georgia.

The five Medals of Honor and eight DSCs awarded to Kontum recon men do not tell the full story. Plenty of men gave their all that were equally deserving of America's highest honors. Some declined attention. Former CCC One-Zero Larry White related that some of the heroes he knew received no awards at all, simply because no one bothered to write them up for actions they performed that were certainly worthy of official recognition. White could look at a man and know what he had done but see that he received no medals. Many Vietnam heroes simply did not come home or had no witnesses to their final actions of courage.

Many other heroes from different service branches gave their lives while supporting SOG teams in conflict on the ground as well. Some were killed in action, some fell into enemy hands, and others were never found—written off as MIAs. One case in point was Major Wayne Wolfkeil, whose A-1 Spad was shot down in August 1968 while he was prosecuting an attack to assist with the extraction of a besieged FOB-2 recon team. His body was not recovered, and the Wolfkeil family anguished for years over his MIA status until the military declared in 1979 that he had been killed in action.

Sergeant First Class Wilson Hunt, whose Recon Team Maine ran a Bright Light to attempt the recovery of Major Wolfkeil's body, never even knew the identity of the downed pilot his men risked their lives to search for. As I interviewed my uncle-in-law for this book, he related how troubled he had been for more than forty-five years in not being able to make contact with the Air Force veteran's family. Hunt's hope was that they knew their loved one had most likely perished in the crash and that they had not been harried by the belief that he might have perished years later in captivity.

Uncovering this longstanding mission was among my goals in researching the story of Kontum and its recon men. Hunt had no formal papers to assist with the search and could only provide a rough estimate of the time frame. After fruitless Internet searches, I finally turned to printed material and found my first solid lead in Chris Hobson's brilliantly detailed book, *Vietnam Air Losses*. A quick search of Spad losses in the summer of 1968 revealed the name of Major Wayne Wolfkeil. Everything seemed to fit. Then, turning back to the Internet, I found a family memorial site with stories about this Skyraider pilot and his family. It described how a Green Beret team reached the crash site two weeks later, finding only shards of the plane and a tattered flight helmet. It was exactly what Hunt's RT Maine had found in 1968.

Left to right: SOG veteran Wilson Hunt, General Jack Singlaub (former Chief SOG), and author at 2014 SOAR convention. *Author's collection*

Working closely with Wilson Hunt's brother-in-law, Bob Dumont, and Vietnam veterans Joe Parnar and Don Engebretsen, I connected with Major Wolfkeil's son, David Wolfkeil. In October 2016, Hunt was able to finally meet with the Wolfkeil family in person at the SOAR convention in Las Vegas during a Spad presentation headed by Engebretsen and former One-Zero John Stryker "Tilt" Meyer. Present were five members of Major Wolfkeil's family—his daughter Maura Wolfkeil Procter, his niece Veronica "Alyn" Procter, his daughter Veronica Wolfkeil, his son David Wolfkeil, and David's wife Jennifer Perez-Wolfkeil—as Hunt shared the full story of his team's Bright Light mission.

✦✧✦

The proud SOG veterans who returned home from the Vietnam War found a country that largely did not welcome their return or respect their sacrifices in the way that veterans of previous wars had been honored. Even more troubling to some was the fact that they were bound to an oath of confidentiality that left them unable for decades to fully disclose many of the details of the dangerous missions their elite Special Forces group had carried out.

It was not until 1997, when SOG veteran John Plaster published his first book on this elite Special Forces unit, that America became more widely aware of what the Studies and Observations Group accomplished in the Vietnam War. Once the military records of the secret war in Laos and Cambodia were declassified in 2003, other SOG veterans followed with their own books, including Frank Greco, Joe Parnar, Lionel "Choo-Choo" Pinn, Doug Miller, John "Tilt" Meyer, and Lynne M. Black Jr. Another series of books by SOG historian Jason Hardy presents individual team histories, complete with rare photos and details of recon team missions that might otherwise have been lost to history.

On April 4, 2001, a collection of SOG veterans gathered with a crowd of hundreds in the plaza on Ardennes Street on Fort Bragg, bunching near a statue of SOG veteran Arthur "Bull" Simons. In attendance were two former SOG commanders—Jack Singlaub and Steve Cavanaugh—along with dozens of recon veterans such as Dick Meadows, John Plaster, Roy Bahr, Clyde Sincere, and John Meyer. Twenty-nine years after running its last operations, this covert operations "band of brothers" was being officially recognized by the military for its contributions, in the form of the award of a Presidential Unit Citation. "Pursued by human trackers and even bloodhounds, these small teams outmaneuvered, out-fought and outran their numerically superior foe to uncover key enemy facilities, rescue downed pilots, plant wiretaps, mines and electronic sensors, capture valuable enemy prisoners, ambush convoys, discover and assess targets for B-52 strikes, and inflict casualties all out of proportion to their own losses," the PUC read in part. "The Studies and Observations Group's combat prowess, martial skills and unacknowledged sacrifices saved many American lives, and provide a paragon for America's future special operations forces."[12]

"It's a day that I think most of us thought would never happen," Plaster said at the ceremony. "There were a great many young men that came home that could never quite tell their families, their friends what they did." SOG's high casualty rate is highlighted by the fact that in 1968, the unit had more people killed and injured than it had positions. Former Chief SOG Singlaub felt the award was long overdue, adding, "We had a collection of heroes that was not equaled."[13]

ACKNOWLEDGMENTS

This book is possible thanks to the many dozens of Special Forces veterans who willingly shared their stories with me over the course of several years. My uncle-in-law, Wilson Hunt, had recounted various recon stories for years at family reunions but I was not fully aware of the vast accomplishments of the Studies and Observations Group until reading John Plaster's groundbreaking 1997 book, *SOG: The Secret Wars of America's Commandos in Vietnam.*

The list of those I must thank is lengthy, primarily being the SOG veterans and air support personnel who agreed to sit down with me in person or recount details of certain events over the telephone or via email. That list is too extensive to present here but all who contributed are acknowledged in the bibliography. Each person helped me in some way to understand more of the big picture or some of the small events of what happened on particular missions.

Others went "above and beyond" to help share vital primary documents and their knowledge of various operations. Jason Hardy, a SOG historian who painstakingly compiled team histories for years, was kind enough to share a number of photos and to field questions regarding various team compositions. Joe Parnar and Bob Dumont, co-authors of a book relating Parnar's experiences, served as guides throughout this process, each sharing copious data and photos they have compiled over many years. Steve Sherman, who has amassed an impressive archive of SOG data, generously granted me access to thousands of Vietnam military award citations to help me set the record straight on the dates when various missions took place. Laura Jowdy and Lourdes Bautista of the Congressional Medal of Honor Society assisted with photos of the late Robert L. Howard from their archives.

Wilson Hunt invited me to attend SOAR conventions as his guest, where dozens of SOG veterans recounted missions and opened themselves to interviews. Former chopper pilot Rick Griffith invited me to the 57th Assault Helicopter Reunion in 2015 and orchestrated interview sessions with his fellow aviators who participated in various Kontum team missions.

Several veterans reviewed chapters for accuracy, including Alan Keller, Steve Goth, Rick Griffith, David Wolfkeil (Wayne Wolfkeil's son), Don Engebretsen, Wilson Hunt, Ed Wolcoff, Bud Williams, and Ed Blyth. John Stryker "Tilt" Meyer took the time to carefully read an early draft of the manuscript and was a constant resource for putting me in touch with key SOG veterans.

I am indebted to Rick Russell of the Naval Institute Press for his eagerness to work with me once again through the publishing process and to Aden Nichols for his expert editing of such challenging subject matter. This book is dedicated to the many people who agreed to share some of their experiences, actions for which most have not fully received the recognition from their country that they so richly deserve.

APPENDIX

FOB-2 / CCC KONTUM ROSTER: MAY 1966–JANUARY 1970

Key to Codes

MOH	Medal of Honor	AM(v)	Air Medal with "V" device
DSC	Distinguished Service Cross	SM	Soldier's Medal
SS	Silver Star	PH	Purple Heart
DFC	Distinguished Flying Cross	MIA	Missing in Action
BS(v)	Bronze Star with "V" device	KIA	Killed in action (indicated
AC(v)	Army Commendation medal with "V" device		by *)

Key to Base Assignment Codes

B-50	Project Omega Detachment, FOB-2, June–November 1967	S1	Personnel and Administration
		S2	Intelligence
HF	Hatchet Force (Reaction Battalion), Recon Company	S3	Operations and Training
		S4	Logistics
MS	Medical Section	ST	Spike Team (1966–68)
RT	Recon Team (1968–70)	STP	Straphanger

Note: This compilation does not include personnel from the Signal Section, Launch Site/Covey Rider, etc. American service awards shown are based on input received from the veterans and from SOG historians Steve Sherman and Jason Hardy. The author regrets any omissions or mistakes.

BASE COMMANDERS: FOB-2 AND CCC

Name	Rank/Tenure		Awards
Norton, Charles William, Jr.	MAJ	May–June 1966	
Crerar, John Heuches	MAJ	June–Sept. 1966	
Sova, Francis Joseph	MAJ	Oct. 1966–April 1967	
Kilburn, Gerald	MAJ	May 1967–June 1967	
Leach, Frank	MAJ	June 1967–July 20, 1967	
Hart, Roxie Ray	MAJ	July 21, 1967–May 4, 1968	
Smith, Donald L.	LTC	May 4, 1968–Dec. 1968	BS(v), AC(v), PH
Bahr, Roy Wilmur	LTC	Dec. 1968–March 6, 1969	
Abt, Frederick Troili	LTC	March 7, 1969–Jan. 25, 1970	

RECON TEAMS, REACTION BATTALION (HATCHET FORCE), AND OTHER BASE PERSONNEL
July 1966–January 1970

Name	Rank	Base Assignment or Team(s)	Awards/Notes
Adams, Bruce D.	SGT	Ford Drum	
Adams, Lloyd	SSG	ST KY, ST TX	SS
Adams, Richard E.	SSG	RT TX	
Adanio, Roger G.	1LT	HF, CO B	
Adcock, Ralph Gene	SFC	ST KY	PH
Addison, George I., Jr.	SFC	S4	
Ahles, Vincent Christian	SGT	HF	
Alberigo, Gaetano L.	SFC	RT WY	
Allen, John J., Jr.	SSG	RT IL	AC(v), SS
Allen, Ronnie L.	SGT	B-50	
Allickson, Henry O.	MSG	HF, CO A	
Ambrose, Floyd, Jr.	SSG	RT WA, RT OH, RT KY	SS, AC(v), BS(v), PH
Ancho, Ramon, Jr.	SFC	HF	
Anderson, Eric E.	SFC	HF	
Anderson, Harry J.	1LT	RT TX, RT NH	PH
Anderson, Wayne Marshall*	SGT	HF	SS(2), BS(v), KIA 12/3/69
Angeles, Ruben	SGT	ST CO	
Angster, Robert C., Jr.	SP4	HF, RT TX	PH

Name	Rank	Base Assignment or Team(s)	Awards/Notes
Anthony, Billy Joe	SFC	ST OH	
Apperson, Gerald Franklin*	SFC	HF	KIA 1/8/69
Armstrong, Donald G.	SFC	Ford Drum	
Arrowood, Steve, Jr.	SGM	command section	
Arvai, Johnny	SFC	ST ME, ST NV	
Arzola, Jorge	CPT	HF	
Ashley, William G.	SGT	MS	
Attebery, Francis S.	SFC	RT NM	BS(v)
Austin, Leon	SFC	RT AR	
Austria, Louis	SFC	S4	
Aycock, Charles A.	1LT	S2	
Bacon, Charles W.	SFC	S1	
Bacon, George Washington, III	SSG	RT IL	PH
Bagby, Jack A.	SFC	RT CA	
Baker, David C.	SSG	RT ME	BS(v), PH(2), AC(v), AM(v)
Ballard, Asa R.	SFC	RT NM	BS(v), AC(v)
Barnatowicz, John	SGT	RT TX, RT OH	
Barnes, Robert William	SFC	S1, RT CA	SS
Barnes, Wesley H.	SFC	ST NV	
Barnes, William G.	SFC	HF	BS(v)
Barras, Samuel J.	SP5	RT AK	
Barrett, Edmont Thomas	SP4	HF, CO A	
Bartlett, Arthur W.	SFC	HF	BS(2), PH
Barton, Jack W.	1LT	HF	
Bath, James David	SFC	ST NV, ST CO	BS(v), AC(v)
Batman, Sherman Richard	SFC	ST IL	PH(2), SS, BS(v)
Bean, Billy Vance	SFC	ST ME	PH(2), SS, BS
Beaton, Peter D.	SGT	RT NH, RT NV	
Bednar, Gerald, III	1LT	RT AZ	
Belletire, Frank Lee, Jr.	SSG	RT NH (STP), RT OH, HF	SS, PH(2), AC(2), BS(4)
Bemis, Donald W.	SGT	RT VT	
Benesh, Don W.	SP5	S2, RT AZ, RT NY	
Bernard, Newell Woodrow	SP5	HF	
Bessner, Harry Baily	SFC	HF	BS(2)
Bettis, Gaylon Eugene	SFC	RT CA	BS, PH
Bingham, Dennis William*	SP4	ST HI	SS, KIA 7/17/69

Name	Rank	Base Assignment or Team(s)	Awards/Notes
Bingham, Oran L., Jr.	SGT	HF	BS(v), SS(2), PH
Bingo, Michael Joseph, Jr.	SSG	RT TX (STP), RT CO	PH
Birchim, James Douglas*	CPT	RT CA, RT NH	DSC, PH, KIA 11/15/68
Bishop, Charles M.	SFC	HF, Co B	BS(v)
Blaauw, John Godfrey	SGT	RT NY	BS(v), PH
Blackwell, Michael R.	SGT	RT HI	
Blankenship, Bennet Lee	MSG	HF	
Blatney, Joseph R.	SFC	RT NV	
Bless, Charles A.	SFC	RT OH	BS(v), PH
Blyth, Edward Lee	SSG	RT VT	BS, PH
Bobroske, Mizuho	SSG	HF	
Booth, Jesse E.	SSG	HF, CO C	PH
Borek, Jan	SFC	ST CO, ST OH	
Boronski, John Arthur*	SSG	RT CO, RT PA	KIA 3/24/70
Borowski, Janusz S.	1SG	S4	
Bottemiller, Clifton John	SP5	RT NV	
Bourgeois, Joseph M.	SGT	HF	
Bowling, Ronald	SGT	ST DK	
Boyd, Kenneth M.	1LT	HF	PH(2), BS(v)
Boyd, Paul L.	SGT	RT MT	BS(v)
Boyd, Stephen T.	SGT	HF	
Boyd, William D.	SP4		
Boyer, George E.	SFC	RT SC	BS, SS
Boyle, William*	SFC	ST ME	BS(2), PH, AM, SS, KIA 2/28/70
Bozikis, Ronald Henry*	SSG	RT NH	BS(v), SS, KIA 10/25/69
Braddock, Jimmie L.	CPT	S2	
Braden, Ted B.	SFC	ST ID, ST CO	
Bradford, Alfred	SSG	RT NV, RT FL	
Brady, Jan	SGT	HF, CO A	AC(v)
Brady, Martin	SSG	HF	
Bragg, Percell	SSG	ST ME	SS
Bramlette, David L., Jr.	1LT	HF, CO A	AC(2), BS(v)
Brents, Terry Ray	SGT	RT CA	BS(v), PH
Briggs, Larry G.	SGT	RT NV	
Brilliante, Felix, Jr.	SFC	S1	

Name	Rank	Base Assignment or Team(s)	Awards/Notes
Brinkman, Paul Leslie	SP4	RT WY	
Brock, David L.	SP4	HF, CO B	BS(v)
Brown, Andrew Marion	SFC	HF, CO B	BS(v), PH
Brown, Donald W.	SSG	HF	
Brown, Edwin O.	SSG	MS	BS, AM, SM
Brown, Philip McIntire	SSG	RT NY	PH
Brown, Robert C.	SP5	RT VT	BS
Brown, Robert R.	SSG	RT CO, RT FL	BS, AC(v)
Brown, Ronald	SGT	HF	AM(v), BS, PH
Brown, Waddell	SFC		
Brown, William	SFC	HF	BS(v)
Broz, Charles F.	SP5	RT SC, RT HI	
Bryant, Floyd	SGT	HF	PH
Buchanan, Larry D.	SFC	HF, CO A	PH(2)
Buckland, Michael Patrick	SP4	RT ME	AC(v)
Bulin, Jerrald J.	SP4	HF	SS, PH
Bullard, Charles Dorian*	SSG	RT HI, RT DE, RT NM (STP)	BS(v), PH, KIA 1/29/69
Bumps, William Roger	SGT	RT NY	BS, PH
Burkins, Lee Charles	SP4	RT IA, RT VT	
Bustamente, Manuel C.	SFC	HF	PH
Butrim, Thomas J.	SFC	ST IL	
Cadenbach, Charles Terry	SSG	HF, CO B	BS(2), PH
Callahan, Frederick D.	SSG	HF	
Calloway, Oscar A.	MSG	S4	
Campbell, Desker M.	SGM	command section	
Cantrell, Verlon Louis	SSG	MS	SS
Caro, Carlos David	SFC	RT (team unknown)	
Carnagey, Richard Dale	MSG	HF, CO A	AC(v)
Carpenter, Howard Bruce*	SGT	B-50	KIA 3/6/67
Carpenter, Kenneth J.	SFC	B-50	BS(v)
Carr, Thomas Andrew	SSG	RT OH, RT WY	BS(v), AM(v), PH
Carter, Lee B.	SFC	HF	
Cassady, John R., II	CPT	S3	
Cavin, Arlen D., Jr.	CPT	HF, battalion commander	
Chambers, Buddy Ray	SFC	RT HI, RT NV	
Chandler, Kenneth J.	SGT	HF, RT CO	
Chapa, Daniel Vasques	SFC	RT TX, RB CO A	

Name	Rank	Base Assignment or Team(s)	Awards/Notes
Chilson, Duane	SGT	RT IL	PH
Clough, Robert E.	SGT	RT (team unknown)	AM(v), PH
Collar, Roy Allen	CPT	S4	
Collier, James D.	SSG	HF	AC(v)
Colvin, Harold Dean	SFC	staff section	
Comerford, Steven Ward	MSG	HF	BS(v), DSC, PH
Conroy, Paul Ames, Jr.*	MSG	ST ME	KIA 3/23/67
Copley, William Michael*	SSG	RT VT	KIA 11/68
Corbett, Thomas E.	SFC	RT IL (STP), RT WY	
Corley, John A.	CPT	HF, company cdr.	
Corpuz, Edward	SFC	HF	
Corren, Sherman Bernard	SFC	RT TX, RT AZ	SS
Cottrell, George A., Jr.	SGT	RT SC	SS
Couch, John R.	SFC	ST ME	
Crane, Frederick A.	SSG	RT CO, RT HI	
Croy, Roy D., Jr.	CPT	S1	AM(v), BS(v)
Cummings, John H., Jr.	CPT	RT NM	
Cunningham, Dever L.	Seal	ST IA	BS
Cunningham, Thomas Patrick	SP5	RT IL (STP), RT CA, RT CO	BS(v), PH(2)
Curtis, Paul B.	SFC	RT (team unknown)	
Dahling, Terrell Alexander	SSG	ST HI, ST DW, RT CO	BS(v)
Daniels, Mark S.	SP4	HF	
Danio, Roger Gary	1LT	HF	AC(v)
Danos, William N.	SGT	RT IA	AC(v), PH
Darcy, Paul M.	MSG	S3	
Daquino, Anthony J.	SP5	RT AZ	
Daquino, William N.	SGT	HF, CO A	
Davenport, Allen	MS	S4	
Davidson, Donald W.	SSG	RT IA	BS(v), SS, PH
Davidson, Jon Peter	SGT	RT WY	PH
Davis, Clinton R.	1LT	HF, CO B	SS, PH
Davis, Craig Donald	SSG	RT WY, RT AK	
Davis, Frank	SGT	MS	
Davis, Maurice T., Jr.	MAJ	S4, HF	PH
Dawson, Floyd	MAJ	S4, HF	
Dean, Kyle Steven	SGT	RT AZ, RT SC (STP)	AC(v), PH(2)
DeLima, William	SFC	RT HI	BS(2), AM(v), AC(v), PH

Name	Rank	Base Assignment or Team(s)	Awards/Notes
DeMesme, Egan Andrew, Jr.	SGT	RT HI	
Dennis, Timothy H.	1LT	S1	
Denison, Gerald Edward	SFC	ST OH, ST NV	BS(v)
Descheeny, Wilford D.	SSG	RT HI	BS(v), PH
DeSeta, Louis Joseph	SGT	ST NV	BS(2), AC
Desoto, William	SGM	command staff	
De Vaull, Charles C.	SSG	S1	
Devaull, David	SSG	HF, CO B	
Devere, Donald	MSG	ST OR	
Dias, George H., Jr.	CPT	HF	
Dickerson, Lee M.	SFC	HF	PH
DiGiovanni, Dennis	SGT	HF, CO B	BS(v)
Dimond, Robert E.	SSG	RT AR	
Dixon, Warren E.	CPT	HF	AC(v)
Doll, Donald A., Jr.	CPT	S3	SS, PH(2)
Domingue, Chester Paul	SSG	ST IA	AC(v)
Doney, Norman Allen	MSG	RT FL, HF	BS, PH
Donohue, Michael B.	SSG	RT AR	
Dorff, Anthony Cleveland	SSG	MS, RT WA (STP)	PH, AC(v), BS(v), SM
Doss, Freddie D.	SFC	HF, ST ME	PH
Doughty, David H.	SSG	HF, ST HI	
Douglas, Paul Melvyn*	SSG	RT CO, RT HI	BS(v), KIA 8/23/68
Dove, Luther Murray, Jr.	SSG	ST HI, RT DE, RT OH	AM
Dowling, James M.	SP5	RT (team unknown)	
Duffield, Ethyl Wilson, Jr.	SFC	RT HI	BS(v), PH
Duncan, James Henry	SFC	HF	WIA 2/2/67, died 2/7/67
Duncan, James L.	CPT	S2, RT TX, RT NV	
Duncan, Wade A.	SFC	S4	
Dunlap, Charles E.	SP5	ST AR	AC(v), BS(v)
Duttlinger, Evald F.	MSG	S2	
Eagle, Cole Wesley	MSG	S2	
Earley, Hugh E.	SSG	HF	
Eggerton, Willie W.	SSG	HF	PH
Elswick, Estil	SGM	command section	
Erickson, Albert Mathew	SSG	ST TX, RT IA, RT NM	
Erickson, Charles G.	SSG	RT CO	BS(v)

Name	Rank	Base Assignment or Team(s)	Awards/Notes
Ernst, William J., Jr.	SGT	HF	
Etheredge, Kenneth Ray	1LT	HF	AM(v), 2
Evans, Billy D.	SFC	RT CO	DSC, PH
Evans, Bobby G.	CPT	HF, CO A	SS, PH
Fails, George Lawson	SGT	RT HI, RT NH, RT NY	AC(v)
Fanning, Ronald L.	SSG	ST FL, RT CA	
Farmer, Roger D.	SGT	S4	
Farrell, Alan Ford	SGT	HF	AC(v), PH
Fawcett, Donald James*	SSG	RT DK, RT NV	KIA 7/3/66
Fedor, Howard R., Jr.	SSG	MS	
Fernea, David Palmer	SSG	RT HI	
Files, Albert Clifton, Jr.*	SGT	HF	KIA 3/25/67
Fitzgerald, Francis C.	SFC	MS	
Flint, Edward Lee	SFC	RT CO, RT WV	
Flynn, Thomas Arthur	SSG	HF	PH
Follini, Peter A.	SSG	ST FL, MS	PH(2)
Fontes, Alex N.	SFC	MS, RT IA	
Ford, Horace	MSG	HF	BS, PH
Foster, Jimmie Allen	SSG	RT AZ, RT TX	PH
Fowler, Donald I.	MSG	ST DK	
Franke, Robert F.	SFC	ST NY, ST NV	BS
Frederickson, Joseph A.	SFC	RT DE, RT HI	
Freeman, Cecil L.	SFC	RT (team unknown)	
Frescura, John L.	SP5	HF	SS
Friess, Nick Dean	SP4	MS	BS(v)
Fritz, David L.	SGT	RT CA	
Frye, Billy Joe	MSG	command section	
Galasso, James Richard	SGT	MS	AC(v)
Gant, James	CPT	RT MN	
Garbett, Edward Gerald	MSG	HF, CO A	PH
Garcia, Geoffrey B.	SGT	RT IL	
Garcia, Oliver R.	SSG	MS	AC(v)
Garcia, Robert, II	SGT	ST FL (STP), RT DE, RT HI	
Gardner, Kenneth C.	SFC	S1, HF	AM(v), PH
Garner, James E., Jr.	SFC	RT OH, HF CO A	
Garvey, James E.	1LT	S4	
Gase, George Robert	SGT	HF	

Name	Rank	Base Assignment or Team(s)	Awards/Notes
Gaston, Chester Robert	SGT	RT CO	PH
Gates, Phillip E.	SP4	HF	
Gaylor, Rodney	SSG	ST OR	
Gayner, James P	MSG	HF	BS(v)
Gayol, Amado	CPT	command section	
Giaco, James M.	SGT	RT AZ, RT NH	
Gibbs, Elzie	SGM	command section	
Gilmer, David Lee	SSG	RT DE, RT CA, RT TX, RT HI	BS(2), AC(v)
Gilreath, Johnnie Baskel, Jr.	SFC	RT CO	BS, SS
Girard, Richard W.	SFC	HF	PH
Glashauser, Gregory Gary	1LT	RT HI, OH	BS(2), PH
Glass, Wendell L.	SFC	RT IL	SS(3), PH(4)
Glover, Douglas John	SSG	ST ME	MIA 2/19/68
Golden, Foyle N.	MSG	ST TX	
Golding, James Richard*	SSG	HF	PH, KIA 11/68
Good, John W.	SSG	RT AZ	
Goodhue, Marlin James*	SFC	RT NY	KIA 7/67
Goodwin, Raymond B.	SP4	RT OH	BS(v)
Goth, Stephen Martin	SP4	RT ME, HF	
Goulet, Ronald Mercel*	CPT	HF, CO B	BS(2), PH, KIA 9/26/69
Grant, John A.	SGT	RT HI, HF	BS(v), AC(v)
Graves, Garrett Van	SGT	MS	PH
Gravett, Ronald Charles	SSG	RT KY	BS(v), PH
Gray, James Junius*	SFC	RT FL	KIA 7/15/67
Greco, Frank	SP4	RT CO	BS
Green, Donald A.	SGT	RT VT, RT TX	
Green, Donald L.	SGT	MS	
Greene, Calvin Arthur*	1LT	HF	KIA 12/67
Greeney, Claude L.	SFC	S1	
Gribble, Robert	SSG	MS	
Griffin, Jerome	SGT	HF, CO C	BS(v)
Grimes, William R.	SFC	ST CO	
Gron, Robert Michael	SSG	HF, CO C	BS(v), PH
Gross, Richard R.	SFC	RT CA	BS(2), PH
Groves, William J., Jr.	1LT	HF, CO C	SS, PH(2), AM
Hall, Marshall D.	SSG	RT WY	PH, BS

Name	Rank	Base Assignment or Team(s)	Awards/Notes
Halpin, Richard William	SP4	RT NH	BS(v), PH
Hamilton, Karl K.	SSG	RT KY, RT WA	AC(v), PH(3), BS(v)
Hamric, Terry Lee	1LT	S3, RT NV, RT HI	BS(v), PH(2)
Hanson, Dale H.	SSG	RT FL	BS(v), PH
Hanson, William Henry	SFC	RT FL, RT HI, RT CO	BS(v)
Harbaugh, Bryce Gilbert	1LT	S2	
Harned, Gary Alan*	SSG	RT PA, RT HI	KIA 3/24/70
Harold, Charles T.	SGT	ST IL	
Harris, Raymond D.	SGT	RT IA	
Hart, James P.	MSG	HF	
Hart, John J.	1LT	HF	
Hartwig, Oliver Edwin	SP4	RT OH	AC(v), BS(2)
Harvey, Daniel R.	SGT	RT CO (STP), RT FL	AC(v)
Hatchett, William M.	1LT	HF, CO B, RT HI	BS(v), PH
Hause, David Woodland	SGT	ST WY	AM, PH
Hayes, Willard, Jr.	1LT	ST IL, RT WY, RT FL	
Haynes, Joel S.	SSG	ST IL	BS(v)
Haynes, Ratchford P.	SFC	HF	BS
Hays, David B.*	SFC	RT CA	SS, KIA 7/13/70
Hebron, Clarence A., Jr.	SGT	RT IA, RT TX	
Henderson, Charles W., Jr.	SSG	ST TX	
Henderson, Jerald D.	1LT	S4, FAC	AM
Henry, John E.	SGT	HF	PH
Herald, Charles T.	SP5	S1	
Hernandez, Samuel D.	SFC	RT FL	BS(v), PH
Hetrick, James Floyd	SFC	ST ID, ST CO	
Hicks, Audel Harrison, Jr.	CPT	S1	
Higgins, David L.	SFC	S1	
Hill, Melvin	SSG	RT FL (STP)	SS, BS, AM
Hill, Ray E.	SGT	RT SC	SS
Hoffman, Richard F.	SSG	RT ME, RT HI	
Hoglund, Michael August*	SGT	B-50	KIA 11/10/67
Holan, John F.	SFC	HF	BS(v)
Holland, John J.	1LT	HF, RT OH	BS(3), PH
Honeycutt, David J.	CPT	RT AZ, RT IA	PH
Hopkins, Michael K.	1LT	HF	
Horion, Walter R.	SSG	RT NH, RT HI	
Howard, Frederick R.	SGT	S4	

Name	Rank	Base Assignment or Team(s)	Awards/Notes
Howard, Robert Lewis	SFC	HF, CO C, ST WY (STP), ST CO (STP)	MOH, PH(7), DSC, BS(v), AC(2), SS, AM
Howes, James D.	SP4	RT FL	BS(v)
Howland, Gerald Jerome	MSG	ST CO, ST HI	SS, BS, AM, PH
Hubel, Frederick Lance	SSG	HF	PH
Huczko, Walter	1LT	HF, CO C	AC(v), PH
Hudson, Herbert T., Jr.	SFC	S4, command section	
Hullinger, Eugene F.	SGT	HF	
Humble, Charlie Adolphus	SFC	ST NV, ST HI	
Hungerford, Homer	SSG	RT DE, RT HI	
Hunt, George Wilson	SFC	RT CA, RT NV (STP), RT ME	BS, ACM, SS, PH(2)
Hurley, Charles J.	MSG	ST NV	
Jaco, Rex Lee	SSG	RT CA	AC(2)
Jaeger, Thomas Wayne	CPT	HF, CO B, RT KY	DSC, SS, PH
Jaks, Frank	CPT	S3, command section	BS, AM(8), PH
Janc, Daniel William	SSG	RT ME	AC(2)
Jenkins, Richard E.	SGT	ST IA	
Jennings, Henry Dale	SSG	RT NM	PH
Jensen, Glen Willard	SFC	ST NV	
Jerson, James Ray*	1LT	HF, CO C	SS, PH, KIA 12/30/68
Joecken, Richard Kenneth*	SP4	HF	SS, KIA 8/28/69
Johanningmeier, Luther	1LT	HF, CO A	BS(v), PH
Johannsson, Thorgrimur	SFC	RT NH	
Johnson, Joe P.	SP4	RT OH	
Johnson, Roy Lee	MSG	HF	BS, AM, PH
Johnston, Emery Peter	CPT	HF	
Jones, Dannie L.	CPT	S1, S4	
Jones, Henry H.	SGM	command section	
Jones-Shorten, James Henry, Jr.	SGT	RT IL, RT HI	BS(2), AM(2), AC, PH
Jones, Jerry L.	MSG	HF, CO B	
Jones, William A.	SGT		
Kainu, Donald W.	SFC	HF	SS
Karr, Donald G.	SSG	HF, CO B	
Kauhaahaa, David K., Jr.	SFC	ST IA	

Name	Rank	Base Assignment or Team(s)	Awards/Notes
Kedenburg, John James*	SP5	RT NV	MOH, PH, KIA 6/14/68
Keefer, Barry A.	SFC	RT NV	
Keever, Steven Harold	SGT	RT IL, RT CO, RT NH (STP), RT OH (STP), RT IL	AC(v)
Keller, Alan Nelson	SP4	RT CO, RT IA	
Kemp, Henry O.	SFC	HF, CO A	SS, PH
Kendall, William Leroy	SFC	S3, RT CO, RT FL, RT HI, RT IL, RT DW	BS(v), PH, AM, AC(v)
Kennedy, Curtis G.	SSG	RT CO	
Kephart, Timothy Gene	SP4	B-50, ST IA	
Kerns, Charles Nathan	SFC	ST OH, ST IA	BS
Keyton, Cecil William	SP4	HF	AC(v)
Kieff, Nelson Richard	SP4	RT NY	
King, Wilbert	SSG	ST DW	
Kinnear, Michael E.	SGT	RT HI, RT NY	AC(2)
Kinnebrew, James M.	1LT	S1	
Kirschbaum, David Paul	SFC	RT KY, RT ME	
Kline, Robert M.	SSG	RT NY, ST CO	BS(2)
Kotin, Robert Charles	SSG	ST OH, HF	BS(v)
Kramps, Henry A.	SGT	S4	PH
Krupa, Frederick	1LT	HF	BS(v)
Krutina, Danny Lamir	SGT	RT DE, RT HI	
Kuhl, Clifford Rees	CPT	HF, CO A	
Kuropas, Michael V.	SSG	RT OH, RT VT	SS
Kuster, Steven Mark*	SP5	HF	KIA 2/7/70
Ladner, Milton Ray	SSG	S4	
Lake, Michael T.	SFC	RT (team unknown)	
Lambert, Lindon G.	SP4	HF	AC(v)
Lamphier, Roy D.	CPL	HF, CO A	SS
Lavoie, Richard A.	SFC	RT NM	SS, PH, BS(v), AC(v)
Lee, Jerry	SFC	RT CO	
Legate, Richard Edward*	CPT	S3, ST CO, HF	KIA 3/25/67
Leites, Robert Lawrence	MAJ	command section	
Lenchner, David Allen*	1LT	ST AZ	KIA 12/15/68
Lensch, William J.	SGT	MS	PH
Lesesne, Edward Rutledge	CPT	HF	PH(3), SS(2), BS(3), AM(v), Legion of Merit

Name	Rank	Base Assignment or Team(s)	Awards/Notes
Leverington, Leon I.	SSG	ST ME	
Lewis, Frederick Harry*	SFC	ST OR	PH, KIA 10/18/66
Lewis, James D.	SP4	RT CA	PH
Lewis, Samuel	PFC	HF	BS(v)
Lindblom, Daniel L.	SGT	RT KY (STP), RT NH	AC(2)
Lishchynsky, George*	SFC	RT NH	KIA 7/5/70
Lively, James R.	SFC	ST NV	
Livingston, Thomas Oliver, Jr.	SSG	ST HI	BS(v)
Loe, Roger T.	SSG	RT ME, RT VT	
Lois, Thomas R.	SGT	RT IA	
Long, Clarence W., Jr.	SGT	RT TX, MS	
Long, Joseph G.	SGT	HF	
Longaker, Francis E.	1LT	HF, CO A	AC(2), BS(v), PH
Longstreath, Dallas Richard, III	SSG	RT FL, RT IL	
Loucks, Bryon Waldo	SGT	MS, RT OH, RT WA	BS(v), PH(2)
Louk, Thomas Neil	SFC	S1, HF	
Love, Anthony Hoyt	SGT	ST IA, RT CA	BS(v)
Lund, William D.	SSG	HF	
Lynch, Timothy M.	SP4	RT OH	BS(v)
Machata, Rudolph George*	SSG	RT CA	AC(v), PH, KIA 5/23/69
Mack, Dennis Allen	SGT	RT NY, ST CA, RT CO	BS(v), PH
MacNamara, Edwin Joseph*	CPT	ST NV	PH, KIA 7/3/66
Madison, James C.	CPT	RT MT	
Magana, Jesus N.	SP5		
Magdaleno, Gilbert O.	SSG	HF	
Maggio, Louis J.	SFC	MS	SS, PH
Malott, Charles R.	SFC	RT AZ	
Mane, Siaki	SSG	S4	
Manning, Robert L.	CPT	HF, company CO	
Mansfield, William R.	1LT	S3, HF	BS(v)
Marple, Robert L.	SFC	ST NV, ST AZ	
Marquis, Roland Gilbert	SSG	HF	SS, PH
Marshall, James G.	SP5	RT HI	BS(v)
Martin, John A.	CPT	S1	AC(v)
Martin, Linwood Dwight*	SFC	RT DW, RT HI	DSC, KIA 3/68
Mason, Frank A.	SSG	HF, RT IL	BS(v)
Massey, Tyrone	SFC	HF	PH, AC(v)
Mathews, William K.	SSG	ST IL	BS(v)

Name	Rank	Base Assignment or Team(s)	Awards/Notes
Matteson, Marvin E.	SFC	HF, RT CA	
Maxwell, John N., Jr.	CPT	S3	
Maxwell, Patrick G.	SFC	HF	
May, Geoffrey L.	SP4	RT NM, RT WY	
McCammond, Joseph Edward	SGT	RT AK, RT WY, HF	AC(v), PH, AM, BS
McCarley, Eugene Crouch, Jr.	CPT	RT FL, HF, S4	BS(3), SS, PH(3)
McCaslin, Wesley E.	SFC	RT NM, RT NY	
McCauley, James P.	1LT	HF	AC(v)
McClain, Jerry	SSG	MS	
McClaren, Alan L.	SGT	HF	
McClaskey, John R.	1LT	HF	
McClelland, Barre R.	CPT	S3, HF	AC(v), BS(v)
McClure, William L.	SFC	RT NH	
McCormick, Clarence William	SFC	RT NY	
McDade, Silas White	SFC	RT AR	PH
McDonald, Alvin E.	SSG	RT NY, RT IL	
McElroy, William E., III	1LT	HF	BS(v), PH
McFall, Michael M.	1LT	HF, RT HI	BS(v)
McGeary, John L.	SFC	RT OR	
McGiffert, Peter H.	SGT	HF	SS
McGirt, John Britton, II	SSG	MS	
McGlon, James Richard	SSG	RT NV, RT NY	
McGuire, Patrick H. T.	CPT	S2	
McKinnear, Mike	SGT	RT NH	
McLemore, Thomas	SSG	RT NV, RT TX	
McLeod, Willie, Jr.	SFC	RT NV, RT CO	BS(v), PH
McNeil, Richard J.	SSG	HF	
McWilliams, James B.	CPT	S1	
Meadows, Richard J.	MSG	ST IA, ST OH	SS
Medina, Francisco	SSG	RT NM	
Mejia, Angel F.	MAJ	DET XO	
Melton, Walter Wayne	SFC	RT HI	BS(v), PH
Merkerson, Willie, Jr.	CPT	RT IL (STP), HF	BS(v), PH
Messer, Joseph	SFC	RT WY, RT CA, RT AZ	PH
Mickelson, Michael L.	SP4	RT SC, RT WY	BS(v)
Mighill, John B.	SGT	HF	
Miles, Grady F.	SFC	HF	

Name	Rank	Base Assignment or Team(s)	Awards/Notes
Miller, Franklin Douglas	SGT	RT VT, RT NH	MOH, SS, BS(2), PH(6)
Miller, John L.	MSG	RT (team unknown)	AC(v)
Miller, Michael A.	CPT	HF	PH
Miller, Sherman Gayle	SGT	RT ME	AC(v)
Milligan, Donald T.	SSG	HF, CO B	AC(v)
Mims, Bernie L.	SSG	RT OH	AC(v), PH(2)
Minnihan, Terry I.	SGT	HF	PH, AC(v)
Minton, Denver G.	SFC	HF	PH
Mitchell, Robert, Jr.	1LT	S1	
Mohs, Robert Paul	SSG	RT CA, RT IA, RT HI	BS(v)
Mongold, Richard Dean	SP4	S4	
Monsees, Stephen K.	CPT	HF, company CO	
Montague, Percell P.	SSG	MS	
Montgomery, Larry R.	SGT	RT WA, RT ME	AC(v), BS(v), PH
Montgomery, Marvin G.	SSG	RT ME	SS
Moore, James R.	SFC	RT HI	
Morales, Edgar J.	SFC	RT NH	
Moreland, Ernest	SSG	RT NV, RT SC	
Morgan, Reuben W.	SSG	HF	PH
Morgan, William L.	SSG	RT IL	
Morris, Joseph F.	SGT	RT FL, RT HI	AC(2)
Morris, Paul Leo, Jr.	SGT	RT TX	AC
Morzenti, John T.	CPT	S1	
Moss, Lynn M.	SGT	RT OH, RT IL	BS(v)
Moss, Richard S.	CPT	HF	AC(v), PH
Motsett, Charles Bourke	1LT	HF, CO A	CIB, BS(v), AC(v), AM(v), PH(2)
Moya, Juan Sr.	SSG	S4	
Murdock, Reed O.	SSG	HF	BS(v), PH
Myers, Robert C.	1LT	S4	
Myrick, Clinton D.	SFC	RT (team unknown)	
Nance, Luke, Jr.	SFC	MS	BS(2), PH
Neese, Paul J.	SSG	HF	
Newkirk, James O.	SSG	S4	
Newman, Clifford M.	SSG	RT FL	AC(v), BS (2)
Niespodziany, Casmir*	1LT	HF	PH, KIA 2/3/67
Noe, Richard L.	SP5	RT IA, HF	BS(v)

Name	Rank	Base Assignment or Team(s)	Awards/Notes
Norris, Richard T.	SFC	ST IL	PH
North, Bruce A.	SSG	ST TX	
Novy, Jan	SFC	RT (team unknown)	PH
Nowack, Richard Rei	SP4	RT NV, RT OH, RT TX	AC(v)
Nubby, Billy Austin	SFC	ST IL, RT NH	BS(v)
Nuqui, Roland	SSG	B-50	SM
Oakland, Gerald Duane	1LT	HF, CO A	
O'Connor, Michael J.	SFC	RT CO	PH
O'Daniel, Lloyd Gerald	SFC	RT CA, HF, RT HI	PH, SS
O'Grady, Thomas L.	SP4		
Ortiz, Luis	SFC	HF, CO B	
Pace, Roy O.	MSG		
Page, Clarence A.	SSG	HF	
Page, Edward J.	MAJ	S4	PH
Palk, Virgil D.	SGT	RT IL	
Palmer, Wilson W.	SFC	S4	
Parker, Carlos	SSG	RT SC	AC(v), BS(v)
Parnar, Joseph Francis	SGT	MS, RT FL (STP), RT TX, RT OH	PH(3), SM, SS, BS(v)
Parrott, Thomas I.	SGT	S4	PH
Patten, Thomas D.	SGT		
Patton, Shephard Hamner	SFC	RT CO	
Payne, Willard, Jr.	SGT	ST FL	
Peck, Michael E.	1LT	HF, CO B	
Perkins, Stuart Lee	CPT	HF, ST OH	
Peterson, John P.	SGT	RT TX, RT WY	
Phillippi, Ralph W.	SSG	HF	
Phillips, Joe W.	SFC	RT TX	
Phipps, Billie F.	SP4	HF	PH
Pike, Walter A.	SP4	HF, CO A	AC(v)
Pimental, Richard	SSG	CO A, HF	AC(v)
Pinn, Lionel Francis	MSG	HF	
Plakans, Juris	CPT	S3	
Plank, Gerald Allan	SGT	RT (team unknown)	SS(2), BS(3), PH
Plaster, John Louis	SSG	RT NM, RT IL, RT CA, RT WA, RT HI	BS(v), AC(v)
Pool, Jerry Lynn*	1LT	RT PA, HF	PH, KIA 3/24/70
Pointon, George E.	SGT	RT IL	

Name	Rank	Base Assignment or Team(s)	Awards/Notes
Poole, Paul Frederick	SSG	RT AK, RT CO	PH(2), AC(v), BS(v), SS
Pope, Reinald Levillian	SSG	RT HI, RT IA, RT DW	PH
Potter, Michael R.	SSG	RT DE, RT NY	AC(v)
Potter, Paul D.*	1LT	S4	PH, KIA 8/23/66
Powers, James P.	SFC	S2	
Presley, Eulis Austin	SFC	RT WA	AC(v)
Price, Robert W.	1LT	HF, CO C	SS, PH
Probart, John Lyman	SFC	MS	SS, PH
Pulliam, Lonnie S.	SGT	RT HI, RT SC	AC(v), PH
Pyle, Frank W.	SFC	ST NV	
Quiroz, Joe H.	SP4	RT WA	BS(v)
Ramiro, Daniel	SGT		
Ramsey, Donald M.	SGT	RT IA, RT HI	
Rasmussen, Delbert Taylor	1LT	B-50	BS
Ray, Richard	Seal	RT OH	
Raybon, John D.	SP4	HF, CO A	
Redman, Darrell Dean	1LT	RT AZ	BS(v)
Reid, James A.	SSG	S4	PH
Reinitzer, Julius	SFC	S2	
Reno, Ralph Joseph*	MSG	ST NV	KIA 7/3/67
Reynolds, Richard M.	CPT	S1	
Rhea, Randolph Vincent*	SP5	S4, RT AK	SS, KIA 11/12/69
Rice, Phillip William	SSG	RT NM, RT IA	AC(v), BS
Richards, Frank L.	SGT	ST HI	
Ringland, James G., III	MSG	HF	
Ripanti, James Lawrence*	1LT	ST HI, RT NH, RT NY	BS(v), KIA 3/14/69
Roche, Stephen Maurice	SP5	RT NV, HF	PH, BS(v)
Rockholt, Eugene	MSG	S1	
Rodd, Ralph Rayburn	SGT	RT FL, RT CO	PH
Roe, Franklin D.	SSG	HF	PH
Rogers, Rafael	SGT	ST IA	
Ross, Donald E.	SFC	S3	AM(v)
Ross, Kenneth J.	SFC	RT NY	AC(v)
Ruane, Francis E.	SP5	S1, ST OH	AC(v)
Ruff, Newman Cooper	SFC	RT AZ	
Ryan, Terrance W.	CPT	S1	
Saal, Harvey W.	SGT	ST KY	PH

Name	Rank	Base Assignment or Team(s)	Awards/Notes
Sample, Joe Deal	SFC	HF, CO A	SS
Sanford, Samuel Spencer	MAJ	HF	BS(v)
Saunders, Alexander P.	SP4	RT (team unknown)	BS(v), PH
Savage, Earl E.	SSG	HF	BS(v), PH
Scherdin, Robert Francis*	SSG	RT (team unknown)	PH, KIA 12/29/68
Scherer, William J.	SSG	HF, CO B	BS(v), PH
Schuler, Hartmut	1LT	HF	BS
Schrack, Donald E.	MSG	HF	BS(v)
Sciriaev, Lolly	CPT	HF	
Scott, Mike J.	SFC	RT (team unknown)	
Scully, Robert L.	SFC	HF	SS
Seaburg, Gary L.	SFC	ST ME	AC
Seibel, Michael S.	SGT	RT CO	AC(v), PH
Sellers, Jesse, Jr.	SFC	HF	
Seper, Robert Earl	SGT	HF, CO B	BS(v)
Sepi, Robert J.	SP4	RT NV	
Setser, Harry Andrew	SFC	HF	BS(v)
Seymour, Leo Earl*	SFC	RT TX	KIA 7/67
Shadduck, Gary Nolan	Seal	RT CO	
Sheppard, James R.	CPT	RT CA	
Sheppard, Michael M.	SGT	RT MT	SS(2), PH
Sheridan, Robert M.	1LT	HF	SS
Sheridan, Thomas A.	SSG	RT NV	
Sherman, Roger P.	1LT	HF	
Shreve, Joseph Linwood, Jr.*	1LT	HF	SS, KIA 5/1/68
Shriver, Jerry Michael	SFC	B-50	BS(7), PH, SS(2), AM, AC(3), MIA 4/24/69
Simenton, Richard M.	MSG	command section	
Simmons, Billy Joe*	SGT	RT NM	BS(v), PH, KIA 1/29/69
Simmons, Robert L.	SFC	HF, CO A	AC(2)
Simon, Daniel J.	SSG	HF, CO B	BS(v)
Simpson, James A.	SFC	HF	
Sincere, Clyde Joseph, Jr.	MAJ	S3	AC(v)
Sisler, George Kenton*	1LT	S2, HF	MOH, KIA 2/7/67
Slade, Raymond R.	SFC	RT (team unknown)	SS
Slagel, Frank Edwards	SSG	HF, CO A	AC(v)

Name	Rank	Base Assignment or Team(s)	Awards/Notes
Smith, David C.	MAJ	FOB XO	PH
Smith, Richard Lee*	MSG	RT (team unknown)	KIA 7/5/70
Smith, Louis, Jr.	SFC	RT DK, RT NV, HF	
Snowden, Ben David*	SFC	B-50	SS, PH, KIA 6/16/67
Snyder, Kenneth O.	1LT	RT IA, RT NV	AC(3), PH
Spencer, William E.	SFC	ST IL	
Spilberg, Paul S.	1LT	HF	BS, PH
Spinaio, Edward W.	1LT	RT (team unknown)	
Spitler, Lawrence Allen	SGT	RT OH (STP), RT WY, RT FL	
Spoon, Terrance J.	SP4	RT HI	BS(v), AC(v)
Sprouse, Robert L.	SFC	HF, ST KY, RT NY, RT WY	SS, BS(v)
Spurgeon, William O.	SSG	RT MN, ST TX	SS
Stamm, Garry Dean	SFC	HF, CO A	
Stanton, Thomas W.	CPT	HF, RT OH, RT NY (STP)	AC(v)
Stapleton, Paul E.	SFC	HF, CO A	AC(v)
Steele, Dean Lee	SSG	MS	
Steele, Don P.	SFC	RT FL	BS(v)
Steel, Raymond P.	SSG	RT (team unknown)	PH
Stephens, Larry Alan*	SP5	RT NM	BS(v), PH, KIA 1/29/69
Ster, Daniel J.	SSG	RT HI, RT NV	BS(2)
Stevens, Lowell Wesley	SFC	HF	SS, BS(v)
Stevenson, Jim	SFC	RT IL	
Stewart, Jimmie Lee	SFC	HF, RT DK	
St. Laurent, Andre Joseph	SFC	HF	BS(v), PH
St. Martin, John M., Jr.	SGT	RT SC, RT AZ, RT NY	AC(v), PH
Stratton, Rupert Gale	SGM	command section	
Straussfogel, Adolph B.	SFC	HF, CO B	BS(v), PH
Strong, George W.	SFC	ST KY	
Stubbs, William Wentworth*	SSG	RT CA	AC(v), KIA 10/20/69
Sullivan, Carl L.	SGT	HF	PH
Sunrich, William Alexander	MSG	S4	
Swain, Lee Robert	1LT	HF, CO C	SS, PH
Sylvester, William A.	CPT	HF	

Name	Rank	Base Assignment or Team(s)	Awards/Notes
Tandy, Peter E.	SFC	HF, CO A	BS(v), PH(2), AC(v)
Tanguileg, Thomas L.	SP5	RT AZ	
Tanona, Chester P.	MSG	ST IA	
Taylor, Floyd D.	SGT	RT WY, HF	BS
Taylor, Howard K., Jr.	SP4	RT NV	BS(v), AM(2), PH
Taylor, James T.	MSG	MS	
Taylor, John C.	SFC	RT TX	
Teeter, Roger L.	SGT	RT HI	BS(2)
Telles, Serafin, Jr.	SSG	RT AZ	
Templin, Thomas Richard	SP4	RT NM	AM(v)
Terrell, Neil W.	CPT	HF	
Terry, Thomas L.*	SFC	RT NY	KIA 7/67
Thomas, Richard L.	MSG	MS	
Thomas, William A.	SGM	command staff	
Thompson, Benjamin E.	SFC	RT IL	
Thompson, Jack D.	MSG	HF	
Tibbit, William T.	SGT	B-50	PH
Tilley, Leonard William	SFC	ST IA	DSC, SS, BS, AM, AC(v), PH
Todd, Allen Earl	SSG	S1	
Todd, Forrest Earl	MSG	HF	SS, BS, AM, PH(2)
Todd, Richard A.	CPT	HF	PH
Tomczak, Thomas James*	SGT	HF	PH, KIA 7/23/68
Torres, Raul	SFC	ST OH	
Townsend, George M., Jr.	MSG	HF	PH, ACM
Trafford, Mel Lloyd	SSG	RT CO, RT HI	ACM
Tramel, James Michael	SP5	ST IL	BS(2), PH
Trujillo, Arthur Hiram	CPT	S2	
Trzos, Frederick	CPT	DET XO	
Turnbull, Turner Bershears, III	SGT	RT NH, RT NV	
Turcotte, Gilbert R.	SGT	HF	
Uemura, Glenn M.	SGT	RT HI, RT TX	BS(v), AC(v)
Urrutia, George H.	SGM	command section	
Vanderzwalm, Richard Louis	SSG	RT FL	BS
Van Dine, Peter W. H.	CPT	S4	
Vandiver, Joe Allen	SSG	RT DE	BS(v)
Van Hall, Robert L., Jr.	SSG	HF, RT TX, RT IA, RT DW	BS(2), SS, PH

Name	Rank	Base Assignment or Team(s)	Awards/Notes
Vasey, Lewis G.	SFC	ST KY	
Vermillion, Michael J.	SGT	RT CA	PH
Vessels, Charles Robert*	SFC	HF, ST IA	KIA 10/18/66
Vigil, Donaciano Manuel	SFC	HF	PH
Villanueva, Vincent	MSG	RT NV	
Vojanec, Karel	SFC	S2	
Wagner, Dan, Jr.	SFC	B-50, RT OH	SS
Wagner, Jackie D.	SSG	HF, CO B	
Walker, Albert C.	SSG	RT IA	BS(v)
Walker, Charles C.	SFC	RT SC	AM(v)
Walker, Joe Johnnie	SSG	RT CA, RT DE	BS(2), PH(2)
Wallace, Robert A.	SSG	HF, CO A	AC(v), PH(2), BS(v)
Wallace, Stephen C.	CPT	RT WA	BS(2), PH
Walthour, Samuel W., Jr.*	SP4	trainee	BS(v), KIA 7/30/69
Walton, John T.	SP4	MS	SS, PH
Wands, Robert E.	MAJ	command section	
Ward, Vernon J. B., Jr.	1LT	HF, CO B	BS(v), PH(2)
Wareing, Gerald Trust	MSG	ST IA	BS
Warrick, James R.	SFC	RT OH, HF	
Warrum, David L.	SSG	RT ME, RT OH	
Waskovich, Thomas R., Jr.	1LT	HF, RT WY, RT SC	AC(v)
Watson, William S.	SFC	HF, RT NV	BS, AC(v)
Watters, James L., Jr.	SGT	RT NY	AC(v)
Webb, Clarence Harold	SFC	ST TX	SS, BS(3)
Weber, Mark E.	1LT	S4	
Weems, Ronald Henry	SSG	RT IL	BS(v), PH
Wells, Charles J.	SFC	S4	
Wells, Ronald B.	SSG	RT AR, RT CO	PH
Whalen, Harry David, Jr.	SGM	RT MT	BS(v)
Whelan, Joseph Vincent*	CPT	HF, CO B	SS, KIA 10/25/69
Whitaker, James P.	CPT	HF, CO C	PH
White, Charles Edward	SFC	MS, HF	MIA 1/29/68
White, Kent B.	SGT	ST IL	
White, Larry Melton	SSG	RT ME, RT HI	AC(v), BS(3), AM(2), PH
Whittaker, Harold Charles*	SSG	B-50	PH, KIA 2/29/68

Name	Rank	Base Assignment or Team(s)	Awards/Notes
Wieprecht, David Earl	SGT	RT VT	
Willey, Lawrence Robert	SSG	RT TX	
Wilcox, Charles E., Jr.	SFC	RT NY	BS(v)
Williams, Bill Fred, Jr.	SP4	HF	KIA 1/8/69
Williams, Gene H.	SGT	ST DW, ST HI	
Williams, Harry A.	PFC	ST IA, ST DE, RT CA	AC(2)
Williams, Larry David	SGT	RT AR, ST CO	SS, BS(v)
Williams, Warren Wellde	CPT	HF, DET XO, RT ME (STP)	BS(v), AC(v), AM(v)
Willis, Billy D.	SSG	RT TX	
Wilson, Burrell Andrew, Jr.	SFC	ST TX, ST NY, ST NV (STP)	
Wilson, Harlan James	SSG	RT NY	
Wilson, Merritt H., Jr.	CPT	HF, S1	
Wilson, Michael P.	SP4	RT AZ	PH
Wilson, Peter Joe*	SFC	RT IL, RT NY	SS, KIA 10/19/70
Wolcoff, Edward	SSG	RT NY	BS(v)
Wolfson, Mark	SP5	RT NV	PH
Wood, James M.	SP5	HF	
Wood, Larry Lee	SP4	RT KY	
Woodworth, Jason T.	SSG	ST IA	
Woody, Richard W.	SSG	RT CA	BS(v), PH
Worley, Morris Gene	SFC	HF, RT NV	DSC, PH
Worthley, Kenneth Wayne*	SSG	RT CO (STP), RT FL	SS, KIA 8/26/69
Yancey, John M., Jr.	SSG	RT CA, RT DW, RT HI	SS, PH, BS(v)
Yeats, Johnny Dayrell	CPL	RT NM	
Young, James L.	1LT	HF, RT DE, RT HI, RT AZ	PH
Young, Ronald E.	1LT	HF	
Zabitosky, Fred William	SSG	ST ME	BS(v), MOH, PH
Zadick, Adrian	SGT	HF	
Zukav, Gary S.	1LT	HF	
Zumbrun, James Henry*	SGT	RT FL	BS(v), KIA 1/10/70

GLOSSARY OF TERMS

A-1	Skyraider ground attack aircraft
A-4	Skyhawk carrier-borne strike aircraft
AA	antiaircraft
ACE	Aviation Company Escort
AH-1	Cobra attack helicopter
AHC	assault helicopter company
AO	area of operations
Arc Light	code name for a B-52 strike
ARVN	Army of the Republic of Vietnam (South Vietnamese Army)
BDA	bomb damage assessment
Bright Light	SOG code name for a cross-border rescue/reaction team
C&C	command and control
CAR-15	Colt Commando (carbine version of the M16)
CBU	cluster bomb units
CCC	Command and Control Central (Kontum); previously known as FOB-2
CCN	Command and Control North (Da Nang)
CCS	Command and Control South (Ban Me Thuot); previously known as FOB-5
CH-47	Chinook cargo/transport helicopter
Claymore	M18A1, a directional antipersonnel mine
CO	commanding officer
Cobra	a military helicopter used as a gun platform ("gunship")
Covey	a USAF detachment flying radio coverage, usually in either a Cessna 0-1 Bird Dog, a Cessna 0-2 Skymaster, or a North American OV-10 Bronco aircraft
Daniel Boone	original SOG code name for Cambodian cross-border operations (code name changed to Salem House in 1969)

DCO	deputy commanding officer
DEROS	date eligible for return from overseas
DMZ	Demilitarized Zone, the dividing line between North and South Vietnam established at the 1954 Geneva Convention
DSC	Distinguished Service Cross
E&E	escape and evasion
Eldest Son	code name for SOG black propaganda project involving the insertion of booby-trapped Chinese ammunition into NVA stockpiles
FAC	forward air controller
fast movers	jet aircraft
FNG	fucking new guy
FOB	forward operating base, a permanent SOG camp that housed and trained Special Forces and mercenary troops
FOB-1	located at Kham Duc from 1965 to mid-1966, Khe Sanh during 1966, and Phu Bai from July 1966 to 1968
FOB-2	located at Kontum from May 1966 into 1970 (became known as CCC in October 1968)
FOB-3	located at Khe Sanh from late 1966 to June 30, 1968; at Mai Loc from July 1 to November 1968
FOB-4	located at Marble Mountain, Da Nang from November 1967 to November 1968
FOB-5	located at Ban Me Thout from November 1967 to November 1968 (became known as CCS in October 1968)
FOB-6	located at Ho Ngoc Tao from 1967 to November 1968
Green Hornets	code name for a U.S. Air Force Huey unit, the 20th Special Operations Squadron
gunships	heavily armed Hueys or Cobras
HALO	high altitude, low opening (an airborne insertion technique)
Hanson rig	developed by FOB-2 One Zero Bill Hanson to replace the McGuire rig as a safer, more reliable method of emergency helo extraction
Hatchet Force	code name for a SOG element specializing in search and destroy missions. Two or more Hatchet Force platoons combined were referred to as a Hornet Force or Havoc Force. Platoon-size elements comprised four to five Green Berets and thirty to forty-two indigenous troops.
HE	high explosive
Hornet Force	two or more platoons of Hatchet Force troops; also called Havoc Force
Huey	nickname for Bell UH-1 Iroquois turbine-powered transport helicopter
JCS	Joint Chiefs of Staff
JPRC	Joint Personnel Recovery Center

Kingbee	code name for Sikorsky H-34 helicopters of South Vietnamese Air Force (VNAF) that supported SOG's cross-border operations
Klick	military slang for kilometer
Leghorn	SOG radio relay and signal intercept site situated atop a pinnacle in southern Laos. Originally known to SOG operators as Heavy Drop.
LLRP	long-range reconnaissance patrol
LZ	landing zone, a site for a helicopter to land
MACV-SOG	Military Assistance Command, Vietnam–Studies and Observations Group
McGuire rig	swing seat attached to a rope, lowered from a helicopter hovering over the treetops used for emergency extractions; also known as "strings"
medevac	medical evacuation of injured personnel
Mike Force	abbreviation of Mobile Strike Force; a reaction team, usually larger than a company
Montagnards	indigenous South Vietnamese hill tribesmen recruited as mercenaries for SOG and other Special Forces units
MOS	military occupational specialty
NCO	noncommissioned officer
Nickel Steel	code name for operations straddling the western DMZ
Nungs	South Vietnamese ethnic group of Chinese origin
NVA	North Vietnamese Army
OCS	Officer Candidate School
OLAA	Operating Location Alpha Alpha
OP	operational plan
OSS	Office of Strategic Services
PAVN	People's Army of Vietnam
PLF	People's Liberation Armed Forces of South Vietnam
Prairie Fire	SOG code name for Laotian operations area; replaced Shining Brass in 1967. Also used as a code word to request emergency extraction of a recon team. A "prairie fire" emergency had priority to divert all available aircraft to assist.
RON	remain overnight
RPG	rocket-propelled grenade
RT	recon team. A SOG recon team generally consisted of three U.S. Special Forces men and nine indigenous members (usually Nungs or Montagnards).
RTO	radio-telephone operator. The RTO was the recon team's "commo man," usually the one-two position on the team.
Salem House	SOG code name for Cambodian operations (replaced Daniel Boone code name in 1969)
SAR	search and rescue
SEAL	Sea, Air, and Land (Navy special operators)

SF	Special Forces
SFG	Special Forces Group
SFTG	Special Forces Training Group
Shining Brass	SOG code name for Laotian operations area (see Prairie Fire)
SLAM mission	Search, locate, annihilate, monitor. Comprising a full company-sized element of Hatchet Force platoons.
Slick	Huey helicopters that carried cargo or personnel. "Slick ships" only carried defensive armament.
SOG	Studies and Observations Group, the Vietnam War's covert special warfare unit
SOW	Special Operations Wing
SPAF	Sneaky Pete Air Force
ST	spike team; later referred to as recon teams (see RT)
STABO	abbreviation of stabilized body; emergency extraction harness/rig used to lift a man from a field location via helicopter.
TA	target area
TAC air	tactical air support
TDY	temporary duty
TF2AE	Task Force 2 Advisory Element
The Bra	target area in southern Laos, so-named because Highway 96 crossed a double bend in the Dak Xou River at this point resembling a woman's brassiere when viewed from the air.
TOC	tactical operations center
VC	Vietcong (indigenous South Vietnamese Communist guerilras)
VR	visual reconnaissance
XO	executive officer
Yard	American slang for Montagnard tribesmen

Enlisted Ranks:
Private first class (E-3 pay grade)
Corporal (E-4 pay grade)
Specialist fourth class (E-4 pay grade)
Specialist fifth class (E-5 pay grade)
Sergeant (E-5 pay grade)
Staff sergeant (E-6 pay grade)
Sergeant first class (E-7 pay grade)
First sergeant (E-8 pay grade)
Master sergeant (E-8 pay grade)
Sergeant major (E-9 pay grade)
Command sergeant major (E-9 pay grade)

NCO	noncommissioned officer
one-zero (1-0)	code name for SOG recon team leader
one-one (1-1)	code name for SOG recon team assistant team leader
one-two (1-2)	code name for SOG recon team radio operator

NOTES

PROLOGUE

1. "Courage under Fire," Recon Series, Medal of Honor profile of Colonel Robert L. Howard. Pritzker Military Library. Robert L. Howard videotaped interview with Ed Tracy, July 27, 2006.
2. Medal of Honor citations for Robert Lewis Howard, Fred William Zabitosky, Franklin Douglas Miller, John James Kedenburg, and George Kenton Sisler.

CHAPTER 1. THE KONTUM THIRTY-THREE

1. Alan Keller, personal interview, October 22, 2014, telephone interview, September 29, 2016, and subsequent follow-up correspondence.
2. Lieutenant Colonel Call's nickname was noted by Sergeant Major Alfred C. Friend, USA (Ret.), a SOG veteran, in his article posted on the MACV-SOG website, "And We Were Once Brave and Foolish (SOG Reconnaissance Missions, Getting Started, B-53, SOG Training)," http://macvsog.cc/a_walk_in_the_indian's_camp.htm.
3. Kelley, *Tales from the Teamhouse*, 93–95.
4. Unless otherwise noted, dialogue from this chapter is derived from author's interviews with Alan Keller, Stephen Goth, and Jimmie Stewart.
5. Sergeant Major Jimmie L. Stewart, USA (Ret.), email correspondence/interview, August 20–21, 2014.
6. Captain Leonard W. Tilley, USA (Ret.), telephone interviews, August 24, 2014, and September 26, 2016, and personal interview, March 27, 2015.

CHAPTER 2. SPIKE TEAMS AND HATCHET FORCE

1. Singlaub, *Hazardous Duty*, 290–92.
2. Schultz, "MACV-SOG Oral History," 2.

3. Plaster, *SOG: A Photo History*, 45.
4. Plaster, *SOG: The Secret Wars*, 30.
5. Ibid., 44.
6. Singlaub, *Hazardous Duty*, 25–46.
7. Ibid., 292–93.
8. Ibid., 294–97.
9. Ibid., 297.
10. Greco, *Running Recon*, 41–42.
11. Plaster, *SOG: The Secret Wars*, 64.
12. Schultz, "MACV-SOG Oral History," 11.
13. Ibid., 1–2.
14. Colonel John H. Crerar, USA (Ret.), telephone interview, January 9, 2015.
15. Schultz, "MACV-SOG Oral History," 7.
16. Plaster, *SOG: The Secret Wars*, 30–31.
17. Greco, *Running Recon*, 238.
18. Plaster, *SOG: A Photo History*, 88, 105.
19. Thomas O. Livingston, personal interview, October 22, 2014, telephone interviews, October 10, 2016, and January 5, 2017, and January 1, 2015, email correspondence.
20. Hoe, *The Quiet Professional*, 13–25. See also P. King, "Meadows Early Life as 'Junior' From Virginia," biographical sketch (April 10, 2000), accessed February 22, 2015, http://sfalx.com/h_meadows_early_life.htm (site discontinued).
21. Hoe, *The Quiet Professional*, 26–56.
22. Ibid., 72–83.
23. Ibid., 85–86.
24. Ibid., 87–88.
25. Thach himself rendered his name as Nguyen Kim Thach and noted in correspondence ca. 2005 that his nickname while serving with Dick Meadows' ST Ohio was "Teddy." However, the SOG veterans interviewed for this book recalled him as simply "Ted." For a scanned facsimile of Thach's letter, see http://macvsog.cc/vernon_t_mock.htm.
26. Sergeant Major Jan Borek, USA (Ret.), telephone interview, August 23, 2014.
27. Plaster, *SOG: The Secret Wars*, 64.
28. "Operation of Command and Control Detachment Center," Frank Jaks interview from SOG Documentation Study, B-O-183.
29. Ibid., 183–84.
30. Ibid., 184.
31. Kelley, *Tales from the Teamhouse*, 98.
32. Ibid., 99–100.
33. Schultz, "MACV-SOG Oral History," 8.
34. Hardy, *MACV SOG: Team History, Vol I*, 203–11.
35. Greco, *Running Recon*, 118.

36. Kelley, *Tales from the Teamhouse*, 263–64.
37. Ibid., 265.

CHAPTER 3. THE MONTAGNARD CAMP AND "OLD BLUE"

1. Plaster, *SOG: The Secret Wars*, 44.
2. Morris G. Worley, telephone interview, August 2, 2014, and email correspondence.
3. Ibid.
4. Master Sergeant James F. Hetrick, USA (Ret.), personal interview, October 22, 2014.
5. Gillespie, *Black Ops, Vietnam*, 79.
6. "Reno, Ralph Joseph," Task Force Omega, accessed August 25, 2014, http://taskforceomegainc.org/r362.html; Plaster, *SOG: The Secret Wars*, 51.
7. Master Sergeant James F. Hetrick, USA (Ret.), telephone interview, October 22, 2014, and Sergeant Major James D. Bath, USA (Ret.), telephone interviews, August 23 and December 24, 2014, are the sources of quotes in the section that follows.
8. Sergeant First Class Lloyd Adams, USA (Ret.), telephone interview, August 24, 2014, and personal interview, October 19, 2016.
9. Plaster, *SOG: The Secret Wars*, 51–54.
10. Sergeant Major James D. Bath, USA (Ret.), telephone interviews, August 23 and December 24, 2014, are the primary source for this narrative. See also "Old Blue," Ballad of America, American Heritage Music, accessed March 6, 2018, www.balladofamerica.com/music/indexes/songs/oldblue/index.htm.

CHAPTER 4. PRISONER SNATCHING AND WIRETAPS

1. Hoe, *The Quiet Professional*, 2–3, 88.
2. Sergeant Major Jan Borek, USA (Ret.), telephone interview, August 23, 2014.
3. Captain Billy Joe Anthony, USA (Ret.), telephone interviews, August 20 and August 23, 2014, and April 15, 2015.
4. Plaster, *SOG: The Secret Wars*, 58.
5. Colonel John H. Crerar, USA (Ret.), telephone interview, January 9, 2015.
6. Alan Keller, personal interview, October 22, 2014, telephone interview, September 29, 2016, and subsequent follow-up correspondence.
7. Sergeant Major James D. Bath, USA (Ret.), telephone interviews, August 23 and December 24, 2014.
8. Alan Keller, personal interview, October 22, 2014, telephone interview, September 29, 2016, and subsequent follow-up correspondence.
9. "Echevarria, Raymond Louis," Task Force Omega, accessed February 25, 2015, www.taskforceomegainc.org/e005.html.

10. Plaster, *SOG: The Secret Wars*, 57, is the source of quotes from this paragraph.
11. "Echevarria, Raymond Louis," Task Force Omega, accessed February 25, 2015, www.taskforceomegainc.org/e005.html.
12. Plaster, *SOG: The Secret Wars*, 57.
13. Alan Keller, personal interview, October 22, 2014, telephone interview, September 29, 2016, and subsequent follow-up correspondence.
14. Plaster, *SOG: A Photo History*, 170.
15. Alan Keller, personal interview, October 22, 2014, telephone interview, September 29, 2016, and subsequent follow-up correspondence.
16. Stephen M. Goth, personal interview, October 22, 2014, telephone interview, September 29, 2016, and subsequent email correspondence.
17. Gillespie, *Black Ops, Vietnam*, 80.
18. Ibid., 80–81.
19. October 13, 1966, roster for FOB-2, courtesy of Steve Goth.
20. Hardy, *MACV SOG: Team History, Vol. II*, 193.

CHAPTER 5. CODE NAME BRIGHT LIGHT

1. Veith, *Code-Name Bright Light*, 123.
2. Plaster, *SOG: The Secret Wars*, 63; Veith, *Code-Name Bright Light*, 123.
3. Captain Billy Joe Anthony, USA (Ret.), telephone interviews, August 20 and 23, 2014, and April 15, 2015.
4. Hoe, *The Quiet Professional*, 92.
5. Veith, *Code-Name Bright Light*, 124–25.
6. Galdorisi and Phillips, *Leave No Man Behind*, 281; "Indian Gal 69 Down, October 16, 1966. Steve Caple's Account of the Mission," Raunchy Redskins, accessed March 1, 2015, http://raunchyredskins.us/operations/IG%2069%20 Down/IG_69_Down_Caple.htm.
7. U.S. MACV-SOG, *Annex M, Command History*, 1966; Hoe, *The Quiet Professional*, 92. Hoe says the team went in under fire. Anthony says this is false. The Caple account says nothing of gunfire going in.
8. Billy Joe Anthony, USA (Ret.), telephone interviews, August 20 and 23, 2014, and April 15, 2015. are the primary source for quotes from him in this narrative.
9. Galdorisi and Phillips, *Leave No Man Behind*, 281.
10. Hoe, *The Quiet Professional*, 93.
11. Galdorisi and Phillips, *Leave No Man Behind*, 282; Hoe, *The Quiet Professional*, 94.
12. Hoe, *The Quiet Professional*, 89–90.
13. Singlaub, *Hazardous Duty*, 308; Hoe, *The Quiet Professional*, 94–96.
14. Plaster, *SOG: The Secret Wars*, 63.
15. Veith, *Code-Name Bright Light*, xiii–xiv.

16. Ibid., xiv–xvii.
17. Ibid., xviii.
18. Ibid., xviii.
19. Ibid., xx.
20. Ibid., xxi.
21. Ibid., 137.
22. Plaster, *SOG: The Secret Wars*, 66.
23. Veith, *Code-Name Bright Light*, 137–38.
24. Plaster, *SOG: The Secret Wars*, 66.
25. Veith, *Code-Name Bright Light*, 138.
26. Plaster, *SOG: The Secret Wars*, 66.
27. PACAF Evasion and Recovery Report No. 76., Part I: Robert E. Kline, Vietnam Center and Archive, Texas Tech University.
28. Veith, *Code-Name Bright Light*, 137–38.
29. Ibid., 138.
30. Plaster, *SOG: The Secret Wars*, 67.
31. Veith, *Code-Name Bright Light*, 139.
32. PACAF Evasion and Recovery Report No. 76, Part I: Robert E. Kline, Vietnam Center and Archive, Texas Tech University. Frank Jaks was promised a Silver Star for the rescue by Colonel Aderholt, but it was not forthcoming.

CHAPTER 6. HEAVY DROP
1. Braden, "Mercenary Job Wanted," 23–26.
2. Murphy, *Medal of Honor Heroes*, 75.
3. Major Hartmut Schuler, USA (Ret.), telephone interviews, January 3 and February 28, 2015.
4. Ibid.
5. Sergeant Major James D. Bath, USA (Ret.), telephone interviews, August 23 and December 24, 2014.
6. Ibid.
7. Plaster, *SOG: The Secret Wars*, 77; Greco, *Running Recon*, 44.
8. Plaster, *SOG: The Secret Wars*, 77.
9. Ibid., 77.
10. Sergeant Major James D. Bath, USA (Ret.), telephone interviews, August 23 and December 24, 2014.
11. Singlaub, *Hazardous Duty*, 314.
12. Sergeant Major James D. Bath, USA (Ret.), telephone interviews, August 23 and December 24, 2014.
13. Singlaub, *Hazardous Duty*, 315, is the source for quotations in this section.
14. Stephen M. Goth, personal interview, October 22, 2014, telephone interview, September 29, 2016, and subsequent email correspondence.

15. Plaster, *Secret Commandos*, 114.
16. Morris G. Worley, telephone interview, August 2, 2014, and subsequent email correspondence are the key sources for this section.
17. Morris Worley Distinguished Service Cross citation; Plaster, *Secret Commandos*, 115.
18. Plaster, *Secret Commandos*, 115.
19. Morris Worley Distinguished Service Cross citation.
20. Morris G. Worley, telephone interview, August 2, 2014, and subsequent email correspondence.
21. Plaster, *Secret Commandos*, 116.
22. Morris G. Worley, telephone interview, August 2, 2014, and subsequent email correspondence.
23. Plaster, *Secret Commandos*, 7–8, 116.
24. Gillespie, *Black Ops, Vietnam*, 112.
25. Ibid.
26. Plaster, *SOG: The Secret Wars*, 78.
27. Sergeant Major James D. Bath, USA (Ret.), telephone interviews, August 23 and December 24, 2014.
28. Major Hartmut Schuler, USA (Ret.), telephone interviews, January 3 and February 28, 2015, are the source for the dialogue that follows.
29. Official statement of Specialist Fifth Class James M. Wood. Also included in this recounting of the George K. Sisler Medal of Honor mission are statements transcribed from Sergeant William Ernst, Sergeant First Class Leonard Tilley, Paul Darcy, and Frank Jaks.
30. Major Frank Jaks, USA (Ret.), telephone interview, October 26, 2016.
31. Official statement of Paul M. Darcy; Sergeant William J. Ernst Jr. official statement.
32. Some Internet accounts mistakenly list Sergeant First Class James Henry Duncan as being part of the Tilley/Sisler mission. Tilley says that only three other Americans were part of his mission, and Medal of Honor paperwork for Sisler supports this. Further research by the author found that Duncan was wounded in action on February 2 by small-arms fire and died in a Vietnam hospital on February 7, the date of death likely the source of later confusion.
33. Captain Leonard W. Tilley, USA (Ret.), telephone interviews, August 24, 2014, and September 26, 2016, and personal interview, October 19, 2016.
34. Ibid.
35. Gillespie, *Black Ops, Vietnam*, 113.
36. Colonel Edward R. Lesesne, USA (Ret.), email correspondence, August 13–21, 2014, is the source for the dialogue in this section.

CHAPTER 7. DANIEL BOONE AND BOB HOWARD

1. Plaster, *SOG: The Secret Wars*, 74.
2. Singlaub, *Hazardous Duty*, 309–10.
3. Plaster, *SOG: A Photo History*, 233.
4. Billy D. Evans Distinguished Service Cross citation, September 17, 1967.
5. Alan Keller, personal interview, October 22, 2014, telephone interview, September 29, 2016, and subsequent follow-up correspondence.
6. Captain Billy Joe Anthony, USA (Ret.), telephone interviews, August 20 and August 23, 2014, and April 15, 2015.
7. Joseph Messer, telephone interview, December 16, 2014.
8. Sergeant Major James D. Bath, USA (Ret.), telephone interviews, August 23 and December 24, 2014.
9. Prairie Fire/Nickel Steel Weekly Report, March 23–29, 1967.
10. Sergeant Major James D. Bath, USA (Ret.), telephone interviews, August 23 and December 24, 2014, are the source for the section that follows.
11. Major Frank Jaks, USA (Ret.), telephone interview, October 26, 2016, is the source for quotes in this narrative.
12. Gillespie, *Black Ops, Vietnam*, 113–14.
13. Plaster, "Wreaking Havoc One Round at a Time," 68–72.
14. Plaster, *SOG: The Secret Wars*, 128.
15. Ibid., 96–97.
16. Singlaub, *Hazardous Duty*, 310; Prados, *The Blood Road*, 153, 197–98.
17. "Cross Border Operations in Cambodia," U.S. Military Assistance Command, Vietnam, Studies and Observations Group, Documentation Study, July 10, 1970, E-9, E-15.
18. Plaster, *SOG: The Secret Wars*, 98–99.
19. Ibid., 101.
20. "Case Files Regarding MIAs Staff Sergeant Leo E. Seymour and SFC William Boyle." Eyewitness statements of Warrant Officer 1 Gregory Waltz, Sergeant First Class Joe W. Phillips, Staff Sergeant Charles W. Henderson Jr., Nguyen Cong-Cu, Tran Van Nga, Tran Van Tim, Duong Van Bac, and Tran Duc An.
21. Ibid.
22. Lawrence A. Spitler, telephone interview, August 30, 2014, and personal interview, October 19, 2016.
23. "Courage under Fire," profile of Colonel Robert L. Howard.
24. Ibid.
25. Bissell, "Special Forces Operation Complex Becomes Howard Hall."
26. Willbanks, *America's Heroes*, 148; "Courage under Fire," profile of Colonel Robert L. Howard.
27. Lieutenant Colonel Eugene C. McCarley, USA (Ret.), telephone interview, March 16, 2015.
28. Plaster, *SOG: The Secret Wars*, 204.

CHAPTER 8. INTO THE HORNET'S NEST

1. DeLong, "Fred Zabitosky," 8; DeLong, *War Heroes*, 71–72.
2. Master Sergeant Jose D. Ortiz, "History of the NCO: SSG Fred W. Zabitosky," 3.
3. Graves, "SLAM Mission into Laos," 48; DeLong, *War Heroes*, 77–80.
4. Albert M. Erickson, telephone interviews, August 10 and 16, 2014.
5. "1967 Gladiators—Cougars," 57th Assault Helicopter Co., accessed August 28, 2015, www.57thahc.com/unit_history.php?year=1967.
6. Richard J. Griffith, telephone interview, January 6, 2015, and personal interview, August 29, 2015.
7. Williams, "Stand Up, Hook Up," chap. 1, 4.
8. Ibid.
9. Ibid., chap. 1, 10.
10. Ibid.
11. Plaster, *SOG: The Secret Wars*, 204.
12. Sergeant First Class Larry D. Williams, USA (Ret.), telephone interview, January 16, 2014.
13. Colonel Johnnie B. Gilreath Jr., USA (Ret.), telephone interviews, January 15 and 16, 2015.
14. Robert Lewis Howard Distinguished Service Cross citation.
15. Gillespie, *Black Ops Vietnam*, 123–26, 142.
16. Tim Schaaf, notes on Spike Team Asp MIAs, accessed July 14, 2015, http://www.macvsog.cc/1968.htm. "Sgt Paul Herman Villarosa," Find a Grave, accessed August 31, 2015, http://www.findagrave.com/cgi-binfg.cgi ?page=gr&GRid=104401222.
17. Plaster, *SOG: The Secret Wars*, 88–89.
18. Plaster, *SOG: The Secret Wars*, 89.
19. Fred Zabitosky and William Boyle Bronze Star citations.

CHAPTER 9. "THEY WON'T TAKE US ALIVE"

1. "White, Charles Edward," P.O.W. Network, accessed June 29, 2015, http://www.pownetwork.org/bios/w/w019.htm.
2. Prados, *The Blood Road*, 248.
3. Williams, "Stand Up, Hook Up" chap. 15, 1–7; Bronze Star citation for Captain Warren W. Williams, General Order No. 1235, July 17, 1968.
4. Prados, *The Blood Road*, 248.
5. Willbanks, *The Tet Offensive*, 54–55.
6. This body of water is known as the Xe Xou River in Laos. SOG veteran Joe Parnar informed the author that the Vietnamese call it the Dak Xou, and it was therefore referred to as the Dak Xou by SOG operators.
7. Plaster, *SOG: The Secret Wars*, 197.
8. DeLong, "Fred Zabitosky," 54–55. See also DeLong, *War Heroes*, 82.

9. Graves, "SLAM Mission into Laos," 48.
10. DeLong, *War Heroes*, 83.
11. Plaster, *SOG: The Secret Wars*, 198.
12. Graves, "SLAM Mission into Laos," 48.
13. Plaster, *SOG: The Secret Wars*, 199.
14. Graves, "SLAM Mission into Laos," 49.
15. Ibid.
16. Plaster, *SOG: The Secret Wars*, 200.
17. Graves, "SLAM Mission into Laos," 49.
18. Ibid., 49.
19. Henry Heberlein, personal interview, August 29, 2015.
20. Graves, "SLAM Mission into Laos," 49–50.

CHAPTER 10. NEW FACES AT FOB-2

1. Unless otherwise noted, quoted dialogue in this section is derived from author's personal interview with Sergeant Louis J. DeSeta, October 21–22, 2014.
2. Thomas P. Cunningham, telephone interview, February 6, 2015.
3. Dumont and Parnar, comps., "Tribute Notebook," Louis DeSeta, "John Kedenburg . . . Things I Think About."
4. Pinn, *Hear the Bugles Calling*, 17, 20, 58.
5. Ibid., 11, 165–71.
6. Ibid., 172–79.
7. Ibid., 182.
8. Gerald E. Denison, telephone interview, January 14, 2015, and subsequent email correspondence, and Robert Kotin, telephone interview, January 1, 2015, are the sources of quotes in the section that follows.
9. Dahling, "Life before Special Forces," Memories of a Special Forces Soldier, accessed January 10, 2015, http://tadahling.tripod.com/memoriesofaspecial-forcessoldier/id7.html on.
10. Kelley, *Tales from the Teamhouse*, 173–74, is the source for Webb's quotes that follow.
11. Kelley, *Tales from the Teamhouse*, 176–78; additional details of the mission from website http://www.macvsog.cc/1968.htm, accessed January 11, 2015.
12. Kelley, *Tales from the Teamhouse*, 173–78.
13. Ibid., 178.
14. David H. Hunt, personal interviews, July 24 and December 5, 2014.
15. Unless otherwise noted, all dialogue from this section on Hunt is derived from author's interviews with George Wilson Hunt, July 24–25 and August 14, 2014.

CHAPTER 11. "THE BIG ONE"

1. Plaster, *SOG: The Secret Wars*, 151.
2. Master Sergeant Sherman R. Batman, USA (Ret.), telephone interview, March 28, 2015.
3. Unless otherwise noted, dialogue from this chapter is derived from author's personal interviews with George Wilson Hunt, July 24–25, August 14 and 18, 2014, and January 25, 2015.
4. Dumont and Parnar, *SOG Medic*, 23–25.
5. Ibid.
6. Sergeant Stephen M. Roche, USA (Ret.), telephone interview, March 26, 2015.
7. Dumont and Parnar, comps., "Tribute Notebook," Stephen Roche 1968 statement.
8. Roche unpublished memoirs (unpaginated), courtesy of Robert Dumont.
9. Ibid.
10. Sergeant Stephen M. Roche, USA (Ret.), telephone interview, March 26, 2015.
11. Dumont and Parnar, comps., "Tribute Notebook," Stephen Roche 1968 statement.
12. Dumont and Parnar, comps., "Tribute Notebook," Gerald Denison 1968 statement.
13. Dumont and Parnar, comps., "Tribute Notebook," Stephen Roche 1968 statement.
14. Roche memoirs.
15. Dumont and Parnar, comps., "Tribute Notebook," Gerald Denison 1968 statement; Uwe Linder DFC citation.
16. Special thanks to Joe Parnar and Steve Roche for clarifying details of the extraction of RT Nevada. This extraction would have included the body of one indigenous trooper who had been killed in action.
17. By the best sleuth work of Joe Parnar, it appears that one of these two indigenous men Winder pulled out was either Dic or Vu, the South Vietnamese members who had first opened fire on the NVA. Covey Rider Denison's report does not state how many men Winder pulled out.
18. Dumont and Parnar, *SOG Medic*, 31.
19. Dumont and Parnar, comps., "Tribute Notebook," William T. Snow and Stephen Roche statements of 1968. Snow says his vantage point did not offer him the chance to see Kedenburg give up his rig, as was written by an intelligence officer as part of the eyewitness statements.
20. Denison to Dumont, April 16, 2005, email, and Denison to Parnar email, July 29, 2008; Denison to author, July 11, 2015, email.
21. Denison to Robert Dumont account, April 16, 2005, email.
22. Dumont and Parnar, *SOG Medic*, 32.
23. Ibid., 33.
24. Roche memoirs.

25. Gerald E. Denison, telephone interview, March 17, 2015.
26. The Air Medal with "V" device was awarded to eight 189th AHC men for their actions on June 13: SP4 Gilbert Carrillo, SP4 Frederick C. Herres, SP4 James T. Huskisson, SP4 Grover D. Ledbetter, SP4 Charles P. Skidmore, SP4 William Snow, PVT Lawrence E. Morrison, and SP5 Lawrence J. Wilcousky. The four co-pilots that day—1LT Stanley B. Albrecht, 1LT Daniel L. Bradshaw, WO1 William C. Haller, and CW2 Robert N. Steinbrunn—each received an Air Medal for heroism.
27. It should be noted that some accounts have this Bright Light inserting the same evening to search for Kedenburg, but Gerald Denison, Joe Parnar, Bryon Loucks, and Tom Cunningham all were clear in the saying that the Bright Light took place early the next morning.
28. Sherman R. Batman, "Kedenburg Britelite," accessed March 25, 2015, http://www.macvsog.cc/britelight-kedenburg.htm.
29. Bryon Loucks, "Memories of John Kedenburg–1968, FOB-2 Kontum, Republic of Vietnam."
30. James M. Tramel, telephone interview, March 27, 2015.
31. Bryon W. Loucks, "John Kedenburg Bright Light Mission: 14 June 1968." Personal account of events written July 6, 2002, with input from Gerald E. Denison, Sherman R. Batman, and James McGlon.
32. Bryon W. Loucks, telephone interview, March 3, 2015.
33. Gerald Denison email to Loucks, April 2, 2002.
34. Dumont and Parnar, comps., "Tribute Notebook," Cunningham letter to John Merritt, July 12, 1968.
35. Roche memoirs.
36. Donald L. Smith narrative, Recommendation for Award for Achievement or Service, John J. Kedenburg Medal of Honor Award Case File.
37. John J. Kedenburg Medal of Honor citation.
38. Dumont and Parnar, *SOG Medic*, 34.
39. Ibid., 34.
40. Ibid., 34.

CHAPTER 12. ENTER THE GLADIATOR

1. Plaster, *SOG: The Secret Wars*, 191.
2. Dumont and Parnar, *SOG Medic*, 37.
3. Ibid., 37.
4. Gene Williams, "Spike Team Delaware at FOB 4, Kontum, Apr 68–Nov 68," accessed May 2015, http://www.macvsog.cc/spike_team_delaware.htm.
5. Master Sergeant Sherman R. Batman, telephone interview, March 28, 2015.
6. George Wilson Hunt, personal interviews, July 24–25, August 14 and 18, 2014, and January 25, 2015.

7. Ibid.
8. Dumont and Parnar, *SOG Medic*, 40–41.
9. Unless otherwise noted, dialogue in this section is derived from author's telephone interviews with W. Wayne Melton, November 12 and December 5, 2014.
10. Unless otherwise noted, dialogue and quotes in this section are derived from author's telephone interviews with Sergeant Major Joe J. Walker, USA (Ret.), December 7, 2014, January 19 and July 19, 2015.
11. Thomas P. Cunningham, telephone interviews, February 6 and April 15, 2015.
12. Plaster, *Secret Commandos*, 53; Plaster, *SOG: The Secret Wars*, 142.
13. Plaster, *Secret Commandos*, 52.

CHAPTER 13. THE WOLFKEIL BRIGHT LIGHT

1. "Col Wayne Benjamin Wolfkeil," Find a Grave, accessed March 3, 2015, http://www.findagrave.com/cgi-bin/fg.cgi?page=gr&GRid=60743439. See also Hobson, *Vietnam Air Losses*, 158.
2. Staff Sergeant Gerald E. Denison statement of action for August 9, 1968.
3. Gerald E. Denison, telephone interview, March 17, 2015, and subsequent email exchanges.
4. Major Richard L. Vanderzwalm, USA (Ret.), telephone interview, March 19, 2015.
5. Major Wayne Wolfkeil incident report, courtesy of David Wolfkeil.
6. Unless otherwise noted, dialogue in this chapter is derived from author's interviews with George Wilson Hunt, July 24–25, August 14 and 18, 2014, and January 25, 2015.
7. Thomas P. Cunningham, telephone interviews, February 6 and April 15, 2015; Michael Bingo, telephone interview, October 21, 2014.
8. Master Sergeant Daniel W. Janc, USA (Ret.), telephone interviews, August 3 and November 26, 2017.
9. Lieutenant Colonel Linden L. Gill, USAF (Ret.), telephone interview, March 10, 2015.

CHAPTER 14. DOUBLE TAKE

1. Dumont and Parnar, *SOG Medic*, 69.
2. Ibid., 74.
3. Master Sergeant Daniel W. Janc, USA (Ret.), telephone interviews, August 3 and November 26, 2017.
4. Unless otherwise noted, dialogue from this chapter is derived from author's personal interviews with George Wilson Hunt, July 24–25, August 14 and 18, 2014, and January 25, 2015.

5. Ibid.
6. Dumont and Parnar, *SOG Medic*, 76.
7. U.S. MACV-SOG, *Annex F, Command History*, 1968, F-II-1-16.

CHAPTER 15. CLOSE SHAVES
1. Unless otherwise noted, dialogue in this section is derived from author's personal interview with Sergeant William R. Bumps, USA (Ret.), October 21, 2014.
2. Kendall diary, courtesy of William L. Kendall.
3. Ibid., October 3, 1968.
4. Master Sergeant William H. Hanson, USA (Ret.), telephone interview, March 22, 2015.
5. Dialogue for this section is derived from author's telephone interview with Gerald E. Denison, March 17, 2015, and subsequent email exchanges.
6. Dialogue for this section is derived from author's interviews with Master Sergeant William H. Hanson, USA (Ret.), March 22, 2015, and First Sergeant William L. Kendall, USA (Ret.), March 22, 2015.
7. Kendall diary, October 8–14, 1968.
8. George Wilson Hunt, personal interviews, July 24–25, August 14 and 18, 2014, and January 25, 2015.
9. Halberstadt, *War Stories*, 20.
10. Ibid., 21.
11. Ibid., 22. It should be noted that in his account, Mack never mentions Bryant being separated from his team. He instead talks about hunting for a black soldier believed to have been cooperating with the NVA. Hunt and others believe it was Mack's RT Colorado that Bryant had been detached from as the result of a grenade attack.
12. W. Wayne Melton, telephone interviews, November 12 and December 5, 2014.
13. Dialogue from this section is largely derived from author's interviews with George Wilson Hunt, July 24–25, August 14 and 18, 2014, and January 25, 2015.
14. William J. Groves, personal interview, October 21, 2014.
15. Craig Collier, unpublished memoirs, 22.
16. Ibid., 22.
17. Ibid., 23.
18. Dumont and Parnar, *SOG Medic*, 80.
19. Ibid., 80.

CHAPTER 16. SLAM VII

1. Plaster, *SOG: A Photo History*, 187–88.
2. Ibid., 189–90.
3. Greco, *Kontum: Command and Control*, 28.
4. Sergeant Major Joe J. Walker, USA (Ret.), telephone interviews, December 7, 2014, January 19 and July 19, 2015.
5. Dumont and Parnar, *SOG Medic*, 83.
6. Lee R. Swain, personal interviews, October 21, 2014, and October 19, 2016, and email correspondence.
7. Ibid.
8. Kendall diary notes for November 14, 1968. In his diary, Kendall lists Bryant as "Bryon" and Brents, of course, had already been medevaced before this attack in the early morning of November 14.
9. "In Memory of Specialist Fourth Class William Michael Copley," accessed February 1, 2015, http://www.macvsog.cc/william_copley.htm; Roger T. Loe sworn statement, November 29, 1971, courtesy of Robert Dumont.
10. Unless otherwise noted, the Loe sworn statement is the key source for quotes used in this section.
11. "Birchim, James Douglas 'Jim,'" Task Force Omega, accessed February 3, 2015, http://taskforceomegainc.org/b387.html.
12. Loe statement.
13. Dumont and Parnar, *SOG Medic*, 84.
14. Ibid., 84.
15. Sergeant Major Joe J. Walker, USA (Ret.), telephone interviews, December 7, 2014, January 19 and July 19, 2015.
16. Master Sergeant Lloyd G. O'Daniel, USA (Ret.), telephone interview, August 6, 2014.
17. Alan F. Farrell, telephone interview, April 2, 2015.
18. Dumont and Parnar, *SOG Medic*, 85.
19. Kendall diary notes for November 14, 1968.
20. Ibid., 85.
21. Collier, unpublished memoirs, 15.
22. Ibid., 16.
23. "Birchim, James Douglas 'Jim,'" Belletire statement, Task Force Omega, accessed February 3, 2015, http://taskforceomegainc.org/b387.html.
24. Dumont and Parnar, *SOG Medic*, 85.
25. Ibid., 86.
26. Collier, unpublished memoirs, 16.
27. Kendall diary notes for November 17, 1968.
28. Lieutenant Colonel Thomas W. Jaeger, telephone interview, January 31, 2015.
29. Dumont and Parnar, *SOG Medic*, 86.
30. Ibid., 88.

31. Ibid., 89.
32. Lee R. Swain, personal interviews, October 21, 2014, and October 19, 2016, and email correspondence.
33. Lieutenant Colonel Thomas W. Jaeger, telephone interview, January 31, 2015.
34. Dumont and Parnar, *SOG Medic*, 90.
35. Lieutenant Colonel Thomas W. Jaeger, telephone interview, January 31, 2015.
36. Collier, unpublished memoirs, 1–2.
37. Hoeck, "Shot Down," 2–3.
38. Ibid., 4.
39. Ibid., 5.
40. Dumont and Parnar, *SOG Medic*, 92.
41. Hoeck, "Shot Down," 5–7.
42. Dumont and Parnar, *SOG Medic*, 93.
43. Ibid., 94.
44. Ibid., 94.
45. Robert M. Gron, telephone interview, April 4, 2015.
46. Sergeant Stephen M. Roche, USA (Ret.), telephone interview, March 26, 2015.
47. Alan F. Farrell, telephone interview, April 2, 2015.
48. Collier, unpublished memoirs, 21.
49. Dumont and Parnar, *SOG Medic*, 94.
50. Gillespie, *Black Ops, Vietnam*, 144.
51. U.S. MACV-SOG, *Annex F, Command History,* 1968, F-II-1–13.
52. Plaster, *SOG: The Secret Wars*, 208.

CHAPTER 17. HOWARD'S MIRACLE MISSION

1. Hardy, *MACV SOG: Team History, Vol. 7*, 100.
2. Unless otherwise noted, dialogue in this section is derived from author's personal interview with Philip M. Brown, October 21, 2014.
3. Dumont and Parnar, *SOG Medic*, 97; Hardy, *MACV SOG: Team History, Vol. VII*, 100.
4. Hardy, *MACV SOG: Team History, Vol. VII*, 100.
5. Cosmas, *MACV: The Joint Command*, 280–81.
6. Lieutenant Colonel Eugene C. McCarley, telephone interview, March 16, 2015, is the source for quotes in this paragraph.
7. Command Sergeant Major Larry M. White, USA (Ret.), telephone interview, September 20, 2016.
8. Plaster, *SOG: The Secret Wars*, 213.
9. Air Medal citation for Robert E. Clough, April 8, 1969.
10. Bronze Star medal citation for Larry M. White, April 7, 1969; Air Medal citation for Robert L. Howard, April 7, 1969.
11. Plaster, *Secret Commandos*, 249.

12. Dumont and Parnar, *SOG Medic*, 98–102.

13. Plaster, *Secret Commandos*, 5–37.

14. Ibid., 38.

15. Ibid., 38.

16. "Scherdin, Robert Francis," Task Force Omega, accessed September 12, 2016, www.taskforceomegainc.org/s005.html.

17. Plaster, *Secret Commandos*, 39.

18. "Courage under Fire," Robert L. Howard.

19. Ibid.

20. Ibid.

21. Mission details from Robert L. Howard Medal of Honor recommendations, December 9, 1969. Further details of the mission come from Robert Gron and Jerome Griffin eyewitness statements and author's telephone interview with Robert M. Gron, April 4, 2015.

22. Robert M. Gron, telephone interview, April 4, 2015.

23. "Courage under Fire," Robert L. Howard.

24. Ibid.

25. Ibid.

26. Plaster, *SOG: The Secret Wars*, 215.

27. "Courage under Fire," Robert L. Howard.

28. Robert M. Gron, telephone interview, April 4, 2015.

29. "Courage under Fire," Robert L. Howard.

30. Robert M. Gron, telephone interview, April 4, 2015.

31. "Courage under Fire," Robert L. Howard.

32. Eyewitness statements of Captain Lyle R. Hill and First Lieutenant Terry L. Hamric regarding the actions of Robert L. Howard on December 30, 1968.

33. Unless otherwise noted, dialogue in this section is based on telephone interview with Robert M. Gron, April 4, 2015.

CHAPTER 18. "NO LONGER A CHERRY"

1. Dumont and Parnar, *SOG Medic*, 106.

2. Ibid., 108–10.

3. Ibid., 112–16.

4. Colonel Roy W. Bahr, USA (Ret.), telephone interview, January 3, 2017, and email correspondence.

5. Plaster, *Secret Commandos*, 131.

6. Thomas R. Templin, telephone interview, August 8, 2014.

7. Plaster, *Secret Commandos*, 43.

8. Ibid., 44–47.

9. Gillespie, *Black Ops, Vietnam*, 167.

10. Ibid., 182.

11. Plaster, *SOG: The Secret Wars*, 239.
12. Gillespie, *Black Ops, Vietnam*, 173–74.
13. Plaster, *Secret Commandos*, 57–60.
14. Ibid., 62–72.
15. Graves, "SLAM Mission into Laos," 50.
16. DeLong, "Fred Zabitosky."
17. Dumont and Parnar, *SOG Medic*, 125.
18. Plaster, *Secret Commandos*, 84–86.
19. Ibid., 87.
20. Dumont and Parnar, "Operation Nightcap," 4.
21. Kyle S. Dean, unpublished mission notes, "Mission One," 1.
22. Ibid.
23. Ibid., 2–3.
24. Dumont and Parnar, "Operation Nightcap," 18.

CHAPTER 19. "IN THE FRYING PAN"

1. Pinn, *Hear the Bugles Calling*, 189–93.
2. Greco, *Running Recon*, 41.
3. Ibid., 50.
4. Ibid., 50.
5. Kyle S. Dean, unpublished mission notes, "Mission 2," 1.
6. Sergeant Major Joe J. Walker, USA (Ret.), telephone interviews, December 7, 2014, January 19 and July 19, 2015.
7. Plaster, *Secret Commandos*, 121–22; Greco, *Running Recon*, 49.
8. Plaster, *Secret Commandos*, 123.
9. William W. Stubbs Army Commendation Medal for Heroism citation, Number 1241, August 5, 1969.
10. Walker Bronze Star citation No. 1243 and Stubbs Army Commendation citation No. 1241, August 5, 1969.
11. Plaster, *Secret Commandos*, 121–31.
12. Ibid., 134.
13. Plaster, *SOG: The Secret Wars*, 155–56; Plaster, *Secret Commandos*, 134.
14. David L. Gilmer, telephone interview, September 13, 2016.
15. Major Clyde J. Sincere, personal interviews, October 22, 2014, and October 20, 2016.
16. Greco, *Running Recon*, 45.
17. Plaster, *Secret Commandos*, 143–44.
18. Ibid., 145.
19. Phillip W. Rice, unpublished mission notes, "Mission Number Three: The Perfect Mission," 1.
20. Ibid., 1–2.

21. Ibid., 2.
22. Greco, *Running Recon*, 198.
23. Ibid., 199.
24. Unless otherwise noted, dialogue in this section is derived from personal interview with Lieutenant Colonel Edward Wolcoff, USA (Ret.), October 22, 2014, and telephone interview, January 22, 2015.
25. Captain Donald F. Fulton, USAF (Ret.), personal interview, October 22, 2014.
26. Plaster, *SOG: The Secret Wars*, 152.

CHAPTER 20. CASUALTIES OF THE FALL

1. Plaster, *SOG: The Secret Wars*, 132.
2. Ibid., 133.
3. Ibid., 134.
4. Ibid., 240–41.
5. Ibid., 242–43. Silver Star citation for Sergeant Kenneth W. Worthley, October 14, 1969; Bronze Star citation for SP4 Dale H. Hanson, September 9, 1969.
6. Plaster, *Secret Commandos*, 154–55.
7. Lieutenant Colonel Edward Wolcoff, USA (Ret.), personal interview, October 22, 2014, and telephone interviews, January 22, 2015, and March 12, 2018.
8. Ibid.
9. Ibid.
10. Plaster, *Secret Commandos*, 166.
11. Ibid., 166–67.
12. Ibid., 168–69; "Stubbs, William Wentworth," P.O.W. Network, www.pownet work.org/bios/s/s154.htm, accessed September 4, 2016.
13. Frank L. Belletire, telephone interview, August 17, 2014.
14. Plaster, *Secret Commandos*, 170–72.
15. Ibid., 187.
16. Miller, *Reflections*, 16, 33.
17. Ibid., 47–49, 52–63; Franklin D. Miller commendation citations.
18. Miller, *Reflections*, 106–12.
19. Ibid., 85–88.
20. Ibid., 75–80.
21. U.S. MACV-SOG, *Annex F, Command History,* 1969, F-II-8–13.
22. Ibid., F-III-4-A-1–2; F-III-4-B-2; F-X-22–23.
23. Plaster, *Secret Commandos*, 180.
24. Ibid., 172, 181.
25. Ibid., 183–84.

CHAPTER 21. "VIETNAMESE ALAMO"

1. Ross, "Prairie Fire, Prairie Fire!," 24.
2. Plaster, *SOG: A Photo History*, 316; Miller, *Reflections*, 145.
3. Miller, *Reflections*, 147. Miller uses pseudonyms for Brown and Blyth in his book and lists point man Hyuk as "Dang."
4. Details of the Hatchet Force operation derived from personal interview with medic Andrew M. Brown, October 21–22, 2014, and telephone interview, January 29, 2017, and personal interview with Hatchet Force team member Charles Terry Cadenbach, October 20, 2016. Brown verifies that Colonel Abt was across the fence that day, a highly unorthodox move for an FOB commander.
5. Miller, *Reflections*, 151–53.
6. Edward L. Blyth, telephone interviews, December 22, 2014, March 29, 2016, and March 19, 2017.
7. Miller, *Reflections*, 156.
8. Franklin D. Miller, "Summary of Recommendations for Award of Medal of Honor"; Miller, *Reflections*, 159.
9. Silver Star Recommendation for Decoration Narrative Description for First Lieutenant Donald L. Engebretsen, January 5, 1970.
10. Miller, *Reflections*, 162–63.
11. Ross, "Prairie Fire, Prairie Fire!," 24–26. Sergeant Ster's one-one, Jim Jones-Shorten, was making his first SOG mission across the fence. He later related that his team was forced to blow down a tree in order to be extracted by choppers under fire. He was literally hanging onto the Huey's skid at three hundred feet before the slick's door gunner helped pull him on board. "That was a close call," Jones-Shorten said.
12. Miller, *Reflections*, 167.
13. Andrew M. Brown, personal interviews, October 21–22, 2014, and telephone interview, January 29, 2017.
14. Ibid.
15. Miller, *Reflections*, 168–69.
16. Ross, "Prairie Fire, Prairie Fire!," 27.
17. Coryell, "Army Hero."
18. Miller, *Reflections*, 171; 1LT Jerry L. Pool statement.
19. First Lieutenant Engebretsen Silver Star recommendation narrative description.
20. In his eyewitness statement to Doug Miller's Medal of Honor paperwork, Robert Brown lists the time of extraction as 1340.
21. Ross, "Prairie Fire, Prairie Fire!," 27.
22. Miller, *Reflections*, 172.
23. Ibid., 172–73.

24. Captain Donald Engebretsen, personal interviews, October 22, 2014, and October 20, 2016, email correspondence, March 7, 2015, and telephone interview, December 20, 2016.

EPILOGUE.
1. "Franklin D. Miller," Wikipedia, last modified December 22, 2017, 21:09, https://en.wikipedia.org/w/index.php?title=Franklin_DMiller&oldid=816662244.
2. Collier and Del Calzo, *Medal of Honor*, 11–14.
3. "Courage under Fire," Robert L. Howard.
4. Ibid.
5. Ibid.
6. Ibid.
7. Bottoms, "MoH Recipient."
8. Ibid.
9. Miller, *Reflections*, 189–91.
10. "Courage under Fire," Robert L. Howard, part 3.
11. Ibid., part 2.
12. Citation for the Presidential Unit Citation given to the Studies and Observations Group, United States Military Assistance Command, Vietnam, 24 January 1964 to 30 April 1972.
13. Cunningham, "SOG Awarded Presidential Unit Citation."

BIBLIOGRAPHY

INTERVIEWS CONDUCTED BY THE AUTHOR

Adams, Sergeant First Class Lloyd. Telephone interview, August 24, 2014, and personal interview, October 19, 2016.

Anthony, Billy Joe, Captain, USA (Ret.). Telephone interviews, August 20 and 23, 2014, and April 15, 2015.

Bahr, Roy W., Colonel, USA (Ret.). Telephone interview, January 3, 2017, and email correspondence.

Barnatowicz, John, USA (Ret.). Personal interview, October 19, 2016.

Bath, James D., Sergeant Major, USA (Ret.). Telephone interviews, August 23 and December 24, 2014.

Batman, Sherman R., Master Sergeant, USA (Ret.). Telephone interview, March 28, 2015.

Belletire, Frank L. Telephone interview, August 17, 2014.

Billings, John. 57th AHC. Personal interview, August 29, 2015.

Bingo, Michael J. Jr., Sergeant Major, USA (Ret.). Personal interview, October 21, 2014.

Birchim, Barbara. Telephone interview, October 19, 2016, and email correspondence.

Blyth, Edward L. Telephone interviews, December 22, 2014, March 29, 2016, and March 19, 2017.

Borek, Jan, Sergeant Major, USA (Ret.). Telephone interview, August 23, 2014.

Brown, Andrew M. Personal interview, October 21–22, 2014, and telephone interview, January 29, 2017.

Brown, Philip M. Personal interview, October 21, 2014.

Buckland, Michael P., Sergeant, USA (Ret.). Telephone interview, April 3, 2015, and subsequent email correspondence.

Bumps, William R., Sergeant, USA (Ret.). Personal interview, October 21, 2014.

Cadenbach, Charles Terry, Master Sergeant, USA (Ret.). Personal interview, October 20, 2016.

Carr, Thomas A., USA (Ret.). Telephone interviews, August 6, 2014, and April 11, 2015.

Chilson, Duane L. Telephone interview, January 21, 2015.

Corren, Sherman B. Telephone interview, August 6, 2014.

Crerar, John H., Colonel, USA (Ret.). Telephone interview, January 19, 2015.

Cunningham, Thomas P. Telephone interviews, February 6 and April 15, 2015.

Davidson, Jon P., Sergeant, USA. Telephone interview, April 2, 2015.

Dean, Kyle S. Telephone interview, January 14, 2015, and subsequent correspondence and emails.

Denison, Gerald E., USA (Ret.). Telephone interviews, January 14 and March 17, 2015, and subsequent emails and telephone exchanges.

DeSeta, Louis J., Sergeant, USA. Personal interviews, October 21–22, 2014.

Dorff, Anthony C., Staff Sergeant, USA. Telephone interview, April 3, 2015.

Downes, Charlie. 57th AHC. Personal interview, August 29, 2015.

Engebretsen, Donald, Captain, USAF (A1E pilot) Personal interviews, October 22, 2014, and October 20, 2016; email interview questions, March 7, 2015, subsequent correspondence; and telephone interview, December 10, 2016.

Erickson, Albert M. Telephone interviews, August 10 and 16, 2014.

Farrell, Alan F. Telephone interview, April 2, 2015.

Fulton, Donald F., Captain, USAF (Ret.). Personal interview, October 22, 2014.

Gill, Linden L., Lieutenant Colonel, USAF (Ret.). Telephone interview, March 10, 2015.

Gilmer, David L. Telephone interview, September 13, 2016.

Gilreath, Johnnie B., Jr., Colonel, USA (Ret.). Telephone interviews, January 15 and 16, 2015.

Glass, Wendell L. Telephone interview, August 4, 2014.

Good, John. Personal interview, October 21, 2014.

Goth, Stephen M. Personal interview, October 22, 2014. Telephone interview, September 29, 2016, and subsequent email correspondence.

Gravett, Ronald W. Telephone interview, January 23, 2015.

Greco, Frank. Telephone interview, March 10, 2015, and subsequent email correspondence.

Griffith, Richard J. Telephone interview, January 6, 2015, and subsequent email exchanges; personal interview, August 29, 2015.

Gron, Robert M. Telephone interview, April 4, 2015, and subsequent email exchanges.

Groves, William J. Jr. Personal interview, October 21, 2014.

Hanson, William H., Master Sergeant, USA (Ret.). Telephone interview, March 22, 2015.

Hardy, Jason M. Interview sessions, October 23 and 30, 2014, and subsequent email correspondence, telephone conversations, and reunion meetings.

Heberlein, Henry. 57th AHC. Personal interview, August 29, 2015.

Hetrick, James F., Master Sergeant, USA (Ret.). Personal interview, October 22, 2014.

Hill, Melvin, Master Sergeant, USA (Ret.). Personal interview, October 20, 2016.

Hunt, David H. Personal interviews, July 24 and December 5, 2014.

Hunt, George Wilson. Personal interviews, July 24 and 25, 2014, August 14 and 18, 2014, and January 25, 2015. Additional material supplied included the use of books, maps, and photos.

Jaeger, Thomas W., Lieutenant Colonel, USA (Ret.). Telephone interview, January 31, 2015.

Jaks, Frank, Major, USA (Ret.). Telephone interview, October 26, 2016.

Janc, Daniel W., Master Sergeant, USA (Ret.). Telephone interviews, August 3 and November 26, 2017.

Jensen, Glen W. Telephone interview, August 19, 2014.

Jones-Shorten, James H. Jr., USA/USAF (Ret.). Telephone interview of January 2, 2017.

Keller, Alan. Personal interview, October 22, 2014, telephone interview, September 29, 2016, and subsequent follow-up correspondence.

Kendall, William L., First Sergeant, USA (Ret.). Telephone interview, March 22, 2015, and subsequent email correspondence.

Kirschbaum, David P., Sergeant Major, USA (Ret.). Telephone interview, April 11, 2015.

Kotin, Robert. Telephone interview, January 1, 2015.

Leites, Robert L., Lieutenant Colonel, USA (Ret.). Personal interview, October 20, 2016.

Lesesne, Edward R., Colonel, USA (Ret.). Email correspondence/interview, August 13–21, 2014.

Livingston, Thomas O. Personal conversation, October 22, 2104, telephone interviews, October 10, 2016, and January 5, 2017, and January 1, 2015, email questions.

Loucks, Bryon W. Telephone interview, March 3, 2015.

McCammond, Joseph E. Telephone interview, January 11, 2015, and subsequent email exchanges.

McCarley, Eugene C., Lieutenant Colonel, USA (Ret.). Telephone interview, March 16, 2015.

McCormick, Clarence W., Sergeant Major, USA (Ret.). Telephone interview, January 1, 2015.

Melton, W. Wayne. Telephone interviews, November 12 and December 5, 2014.

Messer, Joseph. Telephone interview, December 16, 2014.

Meyer, John S., Staff Sergeant, USA (Ret.). Personal interview, October 20, 2016.

Morris, Paul L. Jr., USA (Ret.). Personal interview, October 19, 2016.

Motsett, Charles B., Captain, USA (Ret.). Personal interview, October 20, 2016.

Nesbitt, Charles. 57th AHC. Personal interview, August 29, 2015.

Nowack, Richard R., USA. Telephone interview, September 7, 2016.

O'Daniel, Lloyd G., Master Sergeant, USA (Ret.). Telephone interview, August 6, 2014.

Pagan, Joseph. 57th AHC. Personal interview, August 29, 2015.

Parnar, Joseph F., USA (Ret.). Personal interview, October 19, 2016; telephone and email correspondence from 2014–16.

Perkins, Stuart L., Colonel, USA (Ret.). Telephone interview, August 13, 2014.

Plaster, John L., Major, USA (Ret.). Personal meeting, August 29, 2015, and subsequent telephone follow-up calls.

Rice, Phillip W. Telephone interview, January 21, 2015.

Robertson, Seth, USA (Ret.). Personal interview, October 19, 2016.

Roche, Stephen M., Sergeant, USA (Ret.). Telephone interview, March 26, 2015.

Rodd, Ralph R., Staff Sergeant, USA (Ret.). Telephone interview, March 18, 2015.

Schuler, Hartmut, Major, USA (Ret.). Telephone interviews, January 3 and February 28, 2015.

Sincere, Clyde J., Major, USA (Ret.). Personal interviews, October 22, 2014, and October 20, 2016.

Singlaub, John K., Brigadier General, USA (Ret.). Personal interview, October 22, 2014.

Smith, Dean. 57th AHC. Personal interview, August 29, 2015.

Snow, William T., Master Sergeant, USA (Ret.). Telephone interview, July 11, 2015.

Spitler, Lawrence A. Telephone interview, August 30, 2014, personal interview, October 19, 2016.

Steenbock, Stan. 57th AHC. Personal interview, August 29, 2015.

Stewart, Jimmie L., Sergeant Major, USA (Ret.). Email correspondence/interview, August 20–21, 2014.

St. Laurent, Andre J., Sergeant Major, USA (Ret.). Telephone interview, January 4, 2015.

Sullivan, Stephen. 57th AHC. Personal interview, August 29, 2015, and subsequent email correspondence.

Swain, Lee R. Personal interviews, October 21, 2014, and October 19, 2106, and subsequent email correspondence.

Swanson, Melvin, Lieutenant Colonel, USAF (Ret.). Presentation given to SOG veterans on October 21, 2014.

Templin, Thomas R. Telephone interview, August 8, 2014.

Tilley, Leonard W., Captain, USA (Ret.). Telephone interviews, August 24, 2014, and September 26, 2016, personal interview, October 19, 2016.

Tramel, James M. Telephone interview, March 27, 2015.

Vanderzwalm, Richard L., Major, USA (Ret.). Telephone interview, March 19, 2015.

Walker, Joe J., Sergeant Major, USA (Ret.). Telephone interviews, December 7, 2014, and January 19 and July 19, 2015.

White, Larry M., Command Sergeant Major, USA (Ret.). Telephone interview, September 20, 2016.

Williams, Larry D., Sergeant First Class, USA (Ret.). Telephone interview, January 16, 2014.

Williams, Warren W., Major, USA (Ret.). Telephone interview, February 27, 2017, and follow-up email correspondence.

Wolcoff, Edward, Lieutenant Colonel, USA (Ret.). Personal interview, October 22, 2014, telephone interviews, January 22, 2015, and March 12, 2018, and subsequent email correspondence.

Wolfkeil, David W. Telephone interview, March 6, 2015, and subsequent email correspondence and meeting in October 2016.

Worley, Morris G. Telephone interview, August 2, 2014, and subsequent email correspondence.

Yoakum, Tony. 57th AHC. Personal interview, August 29, 2015.

ARTICLES / MEMOIRS / OFFICIAL REPORTS / COMPILATIONS

Batman, Sherman R. "Kedenburg Brightlite." Accessed March 25, 2015. http://www.macvsog.cc/britelight-kedenburg.htm.

Bissell, Maj. Brandon. "Special Forces Operation Complex Becomes Howard Hall." *Fort Campbell Courier*, July 11, 2013.

Bottoms, Mike. "MoH Recipient, Special Ops Legend Receives Simons Award." *Fort Campbell Courier*, June 5, 2014.

Braden, Ted B. "Mercenary Job Wanted." *Ramparts*, October 1967.

Collier, Craig. Unpublished memoirs, courtesy of Joe Parnar and Robert Dumont.

Coryell, George. "Army Hero of Vietnam War Dies at Age 55." *Tampa Tribune*, July 3, 2000.

"Courage under Fire," Recon Series, Medal of Honor profile of Colonel Robert L. Howard. Pritzker Military Library. Robert L. Howard videotaped interview with Ed Tracy, July 27, 2006.

"Cross Border Operations in Cambodia." U.S. Military Assistance Command, Vietnam, Studies and Observations Group, Documentation Study. July 10, 1970.

Cunningham, Henry. "SOG Awarded Presidential Unit Citation." *Fayetteville Online*. April 5, 2001. http://www.macvsog.cc/presidential_unit_citation.htm (link discontinued).

Dean, Kyle S. Unpublished mission notes.

DeLong, Dr. Kent. "Fred Zabitosky: Vietnam Veteran and Medal of Honor Winner." *Vietnam*, February 1996, 8, 54–56.

Dumont, Robert, and Joe Parnar. "Operation Nightcap. SOG SLAM 9, 15–24 March 1969." Narrative of operation including testimony from thirteen of the twenty participants, award orders, photos, maps. Copyright 2013.

Dumont, Robert, and Joe Parnar, comps. "John James Kedenburg Medal of Honor Recipient Tribute Notebook." Compiled in 2011 by Joe Parnar and Robert Dumont. Compilation of stories, official reports and eyewitness statements. Contributors included Michael D. Berry, Thomas P. Cunningham, Gerald E. Denison, Louis J. DeSeta, Jason Hardy, George W. Hunt, Bryon Loucks, Robert L. Noe, John L. Plaster, and William T. Snow.

Graves, Jim. "SLAM Mission into Laos. SOG Sergeant Wins Medal of Honor." *Soldier of Fortune*, June 1981.

Hoeck, Carl. "Shot Down." Personal narrative of Hoeck's involvement in November 1968 SLAM Mission, 2014. Courtesy of Joe Parnar and Robert Dumont.

Kendall, William L. Personal diary/team notes written during period of September 1968–January 1969. Courtesy of Bill Kendall.

King, P. "Meadows Early Life as 'Junior' from Virginia." April 10, 2000 (accessed February 22, 2015). http://sfalx.com/h_meadows_early_life.htm (site discontinued).

Loucks, Bryon W. "John Kedenburg Bright Light Mission: 14 June 1968." Personal account of events written July 6, 2002, with input from Gerald E. Denison, Sherman R. Batman, and James McGlon.

"Operation of Command and Control Detachment Center." Frank Jaks interview from SOG *Documentation Study*, B-O-183.

Ortiz, Master Sergeant Jose D., "History of the NCO: SSG Fred W. Zabitosky," 3.

PACAF (Pacific Air Forces) Evasion and Recovery Report No. 76., Part I: Robert E. Kline, Vietnam Center and Archive, Texas Tech University.

Plaster, Major John L. "Wreaking Havoc One Round at a Time." *American Rifleman*, May 2008.

Prairie Fire/Nickel Steel Weekly Reports, October 1965–November 1968. U.S. Military Assistance Command, Vietnam, Studies and Observations Group. MACVSOG *Documentation Study*, Appendix D.

Rice, Phillip W. Unpublished mission notes.

Ross, Vaughan R. "Prairie Fire, Prairie Fire!—57th AHC 'Gladiators' Make Desperate Attempt to Save SOG Team." *Behind the Lines: The Journal of U.S. Military Special Operations* 15 (March/April 1995): 24–29.

Schultz, Richard H. Jr. "MACV-SOG Oral History Interviews with Officers Who Served in MACVSOG OP35 (Clandestine Operations in Laos and Cambodia Along the Ho Chi Minh Trail)," International Security Studies Program, Fletcher School of Law and Diplomacy, Tufts University, January 1997.

Swain, Lee R. "Lee's Recollection Nov. 1968." Personal account written to Joe Parnar, August 31, 2010. Courtesy of Parnar and Robert Dumont.

U.S. Military Assistance Command, Vietnam, Studies and Observations Group. *Annex M, Command History, 1966.* Saigon: MACV-SOG, May 5, 1967.

———. *Annex G, Command History, 1967.* Saigon: MACV-SOG, September 3, 1968.

———. *Annex F, Command History, 1968.* Saigon: MACV-SOG, March 7, 1969.

————. *Annex F, Command History, 1969.* Saigon: MACV-SOG, April 6, 1970.

Williams, Warren W. "Stand Up, Hook Up, Shuffle to the Door: A Collection of Autobiographical Sketches." Unpublished memoirs.

BOOKS/EBOOKS

Collier, Peter, and Nick Del Calzo. *Medal of Honor: Portraits of Valor beyond the Call of Duty,* 3rd ed. New York: Artisan, 2011.

Cosmas, Graham A. *MACV: The Joint Command in the Years of Withdrawal, 1968–1973.* Washington, DC: Center of American History, United States Army, 2006.

DeLong, Kent. *War Heroes: True Stories of Congressional Medal of Honor Recipients.* Westport, CT: Praeger, 1993.

Dumont, Robert, and Joe Parnar. *SOG Medic: Stories from Vietnam and Over the Fence.* Boulder, CO: Paladin Press, 2007.

Galdorisi, George, and Tom Phillips. *Leave No Man Behind: The Saga of Combat Search and Rescue.* Minneapolis: Zenith Press, 2009.

Gillespie, Robert M. *Black Ops Vietnam: The Operational History of MACVSOG.* Annapolis, MD: Naval Institute Press, 2011.

Greco, Frank. Kontum: *Command and Control. Select Photographs of SOG Special Ops during the Vietnam War.* Xlibris Corporation, 2005.

————. *Running Recon: A Photo Journey with SOG Special Ops along the Ho Chi Minh Trail.* Boulder, CO: Paladin Press, 2004.

Halberstadt, Hans. *War Stories of the Green Berets.* St. Paul, MN: Zenith Press, 2004.

Hardy, Jason M. *MACV SOG: Team History of a Clandestine Army, Vol. I.* Spencer, NC: Hardy Publications, 2011. Includes histories of RT Arizona, RT California, RT Iowa, and RT North Carolina.

————. *MACV SOG: Team History of a Clandestine Army, Vol. II.* Spencer, NC: Hardy Publications, 2012. Includes histories of RT Krait, RT New Mexico, RT Ohio, and RT Washington.

————. *MACV SOG: Team History of a Clandestine Army, Vol. III.* Spencer, NC: Hardy Publications, 2012. Includes histories of RT Crusader, RT Sidewinder, and RT Texas.

————. *MACV SOG: Team History of a Clandestine Army, Vol. IV.* Spencer, NC: Hardy Publications, 2013. Includes histories of RT Auger, RT Illinois, RT Le Loi, and RT New Hampshire.

————. *MACV SOG: Team History of a Clandestine Army, Vol. V.* Spencer, NC: Hardy Publications, 2013. Includes histories of RT Alabama, RT Habu, and RT Michigan.

————. *MACV SOG: Team History of a Clandestine Army, Vol. VI.* Spencer, NC: Hardy Publications, 2013. Includes histories of RT Adder, RT Louisiana, RT Nebraska, and RT Wyoming.

———. *MACV SOG: Team History of a Clandestine Army, Vol. VII.* Spencer, NC: Hardy Publications, 2014. Includes histories of RT Nevada, RT Oklahoma, RT Pick, and RT South Carolina.

———. *MACV SOG: Team History of a Clandestine Army, Vol. VIII.* Spencer, NC: Hardy Publications, 2015. Includes histories of RT Delaware, RT Hawaii, and RT Intruder.

———. *MACV SOG: Team History of a Clandestine Army, Vol. IX.* Spencer, NC: Hardy Publications, 2016. Includes histories of RT Arkansas, RT Moccasin, RT Ohio, and RT Rattler.

Hardy, Jason, and Michael Tucker. *SOG: Team History and Insignia of a Clandestine Army.* Port St. Lucie, FL: MilSpec Publishing, 2008. Includes histories of RT Asp, RT Colorado, RT Hawaii, RT Idaho, RT Indigo, RT Montana, and RT Rattler.

Hobson, Chris. *Vietnam Air Losses. United States Air Force, Navy and Marine Corps Fixed-Wing Aircraft Losses in Southeast Asia, 1961–1973.* Hinckley, England: Midland Publishing, 2001.

Hoe, Alan. *The Quiet Professional: Major Richard J. Meadows of the U.S. Army Special Forces.* Lexington: University Press of Kentucky, 2011.

Kelley, Jim. *Tales from the Teamhouse.* Kearney, NE: Morris Publishing, 2004.

Meyer, John Stryker. *Across the Fence: The Secret War in Vietnam.* Expanded ed. Oceanside, CA: SOG Publishing, 2013.

Miller, Franklin D., with Elwood J. C. Kureth. *Reflections of a Warrior.* Novato, CA: Presidio Press, 1991.

Murphy, Edward F. *Medal of Honor Heroes.* New York: Presidio Press, 1987.

Pinn, Lionel F. Sr., with Frank Sikora. *Hear the Bugles Calling. My Three Wars as a Combat Infantryman.* Montgomery, AL: NewSouth Books, 2007.

Plaster, John L. *Secret Commandos: Behind Enemy Lines with the Elite Warriors of SOG.* New York: NAL Caliber, 2004.

———. *SOG: A Photo History of the Secret Wars.* Boulder, CO: Paladin Press, 2000.

———. *SOG: The Secret Wars of America's Commandos in Vietnam.* New York: Simon & Schuster, 1997.

Prados, John. *The Blood Road: The Ho Chi Minh Trail and the Vietnam War.* New York: John Wiley & Sons, 1999.

Sherman, Steve. *Who's Who from MACV-SOG.* Houston, TX: The Radix Press, 1996.

Singlaub, Major General John K., U.S. Army (Ret.), with Malcolm McConnell. *Hazardous Duty: An American Soldier in the Twentieth Century.* New York: Summit Books, 1991.

Veith, George J. *Code-Name Bright Light: The Untold Story of U.S. POW Rescue Efforts During the Vietnam War.* New York: Dell Publishing, 1998.

Willbanks, James H. *America's Heroes: Medal of Honor Recipients from the Civil War to Afghanistan.* Santa Barbara, CA: ABC-CLIO, 2011.

———. *The Tet Offensive: A Concise History.* New York: Columbia University Press, 1988.

INDEX

Note: Page numbers in *italics* indicate photographs.

ABOUT THE AUTHOR

Stephen L. Moore, a sixth generation Texan, is the author of two previous Naval Institute Press books and sixteen other publications on World War II and Texas history. He is a contributing writer for the *Dallas Morning News* and has reviewed historical titles for a number of other publications.

Steve graduated from Stephen F. Austin State University in Nacogdoches, Texas, where he studied advertising, marketing, and journalism. He lives north of Dallas in Lantana, Texas, with his wife and three children.